UTOPIAN IMAGINATION AND EIGHTEENTH-CENTURY FICTION

Christine Rees

LONDON AND NEW YORK

Longman Group Limited
Longman House, Burnt Mill,
Harlow, Essex CM20 2JE, England
and Associated Companies throughout the world.

Published in the United States of America
by Longman Publishing, New York

Transferred to digital print on demand 2001

First published 1996   EG 26876

British Library Cataloguing-in-Publication Data

A catalogue record for this book is
available from the British Library

Library of Congress Cataloging-in-Publication Data

Rees, Christine.
    Utopian imagination and eighteenth-century fiction / Christine
Rees.
    p. cm. -- (Studies in eighteenth- and nineteenth-century
literature)
    Includes bibliographical references (p.) and index.
    ISBN 0-582-06735-9 (csd). -- ISBN 0-582-06736-7 (ppr)
    1. English fiction--18th century--History and criticism.
2. Fantastic fiction, English--History and criticism. 3. Utopias in
literature. 4. Imagination. I. Title. II. Series.
    PR858.U7R44 1996
823'.509372--dc20   95-13096
                                                 CIP

Set by 7.00 in 10/12 Goudy Oldstyle
Produced by Longman Singapore Publishers (Pte) Ltd.

Printed and bound by Antony Rowe Ltd, Eastbourne

UTOPIAN IMAGINATION AND
EIGHTEENTH-CENTURY FICTION

Studies in Eighteenth- and Nineteenth-Century Literature

General Editors

Andrew Sanders, Reader in English, Birkbeck College London
David Nokes, Reader in English, King's College London

Published titles

Forms of Speech in Victorian Fiction Raymond Chapman
Henry Fielding: Authorship and Authority Ian A. Bell
Language and Relationship in Wordsworth's Writing: Elective Affinities
Michael Baron
Utopian Imagination and Eighteenth-Century Fiction from Robinson
Crusoe *to* Rasselas Christine Rees

Contents

'Elsewhere is a negative mirror. The traveller recognizes the little that is his, discovering the much he has not had and will never have.'

Italo Calvino tr William Weaver

Introduction

The shortest utopian fiction I know (it is transmitted in more than one version) is the story about a group of shipwrecked sailors adrift in a small boat in unknown seas.[1] At last a distant coastline comes into sight. Outlined against the sky is a single landmark – a gibbet. 'Thank God!' cries one of the sailors. 'It's a civilised country!' Why call this a utopian fiction? In this form at least, it could serve as a brief generic paradigm. Obviously, the narrative structure condenses a sequence of events that are commonplace in voyage literature: a group of unfortunate travellers, thrown on their own resources, brace themselves for the shock of the new, and are taken unawares with a shock of recognition. However, what makes it a utopian story is the sardonic punchline. 'Civilisation' is represented by the sign of the gibbet.

Most utopian writers, certainly in earlier periods, are passionately interested in defining an idea of civilisation (and its opposite). From one point of view, the sailor is right: the gibbet does signify civilisation, that is a society that is sufficiently organised to invest its penal code with ritual symbolism when executing transgressors. From the ancient Greeks to modern interpreters of cultural history like Foucault, the way in which a society disciplines and punishes its citizens is an index of its ideology.[2] From another point of view, the sailor is grotesquely wrong. The gibbet is the visible sign of civilised society's failure, not its success. It mutely calls into question the relativity of our standards of civility and barbarism. And this kind of challenge, implicit or explicit, runs right through utopian fiction. However absolute the judgments may seem to be, they are always relative so far as the reader is concerned. He or she always stands at a slight angle to the utopian universe. To put it another way, eu-topia (good place) and dystopia (bad place) are always, in Thomas More's pun, ou-topia or no-place.[3]

The difficulties of defining utopia as a concept are notorious, and much depends on whether you are discussing it as an historian, a philosopher, or (as in my case) a literary critic. My interest is in the texts that reflect the workings of utopian imagination, whether that of an implied author or a created character like Robinson Crusoe or Rasselas. I've indicated that one central theoretic concern of the genre is the nature of civilisation. For the creator of fictional utopias, this translates into Gonzalo's rhetorical question in *The Tempest*: 'Had I plantation of this isle, my lord . . . And wert the King on't, what would I do?'[4] Even Socrates, according to Plato in the *Timaeus*, is not satisfied with the purely theoretic discourse of the *Republic*, and asks for a representation of the ideal state in action.[5] In this instance, the response is the haunting, incomplete legend of the conflict between ancient Athens and the lost continent of Atlantis. However, all utopian fictions are a response in some form or other to this need for narrative particularity, an exercise of the creative writer's traditional function of delivering a golden world in words.

Nor, it seems to me, should critics legislate too far about what kind of world/text that ought to be. A great deal of scholarly effort has already gone into creating a taxonomy of utopian literature, and differentiating 'utopia' from related types such as the Golden Age or the Millennium. Like other students of the subject, I am much indebted to the work of historians and theorists of the genre.[6] But because I have concentrated on eighteenth-century fiction in English especially, my emphasis is rather different from theirs. I have no intention of engaging in demarcation disputes, since the object of this study isn't to stake out a particular generic territory, but to retain flexibility in dealing with texts, where different genres fuse to produce new kinds of reading experience (as in that relatively recent literary phenomenon, the English novel).

As in earlier periods, a utopia may be ideal, satiric, or ambiguous. It may have traces of pastoral idyll, millennial faith, or Rabelaisian indulgence. Whatever else it reflects, it acts as a mirror tilted by the author to catch new angles on familiar aspects of his or her society. It sets out to induce culture shock, and often succeeds. But it's also self-referential. Since utopian writing in this period frequently constitutes only a part, not the whole, of a given text, it raises interesting questions about its own literary role in relation to its hosts. Is it simply a marginal mode, the poor relation that can be overlooked at the feast of Fielding's or Richardson's fiction for instance? If that's the case – and utopian discourse is disowned by a number of 'serious' eighteenth-century writers – then it is still a surprisingly ubiquitous presence, given a hospitable reception not only in the novel, but in other literary forms: satire, the imaginary voyage, the proto-feminist tract, the eastern tale, and the philosophical fable. It is, therefore, not easy to categorise, because the very essence of utopia depends on perceptive comparison across categories: qualities which should be inseparable from the skill of reading itself.[7]

If formal definitions need to be generously interpreted in an eighteenth-century context, so do definitions by subject. Even describing the classic features of a traditional utopia tends to beg a number of questions. Most readers probably think of utopia as an imaginary society that constitutes, in Miriam Eliav-Feldon's words, 'a presentation of a positive and possible alternative to the social reality, intended as a model to be emulated or aspired to'.[8] The most useful word in this formula is 'alternative': all the other terms – positive? possible? to be emulated? – can be queried (even 'social reality') or subverted. The negative equivalent of utopia is so powerful that other terms have had to come into general use: anti-utopia, or (a term I usually try to avoid) dystopia. Perhaps the only description that applies to all the eighteenth-century variations under discussion is that they involve the imagining of fictional alternatives – whether entire social structures, or different modes of living – which are deliberately designed to contrast with, and comment on, dominant cultural forms. These examples don't necessarily include a package deal of 'politics, laws, customs, and conditions',[9] though some do, like Swift's countries in *Gulliver's Travels*. Nor do they have to be located at a geographical distance, though there are obvious and traditional reasons for this practice. It is possible for an experiment in utopian living to exist within the dominant society, like Sarah Scott's *Millenium Hall*. (In fact, I utilise the distinction between utopia overseas and domestic utopias as a way of organising complicated material.) Nor, most radical of all, does eighteenth-century utopian fiction even need to centre on communal life. A utopian solitude may appear a contradiction in terms, but it depends very much on the treatment of that solitude, and this, most strikingly in *Robinson Crusoe*, can address the same fundamental concerns as more conventional utopianism.

What are these concerns? Surprisingly, most eighteenth-century writers of utopian fiction don't seem to put politics, in the technical sense, very high on their agenda. Few engage in inventing alternative constitutions or political practices in the kind of detail found in the writings of Gerrard Winstanley or James Harrington in the previous century. Of course, this may be explained by the difference of historical context, the eighteenth-century distrust of revolutionary remedies for perennial problems. However, if the later writers have relatively little to say, in the utopian mode at least, on the subject of reforming the system of government, they are less reticent on the subject of social and economic reforms which might or might not be called utopian. They are extremely interested in 'the political', as distinguished from politics: power, property, and privilege inevitably shape human relations in eighteenth-century fiction, and it is the business of the utopian imagination to conceive ways of turning these to good account and to ameliorate the conditions that distort and inflict suffering on individual lives. As we might expect, sexual politics, as the subject would now be termed, figures dramatically in the novel; and I have devoted two chapters to comparing and contrasting utopian schemes in works by male and female novelists.

Just as basic to the quality of civilisation are the other material topics – diet, clothes, money – addressed by the creators of utopia. Like the ancient Greeks, some eighteenth-century utopists are allegedly more interested in food than sex[10] (Robinson Crusoe certainly is; Paltock's Peter Wilkins enjoys both). The age-old conflict between the simple-life state and the luxurious state generates an appreciable amount of utopian discussion in the eighteenth century. Predictably, the needs and image of the body play a large part in utopian satire such as that of Swift. But if the utopian imagination is seduced, for better or worse, by the material world, its natural habitat is the life of the intellect, which also has to be catered for. Since the classical and Renaissance utopia equates the good life with the examined life, and since any ideal society has to perpetuate itself through conditioning its citizens, it follows that the training of mind and spirit is indispensable to the humanist tradition. A number of eighteenth-century utopian schemes, like their predecessors, centre on education, with a special emphasis on the education of women. Perhaps, indeed, it is in this area that eighteenth-century utopianism makes one of its most distinctive contributions to the genre.

This raises the whole question of origins and influences. Where, from the literary and historical point of view, does eighteenth-century utopian fiction fit in? Obviously the idea of utopia, in any period, has to begin somewhere. One way of tackling its origins is to look at what writers are responding to, or reacting against, in their own society.

Like the sailor and the gibbet, each writer interprets cultural signs in relation to what is familiar. The imagined locations of eighteenth-century utopias differ wildly, from desert islands to cities, from the Orient to the Americas, from fantasies of countries populated by ghosts, giants, talking birds or horses, to the sober landscape of an English country estate. What unites all these is the dream of an environment under creative control, programmed to produce not only wonders, but also practical analysis of the workings of society in eighteenth-century Britain. Utopia may be the idealised version or the complete antithesis of its creator's own culture (like the Greek city-state or More's island) but it is seldom, if ever, totally disconnected from it even in fantasy.

The other place to begin is not with what a writer experiences at first hand, but with what he or she has read. From Plato and Aristotle onwards, new utopian texts grow out of dialogue with older ones: critiques and reconstructions of other people's utopias are virtually as old as the genre itself.[11] To construct a map of the literary world with any given utopia in it, it's necessary to proceed by charting the latitude and longitude of the writer's position in relation to existing texts. Because the original map is that of the ancient world, which More redraws for the Renaissance, that is where this study begins. However, it isn't a source study as such, although it is a comparative one. The attitude to sources is more that of rounding up the usual suspects – Plato, Lucian, More – than of establishing evidence beyond a reasonable doubt. However, throughout the discussion of eighteenth-century texts, it should prove illuminating to keep in mind suggestive parallels, not just with classical and Renaissance texts, but with the variety of seventeenth-century ones as well. In spite of historical shifts, the emphasis tends to fall on continuity and creative adaptation.

To that extent, chronology is significant: but, as will become clear from the contents, I have chosen not to treat the eighteenth-century texts themselves in strictly chronological order. Instead, they are grouped by kind. 'From *Robinson Crusoe* to *Rasselas*' doesn't represent temporal brackets but conceptual ones. From possibly the most individual – in all senses – version of one man's utopia, published in 1719, we come in a cycle of four decades to one of the most classical of eighteenth-century utopian fictions, published in 1759. Although some of the fictions considered fall well outside these dates, it makes sense to include them within these generic extremities, just as it makes sense to separate, yet keep in proximity, the two greatest utopian travellers in this period, Crusoe and Gulliver.

Neither Defoe nor Swift, incidentally, would have been astonished by the tale of the sailor's reaction to the gibbet. In different ways, their fictions expose the fallacy of taking it for granted that we know what civilisation is, whether in the eighteenth or the twentieth or indeed the twenty-first century. Utopian fiction goes on testing our imaginative reflexes: that is its function.[12] The following chapters attempt to explore, in a literary context, how it works.

Notes and references

1. I have chosen the version representing a group: it is also related of a lone sailor who is castaway, Crusoe-like, on a strange shore (v A. Dymond, 1865 pp. 287–8 cit H. Potter, 1993 p. 16).

2. cf M. Foucault, 1975/1977.

3. v T. More, 1516/1989 p. xi.

4. W. Shakespeare, 1623/1961 p. 50, II : i : 139. 41.

5. v Plato, 1965/1977 p. 31.

6. eg K. Mannheim, 1936; A.L. Morton, 1952; F.E. Manuel 1965 (ed); F. Venturi, 1971; D. Suvin, 1973; J. Ferguson, 1975; F.E. Manuel, F.P. Manuel, 1979; J.C. Davis, 1981; M. Eliav-Feldon, 1982; L. Marin, 1984; P. Alexander, R. Gill, 1984 (eds); P. Ricoeur, 1986; P. Ruppert, 1986; D. Baker-Smith, C.C. Barfoot, 1987 (eds): K. Kumar, 1987, 1991; P. Neville-Sington, D. Sington, 1993.

7. cf Ruppert's critical method (P. Ruppert, 1986).

8. M. Eliav-Feldon, 1982 p. 1.

9. *Oxford English Dictionary* definition: utopia 2.

10. cf M. Foucault, 1984/1986b p. 340.

11. cf Mannheim's concept of the 'counter-utopia': K. Mannheim, 1936 p. 208.

12. cf Ricoeur's suggestion that 'perhaps we need to find a link between . . . different utopias in the structure of imagination': P. Ricoeur, 1986 p. 271.

CHAPTER 1

Classical origins and Renaissance locations

No age or ideology can lay an exclusive claim to utopian territory; but certain conditions seem particularly to favour experimenting with radical alternatives to the prevailing culture. Periods of rapid change and instability, when the previously unthinkable explodes into people's consciousness and basic assumptions disintegrate under the impact of social, sexual, or scientific revolution, tend to generate varieties of utopian text. On the other hand, total disintegration defeats the purpose. A certain level of intellectual activity, and confidence in intellectual debate as a productive and relevant contribution to society, also seem to be a prerequisite. The utopian creator isn't normally talking to himself or herself. It's hardly accidental that a number of seminal utopian texts should spring from groups functioning as a kind of self-appointed think tank within their cultures, such as the Socratic circle in fifth-century Athens, which became institutionalised in Plato's Academy, or the humanists of early sixteenth-century Europe. At a later date, seventeenth-century sectarians, eighteenth-century savants, nineteenth-century socialists or twentieth-century feminists exhibit a similar phenomenon. The creative temperature rises within a furnace of personalities, fuelled from outside, but fired inwardly by a shared vision: and it fuses together the disparate materials which go to make a utopia. Nor, consequently, is it surprising that formal dialogue and discourse structure utopian writing, even prior to narrative. For all its fantastic imaginings, the genre depends on engaging the ratiocinative powers of the mind (however sceptically these powers may be regarded).

If utopianism is wishful thinking, it is also sophisticated and, in one sense at least, secularised thinking. It concentrates on what might be made of this world, although the otherworldliness of the fictive state is often emphasised. The founders of ancient and early modern utopias, Plato, 'who knew this life was not worth a potato', and the Catholic saint, Thomas More, agree that the ideal commonwealth is not of this world:[1] but, paradoxically, they each offer a controversial model of secular life grounded in mundane physical needs and social mechanisms – what the inhabitants of utopia eat and wear, how they spend their time in work, education and recreation, how they conduct relationships and bring up children, their duties to the state in peace and war, how they deal with those who violate their codes, and their ways of coming to terms with sickness, old age, and finally death. Both Plato and More set a demanding agenda. And no matter how diverse the answers given to the problems they pose, the recurrence of the same questions ensures a fundamental continuity in utopian textual structures. Informing these structures are concerns that are theoretically universal, and certainly in the height of present intellectual fashion, from the history of the body (its food, sexuality, capacity to reproduce, and eventual decay and disposal) to the intellectual history of humanity (language, education, sciences, arts, and religious beliefs and practices).

Although utopia is dauntingly inclusive as theory, as fiction it can only work by giving these huge topics a *topos*, a local habitation and – usually – a name. To plot the exact site of an eighteenth-century utopian fiction on the cultural and literary map, we need the coordinates of classical and Renaissance texts.[2] Classical texts represent origins; Renaissance texts, products of an expanding world geography, create new locations. Together they systematise the genre, so that seventeenth-century and eighteenth-century writers can apply it imaginatively to construct their own alternative fictions. To sketch the options available, the most convenient, and Platonic, method is to start with a clean canvas and block in an outline of the commonest topics, beginning with the idea of origins. What makes a human community, and what does it need in order to survive at all?

Golden Age or state of nature? the simple-life utopia

In *The Republic*, Socrates presents his philosopher ruler as the type of the artist:

> He will take society and human character as his canvas, and begin by scraping it clean. That is no easy matter; but, as you know, unlike other reformers, he will not consent to take in hand either an individual or a state or to draft laws, until he is given a clean surface to work on or has cleansed it himself.[3]

The scraping clean of the canvas might imply a number of procedures, the political ones being the most ominous. However, in a literary context, it marks out a procedure followed by many utopian creators. Since one function of utopian fiction is to return to the pristine state of 'society and human character' and to reassess the basic definition of what it is to be human, many such fictions incorporate an aetiological myth – an explanation of origin. Although theorists make a valid distinction between utopia and the Golden Age, the frontier between them isn't closed, especially to anyone travelling on a creative writer's passport. The simple-life utopia, in particular, has much in common with the classical version of the Golden Age described by Hesiod, Virgil, and Ovid.

Typically, both states are defined as much by what they lack as by their positive attributes: the absence of aggression, competitiveness, stress, fear, exploitation of fellow human beings or the natural world – an absence which is conditional upon not having a money economy or an advanced technology. According to Ovid, 'men of their own accord, without threat of punishment, without laws, maintained good faith and did what was right', so that lawyers and soldiers aren't necessary.[4] However, at this point, Golden Age and utopia diverge. The blessings of the former aren't attributable to social organisation, but to the spontaneous abundance of an earth that requires no cultivation, and to the universally eirenic temperament which is the result. In contrast, even the simplest utopia usually postulates both labour (and the division of labour) and laws. We might expect that the creators of ideal states would prefer to have their military professionals, for example, underemployed if not actually redundant, yet in ancient utopias the reverse is often the case. Indeed, the utopian imagination thrives on precisely the requirements that Ovid excludes from the Golden Age: the framing and execution of laws, civic and military discipline, the regulation of useful and productive work; in short, the belief that human thought and action make a *difference* to the world. The rationale of a utopia has to be post-Golden Age, conceptually if not chronologically.

It is, of course, possible to politicise the Golden Age myth by projecting it into the future, as Virgil does in his fourth Eclogue, where it merges with the millennium. However, the utopian debate between simplicity and luxury tends to presuppose that the simple-life state is primary in more senses than one, preceding and morally superior to the luxurious state. Certainly that's the sequence in Plato's

Republic, though the presence of irony cannot be discounted. At the primitive level of social organisation based on the division of labour, what bulks largest is the satisfaction of physical needs. Whether or not, as Foucault claims, there has taken place over centuries a 'very slow move, from the privileging of food, which was overwhelming in Greece, to interest in sex',[5] food remains perhaps the most basic and reliable index of utopian status, from the ancient world to the eighteenth century. Not just ensuring enough for everyone without back-breaking drudgery – the importance of which can't be over-estimated – but sharing food, in rituals that bring the community together, remain priorities in all kinds of ideal commonwealth. Already in Socrates' version of the simple-life state, the catering for civic feasts goes beyond Golden Age crudités to the baking of loaves and cakes. (Incidentally, a possible further distinction between Golden Age and simple-life utopia could fit Lévi-Strauss's formulation of the raw versus the cooked.[6]) When Glaucon objects to such austerity, Socrates improves his menu with a list of additional relishes, headed by salt: identifying the use of salt as a marker of civilised taste is still current in eighteenth-century fiction. But even with these concessions, Glaucon isn't satisfied, dismissing this vegetarian diet as fit only for 'a community of pigs'[7] – so giving Socrates his cue to make a vital transition in the discussion. Again, the connection of a predominantly vegetarian diet with simple-life utopianism and meat-eating with luxury is a motif which will have a long history.

Plato's 'simple' state evolves into an increasingly complicated organism as requirements proliferate, so creating a need for greater specialisation. The citizens' diet changes to include meat; doctors are more in demand; the population grows beyond the capacity of the land to support it; and the outcome is war. But for one state in the ancient world, which was to prove enormously influential as a utopian model, war and the simple life are ideologically inseparable from the outset. This state is the Sparta of Lycurgus.[8] The notorious Spartan rigour in matters of diet begins in infancy, when babies are trained not to be fussy about their food, and continues with keeping Spartan boys on short commons to make them tough (and skilled in theft). Since the entire object is to produce a military élite, girls however are better fed than elsewhere in Greece, so that they will bear strong children. In adulthood, the communal mess exemplifies the same principle, and its fare, particularly the black broth – the Spartan idea of a delicacy – became the butt of jokes that are still circulating in early modern England. Robert Burton cites the wry anecdote told of the Sybarite who 'supping . . . [at the public tables] in Sparta, and observing their hard fare, said it was no marvel if the Lacedaemonians were valiant men; "for his part, he would rather run upon a sword-point (and so would any man in his wits), than live with such base diet, or lead so wretched a life".[9] In spite of this resistance to Spartan food – and although the military ethos it represents is often rejected or modified in later utopias – nevertheless the Spartan communal meal is much admired and imitated. It is, indeed, largely responsible for the continuing emphasis on the communal meal as a central rite of the ideal commonwealth. And the idea of plain living allied to social unity, whether located in a mythical golden world or a 'historical' culture, clearly attracts writers and readers who feel that they inhabit a more sophisticated but socially divisive existence: in other words, perhaps the majority of the human race in every period on record, including the eighteenth century. Primitivism, as well as progress, is a powerful element in utopian thinking. The two forms of ideal state – simple and luxurious – continue to define each other from *The Republic* onwards.

With the virtual re-invention of the classical utopia in the Renaissance, this debate becomes as much centred on cultural location as on cultural origins. The expansion of world horizons rewrites the old myths of the Golden Age and the lost island of Atlantis.[10] One tempting but possibly misleading way of formulating the new perspective is to express it as Old World luxury versus New World simplicity: but it's more complicated than that suggests. Again, however, what the inhabitants eat and (especially perhaps in Renaissance texts) what they wear, as well as their physical surroundings, help to identify which kind of utopia we are observing.

For example, in a sixteenth-century context, both More's Utopians and Rabelais' Thélèmites profess a philosophy of pleasure, subscribing to the Golden Age principle that whatever is good pleases, whatever pleases is good.[11] However, since they often disagree on what is truly pleasurable, the dissimilarities between the two locations are far more pronounced than the similarities. If Utopia resembles the monastic ideal in aiming at simplicity, the anti-monastic Abbey of Thélème anticipates a modern luxury hotel, with its elegant apartments including full-length mirrors and daily replenished perfume caskets, its excellent service and superb sports facilities. The Rabelaisian 'friars' and 'nuns' depend on an extensive support system of service and suppliers, reflecting that which maintained the courtly world of sixteenth-century Europe. Their dress is a rainbow dazzle of colour and jewels, creating employment for all the luxury trades explicitly debarred from More's Utopia.[12] In contrast, the Utopians' austere dress is a reaction against a culture in which power is signalled by rank and conspicuous consumption: like other simple-life idealists, they oppose extravagant fashion in any form.[13] Yet they aren't averse to the harmless pleasures of the senses, turning the ancient institution of the communal meal into more than a merely utilitarian function. Ralph Robinson's translation lends an authentic Tudor flavour to the proceedings: 'no supper is passed without music, nor their banquets lack no conceits nor junkets. They burn sweet gums and spices or perfumes . . . and sprinkle about sweet ointments and waters, yea, they leave nothing undone that maketh for the cheering of the company.'[14] Although More is concerned with the rituals of eating rather than with what is eaten, the Utopian diet evidently includes meat. They aren't Golden Age vegetarians, which might seem a trifle inconsistent for people who deplore hunting (a favourite recreation of the aristocratic Thélèmites) and who leave the distasteful business of the abattoir to bondsmen, to protect their own sensibilities. Campanella's citizens, faced with the logical dilemma that if it's cruel to kill animals then it's 'also cruel to kill plants, which have feelings' (which leaves starvation as the only option), prefer to justify an omnivorous diet on the grounds 'that lowly things are made for noble ones'.[15]

In such matters as food and clothes, Renaissance utopias keep alive the debate on whether the ideal society should espouse simplicity or luxury, or negotiate a compromise between the two – a debate that continues into the eighteenth century with the rise of economic science. But a new factor that modifies the Renaissance view of this subject develops from the perception of New World cultures as surviving examples of a Golden Age or state of nature. This may be read either positively or negatively, depending on presentation.

In his essay On the Cannibals, Montaigne uses relative concepts of barbarous and civilised customs in a manner that anticipates much eighteenth-century discourse on the topic, including Swift's. To the Greeks, barbarians were alien by definition: Montaigne challenges cultural preconceptions by assimilating his cannibals to precisely the received utopian myths derived from ancient Greece and current in his own society:

It irritates me that neither Lycurgus nor Plato had any knowledge
of them, for it seems to me that what experience has taught us
about those peoples surpasses not only all the descriptions with
which poetry has beautifully painted the Age of Gold and all its
ingenious fictions about Man's blessed early state, but also the
very conceptions and yearnings of philosophy. They could not
even imagine a state of nature so simple and so pure as the one
we have learned about from experience; they could not even
believe that societies of men could be maintained with so little
artifice, so little in the way of human solder.[16]

He subsequently addresses Plato, expanding the familiar negative
formula of everything that this fortunate nation lacks. It all seems
sufficiently conventional (though the reader of *Gulliver's Travels*
might note with interest that they have 'no words for treachery, lying,
cheating . . . '). However, on the crucial points of diet and clothes,
Montaigne reserves his most radical challenge to idealised notions of
the state of nature. In the section on the treatment of enemy
prisoners, he remarks that this includes the ritual consumption of
corpses, not for their food value but for revenge. Eating people is
wrong: but how wrong – relatively – is it? He makes the very Swiftian
point that 'there is more barbarity in eating a man alive than in
eating him dead'.[17] Indeed, the cannibal feast continues the sociable
tradition of the utopian communal meal (and the tone contrasts
piquantly with the revulsion experienced by Robinson Crusoe): after
executing a prisoner 'they roast him and make a common meal of
him, sending chunks of his flesh to absent friends'. As with Swift's
Yahoos, we are entitled to 'call those folk barbarians by the rules of
reason, but not in comparison with ourselves, who surpass them in
every kind of barbarism'.[18]

    Similarly, clothes signify a misleading and literally superficial
separation between the barbarous and the civilised. Both in this essay,
and in *On the custom of wearing clothes*, Montaigne takes the argument
for utopian simplicity to its logical conclusion, that nakedness is the
most natural state of all. He ends *On the Cannibals* with a brilliant
Parthian shot – 'Not at all bad, that. – Ah! But they wear no breeches
. . . .' Only civilised man needs the luxury of '*a Pair of Breeches*,
which, tho' a Cover for Lewdness as well as Nastiness,' as Swift
remarks in another context, 'is easily slipt down for the Service of
Both'.[19]

    The sophisticated relativism of Montaigne leaves judgments on

Golden Age primitivism and the state of nature open. But these are by no means synonymous, and for eighteenth-century writers it is Hobbes who turns the state of nature into a travesty Golden Age which is the reverse of utopian:

> In such condition, there is no place for Industry; because the fruit thereof is uncertain: and consequently no Culture of the Earth; no Navigation, nor use of the commodities that may be imported by Sea; no commodious Building; no Instruments of moving, and removing such things as require much force; no Knowledge of the face of the Earth; no account of Time; no Arts; no Letters; no Society; and which is worst of all, continuall feare, and danger of violent death; And the life of man, solitary, poore, nasty, brutish, and short.[20]

Post-Hobbes, the primitivist ideal can never seem quite the same. Yet it's a matter of definition. For Hobbes, the hypothetical state of nature is pre-social and pre-political, Plato's blank canvas, whereas for Aristotle the state of nature is itself political because 'the state is a creation of nature, and . . . man is by nature a political animal'.[21] In the early eighteenth century, Defoe and Swift, using utopian means, invite or force readers to interrogate such assumptions, to consider what kind of animal unaccommodated man actually is. However, even the simplest utopia requires an idea of social structure. The supply of necessities for the body is only the beginning: the next level of utopian fiction is the construction of the politics of the imaginary state, and for this the inventor needs to manipulate the levers of power and property.

Politics, power, property

After Plato's artist-ruler has restored his canvas to pristine simplicity, 'the first step will be to sketch in the outline of the social system' or, in an alternative translation, 'the outline of the constitution'.[22] Not all later utopian writers concern themselves with the question which was of such pressing interest to the intellectual Greek world: should the ideal state be a monarchy, an oligarchy, a democracy, or should it attempt to combine different elements? Yet almost all utopias presuppose or imply some kind of answer to the political question. Even Alexander Selkirk, the prototype of Crusoe, is monarch of all he surveys, whose 'right there is none to dispute'.[23] Further, the constitutional arrangements tend to mirror the writer's assumptions about the deep structures of human existence. For Plato and Aristotle, the constitution of the just state parallels the constitution of the just man: the different social classes correspond to the divided and specialised faculties of the individual, superior and inferior.

In Plato's *Republic*, the ruling élite represents reason, and is qualified by nature, age and experience to act as the Guardians of the commonwealth (their more youthful colleagues, the Auxiliaries, are responsible for executing their decisions). To sustain the system, Plato proposes a controlling fiction of gods creating human beings in the image of different metals, gold, silver, iron, brass, the predominance of which determines each person's social status. It's a fable designed to condition the acceptance of social division as psychological fact. An individual's class – which is usually, but not necessarily, that of the parents – is as inalienable as his or her own psyche. Aristotle also uses the analogy between individual and social constitution to explain and justify the power of the free man over the slave.[24]

However, Aristotle deploys another very influential model for political power structures, developed from the theory that the state originates in the family. Although he asserts that 'the state is clearly prior to the family and to the individual, since the whole is of necessity prior to the part',[25] the analogy is suggestive in ways that go beyond the purely political. Such a model reinforces a hierarchy in which older dominates younger, male dominates female. Both analogies – with the individual and with the family – make flesh the abstraction of 'the state', and therefore activate feelings of authority and helplessness buried deep in the collective consciousness. It is incumbent on the writer of utopian fiction to address these feelings in devising power structures that will reduce as far as possible inherent tension, conflict and oppression.

One method of doing this is through the control of property rights, for wealth creates one of the most powerful motivating forces in public and personal life. If the ideal state is to achieve the unity and harmony at which it aims, some way must be found to keep the acquisitive, aggressive and competitive instincts in check. Self-interest has to give way to the common good, or at least be harnessed to it. Outside the Golden Age, the means to this end has to be a political one. In Plato's Republic, Lycurgus' Sparta, and More's Utopia (to mention only the most familiar examples) the solution takes a similar though not identical form: eliminate the universal currency of gold and silver, and replace material values with intangible ones. In a sense, this is the Midas touch in reverse. Instead of wanting to turn everything into actual gold, the utopian legislators want to transmute gold into invisible assets – their gold standard is measured by the quality of human beings the state produces.

Plato confines this ideal to his Guardians: 'they alone . . . of all the citizens are forbidden to touch or handle silver or gold'.[26] They own nothing but minimal essentials, their living quarters are communal, and, as in Sparta, they share a common table. This is presented not as deprivation but as privilege, setting the Guardians apart and making them responsible for the economic and moral guidance of the class which is permitted to own property. Later, in *The Laws*, Plato seems to acknowledge that this is a literally utopian ideal, arguing only that the best code is to 'put into practice [the principle of sharing] as widely as possible *throughout the entire state*' (my italics).[27]

Not surprisingly, however, the radical devaluation of gold and silver continues to be a potent symbol of states which have retained or (if it isn't a contradiction in terms) regained their economic virginity. These include Sparta, with its iron currency, described by Xenophon, and the Germania described by Tacitus.[28] In Renaissance Europe, about to be flooded Danae-like with New World gold, Thomas More executes one of the wittiest variations on the theme. His fictional Utopians have the same attitude to gold and silver as their ancient counterparts, but a more sophisticated way of registering their contempt: they eat and drink from plain pottery and glass but defecate into gold chamberpots; they give precious stones to toddlers as playthings and hang gold chains on slaves, a practice precipitating the famous cultural misunderstanding when Utopian children and their mothers unwittingly expose the delusions of grandeur paraded by the heavily bejewelled foreign ambassadors.[29] Arguably, More is the utopian writer who embodies most imaginatively the idea of an entire community based on genuine property-sharing and an unprecedented degree of power-sharing. Yet even More is demonstrably conscious of the theoretic and practical difficulties in the way of ever implementing such a system, making ironic use of his persona 'More' to voice them within the dialogue.

These difficulties had been originally formulated by Aristotle in direct response to Plato's *Republic*. Aristotle doesn't construct a full-scale fictional alternative to Socrates' ideal state, but proceeds by testing the model already set up, particularly in relation to the proposition of possessing everything in common, which he treats as a general principle rather than one confined to an élite. The objections to common ownership and the arguments for it rest paradoxically on the same reading of human nature as essentially self-interested, yet needing to learn how to cooperate. Aristotle wants the incentive that comes from private property combined with a generosity that springs from having something to share. His is a dual ethic, intended to make the best of both systems:

> Property should be in a certain sense common, but, as a general rule, private; for, when everyone has a distinct interest, men will not complain of one another, and they will make more progress, because everyone will be attending to his own business. And yet by reason of goodness, and in respect of use, 'Friends', as the proverb says, 'will have all things common'.[30]

Plato had cited the same proverb in the passage from *The Laws*. Aristotle summarises, 'It is clearly better that property should be private, but the use of it common; and the special business of the legislator is to create in men this benevolent disposition.' Whatever political means they adopt, most utopian legislators believe that it's possible to create such a disposition. Plato and More take the radical option of removing material incentives. For Aristotle, on the contrary, private property is a condition of liberality, a view with which most eighteenth-century writers would concur. The moral evils said to be the result of private property are, as he crisply remarks, 'due not to the absence of communism but to wickedness'.[31]

If property isn't the source of political power in a utopian society, then what is its source? According to Plato, authority should derive from a different kind of wealth, that of wisdom. This results in the paradox that the only human beings fit to exercise power are those who don't want it, or at least those who 'are not in love with it'. Socrates asks rhetorically 'Who else, then, will you compel to undertake the responsibilities of Guardians of our state, if it is not to be those who know most about the principles of good government and who have other rewards and a better life than the politician's?'[32] On this point, Aristotle is in general agreement: neither ambition nor wealth should be the main qualifications for high office, and 'the worthiest should be appointed, whether he chooses or not'.[33] However, Aristotle recognises that although politicians shouldn't buy power or exploit their position for material gain, wealth is a factor because it buys the time to devote to government. If a state wants the best, it has to pay. This is not, of course, a problem in a fully communal system like More's Utopia, where, because of the distribution of labour, everyone has sufficient leisure and the state officials can be exempted from other demands. Yet even More's Utopia has an element of privilege, in the form of this exemption, which depends not on property but on intellectual attainment, and which can be withdrawn.[34] (More problematically, at the other end of the scale, it includes the ancient institution of slavery, which has a wholly penal function.)

Neither classical nor Renaissance utopias are egalitarian when it comes to the exercise of power. All have some principle of exclusion from the rights of citizenship, whether on the grounds of class or of crime. Reading accounts of utopian constitutions from Plato to More and beyond, we can see an identikit picture emerging of the type of person considered fittest for the responsibilities of ruling. In theory, government is a career open to all the talents, including, in Plato's case, female talents; but in practice, the preferred member of the ideal governing class is likely to be male, middle-aged or older, highly educated, and born to the job in the sense of having innate qualities identifiable as the raw material of excellence. In itself, this ideal doesn't appear particularly utopian. What makes it so is the insistence 'that the excellence of the citizen and ruler is the same as that of the good man, and that the same person must first be a subject and then a ruler',[35] a principle that tends towards a kind of spiritual gerontocracy. Virtue immunises the individual against the virus of ambition and prevents addiction to the drug of power. Whether or not he needs the further safeguard of lacking private property is a matter of dispute. His gifts combine those of the thinker and the doer, but he is seen more in the light of a great legislator – a Lycurgus or a Solon – than a great commander. Yet in spite of these utopian archetypes, individual leadership is less important than a collective ideal, for a utopian state depends on a plurality of ideal citizens. How are they to be produced? This burning question is answered in two ways: control of human reproduction and control of education.

Sex and reproduction

Utopian states may or may not privatise the means of production; but we tend to assume that the means of reproduction are already

privatised. However, few utopian legislators are willing to allow
citizens to conduct their own sex lives as they see fit. Too much is at
stake. And since sexual compulsion – a more convincing proof of
necessity to most of us than any mathematical demonstration, as
Glaucon observes – can't be legislated out of existence, it has to be
regulated. According to Socrates, 'it would be a sin either for mating
or for anything else in a truly happy society to take place without
regulation. Our Rulers would not allow it.'[36] Plato's eugenic theories
have become notorious, but their ominous implications are entirely
consistent with utopian logic. On the one hand, human unions
require ritual sanctification; on the other, they must meet the same
criteria that apply to breeding from animals, which means selecting
for superior strains. The analogy between the human animal and other
species will have a long history in utopian discourse, and not only in
the context of reproduction. However, in that context it starkly
exposes the fraud perpetrated by the utopian imagination in the name
of the greater good of society. The marriage festivals in *The Republic*,
with their ceremonies and songs, glorify a biological function which is
at the same time being clinically supervised without the participants'
awareness.

At another level, the Guardians themselves have unawareness
imposed on them by their own myth. By separating children from
their mothers immediately after birth, and either assigning them to
professional child-carers or quietly relegating them to an unspecified
limbo if they are substandard, the state cuts the cord of personal
relationships between parent and child, man and woman (something
that Swift, for one, seems to admire). Plato's Guardians literally don't
know who they are in uniquely individual terms: each person is an
organic part of a supraidentity, the state, and stands in a familial
relationship to all members of his or her class.[37] In a sense, this system
reinforces the 'family' model by extending it to a whole community. It
also has suggestive implications for the position of women (and no
arrangements for sex and reproduction in utopias can be free from
such implications).

In relation to childbearing, Guardian women might appear either
privileged or deprived, according to viewpoint: Glaucon hasn't any
doubts – 'Child-bearing will be an easy job for the Guardians' wives
on those conditions.'[38] What is certain is that the system radically
challenges sexual roles, including the definition of 'wives'. If the
utopian principle of having women and children in common isn't

necessarily liberating (and the aim isn't personal happiness in any case) nevertheless it does remove the traditional justification for treating women as chattels. Even the animal analogy works as part of the Socratic argument for a reassessment of female status in the ideal commonwealth, which culminates in the proposition

> that the best arrangement is for our men and women to share a common education, to bring up their children in common and to have a common responsibility, as Guardians, for their fellow-citizens . . . That women should in fact, so far as possible, take part in all the same occupations as men, both in peace within the city and on campaign in war, acting as Guardians and hunting with the men like hounds, that this is the best course for them and that there is nothing unwomanly in this natural partnership of the sexes?[39]

Yet, though Glaucon agrees, belief in the innate inferiority of women as a sex is far too deep-rooted to be easily shaken. Aristotle's objections to the status of women in *The Republic*, as well as Plato's own later work, *The Laws*, reveal just how utopian even the idea of equal opportunity is perceived to be. Whether or not Plato was a feminist, he undeniably puts feminism – and anti-feminism – on the utopian agenda for his successors.

In his *Politics*, Aristotle reasserts the traditional emphasis on the subordination of women and their essentially domestic role, criticising the latitude given to them in states such as Sparta. He rejects the Socratic proposal of putting relationships on an entirely communal basis, because it goes against the grain of human psychology and devalues emotional ties which can be a powerful force for good in the state. Also, he raises a point which tends to be taken lightly by creators of sexually egalitarian utopias: who will look after the house? 'It is absurd' he claims 'to argue, from the analogy of animals, that men and women should follow the same pursuits, for animals have not to manage a household.'[40] Nonetheless, for Aristotle, biology is the factor that determines culture so far as sex and reproduction are concerned (he appeals to it, for instance, when like Johnson in *Rasselas* he discusses the controversial question of the best age for marriage and procreation).[41] It is the legislator's duty to control the biological processes that create future citizens, so far as is humanly possible. On this point at least he is at one with Plato. To sum up, the political wellbeing of Plato's state requires a limited form of sexual equality, whereas Aristotle's requires the subordination of women to men: but neither would dispute that the interests of the community come before those of individuals.

Other ancient writers on the ideal state may modify either the Platonic or the Aristotelian view of these issues. Xenophon, and later Plutarch, depart from Aristotle in their belief that they order these matters better in Sparta – in the golden age of Lycurgus at any rate. Athletic Spartan girls, who exercise naked alongside men, make fitter mothers in every sense. As for sex, the law does its best to intrude into the couple's bed, recommending restraint even in marriage. 'Adultery was wholly unknown among them' declares Plutarch confidently, though what constitutes adultery becomes an interesting question in a society which permits arrangements for surrogate parenthood in certain circumstances.[42] Generally, in 'ideal' societies which don't adopt the Platonic model of having women and children in common, sexual fidelity is not only admired but severely enforced. Tacitus singles out the Germanic marriage code for particular commendation on this score. 'Adultery is extremely rare', not perhaps astonishingly given the violence of the punishment meted out to the erring wife by her outraged husband: 'he cuts off her hair, strips her naked, and in the presence of kinsmen turns her out of his house and flogs her all through the village.'[43] (There is no mention of the punishment for male adulterers.) Unlike the Greeks or Romans, these barbarians refuse to countenance measures to control reproduction. And, far from separating child from mother at birth, they strengthen the maternal bond by having every mother breastfeed her own infant. The extended family bolsters the patriarchal authority of the elder male: clearly, 'there is nothing to be gained by childlessness in Germany'.[44] Tacitus, of course, is here using the example of barbarians rather as Montaigne will later use the example of cannibals: to shock a sophisticated civilisation – in this case, imperial Rome – into a reappraisal of its own *mores*.[45]

Whether the paradigm is Sparta or Germania, these representations of sexual and parental practices have more to do with utopian idealism than with anthropological interest. Implicitly or explicitly, these writers are contrasting a rigid and successful disciplining of instinct in quasi-utopian societies with the messier lives of actual human beings in actual societies. Yet the ideal itself is still in touch with a recognisable reality, ideologically closer to Aristotle than to Plato.

When the societies described are frankly fictional, however, there are fewer constraints on the utopian imagination. For instance, the Platonic model can be tried out, and its positive results taken for granted, as in the utopia of Iambulus. There 'not even the mothers may know their own offspring. Consequently, since there is no rivalry among them, they never experience civil disorders and they never cease placing the highest value upon internal harmony.'[46]

Conversely, in his description of the Isle of the Blest, Lucian travesties *The Republic*: indeed, while Socrates is admitted for reasons that are slyly substantiated, Plato himself is absent – 'it was said that he was living in his imaginary city under the constitution and the laws that he himself wrote'.[47] Typically, Lucian's version of the Platonic system which he appropriates is all sex and no reproduction: 'About love-making their attitude is such that they bill-and-coo openly in plain sight of everyone, without any discrimination, and think no shame of it at all.'[48] (Incidentally, the translator is being discreet: the Greek verb rendered as 'bill-and-coo' means to copulate.) Socrates denies being involved in these erotic pursuits, but he isn't believed, Hyacinthus and Narcissus giving evidence to the contrary. Lucian's final flourish is to acknowledge his original: 'they all have their wives in common and nobody is jealous of his neighbour; in this point they out-Plato Plato.' In fact, this idyll has a closer affinity to Golden Age libertinism than to Plato's political model of human relations.

If Lucian's imaginary voyages substitute fantasy for the politics of sex, the same could be said for his treatment of sexual physiology. In the ancient world at least, serious utopian theory can't envisage freeing humanity from biological constraints (that has to wait for the imagination of science). However, a surrealist like Lucian can reinvent sexual physiology at will, creating for example a race of moon people who 'are not born of women but of men: they marry men and do not even know the word woman at all' (though they shift roles from 'wife' to 'husband' at a certain age).[49] Moon children are gestated in the calf of the leg, which replaces the womb. Nor is this Lucian's only bright idea for male self-reproduction: he also devises the method of the Tree-men, who extrude the right testicle, plant it, and wait for a phallic tree to grow, bearing the seeds of a new generation in its enormous acorns. The reason for such inventions might be inferred from the existence of alternative fictions representing female sexuality as a threat to the male, like the entangling vine-women, or the seductive women of the sea, with their concealed asses' legs, who make a habit of dining on passing strangers. Although Lucian's fantasies are on the wilder fringe of the utopian genre, they anticipate not just the utopian satires of later writers, but the very concept of utopias in which the sexual function is radically transformed – and, indeed, the idea of the single-sex utopia.

Renaissance utopists, beginning with More, are well aware of the range of classical precedents on this fascinating topic. Their own choices depend on a combination of factors: they are separated from the ancient world primarily by the cultural impact of Christianity, which reinforces monogamy, but at the same time they are conscious of other cultural norms, such as polygamy, associated with exotic locations. Of the writers who include a discussion of sexual arrangements in their fictional utopias, the most influential is More, who himself is indebted to Plato and Lucian in a number of well-attested respects. Yet on this area of human life he differs quite sharply from both these mentors. Although More can be amusing about sex, he is much less airily satiric than Lucian on the subject, and devotes less imaginative space to it in his scheme of things. On the subject of the family, however, he is deeply engaged; and, as is often observed, this insistence on the monogamous and patriarchal family as the basic social unit more than anything else differentiates More's communist state from Plato's. Both see the virtues of having a state which is 'like a single family',[50] but they disagree on the structure of relationships that will best achieve this desirable end.

As for organising reproduction and parenthood, More's Utopians are less inclined to worry about quality and quantity control or to interfere with nature. Adults can be, and are, shifted around to stabilise the numbers in households, but the Utopians 'do not, of course, try to regulate the number of minor children in a family'.[51] More dispenses with most of the elaborate theorising on the bearing and rearing of healthy children found in his classical predecessors. His description of infant care, inserted in the discussion of communal meals, is simple and commonsensical – a supply of 'cradles, clean water and a warm fire', time for play, and nursing by the mother whenever possible. Clearly it would be a happier fate to be a Utopian baby than a Spartan one subject to a toughening regime from birth.[52]

However, there is one point on which More does seem to follow Plato's lead, and that is the best-remembered comic feature of Utopian courtship: the custom of inspecting each other naked, under respectable supervision, before taking the plunge into matrimony. It's equally revealing in the context of the Utopian attitude to marriage, which is eminently practical. What is perhaps most striking about monogamous relationships in Utopia, given their philosophy of pleasure, is how little pleasure is expected from marriage. Apropos of the mutual inspection, Hythlodaeus comments chillingly 'if some disfiguring accident takes place after marriage, each person must bear his own fate; but the Utopians think everyone should be legally protected from deception beforehand.'[53] Legally protected: what is conspicuously absent from the discussion is any mention of compatibility other than on the physical level – exactly the point that Milton was later to make in his divorce tracts. Utopian rationality also admits grounds for divorce. However, like so much else in Utopia, this freedom is hedged about with stringent conditions, and requires permission from the state: 'divorce is deliberately made difficult because they know that couples will have a hard time settling down if each partner has in mind that a new relation is easily available.'[54] For the same reason, to protect marriage, adultery is punished with 'the strictest form of slavery', and, for the second offence, carries the death penalty. The penalties for premarital intercourse also suggest that the primary motive for marriage is to legitimise sex: 'they suppose few people would join in married love – with confinement to a single partner and all the petty annoyances that married life involves – unless they were strictly restrained from promiscuity.'[55]

The question that the reader is tempted to ask is why all this should be necessary. Why does sex have to be legitimised in a non-Christian communist state, unless it's purely an assertion of state power over individuals? More's utopian creation is not the first, nor the last, to regard the sexual impulse as essentially anarchic and destabilising. In a commonwealth where inheritance is not an issue, why should marriage require such powerful protection against adultery? There seem to be few if any arguments from expediency alone to justify marriage as an institution in a state where the vulnerable citizens, the very old and the very young, are in any case provided for. Yet the Utopians lay particular stress on the importance of fidelity in old age. Practically speaking, there is no reason why Utopia shouldn't adopt the Platonic model of wives and children in common. We may suspect that it is the moral, not the rational argument, that is the real influence. Whatever its drawbacks, marriage is good for the character, and the Utopians prefer its 'comforts' to the hardships of celibacy. They might well concur in the famous Johnsonian aphorism: 'marriage has many pains, but celibacy has no pleasures'.[56]

Among the many pains of Utopian marriage specifically affecting women might be considered the requirement that they kneel and confess their shortcomings to their husbands on a regular basis. Of course, this evidence of female subordination can also explain why the Utopians feel more comfortable with traditional marriage: the two go together. Nevertheless, women in More's *Utopia* aren't confined entirely to reproductive and domestic roles, although these roles are a primary responsibility. If 'women's work' apparently doesn't count as *work*, at least – unlike women in the outside world – they are regarded as productive members of the community, and (if elderly widows safely beyond an active sex life) can even aspire to the priesthood. Like Plato's female Guardians, they can also defend their country. In short, More's *Utopia* is as controversially inconsistent on the status of women as it is on most other utopian topics.[57]

Other Renaissance utopias are perhaps more consistent, if no less controversial, in dealing with the subject of sex and reproduction. The Rabelaisian Abbey of Thélème offers Golden Age joys of freely chosen love, a prolonged courtship which, on re-entry into the outside world, becomes the basis for long and idyllically happy marriage (in stark opposition to the monastic vow of celibacy).[58] It is the Rabelaisian not the Morean utopia which integrates sexual fulfilment with a general philosophy of pleasure, without having to confront any of the more awkward questions about how to sustain that fulfilment.

In contrast, Rabelais' compatriot Montaigne relocates the Golden Age of freedom and tolerance in the New World, pointing a barbed contrast with European custom: 'one beautiful characteristic of their marriages is worth noting: just as our wives are zealous in thwarting our love and tenderness for other women, theirs are equally zealous in obtaining them for them . . . Our wives will scream that that is a marvel, but it is not: it is a virtue proper to matrimony, but at an earlier stage.' Predictably, the women know their place, occupying themselves with ministering to men by 'warming up their drink: that is their main task'.[59] This polygamous paradise, supported by parallels from the Bible and classical antiquity, foreshadows the debate about polygamy which keeps resurfacing in seventeenth- and eighteenth-century contexts, and which has a distinctly utopian tinge.

Finally, perhaps the most complete European utopia of the century following More, Campanella's *City of the Sun* (*La Città del Sole*, or *Civitas Solis*), reverts to Plato and the principle of having women in common. From the care with which the elaborate arrangements for sexual intercourse are worked out, it's clear that Campanella (who incidentally had rebelled against his Dominican training) has thought hard and positively about this aspect of utopian life. As far as possible, sex is divorced from love – which is an affair of minds not bodies – and linked entirely with procreation: 'the only love that is recognised among them is, at the most, that of friendship, not that of burning passion'.[60] Swift's Houyhnhnms would have approved. Young males who find abstinence beyond them are supplied with barren or already impregnated partners to avoid random conception. Campanella sees nothing incongruous in the Socratic analogy between human and animal breeding, and he works out the biological implications: 'tall and beautiful women are coupled only with strong and tall men, fat women with thin men, and thin women with fat men, so as to achieve a balance'.[61] As for male intellectuals, naturally feeble in animal spirits, they have the pick of women with the best physical endowments (a convenient doctrine for the intelligentsia). Campanella slides out of any suggestion of incompatibility by blandly asserting that none of the sun citizens are actually ugly, since health and exercise produce the body beautiful. The actual business of intercourse is conscientiously timed and regulated for maximum efficacy, including scrupulous attention to hygiene. Yet, on the whole, Campanella is less harsh than others in his penalties for sexual mis-demeanour, provided that it doesn't become a habit: the punishment for a first offence of sodomy is public humiliation – 'for two days [they] have to go around with a shoe tied to their necks, signifying that they have perverted the proper order of things and have put their feet on their heads'.[62] Not only does this exhibit the utopian concern with making the punishment fit the crime, but it is also consistent with the emphasis on procreation as the only end of sex.

All these Renaissance variations on the structure of relationships in utopia continue a classical debate which is to remain central to fictional representation. Michel Foucault writes of the ways in which the term 'sexuality' relates to 'other phenomena' defined as

> the development of diverse fields of knowledge (embracing the biological mechanisms of reproduction as well as the individual or social variants of behaviour); the establishment of a set of

rules and norms – in part traditional, in part new – which found support in religious, judicial, pedagogical, and medical institutions; and changes in the way individuals were led to assign meaning and value to their conduct, their duties, their pleasures, their feelings and sensations, their dreams.[63]

The same phenomena are subject to investigation by the utopian theorist and novelist alike, especially in a period when the legal and social concepts of marriage are being questioned.[64] For eighteenth-century writers, marriage and the family occupy an emotional territory where private and public concerns intersect, and in which the novel and utopian fiction both have powerful vested interests.

Education and culture

Logically, the next stage in utopian thinking after control of reproduction is control of education. Once the children of any ideal state have been properly conceived and born, they have to be inducted into their culture: and utopian writers emulate Walter Shandy in their attention to pedagogy. There is relatively little disagreement about the ends of education – to produce better human beings and better citizens – compared with the dispute about means. Aristotle sets out the questions with particular clarity:

> That education should be regulated by law and should be an affair of state is not to be denied, but what should be the character of this public education, and how young persons should be educated, are questions which remain to be considered. As things are, there is disagreement about the subjects. For men are by no means agreed about the things to be taught, whether we look to excellence or the best life. Neither is it clear whether education is more concerned with intellectual or with moral excellence. The existing practice is perplexing; no one knows on what principle we should proceed – should the useful in life, or should excellence, or should the higher knowledge, be the aim of our training? – all three opinions have been entertained. Again about the means there is no agreement; for different persons, starting with different ideas about the nature of excellence, naturally disagree about the practice of it.[65]

The questions are equally relevant inside and outside utopia (in a sense, we could all be said to be utopians when it comes to education). Through Socrates in *The Republic* and the Athenian speaker in *The Laws*, Plato had already offered a number of possible answers. And although the answers change with the centuries, the questions stay remarkably constant, so that the reader finds the same issues being debated in eighteenth-century fiction.

Aristotle assumes that the state should take responsibility for education. But however disputable that may be, there is still greater potential for disagreements over the question of who should be educated. Both Plato and Aristotle are prepared to extend education to women, but Socrates, as has already been observed, is much more emphatic on the necessity for compulsory egalitarian education for Guardians of both sexes. The effect in *The Republic* is to maximise opportunity for developing individual talent, for medicine, say, regardless of gender:[66] an aim which is still an impossibly utopian dream in eighteenth-century Britain. On the other hand, in both *The Republic* and in Aristotle's envisaged society, the right to education is determined by prior assignment to class. Those not deemed worthy of educating, or excluded from the citizen body, are *ipso facto* outside the system. This is another reason for a certain élitism in the curriculum: Aristotle rules out the arts which he terms 'mechanical', defined as those 'which tend to deform the body, and likewise all paid employments, for they absorb and degrade the mind'.[67] Education is for leisure. At the same time, everything taught has a function.

It follows that a certain tension exists between encouraging concentration on special gifts and skills and encouraging the development of the whole human being to become an exemplary citizen – between the vocational and the moral. Utopias aren't the best places to have ambitions as a doctor or lawyer, for instance, and the creator of *The Republic* has little patience with the closed shop of the learned professions.[68] Equally, however, there is a problem about educating human beings to realise their highest potential in intellect and imagination, without taking into account that teaching people to think might also mean that they start to think independently. Few utopists address the full implications of education as a force for change. But Plato certainly recognises the possible subversiveness of the creative arts in particular, and their powerful influence.

His case against admitting poets to the ideal state has been debated from every angle, from the Renaissance to the present.[69] One aspect particularly relevant to eighteenth-century writers is the distrust of the uninhibited power of imagination over reason, expressed by a philosopher who is himself a great creative artist. Both Swift and Johnson voice similar fears.[70] Further, virtually all utopias before the modern period ground culture on the sanctity of religious belief; and part of Plato's indictment of human art is that it can distort and trivialise the sacred. Since the child's mind is especially responsive to fiction, from the very outset, the storytelling of mothers and nurses is to be censored.[71] As the child grows, the danger arises more from active participation in creative art, through the medium of drama. Acting, the fissuring of identity, goes against the whole ethos of the Platonic ideal state, which enjoins unity, integrity, self-respect fixed by role and function (it's significant that Plato is especially anxious about the acting out of female emotions by males). Socrates sums up:

> So we shall be justified in not admitting [the poet] into a well-ordered commonwealth, because he stimulates and strengthens an element which threatens to undermine the reason. As a country may be given over into the power of its worst citizens while the better sort are ruined, so . . . the dramatic poet sets up a vicious form of government in the individual soul . . . and he is an image-maker whose images are phantoms far removed from reality.[72]

Yet in spite of this apparent intransigence, music and poetry still have an ineradicable importance in human life, even under conditions of strictest censorship. In *The Laws*, Plato's Athenian spokesman accepts whatever art is ideologically approved by mature and educated individuals – those who are already among the élite products of the system – and later adds the pleasingly ironic suggestion that the recommended set text which would best fulfil the criteria would be *The Laws* itself.[73] The creators of utopias are not prepared to deny themselves the privilege of exercising imagination.

Although Plato's educational system caters for the body as well as the mind, the supreme example of physical linked to vocational education in the ancient world is Sparta, which gears everything to the military ethos. It is a nation in perpetual training. As a result, it values discipline and team spirit very highly, and puts a relatively low priority on literate skills: 'of reading and writing, they learned only enough to serve their turn; all the rest of their training was calculated to make them obey commands well, endure hardships, and conquer in battle'.[74] Yet, though the Spartans regard verbal incontinence in much the same light as sexual incontinence (hence the derivation of 'laconic'), their education isn't deficient in the arts: 'nor was their training in music and poetry any less serious a concern than the emulous purity of their speech, nay, their very songs had a stimulus that roused the spirit . . . the style of them was simple and unaffected, and their themes were serious and edifying'.[75] If this reminds Swift's readers of the Houyhnhnms, it must be added that the Houyhnhnm republic is designed for peace not war.

In fact, one marked difference between ancient utopias and those of the early modern world, which is relevant to education and culture, might be registered as a growth in anti-war propaganda. This is a productive source of satire from More onwards (although many ideal states reluctantly accept the necessity for self-defence, and the concept of the just war, in a far from ideal world). Ancient utopias, on the other hand, tend to regard war against outsiders as the supreme test of what Socrates calls 'all the qualities one would expect from [their] system of education and training'.[76]

Another significant shift of emphasis in the utopian tradition is the degree to which cultural consciousness becomes overtly linked with linguistic difference. Language is scarcely an issue in ancient utopias, where the distinction between Greek and barbarian is so fundamental that there is no need to spell out which language is privileged, or to invent a specifically 'utopian' tongue. In Renaissance utopias, however, language is an issue, and fascination with its possibilities leads to imaginative word games. Interestingly, Greek is still the benchmark. More's Utopians, we are told, have a special facility in learning ancient Greek, because their own language has an affinity with (perhaps derives from) both it and Persian. In More's world, to assimilate a new language to that of a classical civilisation becomes a deliberate value judgment, resulting in a 'native tongue, which is not deficient in terminology or unpleasant in sound, and adapts itself as well as any to the expression of thought'.[77] Montaigne plays the same card in describing a New World language – which might be assumed to be barbaric – in these terms: 'their language incidentally is a pleasant one with an agreeable sound and has terminations rather like Greek'.[78] But in the case of More's Utopia, the language is an integral part of the fiction, which draws attention to *Utopia* as text (and a text which is itself written in a learned tongue). More's language games, in which his friends collaborated, devising not only tongue-in-cheek names but a Utopian alphabet and a sample of Utopian poetry, aren't simply playful.[79] From More onwards, the invented language of a utopian fiction will be a key to its culture and politics (Swift and Orwell provide notable examples).

Hythlodaeus makes a point of informing his humanist audience that in Utopian education all subjects are taught in the vernacular – and this makes a point not just about the versatility of the Utopian language, but about the accessibility of the educational system. More's curriculum is classically orthodox, but there is no pre-selection of its beneficiaries. Although only a minority are eventually 'assigned to scholarship full time', the entire population is given educational opportunities from childhood, and early morning lectures are a favourite adult pastime.[80] The craftsman can become a scholar through aptitude and application. The moral purpose of education is still paramount – 'instruction in good manners and pure morals is considered no less important than learning proper'[81] – but changes are beginning to take place, not least the fact that the 'mechanical arts', despised by Aristotle, are honoured by More and his successors.

It is in the next century, however, that the advancement of 'learning proper' and a concomitant interest in new educational methods make an impact on utopian literature. With Campanella and Bacon, the so-called 'pansophist' utopia comes into its own, and in turn influences the eighteenth-century utopian tradition either as a positive ideal or as a target of satire. The classical and earlier Renaissance utopian writers are obviously concerned with the quality of human life, but generally speaking they don't imagine the effects of scientific and technological revolution on that life. Yet if a new scientific culture will radically alter the perception of what is possible even for the utopian imagination, the old questions remain. The final one in every sense is also the ultimate test of a utopian society: how it comes to terms with the fact of mortality.

The utopian way of death

Death, like birth, is a concern of the utopian state, partly because it represents the most absolute form of control over its members. Classical and Renaissance utopias usually retain capital punishment as part of their penal code, and death in battle is always a possibility in a world where total pacifism seems almost an unthinkable option. However, that is true of all states. What makes the utopian state different is its management of death in the course of nature, which is directly linked to the concept of the good life. The culture of utopia is designed to make the best of *this* life, and paradoxically that includes aiding the passage out of it (sometimes literally).

Obviously a number of factors shape the utopian perception of the good death. Allowing for certain cultural variables – the Spartan heroic ideal, for instance – primary among these are religious faith and the support of philosophy, which are fundamental to utopias of virtually all persuasions in the ancient and Renaissance worlds. Both Plato and More take the immortality of the soul as the basis for a serene acceptance of personal mortality and bereavement. Citizens of the ideal state should be acclimatised to the idea of an immortal as well as an earthly paradise, and shouldn't indulge in excessive grief for those who exchange one sphere of existence for the other. The Spartans tackle the fear of death most pragmatically, by familiarising the young with all its appurtenances and cutting short the period of mourning.[82]

If the fear of death is distinguishable from the fear of dying, there are also practical ways of dealing with the latter. To a large extent, this involves utopian attitudes to health and growing old. Most utopian states promote good health by all the measures available within contemporary medical knowledge, ranging from prevention – the proper choice of location, good urban planning and so on – to provision of skilled medical care. However, some theorists are much more robust than others in the view they take of the relation between morality and health. Not only does Plato condemn self-induced troubles, given spurious importance by medical terminology (Socrates cites flatulence and catarrh); he also argues that extending professional treatment helps to create chronic sickness and hypochondria, preferring to advocate a kill-or-cure approach. In *The Republic* only useful citizens need apply for medication.[83] This implication that sickness is anti-social foreshadows the kind of utopian thinking that culminates in Samuel Butler's *Erewhon* where physical disease is a crime. More's Utopians are much more humane in their attitude to the sick and their administration of an enlightened hospital system, although they draw the line, as might be expected, at self-abuse. For the Utopians, 'health is crucial to pleasure' and therefore doctrinally central.[84]

However, even if the great majority of utopian citizens enjoy good health and longevity, old age and decay remain to be faced. On the whole, the increase in wisdom is supposed to compensate for decreasing physical powers, and in early utopias the status, dignity, and influence of the old are reinforced by the power structure. Naturally, the prospect of a good death is especially relevant in old age: one way of ensuring this is to suggest a measure of control and choice in the manner of departure. However, here the tension between individual and state decisions, between voluntary and involuntary euthanasia, becomes crucial. A good death – from whose point of view? Euthanasia can take bizarre forms; for example, the practice of the Massagetae, as recorded by Herodotus, might or might not be classified as utopian:

> They have one way only of determining the appropriate time to die, namely this: when a man is very old, all his relatives give a party and include him in a general sacrifice of cattle; then they boil the flesh and eat it. This they consider to be the best sort of death. Those who die of disease are not eaten but buried, and it is held a misfortune not to have lived long enough to be sacrificed.[85]

More appealing is the gentle mode of death available to the island utopians visited by Iambulus, although the time of dying is fixed by law:

> there is . . . a law among them that they should live only for a stipulated number of years, and at the completion of this period they should make away with themselves of their own accord, by a strange manner of death; for there grows among them a plant of a peculiar nature, and whenever a man lies down upon it, imperceptibly and gently he falls asleep and dies.

A *fortiori* (and with more obvious coercion) the unfit are disposed of – 'anyone also among them who has become crippled or suffers, in general, from any physical infirmity is forced by them, in accordance with an inexorable law, to remove himself from life'.[86]

More, writing in the Christian era when both suicide and euthanasia were anathematised, explores the rationale of approved self-killing through his Utopians. In purely utopian terms, without regard to Christian doctrine, he lets them evolve a thoughtful compromise, applicable in cases of painful and incurable illness, between state intervention and personal decision: the religious and secular authorities argue for death as a merciful release in such circumstances:

> Those who have been persuaded by these arguments either starve themselves to death or take a drug which frees them from life without any sensation of dying. But they never force this step on a man against his will; nor, if he decides against it, do they lessen their care of him.[87]

Believing as they do that a peaceful death presages eternal bliss, it is logical for the Utopians to rejoice rather than mourn for those who die 'blithely and full of good hope' (though the reverse also holds). They also have another source of consolation. Utopia isn't just a holy community, it is a community of ghosts who watch, and watch over, the living: a benign or a sinister conception, depending on how it is represented. 'Given their state of bliss, the dead must be able to travel freely where they please, and it would be unkind of them to cast off every desire of seeing those friends to whom in life they had been joined by mutual affection and charity':[88] Utopia is a country for both the dead and the living, a place of stability and continuity across the ephemeral generations.

To put it another way, if generations pass, the utopian state is immortal. But this immortality may be defined in different ways. It's a truism that the fictional ideal commonwealth tends to be a closed system, protected from change once it attains its optimum form. If More's Utopians conform to type in believing their state to be the happiest, they are unusual in the openness of their famous prayer (an openness which may not be totally owing to the necessity of providing for Christian conversion):

> . . . if there is some sort of society or religion more acceptable to God than the present one, they pray that he will, in his goodness, reveal it to them, for they are ready to follow wherever he leads. But if their form of society is the best and their religion the truest, then they pray that God will keep them steadfast, and bring other mortals to the same way of life and the same religious faith – unless, indeed, there is something in this variety of religions which delights his inscrutable will.[89]

As far as bringing other mortals to the utopian way of life is concerned, neither Plato nor More will commit themselves on the feasibility of their 'ideal' societies in real political terms. Through the dialogue form, More in particular hedges his text around with sophisticated reservations, expressed and unexpressed. However, as

Plato has Socrates say, ultimately it doesn't matter: 'perhaps . . . it is laid up as a pattern in heaven, where he who wishes can see it and found it in his own heart. But it doesn't matter whether it exists or ever will exist . . . '[90] The true origin and location of utopia is in the imagination, and its immortality is in literature. In the centuries following More, the genetic codes of these classical and Renaissance texts pass down to writers of other texts, becoming modified in the process, but still recognisable.

Notes and references

1. v Plato 1955/1987 p. 420 (the quotation is from Byron, *Don Juan*, VII: iv): More's religious beliefs imply a similar attitude, although 'More's' comment at the end of *Utopia* seems ironic (v T. More 1516/1989 Book II pp. 110–11).

2. There is a vast secondary literature on Plato, More, and associated writers in the genre: for classical utopias v J. Ferguson 1975; for Renaissance utopias v M. Eliav-Feldon 1982 inter al.

3. Plato 1941 pp. 204–5: for the implications of the aesthetic analogy v K. R. Popper 1945/1966 pp. 164–8.

4. Ovid 1955 p. 31: for the 'negative formula' v H. R. Patch 1950 p. 12. Theorists differ on the necessity of distinguishing between utopia and Golden Age: cf F. E. Manuel, F. P. Manuel 1979 introduction; J. C. Davis 1981 introduction and ch. 1.

5. M. Foucault 1984/1986b p. 340.

6. v Plato 1955/1987 pp. 121–2: cf C. Lévi-Strauss 1964/1970 vol. 1 pp. 334–9.

7. Plato 1955/1987 p. 122.

8. The details are given in Xenophon 1925 and Plutarch 1914 vol. 1.

9. R. Burton 1621/1972 Pt. 1 Sec 2 Mem 4 Subs 6 p. 355.

10. cf preface to H. Levin 1969/1972.

11. The Renaissance *locus classicus* is Torquato Tasso's chorus 'O bella età dell' oro' (*Aminta* I: ii).

12. v *Gargantua* chs 52–7. In F. Rabelais 1564/1991 pp. 116–27.

13. v T. More 1516/1989 Book II pp. 50, 52–3, 54–5, 71: for a survey of the dress topic v A. Ribeiro 1987.

14. T. More 1516/1551/1974 Book II pp. 74–5.

15. v T. More 1516/1989 Book II pp. 57, 73: T. Campanella 1602, 1637/1981 pp. 45–6.

16. M. de Montaigne 1580–1588/1991 pp. 232–3.

17. M. de Montaigne 1580–1588/1991 pp. 235–6: for comparison with Swift v C. H. Flynn 1990 p. 161.

18. M. de Montaigne 1580–1588/1991 p. 236.

19. M. de Montaigne 1580–1588/1991 p. 241: J. Swift 1939–68 vol. 1 p. 47.

20. T. Hobbes 1651/1968 p. 186.

21. Aristotle 1988 p. 3.

22. Plato 1955/1987 p. 297; Plato 1941 p. 205.

23. *Verses, Supposed to be Written by Alexander Selkirk, During his Solitary Abode in the Island of Juan Fernandez.* In W. Cowper 1968 pp. 56–8.

24. v Plato 1955/1987 pp. 177–224; Aristotle 1988 pp. 6–9.

25. Aristotle 1988 p. 4: cf pp. 1–3.

26. Plato 1955/1987 p. 184

27. Plato 1970/1988 p. 207

28. v Xenophon 1925 p. 161: cf Plutarch 1914 vol. 1 pp. 229–31; Tacitus 1948/1970 pp. 104–5.

29. v T. More 1516/1989 Book II pp. 62–5.

30. Aristotle 1988 p. 26: cf Plato 1970/1988 p. 207.

31. Aristotle 1988 p. 27.

32. Plato 1955/1987 p. 325: cf Plato 1941 p. 230.

33. Aristotle 1988 p. 43.

34. v T. More 1516/1989 Book II p. 53: the state officials don't in fact avail themselves of the concession, but scholars do.

35. Aristotle 1988 p. 177.

36. Plato 1955/1987 p. 239.

37. v Plato 1955/1987 pp. 240–3.

38. Plato 1955/1987 p. 241: for different viewpoints on Plato's 'feminism' v G. Vlastos 1989: M. Lefkowitz 1989.

39. Plato 1955/1987 p. 252.

40. Aristotle 1988 p. 29: cf pp. 18–20; 21–5; 40–1.

41. Aristotle 1988 pp. 180–2.

42. Plutarch 1914 vol. 1 p. 253: cf pp. 247–51: also v Xenophon 1925 pp. 139–41.

43. Tacitus 1948/1970 p. 117.

44. Tacitus 1948/1970 p. 119.

45. cf Mattingly's intro to Tacitus 1948/1970 pp. 25–6.

46. Diodorus Siculus 1933–67 vol. 2 p. 75.

47. Lucian 1913 vol. 1 p. 321.

48. Lucian 1913 vol. 1 pp. 321–3.

49. Lucian 1913 vol. 1 p. 275: for Tree-men v vol. 1 pp. 275–7; for Vine-women v vol. 1 pp. 257–9; for Asslegs-women v vol. 1 pp. 353–5.

50. T. More 1516/1989 Book II p. 61.

51. T. More 1516/1989 Book II p. 55.

52. T. More 1516/1989 Book II p. 58: contrast Plutarch 1914 vol. 1 p. 255 (although Spartan babies are at least free from swaddling).

53. v T. More 1516/1989 Book II p. 82: the editors note the parallel with *The Laws* and also compare Utopian emphasis on monogamy with Tacitus' Germans.

54. T. More 1516/1989 Book II p. 83: compare and contrast Milton's arguments in *The Doctrine and Discipline of Divorce* (J. Milton 1953–82 vol. 2 pp. 222–356).

55. T. More 1516/1989 Book II p. 81.

56. S. Johnson 1759/1990 vol II ch. xxvi p. 99.

57. v T. More 1516/1989 Book II pp. 104; 102; 92: revealingly, women's domestic contribution in the world outside Utopia is invisible: v Book II p. 52 and n 31.

58. v F. Rabelais 1564/1991 Book I ch. 52 pp. 116–17; ch. 57 pp. 126–7.

59. M. de Montaigne 1580–1588/1991 pp. 239, 234.

60. T. Campanella 1602, 1637/1981 p. 33.

61. T. Campanella 1602, 1637/1981 p. 29: for animal analogy v p. 20: for detailed discussion of sex and procreation v pp. 28–33.

62. T. Campanella 1602, 1637/1981 p. 29.

63. M. Foucault 1984/1986a vol. 2 introduction pp. 3–4: cf his discussion of marriage 1984/1990 vol. 3 part 5 chs 2, 3.

64. For marriage in the early modern period cf L. Stone 1977; 1990; 1992; 1993: A. Macfarlane 1986.

65. Aristotle 1988 pp. 185–6.

66. v Plato 1955/1987 p. 232: for full discussion v pp. 228–36.

67. Aristotle 1988 p. 186.

68. v Plato 1955/1987 p. 168.

69. For the substance of the case v Plato 1955/1987 parts 3, 10: for a philosophical assessment v I. Murdoch 1977.

70. e.g. Swift in A *Tale of a Tub*, Johnson in *Rasselas*: v J. Swift 1939–68 vol. 1 pp. 108, 114; S. Johnson 1759/1990 vol. II pp. 117–19, 150–3.

71. v Plato 1955/1987 pp. 130–1: Turner cites the Swiftian parallel (J. Swift 1726/1986 p. 320 n 26).

72. Plato 1941 p. 329.

73. v Plato 1970/1988 pp. 94–5, 302.

74. Plutarch 1914 vol. 1 p. 257.

75. Plutarch 1914 vol. 1 p. 271.

76. Plato 1965/1977 p. 31.

77. T. More 1516/1989 Book II p. 66: cf p. 78.

78. M. de Montaigne 1580–1588/1991 p. 240.

79. v T. More 1516/1989 pp. 123–5.

80. v T. More 1516/1989 Book II pp. 65–6: cf p. 51.

81. T. More 1516/1989 Book II p. 102.

82. cf Plato 1955/1987 pp. 140–3, 455: T. More 1516/1989 Book II pp. 99, 106: Plutarch 1914 vol. 1 p. 287.

83. v Plato 1955/1987 pp. 168–71.

84. T. More 1516/1989 Book II pp. 74–7: cf pp. 57–8.

85. Herodotus 1954/1972 p. 128.

86. Diodorus Siculus 1933–67 vol. 2 pp. 73–5.

87. T. More 1516/1989 Book II p. 81.

88. T. More 1516/1989 Book II pp. 99–100.

89. T. More 1516/1989 Book II p. 106.

90. Plato 1955/1987 p. 420.

CHAPTER 2

Seventeenth-century utopias: 'witty fictions, but mere chimeras'

From an English perspective, the seventeenth century appears to offer virtually ideal conditions for a golden age of utopian writing. Looking back to the classical world and Renaissance, and forward to the modern world, this early modern period is fascinatingly poised: sufficiently unstable to dream of lost paradises, yet seduced by a utopian or millenarian vision of progress through revolutionary change. If the utopian genre had not existed, the seventeenth century would have had to invent it. Since it does exist, all kinds of writers rush to re-invent it. Although this isn't an insular phenomenon – Continental Europe makes a significant contribution to the genre in this period – nevertheless, for historical reasons, seventeenth-century England is a particularly propitious intellectual environment for anyone moved by the utopian impulse.[1]

The upheaval of civil war and its extended preliminaries and aftermath; the challenge to authority and the opportunities for social and political experiment; the advances in scientific theory and practice, and the controversies in theology: all throw up more extreme varieties of utopian fiction than even the earlier Renaissance. The characteristic forms and topoi continue, but combinations change. Instead of classical balance, there is a kind of baroque asymmetry, foregrounding specific obsessions: with science, religion, sex or politics. It is in this century that we see the increase of specialist utopias reflecting minority interests.

Yet classification becomes more rather than less difficult as a result. From the vantage point of the following century, it's possible to identify certain fruitful variations which will in time fertilise eighteenth-century satire and the novel; but there is an inevitable untidiness when it comes to placing individual texts, because a number fit more than one category. For example, the same utopia can be rationalist, scientific, and religious; the fantastical and the scientific overlap, as in the subgenre of moon voyages; and sex and politics creep into almost everything in some shape or form. Generic restraints also loosen up, anticipating the emergent novel, so that utopian fictions flourish more and more within texts that are predominantly non-utopian. Not that this is a new idea. Rabelais and Cervantes provide classic examples, and in the seventeenth-century English context Robert Burton includes a characteristically sharp-witted compendium of utopian motifs in the vast *Anatomy of Melancholy*.[2] However, it further dissolves the genre into fragments within a medley of related forms.

Perhaps the basic divide in this century is between those writers who offer a programme for scientific, religious, or political reform, which may be futuristic or specifically millenarian, but which is historically based and has reference to the real world, and those who create surrealistic fantasy worlds which cross the barriers of species or gender and rewrite natural history rather than political history: between, as it were, the Platonic and the Lucianic inspirations. Among the former in the earlier seventeenth century are Francis Bacon, and on the Continent, Campanella (already discussed as a late Renaissance utopist), and Johann Valentin Andreae; and in the heavily politicised English climate of the mid-century, Samuel Gott, Gerrard Winstanley, and James Harrington. Among the latter are the early seventeenth-century satirist, Joseph Hall, the proto-feminist of the 50s and 60s, Margaret Cavendish, Duchess of Newcastle, and the moon voyagers such as Francis Godwin in England and Cyrano de Bergerac in France. Alongside these, fresh versions of the familiar geographical utopia, like the island utopia or the unknown continental utopia, continue to appear: Henry Neville's Isle of Pines (1668), Denis Vairasse's Sevarambia (1675), Gabriel de Foigny's Australia (1676) and a New World example, Aphra Behn's Surinam (1688). Between the rational poles of the scientific and the political seventeenth-century utopias spins a globe of fantastic journeyings, terrestrial and extraterrestrial. To understand what eighteenth-century writers, no less than Burton, perceived as their predecessors' 'witty fictions, but mere chimeras',[3] it's necessary to chart in more detail some representative seventeenth-century ventures.

The scientific utopia

Fittingly, perhaps, for this fissured century, one of its most influential utopias, *New Atlantis*, represents a fragment of a much larger design, an offshore island of an intellectual continent, Bacon's Great Instauration. Its incompleteness seems evidenced by its lack of the orthodox centre of an ideal-commonwealth experiment: 'his Lordship thought also in this present fable, to have composed a frame of laws, or of the best state or mould of a Common-wealth; but foreseeing it would be a long work, his desire of collecting the Natural History diverted him, which he preferred many degrees before it.' What replaces the missing core at the heart of the enterprise is the 'model or description of a College, instituted for the interpreting of Nature, and the producing of great and marvellous works for the benefit of men; under the name of Salomon's House, or the College of the Six Days' Works'.[4]

The idea of a research institution as the power-house of an ideal society suggests a new set of priorities for utopian writing. *New Atlantis* is a recension of the Platonic myth which consciously revises its pessimistic outcome. If the legendary first Atlantis, a great maritime civilisation, collapsed through overweening imperialism, the second establishes an intellectual not a territorial empire, holding the rest of the world in fee for ideas, carrying on a secret trade in light.[5] As importantly, the lost and starving mariners who discover this unknown island in the South Seas are reassured to find that this civilisation is enlightened in Christian truth as well. Bacon takes pains to reinforce the religious and social traditionalism of his progressive scientific utopia. Since knowledge of the secrets of nature inevitably increases human power for good or evil, one built-in safeguard is to make the hierarchy of scientists also a hierarchy of Christian priests (though the connection between science, religion and ethics is by no means as unproblematic as Bacon makes it seem). The story of the conversion of New Atlantis, centred on the miraculous appearance of a pillar of light out at sea, says a good deal about Bacon's preference for a religion that is revealed rather than rationalised.[6] When the mystical revelation takes the material form of a waterproof chest containing the Scriptures – and the Scriptures already conveniently packaged in their canonical form about twenty years after Christ's Ascension – it might be argued that Bacon is manipulating his miracle rather too blatantly to avoid the danger he warns against in *The Advancement of Learning* – 'that they do not unwisely mingle or confound these learnings [theological and natural] together'.[7] Certainly the mariners don't ask any inconvenient questions, but, in contrast to Swift's Gulliver, readily accept that they are in 'a land of angels' not 'a land of magicians'.[8] The powers of the House of Salomon are sanctioned by the divine Truth.

Yet the recurring impression of this utopia is of a society dominated by the need for secrecy. In the rare event of the visitation from the Father of the House of Salomon, 'his coming is in state; but the cause of his coming is secret'. As befits a member of a powerful and mysterious élite, his state is princely. One of many features differentiating Bacon's utopian imagination from Thomas More's is his pleasure in magnificence, and he uses detail of dress to signify status (here pinpointed by the sublimely impractical 'shoes of peach-coloured velvet'). Like the House of Salomon itself, the Fathers are set apart from and seem to pity ordinary humanity.[9]

'The end of our foundation', explains the Father, 'is the knowledge of causes, and secret motions of things; and the enlarging of the bounds of human empire, to the effecting of all things possible.'[10] Just as faith in Christian revelation is unquestioned, so is the scriptural assumption that the natural creation is made for the benefit of humanity, the privileged species: 'we have also parks, and enclosures of all sorts, of beasts and birds; which we use not only for view or rareness, but likewise for dissections and trials, that thereby we may take light what may be wrought upon the body of man.'[11] The simple-life or golden age utopia has been left a long way behind in the extravaganza of experimentation conducted by the College of the Six Days' Works, which acknowledges virtually no limits on human requirements, human inventiveness or human curiosity. The butchered beasts of Utopia belong to an older, simpler agrarian world; the dissected beasts of New Atlantis belong to the modern world. When it comes to research and development, the record of the House of Salomon is technically impressive: genetic engineering, dietary and pharmaceutical improvements, optical instruments, hearing aids, sophisticated machinery and weaponry, and that old utopian dream 'some degrees of flying in the air'.[12] Bacon undeniably conveys a sense of intellectual excitement, which was to dazzle future progressively-minded generations, and which makes him seem extraordinarily prescient. To Abraham Cowley, addressing that most Baconian of institutions the Royal Society, he is the Moses who gives his people the vision of a utopian 'promis'd Land'.[13]

However, this was at a price: although the House of Salomon shouldn't be judged entirely from hindsight, there are certain warning signals inscribed in the text itself, which eighteenth-century readers as well as modern readers could detect. War, for instance, has become a purely technological concern. In the gallery of fame, the invention of gunpowder is undifferentiated from inventions such as navigation, agriculture, music, printing, and so on. There's no allusion to the effects of gunpowder on the human bodies which the medical researchers of the House of Salomon are striving to preserve in health and longevity. Indeed, Swift's satire on the benefits of gunpowder in *Gulliver's Travels* might well strike a reader as relevant comment.[14] More insidious still is the suggestion that science is responsible for the manipulation of human minds. Like other utopians, including Swift's Houyhnhnms, the Fathers consider untruth an abomination, but this relates to a particular concept of scientific integrity. If suppression of truth can be equated with the implication of falsehood (*suppressio veri suggestio falsi*), then the prevalent secrecy of New Atlantis might call into question their occupation of this moral high ground. Not only do the Fathers of the House of Salomon control the sources of knowledge, but also its dissemination. There is no right to freedom of information outside their closed group:

> And this we do also: we have consultations, which of the inventions and experiences which we have discovered shall be published, and which not: and take all an oath of secrecy for the concealing of those which we think fit to keep secret: though some of those we do reveal sometimes to the State, and some not.[15]

Underlying the final clause is a potential conflict of interests between politicians and scientists, which again seems highly prescient, although Bacon papers over the crack by constructing New Atlantis as a benignly paternalistic society. (This paternalism is equally illustrated by the social arrangements, which conform to a standard utopian model of family hierarchy.)[16] The fundamental tensions in this society between tradition and progress are buried in an unfinished text which resists closure – '*the rest was not perfected*' – but which fits Bacon's own phrase a 'knowledge broken' in being a growing point for other texts.[17]

By the eighteenth century, the Baconian vision of the House of Salomon could be satirically interrogated and travestied, to produce the aberrations of Swift's Academy of Lagado. In his own century, however, Bacon's utopia establishes a benchmark for judging not just scientific utopias but any ideal state in which intellectual enlightenment and spiritual faith are indivisible. Light, in fact, is a key symbol, from the solar utopianism of Campanella to Andreae's Christianopolis where adequate street lighting is more than simply a civic convenience since it represents the metaphoric domination of light over darkness, or Gott's Nova Solyma where schoolmasters are 'invested with the order of the Sun'.[18] Although Campanella, and More before him, have their utopian citizens practise a form of natural religion close to Christianity in its fundamental principles, Andreae and Gott make Christianity itself the main plank of their utopian states. Both, like Bacon, see no conflict between this and scientific study. For Gott, 'the special advantage of natural science is to rise from Nature to Nature's God, tracing His footsteps everywhere therein'.[19] However, his principal interest is religion, and the millennial vision of Nova Solyma – the New Jerusalem, inhabited by converted Jews – offers an answer to political and religious conflict by transcending it: a particularly poignant dream in 1648, the year of publication.[20] As J.C. Davis observes of Gott's project, 'it was not necessary to develop a coherent theory of politics' since 'the state was merely a convenience, a device to contain the forces of evil and to enable Christian doctrine and practice to do their work'.[21] The idea of religion as the solution, not as part of the problem, has an attractive simplicity which leaves traces even in the eighteenth century when religious millenarianism, at least for political purposes, had been largely discredited.[22] However, for Gott's immediate contemporaries, the political challenge isn't so easily accommodated. Indeed it becomes an increasingly urgent issue in the Cromwellian state, a state in search of a constitution.

The political utopia

One result of the shake-up of political ideas in the Interregnum was the discussion of utopian constitutional models, presented as practical options by Gerrard Winstanley, The Law of Freedom in a Platform, or True Magistracy Restored (1651), James Harrington, The Commonwealth of Oceana (1656), and John Milton, The Ready and Easy Way to Establish a Free Commonwealth (1660). The last-mentioned, written and published when the sun was finally setting on Cromwell's Protectorate, is the least original, a brief doomed political throw. However, Winstanley and Harrington both take the long-term view, and both are concerned with essentially remoulding seventeenth-

century England into a proposed utopian state in accordance with
their own clearly defined principles. What they have in common,
despite their theoretic differences, is a sense of possibility, a faith that
these are, or could be, *working* political models.

Winstanley in particular shares with later eighteenth-century
writers a distrust of the faculty of fantasy, and the fictions that abuse
the mind.[23] Yet, paradoxically, by eighteenth-century standards he
himself would appear as a wild radical visionary. He believes implicitly
in the plain man, and in the 'creation right' of every human being to
share the labour and the fruits of the Earth with every other human
being – 'true freedom lies in the free enjoyment of the earth'.[24]
Accordingly, he rewrites the myth of the Fall as economic (the fall
into money and commerce) and political (the fall into war and
kingship). Freedom, peace, plenty, brotherly love: it's hard to quarrel
with Winstanley's utopian objectives, but he clearly anticipates
opposition to the revolutionary means he proposes. Specifically, he
wants to uncouple the principle of a common utopia from fears of
idleness, anarchy, and sexual promiscuity.

One measure he takes to try to defuse opposition is to retain the
stability of domestic relationships. So the following passage modulates
skilfully from the familiar present to the utopian future:

> Every family shall live apart, as now they do; every man shall
> enjoy his own wife, and every woman her own husband, as now
> they do; every trade shall be improved to more excellency than
> now it is; all children shall be educated, and be trained up in
> subjection to parents and elder people more than now they are.
> The earth shall be planted, and the fruits reaped and carried into
> store-houses, by common assistance of every family. The riches of
> the store-houses shall be the common stock to every family.
> There shall be no idle person nor beggar in the land.[25]

Again it's a utopia for the plain man, who wants his fair share but
doesn't want his domestic world turned upside down. Winstanley
campaigns on his platform for the rights of the dispossessed, for the
abolition of social and economic privilege and the dismantling of
professional mystique. Yet apparently every Englishman's home is to
remain his castle, in one sense at least. Not that Winstanley ignores
the rights of women: his utopia legislates for freedom *from* as well as
freedom *to*, and that includes freedom from familial or sexual
oppression. Marriage is to be for love and by consent, without

economic or social constraints, a state of affairs which is more aspiration than actuality for many men and women in the seventeenth and eighteenth centuries. It is, of course, an idea which strongly influences the domestic concerns of the eighteenth-century novel. If a man makes a woman pregnant, under Winstanley's laws he is required to marry her; if a man rapes a woman and the case is proved, he is condemned to death, for 'it is robbery of a woman['s] bodily freedom'.[26]

Freedom is indeed the key to Winstanley's thinking, although as with all freedoms there are limits and reciprocal responsibilities. What interests him most is ensuring freedom from want, and that entails shared physical labour. Moreover, his distrust of imagination and of the power of imaginative discourse acts as a restriction on certain kinds of intellectual freedom of expression. He has faith in material and social satisfaction, asking rhetorically (like other utopists before and since), 'And having food and raiment, lodging and the comfortable societies of his own kind, what can a man desire more in these days of his travel?'[27] It is a question that resonates through eighteenth-century debate as well, although most eighteenth-century thinkers would dissociate themselves from Winstanley's brand of radicalism.

James Harrington, too, is less radical than Winstanley. As a classical republican, he trusts more to institutions than to humanity. He argues in the 'Preliminaries' to *Oceana* that ' "Give us good men and they will make us good laws" is the maxim of a demagogue, and . . . exceeding fallible. But "give us good orders, and they will make us good men" is the maxim of a legislator, and the most infallible in the politics'.[28] By getting the balance right between property (the agrarian law) and political power (by rotation) it is possible to create a self-perpetuating commonwealth. Rotation, an electoral system that provides for regular changes in government 'through the suffrage of the people given by the ballot', is Harrington's pet scheme.[29] He expends much ingenuity in devising a fiendishly elaborate secret balloting mechanism (naturally without benefit of a computer, a future invention which would have given him much pleasure). He thinks in technological and medical images: his political engines are designed 'to bite, and with the screws of their rotation, hold and turn a business'; parliament is like a heart with two ventricles.[30] However, unfortunately, Harrington lacks a gift for fiction. His attempt at a fictional framework for his political theory, involving a role for

Cromwell as the Lord Archon with a projected career of truly utopian longevity (he dies, still fully *compos mentis*, at the age of 116) is stiff and lopsided.[31] Also, his social imagination doesn't match his political originality, although he promulgates some familiar and influential themes: opposition to property marriage, support for education – he is an eloquent defender of universities – and respect for liberty of conscience.

Neither Winstanley's nor Harrington's utopias stood a chance of being realised in their own century or *a fortiori* in the next. However, although contemporary history moved in a dramatically different direction, writings of this kind seeded ideas which might germinate in odd places. Defoe and Swift, for instance, connect with Harrington in certain contexts.[32] But the main influence of seventeenth-century political theory on eighteenth-century writers comes not from the overtly utopian inventors, but from the philosophical writings of Hobbes in the mid-century and Locke after the so-called Glorious Revolution of 1688. Although neither Hobbes nor Locke cast their political theories in utopian form, their texts occupy an area bordering on utopian territory.[33] Any thinker who constructs hypotheses about the origins of society and government in order to speculate on the nature of political behaviour provides a potential impetus for utopian fiction.

However, in spite of their apparent affinity, the relation between serious political discourse and utopian fiction is often seen as a mésalliance, or perhaps a shotgun wedding. Milton, for example, has already been identified as the author of what might be called a political utopia, *The Ready and Easy Way*; but years earlier and under different circumstances he had written 'To sequester out of the world into *Atlantick* and *Eutopian* polities, which never can be drawn into use, will not mend our condition; but to ordain wisely as in this world of evil.'[34] He overlooks the fact that theorists, including himself, may engage in forming '*Atlantick* and *Eutopian* polities' in the fond belief that they *are* ordaining wisely for this world. More significantly, Milton in another context distinguishes trenchantly between good and bad utopian writing. On the one hand, there are the philosophically respectable fictions, represented as 'That grave and noble invention which the greatest and sublimest wits in sundry ages, *Plato in Critias*, and our two famous countreymen, the one in his *Utopia*, the other in his *new Atlantis* chose, I may not say as a feild, but as a mighty Continent wherein to display the largenesse of their spirits by teaching this our world better and exacter things, then were yet known, or us'd'. On the other hand, there are the promiscuous fictions from which Milton singles out for opprobrium Joseph Hall's *Mundus alter et idem*, 'the idlest and the paltriest Mime that ever mounted upon banke', 'a meer tankard drollery, a venereous parjectory for a stewes'.[35] It is, however, possible to justify the latter on the grounds of its entertainment value; and this doesn't exclude (*pace* Milton) a serious utopian function.

Other worlds, other species

Unlike Milton, Robert Burton treats the entire genre as entertaining fantasy, and revels, Shandy-like, in his own creative freedom: 'I will yet, to satisfy and please myself, make a Utopia of mine own, a New Atlantis, a poetical commonwealth of mine own, in which I will freely domineer, build cities, make laws, statutes, as I list myself. And why may I not?' Why not indeed? He also casts an ironic eye on the competition: 'Utopian parity is a kind of government to be wished for rather than effected. *Respub. Christianopolitana*, Campanella's City of the Sun, and that *New Atlantis*, witty fictions, but mere chimeras, and Plato's community in many things is impious, absurd, and ridiculous, it takes away all splendour and magnificence.'[36] Burton's own witty fiction is more remarkable for style than content, but it is a reminder that satire and fantasy continue to be a vital element in the utopian tradition. If the Baconian utopia gives a hostage to future satirists as well as an ideal to future scientists, it's salutary to realise that the satiric utopia flourishes in its own right in the seventeenth century.

Joseph Hall's title for the work which Milton targeted with his 'controversial merriment', *Mundus alter et idem* (1605) – *Another world and the same* – epitomises precisely one function of a literary utopia, especially a satire: that is, to negotiate between otherness and identity. Hall, like Swift, was a cleric and a satirist; and his other world, like Swift's in *Gulliver's Travels*, contains distinctive countries, each animated by an apparently simple but inventively proliferating idea and threaded through by the travels and commentary of a single narrator.[37] As in a hall of mirrors, the description squashes, elongates, distorts human reflections to throw back a grotesquely dislocated but still recognisable image. The crude and lively Jacobean idiom of Hall's translator, John Healey, may not accurately represent the educated

Latin of the original, but adapts splendidly to the Rabelaisian, or Swiftian, obsession with bodily functions.

Mundus alter et idem is as crammed with detail as the inhabitants of one of its countries, Tenter-belly, are with food and drink. All the conceivable utopian topics are single-mindedly converted to the prevailing ethos of the various environments, so that (for example) the penal code in a region of Tenter-belly, Eat-allia, grades punishments from the most severe, starvation, to the relatively lenient, loss of a tooth.[38] Life for the Eat-allians and their neighbours, the bleary, bejowled and brain-damaged Drink-allians, is nasty, brutish and short, the medieval dream of Cockaigne turned into nightmare. Even this physiological disaster area is surpassed in the later books by the land of Fooliana with its manifold instances of human incompetency and lunacy, from which Swift may have taken hints for *A Tale of a Tub* and *Gulliver's Travels*.[39] Lacking any kind of skill, reduced to the level of animals or below, not even knowing which orifice they should put food into, the inhabitants of Fooliana constitute a satire on the human claim to be a rational species which possibly isn't surpassed until Swift's Yahoos.[40] And the thieves' utopia of the final book also anticipates a favourite target of eighteenth-century satire, the threat posed by parasites on society (an eighteenth-century reader might particularly relish Hall's paradise of plagiarism, or his comment on this culture of cheats and knaves 'And surely there is no nation vnder heauen so stored with lawiers as this is . . .').[41] Of all the countries in the work, it's this one which we might be most disposed to regard as *idem* not *alter*.

Yet there is one more of Hall's inventions in the Lucianic vein that deserves special mention in the light of later developments in the genre. Shee-landt or Womandeçoia is also a nightmare, this time of misogyny, a utopia in which sexual politics dictates role reversal on various levels. What Hall exploits through his narrator is male fear of female dominance: *femmes fatales* who trap men for sexual gratification and use them like 'stallion horses kept for breede'; female politicians who scream each other down – 'each one yells as if she were horne mad'; a place where men are made to keep house (beautifully, so proving that anything women can do, men can do better) and women make a mess of public works.[42] Interestingly, Hall includes in this gender upheaval an island of hermaphrodites who believe themselves to 'have the perfection of nature amongst them alone': a conceit that Gabriel de Foigny later develops in his imaginary Australia.[43] Of more general significance is the potential of utopian writing for breaking out of gender constraints. If Hall exploits this for conservative satiric purposes, women writers will eventually turn the tables by creating utopian societies in which female dominance is positive not negative, transforming the quality of human life for all concerned.

The most extraordinary seventeenth-century progenitrix of women's utopias is Margaret Cavendish, Duchess of Newcastle, who refuses to confine herself to any unitary utopian idea, but creates a plurality of worlds more strikingly 'other' even than Hall's. *The Description of a New Blazing World* (1666) is preceded by the assortment of *Nature's Pictures Drawn By Fancies Pencill* (1656) in which fancy's pencil heightens nature's pictures to a surrealist level of intensity. In *Assaulted and pursued Chastity*, the heroine Travelia in company with her adoptive 'father' arrives in an alien culture by the classic rite of shipwreck. The predominant impact is of dazzling colour and light, and surrealistic displacement of physical properties: furry parrots, feathered animals, deep purple humans with shining jet black teeth and nails (except, perversely, for those of the blood royal who are bright orange).[44] Finding that these people, with their mixture of good and bad utopian practices, are less enlightened than their colourful environment implies, Travelia (after a hairsbreadth escape from becoming a human sacrifice because of her male attire) becomes the supreme arbiter of king and country and establishes a true utopia, 'forbidding vain and barbarous Customes' and enjoining them to free their slaves.[45]

The common denominator of this fiction and *The Description of a New Blazing World* is the assertion of female power for utopian purposes. The pattern of a female traveller and outsider being entrusted with supreme power over a new world repeats itself.[46] As with other seventeenth-century fantasies, topical concerns are also in evidence. For example, the 1666 fiction has a political application: Margaret Cavendish emphasises the values of peaceable cooperation and religious uniformity in a way that has particular relevance for post-Civil War England; naturally she links these to monarchical government, and in the Second Part depicts the pastimes of a leisured and aristocratic society, an ideal for Restoration London. Not for nothing is the capital of the Blazing World called Paradise. It is not just a secular state but, like many utopias, a holy one. In this context, it's given a feminist slant.[47] When the new Empress sets about converting her people to Christianity, she challenges the male status quo with a question that goes to the painful root of the matter: she 'desir'd to know the reason why the Priests and Governors of their World were made Eunuchs? They answer'd, To keep them from Marriage: For Women and Children most commonly make disturbance both in Church and State.' Her response is to open up access to public life and worship for her own sex, creating 'a Congregation of Women' who because they 'generally had quick wits, subtile conceptions, clear understandings, and solid judgments, became, in a short time, very devout and zealous Sisters; for the Empress had an excellent gift of Preaching . . .'[48] This seems clearly to foreshadow the devout groups under female leadership envisaged by subsequent creators of utopian institutions for women, like Mary Astell and Sarah Scott.

However, perhaps the most distinctively seventeenth-century side of Margaret Cavendish comes through in her devotion to scientific and speculative enquiry. The initial evidence in this text is her interest in inventing and classifying new species combined from elements of existing ones, such as Bear-men and Bird-men.[49] Later, the Empress engages in 'Discourses and Conferences with the . . . Societies of her Vertuoso's' to enlarge her notions regarding the physical sciences and the occult. Much of this reads like variations on the more bizarre proceedings of the Royal Society, or a Swiftian parody of them.[50] Yet the intellectual hunger wins respect, and is given unmistakable edge, because of the restrictions on her sex in an un-utopian world: another factor that recurs in women's utopian writing. It's logical that the Empress should wish to engage in her own research project. Logical also, that in looking for a research assistant among the illustrious spirits of dead white European males she should encounter problems in recruiting one of the ancients ('Aristotle, Pythagoras, Plato, Epicurus, or the like') because they are too 'wedded to their own opinions' (the moderns are likewise too 'self-conceited' to act as scribes for a woman).[51] The successful job applicant has to be female, and turns out to be none other than the Duchess of Newcastle in person, given a glowing reference by the advisory spirits. The two soul-mates embark on the creation of a galaxy of new worlds, the Duchess herself testing and rejecting various masculine models from the Platonic to the Hobbesian, which gives her a raging headache. Finally, she settles for her own 'Imaginary World; which World after it was made, appear'd so curious and full of variety, so well order'd and wisely govern'd, that it cannot possibly be expressed by words, nor the delight and pleasure which the Duchess took in making this world of her own.'[52]

This statement has the recessiveness of the true utopian text: there is always a world beyond, and language can only attempt to constitute it. That difficulty of access can also be metaphorically expressed by choosing a location that is outside our planet altogether. For another group of seventeenth-century writers, the extraterrestrial voyage is the obvious medium for representing a *mundus alter et idem*. Moon travel has the advantage of of being adaptable: it can combine science, fantasy and even theology in a way that is especially attractive to seventeenth-century minds, and the nature and manner of life of extraterrestrial beings allows scope for utopian invention.[53] In 1638 *The Discovery of a World in the Moone* by John Wilkins was first published, its title later expanded into A *Discovery of a New World, or A Discourse Tending to Prove, that 'tis Probable there may be another Habitable World in the Moon. With a Discourse concerning the Probability of a Passage thither*. As befits a bishop, Wilkins is concerned about the theological status of hypothetical lunar inhabitants, and whether they are fallen or unfallen; but he is also absorbed in the development of the new technology that space travel will require, anticipating practical problems such as how to deal with weightlessness and nutrition.[54] Although not actually a utopian fiction, Wilkins's book feeds the appetite for speculation which produces a particular variety of utopian fantasy in his own and the following century (his interest in language, evinced in his *Essay towards a Real Character and a Philosophical Language* (1668), is also part of an influential trend).[55]

A contemporaneous, and celebrated, literary moon voyage, published in the same year as Wilkins's first edition, anticipates Swift in certain of its utopian features. This is Francis Godwin's *The Man in the Moone: or A Discovrse of a Voyage thither by Domingo Gonsales* (1638), in which the Spanish hero reverts to bird transport rather than technology, and discovers marvels in the moon that are likewise more reminiscent of myth than scientific discourse. Among these are an abundant food supply available 'without labour', 'a perpetuall Spring', and beautiful and virtuous people who have no trouble in controlling their instincts: 'I know not how it commeth to passe', remarks the narrator, 'by a secret disposition of nature there, that a man having once knowne a Woman, never desireth any other.'[56] However, if Godwin sidesteps certain problems confronted by utopia-makers, in other respects he represents the moon not as a pure Golden Age pastoral, but as a utopian state needing to be policed. Lacking the sanction of capital punishment in a world where all wounds, even decapitation, are curable by herbal remedy, the lunar authorities rely on detecting moral deviants at birth and expelling them to earth (where else? to be precise, 'a certaine high hill in the North of America') in exchange for terrestrial children.[57]

The uncommonly tall physique of the lunar race prefigures, it is claimed, Swift's Brobdingnagians, and their stoic and cheerful attitude to death is very much in the utopian tradition, of which Swift's Houyhnhnms are also partly a reflection.[58] In addition, Godwin shares the utopian – and Swiftian – preoccupation with imagined languages. Domingo Gonsales at first considers the lunar language to be unique, though he later discovers an affinity with Chinese, and he records examples in musical notation ('yea many wordes there are consisting of tunes onely . . .').[59] But, unlike Swift, Godwin emphasises that his lunar people recognise and respond to the name of Jesus;[60] and this overt identification of a utopian culture with Christianity, typical of seventeenth-century utopianism, also helps to account for a crucial contrast between Gonsales and Gulliver. Although both are powerfully affected by their experiences of an 'ideal' society, the outcome is different. Gonsales may feel a sense of deprivation and emotional conflict, torn as he is between the lunar world and his human responsibilities – 'O my Wife and Children, what wrong haue you done mee to bereave mee of the happinesse of that place'[61] – but he sublimates this feeling into the Christian hope of immortal bliss, and acknowledges the claims of human affection as Gulliver does not. In the end, it is the thought of his children that motivates Gonsales to return to his own imperfect planet.

Across the Channel, Cyrano de Bergerac is also a contender in the figurative race for the moon, and throws in the sun for good measure in his exploration of *L'Autre Monde* of the utopian imagination. A magpie writer who snaps up glittering ideas from every quarter, he inlays his creations with treasured items amassed from a familiar collection of sources: Lucian, More, Rabelais, Montaigne, Campanella, Bacon, and, it seems, Godwin as well.[62] In turn, for readers of English literature, he brings Swift irresistibly to mind. This applies not only to narrative detail (there are some good Swiftian jokes in Cyrano's imaginary voyages) but to the rationalistic conceptual framework. The kinds of utopia described, like the topsy-turvy world of the moon and the bird utopia in the sun, foreground the problem of classification by species, and the nature of relativity. Like Swift, Cyrano challenges humanity's claim to be *animal rationale*, using the weapon of humour.

In *Voyage dans la Lune* and *L'Histoire du Etats et Empires du Soleil*, the narrator is subjected to a variety of physical and intellectual humiliations, scrutinised, for example, by huge lunar beings who go on all-fours and argue that the upright position is unnatural, or by superior birds who are repelled by his featherless state.[63] In the seventeenth-century context, this connects with the philosophical stance sometimes termed theriophily, the argument that beasts are physically and morally superior to humanity.[64] Nor does Cyrano stop at animals and birds when rearranging the boundaries of species. He combines the utopian topic of diet with his rationalistic agenda to develop the argument, after Campanella, that vegetables, particularly cabbages, are an unfallen species, the survival of which is dearer to God than that of human beings (whose sinfulness is logically demonstrated by their propensity to eat innocent cabbages).[65]

Cyrano's moon is indubitably another world; it's also the world turned upside down in the traditional sense of the trope, a place where the old respect the young and fathers obey children as soon as they reach the age of discretion. Moon logic dictates that the badge of honour is the wearing of bronze genitals, to signify the giving of life: earth logic attributes shame to the genitalia or *pudenda*, and conversely attaches honour to that which takes life, the sword. To make a parallel point, in the bird utopia on the sun the dove, not the eagle, is chosen as king.[66] As with Swift's satire, the effect of Cyrano's inventions is to provoke reassessment of received ideas. They entertain, but they also keep the reader constantly off-balance. Both writers use utopian fiction, with its well-developed and often sophisticated techniques of defamiliarising what is taken for granted, to mount a powerful attack on intellectual complacency about human status, knowledge and judgment.

Among Cyrano de Bergerac's seventeenth-century compatriots, whose utopian fictions also apparently found a market among English readers, are Gabriel de Foigny and Denis Vairasse d'Allais. The former's *Les avantures de Jacques Sadeur* (1676) was translated into English as *A New Discovery of Terra Incognita Australis, or the Southern World* (1693). The latter's *Histoire de Severambes/History of the Severambians* (1675 and 1677–79) has a complicated bibliographical record in both French and English, which includes an eighteenth-century version appearing as part of a 1727 text attributed to 'Gulliver'.[67] Both these works have entered into discussions of the authentic *Gulliver's Travels*, although there is no hard evidence that Swift read either of them.[68] Nevertheless, they are still useful as context, since they have a bearing on eighteenth-century readers' expectations and experience of the genre.

Both de Foigny and Vairasse locate their utopias in the Australian continent, to which they export seventeenth-century French rationalism. Of the two, *The History of the Severambians* seems to conform more to a standardised utopian type, as a full-scale project covering every aspect of society. The Severambians are like ourselves, only better: better organised, better disciplined, more virtuous, more reasonable, healthier, cleaner, taller. . . . There's little to astonish any reader versed in utopian literature, from the equitable distribution of goods which ensures that no one is poor or overworked, to the gender stereotyping which ensures that boys and girls are appropriately educated for their roles and that marriage is faithful (with restraints on the frequency of intercourse in the interests of producing strong and thriving children).[69] There are plenty of prohibitions in Severambia, but there are pleasures as well, to be temperately enjoyed: dancing, music, mixed bathing on summer evenings for married couples.[70] As a rationalist utopia, practising toleration in religion and moderation in everything, it seems calculated to appeal to seventeenth- and eighteenth-century readers without unduly disturbing them.

In contrast, Gabriel de Foigny's version of Australia while also rationalist in its philosophy is more bizarre in its fundamental premiss. His narrative takes off in great style with a narrator, Jacques Sadeur, whose parents perish in a shipwreck when he is an infant, who becomes the centre of a child custody case, is abducted, shipwrecked again (twice) and so on, through a bewildering variety of adventures. But the most salient fact about him is his gender: he is born a hermaphrodite, and assigned arbitrarily to 'the *Masculine Party*' by the Jesuits at the age of five. The Australian utopia he discovers is peopled entirely by hermaphrodites, given to killing single-sexed strangers or any mutant among themselves.[71] This hermaphroditism isn't simply biological freakishness, an exotic fictional variation as it might be in Lucian. Instead it serves as a basic symbol of otherness, explaining their whole culture and ideology. As with some of the other seventeenth-century utopias already discussed, this sense of strangeness is functional in opening up discussion of what *is* natural and rational, and where humanity as a species fits into the universal scheme.

In the extended dialogue between Sadeur and the elderly Australian who becomes his protector and mentor, the idea of the complete human being is redefined as one who unites both sexes as well as having the capacity to reason (an idea that accords with one mythic account of the original Adam). *Both* attributes are considered necessary to differentiate humanity from other animals:[72] to de Foigny's Australians, single-sexed human beings regrettably participate in bestial nature, and Sadeur's defensive argument (not unlike Gulliver's in similar situations) is met with the flat rebuttal – 'thou canst never reconcile the use of Reason with the exclusion of both Sexes in one person; and what thou addest, that many reason among you, and that they make publick Lectures in divers places, proves only that reasoning is banished from you.' Conversely, the Australian asserts

> we are entire Men; wherefore we live without being sensible of any of these Animal Ardours one for another, and we cannot hear them spoke of without horrour: Our love has nothing Carnal, nor Brutall in it; we are sufficiently satisfyed in our selves, we have no need to seek any happiness from without, and live contented, as you see we do.[73]

Although their society has other utopian properties, and a utopian environment, it is the sole fact of their being hermaphrodites that is held to account for its harmony and rationality. It also, of course, sweeps away all the problems associated with gender difference, for which so many utopian writers painstakingly legislate. (However, it creates problems for the narrator, who may resemble his hosts physiologically, but who has been conditioned by very different cultural norms – problems which parallel Gulliver's among the Houyhnhnms.)

What is interesting about de Foigny's utopia is the notion of sex as the root of all evil, the extent to which biology is blamed for humanity's failure to live together rationally and lovingly. The 'solution' isn't a feasible one, since we can't turn ourselves into hermaphrodites any more than Gulliver can turn himself into a horse. In most utopian societies, like Vairasse's Severambia, the problem is dealt with by the arrangements relating to marriage. In this connection, there is a growing interest among seventeenth- and eighteenth-century writers and readers in polygamy as a utopian alternative, which is at least more practicable than hermaphroditism. In Vairasse's ideal society, for instance, polygamy is a perquisite of high office.[74] In the last seventeenth-century utopian fictions to be considered in this chapter, polygamy features even more generally.

Polygamous paradises: a coda

The Isle of Pines (1668) shares a geographical area with the utopias of Vairasse and de Foigny, since it is subtitled Or a late discovery of a fourth Island in Terra Australis Incognita; but its political subtext differs from theirs. Indeed it is somewhat unexpected, given that the author, Henry Neville, had been a member of the republican Harrington's Rota Club in 1659–60, which set up a kind of seminar for debating and voting on theoretic constitutional models. On the surface, The Isle of Pines seems to have more in common with wishful thinking about desert-island paradises than with systematic political structures like Oceana. Yet it fictionalises an immensely influential principle in seventeenth-century political theory, the principle of patriarchy as the basis of society and government (a key controversial issue between Robert Filmer and Locke).[75]

The Isle of Pines, a forerunner of Robinson Crusoe, starts from a shipwreck and an uninhabited island. However, in this fiction there are a group of castaways, a microcosm of society including difference of both sex and race. The one man and four women stand in carefully differentiated social relations according to their status in the old world: the male narrator is a book-keeper, and the women consist of his master's daughter, two maid-servants, and 'one negro female slave' – 'in all four persons, beside the negro' he itemises, revealingly.[76]

The story is a simple, even archetypal one. After the shipwreck, their first concern is with physical survival; and like Crusoe, they manage very well. The island turns out to be a natural paradise, or rather an environment that, in the narrator's eyes, can be improved into a paradise by human development: 'the country so very pleasant, being always clothed in green, and full of pleasant fruits, and variety of birds, ever warm, and never colder than in England in September; so that this place, had it the culture that skilful people might bestow on it, would prove a paradise'.[77] Not so much paradise, therefore, as utopia; but he has other priorities than work. Without conscious intention, to begin with, he brings about his utopia by literally creating a population for the island from his other main resource, the four women – which makes polygamy the obvious option. If the interest in food anticipates Crusoe, the asset that most decisively separates the Isle of Pines from Crusoe's island is the ample opportunity for sex and procreation. The two are in fact linked, as the narrator observes: 'idleness and a fulness of every thing begot in me a desire for enjoying the women. Beginning now to grow more familiar, I had persuaded the two maids to let me lie with them, which I did at first in private; but after, custom taking away shame, there being none but us, we did it more openly, as our lust gave us liberty. My master's daughter was also content to do as we did.'[78]

Sexual and social constraints break down in this kind of environment, especially once hope of return to their former world is abandoned. Yet it isn't an entirely fresh start. For instance, racial consciousness pervades the narrative from start to finish – the narrator distinguishes significantly between his sexual relations with the black woman and with the others – and there is still a vestige of class distinction lightly disguised (he has most children by his master's daughter who 'being the youngest and the handsomest, was most fond of me, and I of her').[79] However, despite these undercurrents, what is highlighted is a sexual idyll full of sunshine, easy living, and an abundance of naked healthy children, who in due course themselves reach maturity and procreate.

This is a society relieved by nature, not planning, of most of the anxieties that utopias address: the resources are adequate for the growing population. However, after 40 years on the island, when his descendants number 545, the patriarch does institute certain organisational measures, such as a general assembly for arranging marriages to avoid the sibling incest that was originally unavoidable. Clearly this is a model of the origin and growth of society based on family structure; and another factor now emerges more prominently, namely the religion of this new society. Neville doesn't attempt to reinvent this most sensitive subject: like Defoe, he sees to it that his hero has salvaged a Bible, which becomes the foundation of education and religious observance on the island.[80]

At the age of almost 80, the patriarch prepares for the next world by ensuring the continuance of his utopia in this. He makes his eldest son 'king and governor of all the rest', so establishing traditional primogeniture and the principle of sovereignty.[81] He also establishes cultural continuity, giving his colony its place in the imperial and linguistic map of the world: 'I informed them of the manners of *Europe*, and charged them to remember the Christian religion, after the manner of them that spake the same language, and to admit no other, if hereafter any should come and find them out.' The final census of his descendants amounts to 1789. Somewhat redundantly, one feels, he concludes the ritual by 'praying God to multiply them and send them the true light of the gospel'. However, they are a 'people of the book' in another sense, since his last act is the transmission of his text, 'this narration'. Only at its close does the naming of the utopian society take place, the signifier that joins them to history and to the larger human community: 'I gave this people, descended from me, the name of the ENGLISH PINES, *George Pine* being my name, and my master's daughter's name *Sarah English*.' Yet even here, set against this unifying sign is a dividing practice. The subgroups bear their maternal surname, except for those descended from the slave who, possessing no known surname, can only pass down an abbreviated form of her Christian name, Philippa. This polygamous paradise isn't innocent of the knowledge of human division.

Indeed, the affinity of the fictional Isle of Pines is more with a libertine Golden Age than with Eden. Both Eden and New World utopianism, however, contribute to Aphra Behn's account of another polygamous paradise, the actual colony of Surinam in the West Indies. She romanticises the culture of the flower children of Surinam by assimilating it to the myth of primal innocence:

> They are extreme modest and bashful. . . . And though they are all thus naked, if one lives for ever among them, there is not to be seen an indecent action, or glance; and being continually used to see one another so unadorned, so like our first parents before the Fall, it seems as if they had no wishes; there being nothing to heighten curiosity, but all you can see, you see at once, and every moment see; and where there is no novelty, there can be no curiosity.[82]

The same effect of habitual nakedness on observers had been reported by earlier travellers.[83] Behn colours their courtship with conventions of European romance such as sighs and blushes, ascribing this behaviour entirely to nature – 'and these people represented to me an absolute idea of the first state of innocence, before man knew how to sin' she declares. Apparently nature also favours marriage arrangements alien to European tradition. Like Montaigne, Behn doesn't appear to find anything detrimental in a polygamous system: 'they have plurality of wives, which, when they grow old, they serve those that succeed them, who are young; but with a servitude easy and respected'.[84] Also like Montaigne with his cannibals, Behn uses her version of the Noble Savage as a pointed contrast with European duplicity: 'they have a native justice, which knows no fraud: and they understand no vice, or cunning, but when they are taught by the white men.'[85] She herself behaves like an enlightened tourist, aware of a culture clash, but intensely appreciative of the impact of new experiences on her senses – the wonderful climate, the colours and fragrances, the unfamiliar deliciously aromatic food. What Margaret Cavendish had to invent, Aphra Behn discovers. Although to some extent she is remaking this society in a conventional utopian image, such responsiveness to cultural difference is a valuable asset to a writer.

Behn did not, of course, set out to write a utopian fiction as such in *Oroonoko*. But her incorporation of a utopian element into a mainline narrative, which reflects upon that narrative instead of being a simple digression, anticipates techniques to be developed further in the novel genre. With Behn's work, we come in sight of the still distant but impressive coastline of eighteenth-century fiction. However, before approaching it, it's necessary to take a few preliminary soundings in non-fiction, to test eighteenth-century attitudes to utopian discourse in general.

Notes and references

1. For a survey of utopian experiments in the period v W.H.G. Armytage 1961 Phase I: for discussion of the nature of seventeenth-century English utopianism v J.C. Davis 1981: K. Thomas 1985 (both adopt criteria and reach conclusions which differ somewhat from mine).

2. v F. Rabelais 1564/1991 Book I chs 53–8 (cf Book III ch. 1): M. de Cervantes 1604–1614/1950 part II chs xlv, xlvii, xlix, li: R. Burton 1621/1972 Democritus to the Reader pp. 97–107.

3. R. Burton 1621/1972 Democritus to the Reader p. 101.

4. Rawley 'To the Reader': F. Bacon 1605–1627/1906 p. 256.

5. v Plato 1965/1977 pp. 33–5, 131–45, 146–67: cf Plato 1980: for Bacon's reworking of the myth v F. Bacon 1605–1627/1906 pp. 269–78.

6. v F. Bacon 1605–1627/1906 pp. 266–9.

7. F. Bacon 1605–1627/1906 Book I p. 11.

8. F. Bacon 1605–1627/1906 pp. 265, 270.

9. v F. Bacon 1605–1627/1906 pp. 285–6.

10. F. Bacon 1605–1627/1906 p. 288.

11. F. Bacon 1605–1627/1906 p. 290: for the basis of the attitude to nature v K. Thomas 1983 pp. 17–36.

12. F. Bacon 1605–1627/1906 p. 295: for the full account v pp. 288–98: for science and early utopias v R.P. Adams 1949: J. Bierman 1963.

13. *To the Royal Society* st 5. In A. Cowley 1905 p. 450.

14. F. Bacon 1605–1627/1906 p. 297; cf p. 295: also cf A. Cowley 1906 p. 250: contrast J. Swift 1726/1965 part II ch. vii pp. 134–5; Part IV ch. v pp. 247–8.

15. F. Bacon 1605–1627/1906 p. 297: cf R.P. Adams 1949 pp. 390–2: for a more optimistic emphasis v J. Bierman 1963 pp. 499–500.

16. For family values in *New Atlantis* v F. Bacon 1605–1627/1906 pp. 279–83.

17. F. Bacon 1605–1627/1906 p. 298: for 'knowledge broken' (said of aphorisms) v *Advancement of Learning* Book II p. 164: for the inconclusiveness of Bacon's utopia cf J.C. Davis 1981 ch. 5: among those influenced by Bacon were Samuel Hartlib's circle, which produced another utopian fiction, *Macaria* (v C. Webster 1970; 1972; 1975).

18. v. J.V. Andreae 1619/1916 pp. 172–3: S. Gott 1648/1902 vol. 1 p. 234.

19. S. Gott 1648/1902 vol. 1 p. 172: after religious education, Gott's priority is 'a liberal education, both literary and scientific' (vol. 1 p. 239).

20. For information about *Nova Solyma* v J.M. Patrick 1977: for seventeenth-century millenarianism and utopianism in context v E.L. Tuveson 1949 ch. 3; K. Thomas 1985 pp. 173–5; C. Hill 1988 "Till the Conversion of the Jews". In R.H. Popkin (ed) pp. 12–36.

21. J.C. Davis 1981 p. 164.

22. But eighteenth-century attitudes to millenarianism, utopianism and progress are still the subject of debate: v D. Spadafora 1990 part I ch. 3; cf E.L. Tuveson 1949 chs 4, 5.

23. v. G. Winstanley 1651/1983 ch. iv pp. 347–54.

24. G. Winstanley 1651/1983 Address to Cromwell pp. 283–4: ch. 1 pp. 295–6.

25. G. Winstanley 1651/1983 To the Friendly and Unbiased Reader p. 291.

26. G. Winstanley 1651/1983 ch. vi pp. 388–9.

27. G. Winstanley 1651/1983 ch. v p. 369.

28. J. Harrington 1656/1977 p. 205: for a study of seventeenth-century republicanism v Z.S Fink 1945/1962.

29. J. Harrington 1656/1977 p. 181: cf p. 231.

30. J. Harrington 1656/1977 pp. 249, 287: the latter analogy refers to circulation of the blood.

31. Even so, Pocock perhaps underestimates the extent to which *Oceana* meets the criteria of utopian fiction: v J. Harrington 1656/1977 intro pp. 73–4.

32. For Defoe and Harrington v J. Harrington 1656/1977 intro p. 140: for Swift and Harrington v below p. 135 also v J. Swift 1939–68 vol. 3 pp. 114–15.

33. v T. Hobbes 1651/1968: J. Locke 1690/1988: Thomas considers *Leviathan* as a utopian text (K. Thomas 1985 p. 169).

34. *Areopagitica* 1644. In J. Milton 1953–82 vol. 2 p. 526: Milton criticises those who take Plato's utopianism too literally: v pp. 522–6.

35. *An Apology Against a Pamphlet &c (An Apology for Smectymnuus)* 1642. In J. Milton 1953–82 vol. 1 pp. 880–1.

36. R. Burton 1621/1972 Democritus to the Reader pp. 97, 101: Patrick takes Burton's utopianism more seriously: v J.M. Patrick 1948. For Burton and Swift v A. Ross 1989. In J.I. Fischer, H. Real, J. Woolley (eds) pp. 133–58.

37. 'Controversial merriment': v S. Johnson 1779–1781/1905 vol. 1 p. 104. For Swift and Hall, and for Healey's translation, v Wands's intro to J. Hall 1605/1981.

38. v J. Hall 1605/?1608 Book I ch. 9 pp. 37–9.

39. v J. Hall 1605/1981 intro pp. xxxviii–xli.

40. v J. Hall 1605/?1608 Book III ch. 6.

41. J. Hall 1605/?1608 Book IV ch. 5 p. 236: for plagiarism (*Lurtch-wit*) v ch. 6 pp. 241–2.

42. J. Hall 1605/?1608 Book II ch. 5 p. 109; ch. 3 p. 102; ch. 7 pp. 118–20.

43. J. Hall 1605/?1608 Book II ch. 6 p. 111.

44. M. Cavendish Duchess of Newcastle 1656 pp. 231–4.

45. M. Cavendish Duchess of Newcastle 1656 pp. 239–40.

46. cf. Lilley's intro to M. Cavendish Duchess of Newcastle 1992 p. xxvii.

47. cf K. Lilley on seventeenth-century women's utopianism in C. Brant, D. Purkiss 1992 (eds) pp. 126–9: also her intro to M. Cavendish Duchess of Newcastle 1992 pp. xiv–xv.

48. M. Cavendish Duchess of Newcastle 1666 pp. 17–18, 60.

49. cf Lilley's comments on her interest in hybrids. M. Cavendish Duchess of Newcastle 1992 pp. xi, xiv.

50. v M. Cavendish Duchess of Newcastle 1666 pp. 19–60.

51. M. Cavendish Duchess of Newcastle 1666 p. 89.

52. M. Cavendish Duchess of Newcastle 1666 p. 101: cf M. Cavendish Duchess of Newcastle 1992 intro pp. xxvii–xxviii.

53. v Nicolson's pioneering study (M.H. Nicolson 1948).

54. v J. Wilkins 1638/1684 Proposition XIII pp. 124–35; Proposition XIV pp. 135–60.

55. For the political connections v C. Hill 1965/1980 p. 110: for linguistic connections v E.D. Seeber 1945.

56. F. Godwin 1638 pp. 102, 109, 103.

57. F. Godwin 1638 pp. 103–5: cf M.H. Nicolson 1948 p. 83.

58. v F. Godwin 1638 pp. 70, 73–8, 107–9: for Swiftian parallels v M.H. Nicolson 1948 pp. 81, 84: W.A. Eddy 1923/1963 pp. 124–5.

59. F. Godwin 1638 pp. 93–4: cf E.D. Seeber 1945 p. 587.

60. v F. Godwin 1638 p. 73: cf pp. 82–3.

61. F. Godwin 1638 p. 109.

62. Godwin's Man in the Moone was published in a French edn in 1648: for influences on Cyrano and for Cyrano and Swift v Strachan's intro to Cyrano de Bergerac 1657/1965 pp. x, xiv–xvi.

63. Cyrano de Bergerac 1657/1965 pp. 30, 171.

64. For theriophily v G. Boas 1933 (for Cyrano v pp. 142–5).

65. v Cyrano de Bergerac 1657/1965 pp. 71–3: compare and contrast T. Campanella 1602, 1637/1981 pp. 45–6.

66. v Cyrano de Bergerac 1657/1965 pp. 63–4, 92–3, 175–7.

67.   v F.E. Manuel, F.P. Manuel 1979 pp. 367–81: also [D. d'A Vairasse] 1727 vol. 3 pt II.

68.   e.g. K. Williams 1959 pp. 179–80.

69.   v D. d'A Vairasse 1675–9/1738 Part III pp. 197, 201–7, 207–9.

70.   v D. d'A Vairasse 1675–9/1738 Part IV pp. 216–21.

71.   G. Foigny de 1676/1693 pp. 10–11, 45–6, 63.

72.   v G. de Foigny 1676/1693 pp. 67–70: Hermeticism has a similar emphasis on original hermaphroditic unity.

73.   G. de Foigny 1676/1693 pp. 67, 70.

74.   v D. d'A Vairasse 1675–9/1738 p. 208.

75.   cf R. Filmer 1680/1991: J. Locke 1690/1988: for commentary on Filmer and Locke v Laslett's intro to J. Locke 1690/1988 pp. 67–71. Aldridge suggests different angles on Neville's text and relates it to contemporary attempts to legalise polygamy (A.O. Aldridge 1950 pp. 465–8).

76.   H. Neville 1668/1930 pp. 228–9.

77.   H. Neville 1668/1930 p. 231.

78.   H. Neville 1668/1930 p. 232.

79.   H. Neville 1668/1930 p. 234: cf pp. 232–3.

80.   H. Neville 1668/1930 p. 234.

81.   H. Neville 1668/1930 p. 236 (and subsequent quotations).

82.   A. Behn 1688/1992 p. 76.

83.   e.g. John Lerius cit R. Burton 1621/1972 Pt 3 Sec 2 Mem 2 Subs 3 pp. 88–9.

84.   A. Behn 1688/1992 p. 77: cf M. de Montaigne 1580–1588/1991 p. 239.

85.   A. Behn 1688/1992 p. 77: the bad faith of the white colonists is borne out by Behn's narrative.

CHAPTER 3

Utopian discourse in the eighteenth century: a preliminary view

For various reasons, the intellectual climate of eighteenth-century Britain appears more hostile to utopian writing than the seventeenth century had been. Asked to list English works from the period – fiction or non-fiction – which could be so described, not many readers might get beyond parts of *Gulliver's Travels*, or, stretching a point, *Robinson Crusoe*. Yet the dominant literary genres, satire and the novel, positively invite experiment with imaginative alternatives to the *status quo*; and theories about society, government, economic activity and family values, and how to reform them, proliferate on all sides. However, there is some evidence of a reaction against anything that might be called overtly utopian in this context.[1] Possibly this is part of a deeper historical reaction against a discourse associated with the earlier revolutionary period, or else a self-consciously 'enlightened' rejection of an older form of humanism. Whatever the cause, it has literary repercussions.

'Utopian' itself, if not exactly a dirty word, is a suspect one, often found guilty by association. It tends to occur in contexts which are either dismissive or defensive. 'Chimerical', for example, is a favourite synonym. As John Brown remarks, 'Closet-*Projects* . . . often *are*, and always are *regarded*, as *chimerical*'.[2] Fielding's fictional peer waves away the ideal of social justice with ' "This is all mere *Utopia* . . . the Chimerical system of *Plato's* Commonwealth with which we amused ourselves at the University; Politics which are inconsistent with the State of Human Affairs." '[3]

William Temple echoes a similar sentiment in attacking the utopian principles – as he regards them – of one Mr Bell, who advocated universal employment and an equal division of land and property: 'This would be a pretty scheme truly, but is as impracticable as *Plato's* republick.' He reinforces his point by denigrating the ancient utopian paradigm, the Sparta of Lycurgus:

> Truly when this fine scheme and these political *Lycurgic* institutions are reduced to practice, you will have little or nothing to do, but to follow the example of the disciples of the *Spartan* legislator, that is, to sing, dance, fiddle, wrestle, run, eat black broth, live in huts, and wear sheep-skins, and in the issue, be extinguished or made slaves of by your invading neighbours.[4]

He finally demolishes Bell with a metaphor suggestive of utopian voyaging: 'our author's volatile imagination has carried so much sail, that it has overset his judgment, wreck'd his memory, and sunk him to the bottom of a gulph of stupidity in a shatter'd crazy *theory*.'[5] Temple's hammering is intellectually lightweight, designed (in the case of the Sparta passage) to test the instant reflex of a classically educated reader and provoke anti-primitivist, anti-utopian prejudice. Yet even the heavyweights of eighteenth-century political theory can and do appeal to the same prejudices.

One of the most radical challenges to traditional humanist utopian discourse comes from Bernard Mandeville in *The Fable of the Bees*. The *Moral* of *The Grumbling Hive* literally spells out the meaning of utopia that is targeted:

> . . . Fools only strive
> (X.) To make a Great an Honest Hive
> (Y.) T'enjoy the World's Conveniencies,
>   Be fam'd in War, yet live in Ease,
>   Without great Vices, is a vain
>   EUTOPIA seated in the Brain.[6]

Although Mandeville's philosophy is far from universally accepted, he purveys a highly developed and influential version of anti-utopianism, which is all the more effective because he recognises the utopian terms of reference. In arguing his thesis of *Private Vices, Publick Benefits* – a thesis which would be anathema to most earlier utopian writers for whom the virtuous life and the ideal society are inseparable – Mandeville deliberately exposes the incompatibility of utopian aims. You can have the good life in spiritual terms or the good life in material terms, but not both. He graphically illustrates the conflict of priorities in his preface. London's filthy streets would not be tolerated in any utopian city; but they are an index of public prosperity, which takes precedence over 'private Conveniency'. In this passage Mandeville puts the choice with characteristic trenchancy:

But if, without any regard to the Interest or Happiness of the City, the Question was put, What Place I thought most pleasant to walk in? No body can doubt but, before the stinking Streets of *London*, I would esteem a fragrant Garden, or a shady Grove in the Country. In the same manner, if laying aside all worldly Greatness and Vain-Glory, I should be ask'd where I thought it was most probable that Men might enjoy true Happiness, I would prefer a small peaceable Society, in which Men, neither envy'd not esteem'd by Neighbours, should be contented to live upon the Natural Product of the Spot they inhabit, to a vast Multitude abounding in Wealth and Power, that should always be conquering others by their Arms Abroad, and debauching themselves by Foreign Luxury at Home.[7]

It is the classic utopian answer, but to a loaded question. *The Grumbling Hive* is a brilliant social fable which dismantles the myth of social and moral perfection by driving a wedge between its two complementary concepts. Mandeville's moral recalls Socrates' distinction between the simple and the luxurious state:

Bare Virtue can't make Nations live
In Splendor; they, that would revive
A Golden Age, must be as free,
For Acorns, as for Honesty.[8]

The simple-life utopia pays an economic price: what Mandeville asks is that humanity should stop deceiving itself about the economic consequences of virtuous living.

In subsequent discussions – *An Enquiry into the Origin of Moral Virtue*, the *Remarks*, *An Essay on Charity, and Charity-Schools*, *A Search into the Nature of Society* – he probes sharply and uncomfortably into the received wisdom on a great number of topics also treated in utopian literature, from dress and diet to prostitution and polygamy, and from the regulation of crime to the regulation of education. Read against earlier utopian texts, his opinions gain extra pungency. He exploits this openly in his critique of Plutarch's description of Sparta, the 'ideal state' that violates Mandeville's contention by being praised for greatness *and* frugality. 'But certainly there never was a Nation whose Greatness was more empty than theirs' he sneers, for although 'it is plain, that no Nation on Earth was less effeminate . . . being debarred from all the Comforts of Life, they could have nothing for their Pains but the Glory of being a Warlike People inured to Toils and Hardships, which was a Happiness that few People would have cared for upon the same Terms'.[9] Who would want to live in Sparta? It is an essentially modern approach to the interrogation of utopian texts. Mandeville might equally well have cited More's *Utopia*, though for different reasons, since he reverses its basic principle: that the suppression of whatever incites to pride and luxury produces both communal prosperity and true pleasure. Far from conflating the ideal society with the Golden Age, Mandeville argues that civilisation is the opposite of a primitivist golden age in almost every respect:

> In the first Ages, Man, without doubt, fed on the Fruits of the Earth, without any previous Preparation, and reposed himself naked like other Animals on the Lap of their common Parent: Whatever has contributed since to make Life more comfortable, as it must have been the Result of Thought, Experience, and some Labour, so it more or less deserves the name of Luxury, the more or less trouble it required, and deviated from the primitive Simplicity.[10]

Defoe might dissent from Mandeville's moral philosophy, but Robinson Crusoe's attempts 'to make Life more comfortable' and his sense of how much human effort and ingenuity goes into producing the simplest, most taken for granted adjuncts of civilised living serve to confirm Mandeville's doctrine, in this instance at least. Luxury becomes a different kind of concept on a desert island: the fiction makes the definition more, not less, problematic.

Like Mandeville, David Hume both engages with and presents a critique of utopian discourse in his *Essays Moral, Political, and Literary* of 1742. However, he is less anti-utopian than Mandeville: the psychology and methodology interest him, and he applies a utopian hypothesis on occasion as an incisive analytical tool. For example, in the essay *Of Refinement in the Arts* he explains the tendency 'to declaim against present times, and magnify the virtue of remote ancestors' (one possible starting-point for utopian speculations) as a deep-rooted psychological phenomenon. To counter this fallacy, he proposes an exercise in cultural relativity, 'by comparing different nations that are contemporaries' (again a method that can be adapted to a utopian context).[11] In the same essay, he himself proposes a utopian hypothesis in order to focus ironically on the interrelation of moral, political and economic factors:

Suppose the same number of men, that are present in GREAT BRITAIN, with the same soil and climate; I ask, is it not possible for them to be happier, by the most perfect way of life that can be imagined, and by the greatest reformation that Omnipotence itself could work in their temper and disposition? To assert, that they cannot, appears evidently ridiculous. As the land is able to maintain more than all its present inhabitants, they could never, in such a UTOPIAN state, feel any other ills than those which arise from bodily sickness; and these are not the half of human miseries. All other ills spring from some vice, either in ourselves or others; and even many of our diseases proceed from the same origin. Remove the vices, and the ills follow.

The logic appears impeccable, from a utopian viewpoint, but there is a sting in the tail:

You must only take care to remove all the vices. If you remove part, you may render the matter worse.[12]

For Hume, sceptical of 'such a miraculous transformation of mankind',[13] the issue is a philosophical not a political one – politics being the art of the possible. There are clearly defined limits to utopian engineering.

Moreover, just as he distinguishes between philosophy and politics, so he distinguishes between fiction and fact. According to these categories, utopian discourse is fiction: historical discourse is fact. And he privileges the latter over the former. So when, like Mandeville and Temple, he wants to cite Sparta as an example, he insists on treating it as historical evidence to support an argument which, as he points out, is not 'merely chimerical', however utopian the description might appear:

It is well known with what peculiar laws SPARTA was governed, and what a prodigy that republic is justly esteemed by every one, who has considered human nature as it has displayed itself in other nations, and other ages. Were the testimony of history less positive and circumstantial, such a government would appear a mere philosophical whim or fiction, and impossible ever to be reduced to practice.[14]

Yet, for all his reservations, Hume's interest in the limits and possibilities of the utopian form leads him to experiment with his own ideal-state exercise. His elegantly concise essay, *Idea of a perfect Commonwealth*, evinces an unusual openmindedness towards utopian methodology, though it does concede something to current opinion:

The subject is surely the most worthy curiosity of any the wit of man can possibly devise. And who knows, if this controversy were fixed by the universal consent of the wise and learned, but, in some future age, an opportunity might be afforded of reducing the theory to practice, either by a dissolution of some old government, or by the combination of men to form a new one, in some distant part of the world?[15]

However, he anticipates a familiar criticism, and deliberately excludes works of imaginative literature as a model:

All I pretend to in the present essay is to revive this subject of speculation; and therefore I shall deliver my sentiments in as few words as possible. A long dissertation on that head would not, I apprehend, be very acceptable to the public, who will be apt to regard such disquisitions both as useless and chimerical.

All plans of government, which suppose great reformation in the manners of mankind, are plainly imaginary. Of this nature, are the Republic of PLATO, and the Utopia of Sir THOMAS MORE.[16]

His preferred candidate for 'the only valuable model of a commonwealth, that has yet been offered to the public' is James Harrington's Oceana, and even it falls short in provision of certain political safeguards, a defect that Hume proceeds to rectify. As might be expected, his scheme is methodically thought through, a finely tuned structure of checks and balances devised almost exclusively in terms of constitutional mechanisms. It is scarcely the stuff of which novels are made. Indeed, the eighteenth-century novel is concerned less with the overt politics of utopia than with its creative social possibilities, with alternative ways of restructuring individual and communal life to fulfil the human potential that is warped and frustrated by the writer's own culture. The value of non-fictional utopian discourse is not that it offers practical solutions, but that it keeps open the debate begun by the seminal texts.

As for the pervasive scepticism, the argument that utopia is located only in the ideal world of imagination is inherent in the tradition virtually from the beginning. The greatest creators in the genre, Plato and More, are far too subtle to impale their myths on any crudely pragmatic criteria. So it cannot be claimed that there is anything unprecedented in the general eighteenth-century line of attack, though the tone of such attacks on 'chimerical' systems is more consistently patronising. Scepticism seems to have hardened into a consensus that the utopian writer is not to be taken as a serious intellectual threat, unless, like the pirate vessels of eighteenth-century maritime history, he or she is prepared to sail under misleading colours. That is certainly a feasible option. Writers of fiction, to pursue the pirate analogy, can take on profitable cargo from other legitimate traders in ideas. More, they can carry on such trade themselves. After all, eighteenth-century purveyors of fiction are, as often as not, authors of discursive non-fiction, writing with their other hand. Fiction gives them freedom to plunder the raw material of other discourses, including their own.[17]

It follows that evidence for the degree and slant of a writer's utopianism may be assembled from a variety of sources, which will be considered in due course. Defoe's educational background and *An Essay Upon Projects*; Swift's library and politics; the periodical writings of Fielding and Johnson: all these create a context for their fiction, as does (for example) the *Serious Proposal* of Mary Astell for women's utopias. In addition, the philosophical texts, from Plato and Aristotle to Hobbes and Locke, that infiltrate the thinking of educated eighteenth-century writers must serve both as cargo and ballast for these fictional utopian voyages. However, the utopian imagination travels furthest when it is not over-ballasted by political theory, when it lets the vessel run before the wind, controlled only by the novelist's or satirist's skills, so that it can test the utopian model if need be to destruction.

What is conspicuous in eighteenth-century fiction is the much enhanced role of the individual consciousness in this testing process. The question more rarely posed by earlier practitioners of the 'pure' form of the genre – what would it be like to encounter or inhabit utopia as an individual human being conditioned in specific ways by gender, class, education and culture – is constantly addressed by eighteenth-century writers. One consequence is that the political and constitutional dimension tends to become less prominent. The quality of life is directly associated with an environment that fosters individual creativity and satisfactions, and represents social relationships on a personal rather than institutional level:

> How small, of all that human hearts endure,
> That part which laws or kings can cause or cure.[18]

asserts Johnson, and if not every bosom returns an echo to his sentiment, certainly it appeals to many novelists. Utopia is domesticised as never before. Yet at the same time the exotic location beyond seas draws the utopian imagination as compellingly as ever. Defoe is one writer who marks out an extraordinary personal territory, as unique as the naked footprint on Crusoe's island, but also as centrally human. Eighteenth-century utopian fiction might be said to begin with that most unlikely protagonist for a utopian narrative, the man cut off from society altogether for a critical period and condemned to recreate it: Robinson Crusoe.

Notes and references

1. Arguably, utopianism as such is displaced into theorising about progress: cf E.L. Tuveson 1949 ch. v: D. Spadafora 1990.

2. J. Brown 1757 pp. 212–13.

3. H. Fielding 1751/1983 Book XI ch. ii p. 459.

4. W. Temple 1758 pp. 24–5: cf p. 51.

5. W. Temple 1758 p. 137.

6. B. Mandeville 1705–1725/1924 vol. 1 p. 36: for discussion of Mandeville's thought v M. Goldsmith 1985.

7. B. Mandeville 1705–1725/1924 vol. 1 pp. 12–13.

8. B. Mandeville 1705–1725/1924 vol. 1 p. 37.

9. B. Mandeville 1705–1725/1924 vol. 1 pp. 245–6 (Remark X).

10. B. Mandeville 1705–1725/1924 vol. 1 p. 169 (Remark P): for the eighteenth-century debate on luxury v J. Sekora 1977 part I chs 2, 3.

11. D. Hume 1882/1964 vol. 3 p. 307.

12. D. Hume 1882/1964 vol. 3 p. 308.

13. D. Hume 1882/1964 vol. 3 p. 309.

14. D. Hume 1882/1964 vol. 3 pp. 290–1.

15. D. Hume 1882/1964 vol. 3 pp. 480–1.

16. D. Hume 1882/1964 vol. 3 p. 481.

17. For a demonstration of this in practice, and in relation to utopia, v C. Watts 1990 ch. 7.

18. Johnson's contribution to Goldsmith's The Traveller. In O. Goldsmith 1969 p. 656.

CHAPTER 4

Utopia overseas: Robinson Crusoe;
A General History of the Pyrates;
Gaudentio di Lucca; Peter Wilkins

Defoe's qualifications as a utopian writer start with a background that places him in an ideal position to negotiate between the early eighteenth-century world and worlds elsewhere. His roots are in the seventeenth century (he was born c.1660), in the same soil of religious dissent that traditionally produced thinkers who combine the visionary and the pragmatic. For these earlier utopians, the light of spiritual illumination transfigured English earth and the prospect of the millennium had transiently revolutionised English politics. For Defoe – post-1688 and post-Locke – it was a peaceful property-owning revolution that had triumphed, and that could be exported. Yet he is still a Dissenter, neither a complete insider nor an outsider in his own culture. This background may partly account for the revolutionary zeal he directs into secular reform or 'Projects'.

It certainly accounts for the kind of education he received. At Newington Green Academy, the progressive curriculum didn't only equip Defoe with skills for a modern age – languages, mathematics, science – but also possibly sowed the seed of utopian interests in his imagination. His headmaster, Charles Morton, 'was a great Acquaintance of Bp. W[ilkins], an Ingenious and universally learned Man'[1] – the same Bishop Wilkins who speculated on lunar travel and conditions in the moon, and who made a notable contribution to technological theory. Defoe himself salutes Wilkins as a pioneer in this field (in *An Essay Upon Projects*, 1697),[2] and acknowledges him as the predecessor of the moon voyager in *The Consolidator* (1705).[3] Besides this connection, Morton was an author in his own right of a treatise on politics, the *Eutaxia*, which is no longer extant, but which was allegedly an 'imitation of More's *Utopia*' and which was probably used as a textbook in his school.[4] How many of the books listed in the 1731 sales catalogue of Defoe's and Farewell's libraries actually belonged to Defoe is uncertain, but Robinson's translation of More's *Utopia* is there, as well as a number of other classics of the genre.[5] It's tempting to speculate that Defoe found some literary as well as practical stimuli for utopian imaginings. Certainly he read widely in related genres – travel literature and *voyages imaginaires* – to an extent that helps to explain the balance between pragmatism and fantasy, non-fiction and fiction in his work.

For Defoe's mind seems to have had a naturally utopian bent: his instinct for planning and problem-solving combines with his impulse to make things vivid to produce schemes that transcend the merely feasible. However much he presents himself as a practical thinker, utopianism keeps breaking in. This is the case with *An Essay Upon Projects*, in which Defoe's enthusiasms occasionally recall that of the later projector, Gulliver (for example, on 'The Art of War, which I take to be the highest Perfection of Human Knowledge').[6] The fact that his commitment to social welfare also can recall More's *Utopia* is a tribute to the underlying vision of the *Essay*. Like More in *Utopia*, Defoe addresses the perennial problems that the ideal state is designed to solve: poverty, unemployment, beggary, crime. Like most utopian writers, he is full of proposals for institutional solutions to human ills, errors and inadequacies.[7] He agrees with More that man's reason can tackle most social and natural evils.

However, Defoe's approach differs radically from that praised by Raphael Hythlodaeus. Instead of sweeping away the monetary and property system, Defoe wants to deploy its resources to protect people against 'All the Continenges of Life . . . as Thieves, Floods by Land, Storms by Sea, Losses of all Sorts, and Death it self, in a manner, by making it up to the Survivor'.[8] What he is talking about here is insurance. More's Utopians are locked into a kind of mutual assurance society, metaphorically guaranteed by their ethical investment; Defoe's citizens are to depend on insurance premiums of a more conventional kind. But the preoccupation with taking out insurance, spiritual as well as financial, extends into Defoe's fiction, and is one key to his utopian social vision. For Defoe, God helps those who insure themselves, but society also has a responsibility for organising aid to the deserving. (Those whose ills, like the pox, are self-inflicted, need not apply.) Ultimately, like other utopian writers, he dreams of a social structure embracing an entire population which could 'for ever Banish Beggery [sic] and Poverty out of the Kingdom'.[9]

An Essay Upon Projects further demonstrates its utopian credentials by devoting attention to other categories of disadvantaged human beings. This is traditional: both Defoe and More, for example, make the treatment of 'fools' – those who are mentally incapacitated – a test of a compassionate society. Logically, Defoe argues, they should be maintained by those who have more than their fair share of intellect. In a nicely ironic anticipation of Swift's testatory gesture – 'He gave the little wealth he had, / To build a house for fools and mad' – he proposes the building of a 'Fool-house' at the expense of live authors, through levying 'a Tax upon Learning, to be paid by the Authors of Books'.[10] Where More and Defoe part company is on the entertainment value of those naturally afflicted. More condemns attitudes of mockery or contempt, but encourages kindly amusement, since that confers a kind of social role on 'fools'. Defoe deplores making them any kind of public spectacle. However, his answer is still the institutional one, characteristic of utopian projects.

Another category of the population who are disadvantaged in a different sense, and whose intelligence, in Defoe's eyes, is certainly undervalued, is that of women. An Essay Upon Projects supports female utopian discourse in the late seventeenth and eighteenth centuries by voicing the belief that women are worth educating, and that they should be given access to knowledge as men are, if not necessarily in their company.[11] It is true that in designing his Academy for Women Defoe is consulting male interests at least as much as female: educated women make better companions and managers. Yet that doesn't have to detract from the principle, that the civilised state educates all its members irrespective of gender. One possible test of an eighteenth-century utopia – in the ideal sense of the term – is whether it treats fools and women like human beings.

Among other attributes, it is this capacity for accommodating otherness that turns a writer's imagination towards fiction. It is clear from Defoe's non-fictional works how readily his mind engages with the kind of material that figures largely in utopian discourse. Add the element of imagined narrative, and the generic shift to utopian fiction is achieved. What is unexpected is Defoe's first choice of vehicle, which excludes virtually all the social possibilities developed in An Essay Upon Projects. When he wrote Robinson Crusoe, published in 1719, he not only set the utopian part of the novel beyond seas – a perfectly traditional expedient – but he also set it outside any normal concept of what constitutes society.[12] Almost by definition, utopian writing is expected to centre on the representation of community, man as a political animal. For Aristotle, the state is conceptually prior even to the human family, and the completely solitary human being is a contradiction in terms: he becomes literally dehumanised. Yet the social utopias of literature might be accused of dehumanising the subject in a different sense. In a number of earlier classics of the genre, individual consciousness is erased from utopia itself: Socrates serenely discussing the structure of the ideal state, Raphael Hythlodaeus relaying to somewhat sceptical auditors the practices of a perfectly adjusted community – neither so much as ask, let alone imagine, what it would be like to inhabit the mind of a single citizen and experience everyday utopian living on that basis. The only way to experience utopia as an individual is through the consciousness of the traveller-narrator, who functions as as alien commentator. However, Crusoe combines both roles, as discoverer and creator, man *as* island. As the shipwrecked traveller, he fits one kind of literary expectation; in addition, because the island is uninhabited, he becomes the founder of a utopia and the individual who registers the kind of experience he creates, first for himself then for others.

The implications of Defoe's paradox – a utopia originating with a solitary individual – complicate and transform the investigation of customary utopian topics, such as survival, defence, diet, clothes, control of the environment, politics, war, education, religion and the fear of death. Although Crusoe writes the island as utopian text, it is not a *tabula rasa* and neither is he. His own cultural history interacts with the island's natural history. Even more important than the goods he salvages from the wreck is the model of civilisation that he carries inside his head. To discover the dimensions of this model, the reader needs to look at Crusoe's background, as an Englishman of typically mixed ancestry (his father was a first-generation immigrant) and of mixed experience in the world outside England. The narrative prior to his arrival on the island gives us our bearings, as well as being a conventional feature of voyage narratives.

Before the island

In the opening stages of *The Life and Adventures of Robinson Crusoe*, Crusoe's father defines the model of social living to which his son should aspire. In its supposed perfect adjustment of human desires to available satisfactions, 'the middle Station of Life' might itself rank as a kind of utopian ideal. Certainly it is said to be 'calculated for all kind of Vertues and all kind of Enjoyments' accompanied by 'Peace and Plenty . . . Temperance, Moderation, Quietness, Health, Society, all agreeable Diversions, and all desirable Pleasures': a catalogue which might fit More's Utopians, but which springs from a very different creed from theirs.[13] Essentially, it is a creed based on money and property, enough to protect, not enough to tempt to power. What matters in life is to lubricate its passage, and money – in a reasonable sufficiency – is the prime lubricant. There is no impulse to reform the world. The aim is to evade, not to confront, its demands, and the ideal existence is described in language that slips down the throat as easily as the lives it defines slip through their narrow social channel:

> . . . this Way Men went silently and smoothly thro' the World, and comfortably out of it, not embarass'd with the Labours of the Hands or of the Head, not sold to the Life of Slavery for daily Bread, or harrast with perplex'd Circumstances, which rob the Soul of Peace, and the Body of Rest; not enrag'd with the Passion of Envy, or secret burning Lust of Ambition for great things; but in easy Circumstances sliding gently thro' the World, and sensibly tasting the Sweets of living, without the bitter, feeling that they are happy, and learning by every Day's Experience to know it more sensibly.[14]

Famously, it is an ideal that the youthful Robinson rebels against. Yet it is also one that he internalises, measuring his narrative experience against his father's programme.

In the early sequences of the novel, he learns at first hand what it is like to be both a slave and a slave-owner. For Crusoe, what defines slavery is enforced labour: his father's metaphoric 'Life of Slavery' becomes a literal state. As a slave of the Moors, he is not treated with any particular cruelty, but he has to carry out his master's commands 'to look after his little Garden, and do the common Drudgery of Slaves about his House'.[15] After his escape, when he settles in Brazil, he complains about having to labour for himself, ironically fore-shadowing his future fate: 'I had no body to converse with but now and then this Neighbour; no Work to be done, but by the Labour of my Hands; and I used to say, I liv'd just like a Man cast away upon some desolate Island, that had no body there but himself.'[16] Crusoe has no ideological objection to slavery, despite a passing qualm, as his treatment of Xury shows.[17] He is not concerned with liberty as a human right, only with liberty from drudgery. Once he starts to prosper, he says ' the first thing I did, I bought me a Negro Slave, and an *European* Servant also . . . .'[18] Prosperity tempts him, in accordance with his father's warning, to the other extreme of ambition, 'a rash and immoderate Desire of rising faster than the Nature of the Thing admitted'. Throughout Crusoe's career people persist in making him offers he can't refuse: this one is, all too appropriately, a slaving venture, which is to cast him 'down again into the deepest Gulph of human Misery that ever Man fell into'.[19] The island experience presents itself originally as a kind of hell, his nightmare imaginings realised. Yet it is also a rebirth, as the description of his being driven ashore graphically illustrates: his physical trauma enacts that of an infant, in the struggle to emerge from the womb of the sea:

> The Wave that came upon me again, buried me at once 20 or 30 Foot deep in its own Body; and I could feel my self carried with a mighty Force and Swiftness towards the Shore a very great Way; but I held my Breath, and assisted my self to swim still forward with all my Might. I was ready to burst with holding my Breath, when, as I felt my self rising up, so to my immediate Relief, I found my Head and Hands shoot out above the Surface of the Water . . . .[20]

Crusoe himself feels that he has been rescued from the grave. What awaits him, however, is not paradise, but the state of nature, a return to the pre-social existence of his species.[21] Crusoe's rebirth is the birth of utopia.

On the island: Crusoe in solitude

He reacts to his brave new world as if it were indeed Hobbes's state of nature, an environment condemning him to a life 'solitary, poore, nasty, brutish, and short'[22] – that is, the antithesis of utopia. However, this perception arises from a partial misreading of his situation. As it turns out, he isn't a castaway without resources; nor is the island the hostile place he fears – there are no 'ravenous Beasts' and at least no indigenous ravenous humans.[23] It is not until much later that he can represent to himself 'in the most lively Colours' what true Hobbesian primitivism would have been like, without the supplies, weapons and tools retrieved from the wreck:

How I could not have so much as got any Food, except Fish and
Turtles; and that as it was long before I found any of them, I
must have perish'd first. That I should have liv'd, if I had not
perish'd, like a meer Savage. That if I had kill'd a Goat, or a
Fowl, by any Contrivance, I had no way to flea or open them, or
part the Flesh from the Skin, and the Bowels, or to cut it up; but
must gnaw it with my Teeth, and pull it with my Claws like a
Beast.[24]

This is the condition of bestiality that Aristotle and Hobbes associate
with the hypothetical human being deprived of society. For Crusoe, it
significantly focuses on the image of eating, tearing raw flesh. He can
assure himself that he is not a beast or a savage because of the way in
which he has progressed beyond what is necessary for survival to
regulate his food supply, its preparation and consumption.[25]

It isn't coincidental that the subject of food occupies an important
place in the utopian tradition, and that, in giving it a central place in
the narrative, Robinson Crusoe conforms to type. Many utopian texts
use food and the mode of its consumption as a determinant of the
level of civilisation. In the land of Cockaigne version (usually not
classified as utopia proper, but a related form) and its satirical counterpart like Hall's Tenter-belly, excess is the ideal. However, in other
ideal states, eating is organised as a social discipline as well as a
pleasure. Even before he founds his human society – and he receives
strangers into a communal relation by feeding them – Crusoe observes
this ritual. At the high point of his solitary existence, he translates
the characteristic utopian act of communal eating into biblical and
political metaphor: 'What a Table was here spread for me in a
Wilderness, where I saw nothing at first but to perish for Hunger.'[26]
Nor is it fortuitous that savagery among the human species defines
itself primarily as cannibalism, making literal the Hobbesian metaphor
of men preying on each other.

'Where I saw nothing at first . . . ' Crusoe begins his climb out of
the Hobbesian predicament by salvaging the material legacy of his
civilisation from the wreck. Yet its true legacy is the knowledge
imprinted, however imperfectly, on his brain. He has to know how to
use the arms and tools. With that knowledge comes the capacity to
fulfil the opposite half of the Aristotelian formula. Instead of acting
like a beast, he now has the potential to act like a god – within limits.
He brings to the island the destructive power of European man,
making his first (futile) kill, and so permanently changing his relation

to the environment: 'I believe it was the first Gun that had been fir'd there since the Creation of the World'.[27]

However, what kind of creation is the island? In a sense, it *is* Crusoe's creation, for it is as though he has brought it into being by imagining it beforehand. While he is there, it is structured by his perceptions and his words. Part of Crusoe's psychology is that like a true utopist he is always imagining an elsewhere, and comparing his present state with possible alternatives. He is addicted to 'what if' and 'if only'; and with regard to the island, his moods swing violently between experiencing it as a place of opportunity and as a place of desolation. Indeed there are alternative islands: the solid island of daylight reality, and the 'enchanted Island' of gods and demons that passes into savage legend.[28] As an island utopia, however, it has a significant topography. Like other utopian founders, having ensured the means of survival, Crusoe pays close attention to topography.

In the ancient world, the theoretic creation of a new colony prompts discussion of the best kind of location, taking such factors as climate and natural resources into account. In fictional accounts of utopian discoveries, the description of place often goes beyond the utilitarian to the aesthetic, featuring exotic flora and fauna, paradisal garden landscapes, and shining symmetrical cities. In contrast, Crusoe's island, initially at least, boasts few literary or tourist attractions. His choice of habitation is dictated by the imperatives of physical survival (fresh water, shade, security): a sea view is prized purely because it offers a hope of escape. His first territorial instinct is to enclose and fortify, not to expand. Only after a prolonged period of digging in and establishing a secure base, does he decide to explore 'his' island.

As the prospect opens, so the language becomes more like that of the traditional traveller discovering an earthly paradise: 'the Country appear'd so fresh, so green, so flourishing, every thing being in a constant Verdure, or Flourish of *Spring*, that it looked like a planted Garden.'[29] For readers parched for the delights of the senses, this glimpse of an ancient motif, the *ver perpetuum* or eternal spring, is like an oasis – or a mirage. For Crusoe, it inspires a utopian fantasy with down-to-earth political implications:

> I descended a little on the Side of that delicious Vale, surveying it with a secret Kind of Pleasure, (tho' mixt with my other afflicting Thoughts) to think that this was all my own, that I was King and Lord of all this Country indefeasibly, and had a Right

of Possession; and if I could convey it, I might have it in Inheritance, as compleatly as any Lord of a Mannor in *England*.[30]

This passage raises the issue of power and property central to all political utopias, and requires to be considered in the context of Crusoe's claim to the island.

Since Crusoe believes the island to be not only uninhabited but undiscovered, the case appears simple. But precisely because it is so clear-cut, it goes back to fundamental principle: on what is the 'Right of Possession' based? In the seventeenth century, the connection between property rights and political power triggered the differing utopian theories of Winstanley and Harrington. Winstanley had argued that the Earth should be in common ownership; Harrington wanted a more equitable distribution of land property under his agrarian law. In Crusoe's case, his rights do not conflict with anyone else's, but his claim does raise the question of legitimacy in another sense: what gives a man a right to private ownership of the Earth's resources? It is a question famously addressed by Locke in his *Two Treatises of Government*, 1690, and a number of critics have applied Lockean theory in one way or another to *Robinson Crusoe*.[31] Because it radically affects Crusoe's relation to his environment and his subsequent exercise of power, this theory bears also upon the novel as utopian fiction.

Locke accepts the original common ownership of the Earth through divine dispensation, but argues that private property arises out of the individual's need to provide for his own subsistence: even in the wild, labour in the form of hunting or gathering is necessary to support life. From this he develops his thesis that labour is what appropriates goods from the common stock to individual right of possession: 'He that is nourished by the Acorns he pickt up under an Oak, or the Apples he gathered from the Trees in the Wood, has certainly appropriated them to himself.'[32] The same principle extends from the fruits and beasts of the Earth to the Earth itself when it is cultivated. But is this process without limits? Locke answers in the negative:

> It will perhaps be objected to this, That if gathering the Acorns, or other Fruits of the Earth, &. makes a right to them, then any one may *ingross* as much as he will. To which I Answer, Not so. The same Law of Nature, that does by this means give us Property, does also *bound* that *Property* too. *God has given us all*

things richly . . . . But how far has he given it us? *To enjoy.* As much as any one can make use of to any advantage of life before it spoils; so much he may by his labour fix a Property in. Whatever is beyond this, is more than his share, and belongs to others. Nothing was made by God for Man to spoil or destroy.[33]

Crusoe has already fixed a limited property in his island, but his discovery of the 'delicious Vale' seems exactly the right psychological moment for him to experience the joy of possession – like the first man in Eden – and to have his post-Edenic responsibility brought home to him.[34] For Defoe uses this episode to emphasise the Lockean point that the human being is not given the fruits of the Earth to spoil them, or over-indulge himself. Crusoe, brought up in a northern climate, appreciates the temptation of abundant melons and grapes 'very ripe and rich'. To an Englishman they connote sensuality and expense; and, as Crusoe remembers from experience, gorging on grapes can have disastrous physical consequences. Cautiously, he doesn't behave as if this were the Land of Cockaigne. However, his first attempt to exploit his discovery fails, because he miscalculates the problems of accumulating and transporting heaps of ripe grapes, and they are spoilt and destroyed. The practical answer is to dry them for raisins; but there is a moral point about use, which Crusoe formulates in a later Lockean observation 'That all the good Things of this World, are no farther good to us, than they are for our Use; and that whatever we may heap up indeed to give others, we enjoy just as much as we can use, and no more.'[35]

This is, of course, a principle practised in many utopias, but we might ask how consistently Crusoe actually applies it. He may deplore waste, but he doesn't question the availability of natural resources for his use. While he hoards the civilised products that he can't replace – such as ink – he is prepared to sacrifice an entire tree to make a single plank. Indeed, for the modern reader, Crusoe's relation to the natural environment is complicated, although perfectly explicable in his contemporary terms. The island is hardly a forerunner of the so-called ecotopia. Crusoe's assumed right of exploiting what he possesses is only partly justified by self-preservation. Yet his sense of moral accountability functions even in total solitude. It is that sense of accountability that defines Crusoe's island as belonging to one kind of utopia rather than another – that, and the dominance of the work ethic over the pleasure principle.[36] Not for Crusoe the idle basking of the Isle of Pines.

Nevertheless, the verdant inland valley does offer him a version of ideal living which presents him with a significant choice:

> When I came Home from this Journey, I contemplated with great Pleasure the Fruitfulness of that Valley, and the Pleasantness of the Situation, the Security from Storms on that Side the Water, and the Wood, and concluded, that I had pitch'd upon a Place to fix my Abode, which was by far the worst Part of the Country. Upon the Whole I began to consider of removing my Habitation; and to look out for a Place equally safe, as where I now was situate, if possible, in that pleasant fruitful Part of the Island.
>
> This Thought run long in my Head, and I was exceeding fond of it for some Time, the Pleasantness of the Place tempting me . . . .[37]

These topographical considerations would influence any utopian founder. However, Crusoe rejects the temptation, not primarily because of a puritan conscience, but more specifically because he refuses to commit himself totally to the island experience, to be seduced by nature: in his unconsciously suggestive phrasing – 'to enclose my self among the Hills and Woods, in the Center of the Island, was to anticipate my Bondage'.[38] He needs to stay within sight of a possible sail, to remain open to his own civilisation and the chance of return, however remote the contingency. In the event, he compromises in a fashion that reflects that old civilisation very pointedly, dividing his life between routine work and recreation, between two domiciles 'so that I fancy'd now I had my Country-House, and my Sea-Coast-House' (the second home becomes a status symbol of leisure and affluence).[39]

This is a further sign that the eighteenth-century debate on luxury is by no means irrelevant to Crusoe's circumstances.[40] His property includes not just natural resources, but three kinds of material possessions that he sees as particularly defining his civilised status: his artefacts, his clothes, and, more ambivalently, his money. 'Allow not nature more than nature needs, / Man's life is cheap as beast's':[41] Crusoe's anxiety to distance himself from beasts and savages, apparent in his eating habits, expresses itself in his desire to reproduce as far as he is able the amenities of civilised life which to him are 'necessary'. So he makes the transition from Socrates' simple-life state to that of luxury. As for the subject of clothes – often used to make contentious ideological statements in utopian writing – Montaigne had asked how far the custom arises from natural factors, such as climate, and how far from cultural factors.[42] Crusoe's reasoning suggests two kinds of need, physical and psychological. He plausibly gives protection from sunburn and torrential rain as his first concern; but he also hints that his clothing is related to his sense of identity, differentiating him from the stark naked cannibals: 'I could not go quite naked; no, tho' I had been inclin'd to it, which I was not, nor could not abide the thoughts of it, tho' I was all alone.'[43]

A table and chair make writing and eating more pleasurable; clothes provide protection against the elements. Only in the case of money is it impossible to rationalise its possession, so long as Crusoe remains in a completely solitary state. Defoe's own deep fascination with the power of money is inescapable for any reader of his works, and it is basic to his quasi-utopian schemes. Yet in this particular phase of *Robinson Crusoe*, he reverts to the radical questioning of the value of money that figures in certain communal utopias. What the citizens of Lycurgus' Sparta and More's Utopia had imposed on them by the state, Crusoe had imposed on him by circumstance. Defoe was familiar with Plutarch's life of Lycurgus, which describes how, in order to promote civic virtue, Lycurgus substituted iron for gold and silver currency. Similarly, More's Utopians degrade the value of gold by the imaginative method of putting it to the basest possible use. Crusoe likewise has to relearn his scale of values, at least temporarily. Situated as he is, iron is priceless and gold coin worthless; but his utopian conceptual leap is notoriously half-hearted. His familiar apostrophe to the money he finds on the wreck – 'O Drug! Said I aloud, what art thou good for' – culminates in the 'Second Thoughts' which make him take it away (just in case . . .).[44] A Spartan or a Utopian would not have had second thoughts. However, Crusoe's conditioning is too strong; as with his decision against moving permanently to the island's interior, this signals that he still belongs to an un-utopian civilisation, that his conversion is incomplete. He doesn't, as it were, burn his boats. He does return to meditate on solitude as a cure for materialism after his religious conversion, but he never extrapolates from his individual case to argue for a utopian vision of a moneyless society. And when the episode on the original wreck is recapitulated in the narrative, he requisitions the much larger haul of money on the second wreck, with no second thoughts.

Although Crusoe learns a great deal from being deprived of all human society – including what Johnson calls 'a just sense of . . . artificial plenty'[45] – his solitary state remains deeply unnatural to him. For the Robinson Crusoe of the *Serious Reflections* 'Man is a creature so formed for society, that it may not only be said that it is not good for him to be alone, but 'tis really impossible he should be alone.'[46] If the island is to be transformed into even the semblance of a utopian state prior to the arrival of other human beings, then Crusoe has to create some form of imaginative substitute for society. And this is what he does. Social existence requires communication, and the solitary Crusoe has three options: self communing, communication with other living creatures below him in the chain of being, and communion with God. From these resources he shapes a political and religious discourse, as he had shaped the physical means of civilised living from what the island had to offer.

The utopian genre as such is not introspective, and Crusoe's communication with the self and with God belongs to a different generic history. Its logical extension is the *Serious Reflections*, in which 'Crusoe' becomes privileged reader of, and commentator upon, his former narrative. However, by combining an introspective element with a utopian fiction, on an unprecedented scale, Defoe opens up fresh possibilities for the utopian novel of the future. He examines psychological strategies for creating meaning, order and purpose from the flux of material existence. Crusoe structures his life to accommodate social roles and routines, instead of lapsing into pure solipsism. His fantasy of kingship, which develops and enriches the political dimension of the island, is rehearsed before the formation of a community, with the only subjects he has at his disposal: the animals who survive the wreck, and the native wildlife.

From a very early stage, Crusoe relates to animals in a way that goes beyond the simply utilitarian. He is not the kind of utopian idealist who reverences animal life: he hunts to kill, for self-preservation. Yet if the initial encounter is destructive, the second encapsulates the phase of human history when people learnt to domesticate animals for mutual advantage. Crusoe is disarmed by the feral cat who accepted a precious 'Bit of Bisket' and 'look'd (as pleas'd) for more'.[47] The animal episodes may partly originate with Woodes Rogers's account of Alexander Selkirk singing and dancing with his tame goats and cats.[48] If Crusoe doesn't go quite so far, he does at least enjoy their companionship as sentient beings: not even the goats are regarded as merely a larder on legs. When he is unable to acquire a mate for the first kid he tames, Crusoe records 'I could never find it [in] my Heart to kill her, till she dy'd at last of meer Age.'[49] Naturally, he makes more of the 'Dog and two Cats' rescued from the ship, 'of whose eminent History I may have occasion to say something in its place'.[50] The dog's one deficiency as a companion – 'I only wanted to have him talk to me, but that would not do' – is partly compensated for by the parrot Crusoe teaches to speak. Ironically, however, the effect is to intensify the sense of solitude, since the parrot's speech is a mockery of communication, an attempt to imprint something distinctively human on an alien environment. As a powerful delusion, it provides one of the most striking symbolic moments in the narrative, when Crusoe is startled by the sound of his own name.[51]

If one of his 'Domesticks' parodies human speech, the whole group presents a parody of human politics, centred on the classic utopian ritual of the communal meal:

> It would have made a Stoick smile to have seen, me and my little Family sit down to Dinner; there was my Majesty the Prince and Lord of the whole Island; I had the Lives of all my Subjects at my absolute Command. I could hang, draw, give Liberty, and take it away, and no Rebels among all my Subjects.
>
> Then to see how like a King I din'd too all alone, attended by my Servants, *Poll,* as if he had been my Favourite, was the only Person permitted to talk to me. My Dog who was now grown very old and crazy, and had found no Species to multiply his Kind upon, sat always at my Right Hand, and two Cats, one on one Side the Table, and one on the other, expecting now and then a Bit from my Hand, as a Mark of special Favour.

It's deliberately comic, but also proleptic: 'With this Attendance, and in this plentiful Manner I lived; neither could I be said to want any thing but Society, and of that in some time after this, I was like to have too much.'[52] There may be different kinds of subtext here. One worth noting in a utopian connection is the apparently gratuitous information about Crusoe's subjects' success or failure in propagation. The cats, we are told, are descended from one of the original ship's cats, who mated with an island cat and bred so prolifically that Crusoe was forced to kill a number of them as a means of pest control. The dog has been less lucky, in one sense, in finding 'no Species to multiply his Kind upon'. Taken together, these details suggest a problem with Crusoe's fantasy, apart from the obvious ones. His power is limited, even in the animal kingdom. Sex and reproduction, so much the concern of earlier utopian authorities, are not something that he can wholly regulate. Since, unlike George Pine, he has no female fellow-castaways, his ultimate fate may be to grow old and crazy like his dog. It doesn't happen like that; but the hint is there. If the island is ever to be more than a parody utopia, the means of populating it will need to be supplied.

Meanwhile, Crusoe's absolutism takes the form of power over the lives and liberties of his creatures. As he is to the creatures, so God is to him – except that God's absoluteness has no limits: 'I was not to dispute his Sovereignty, who, as I was his Creature, had an undoubted Right by Creation to govern and dispose of me absolutely as he thought fit'.[53] Much has been written about the importance of religion in *Robinson Crusoe*, and rightly so.[54] However, as far as the utopian imagination is concerned, it is another assertion of cultural identity, a means of giving spiritual structure, first to the individual's experience and then to the colony's way of life. Together with other aspects of his civilisation, Crusoe brings the seeds of his faith already within him, ready to germinate under the right conditions just as the seeds of corn providentially germinate. Solitude is appropriate to his highly individualised form of Christianity, based on the Bible rather than the institution of the Church. Only with the transition from solitude to society does religion become fully integral to the utopian discourse.

On the island: Crusoe and society

For all his longing for 'the Conversation of one of [his] Fellow-Christians', Crusoe is ill-prepared for the intrusion of human beings who are not fellow-Christians upon territory where he has no rivals in his sovereignty.[55] His confusion and terror at the sign of the naked footprint seem to be confirmed by his discovery of the cannibals. He has constructed his island on the paradigm of European Christianity: he now faces a culture which he scarcely recognises as such, radically different from his own, yet making ironically literal the predatory nature of his former society. Like Gulliver encountering the Yahoos, his first reaction is to differentiate himself 'from such dreadful Creatures as these'.[56] However, again like Gulliver, he finds that it is not so simple.

His discovery confronts him with one of the fundamental problems of a utopian sovereign, how to maintain the integrity of his state in a hostile world. To begin with, largely from instinct, he retreats into a concealed fastness, pursues an isolationist policy. However, then he begins to consider intervention between the cannibals and their victims, which leads to arguments for and against making war. The issue of the just war is naturally one that occupies utopian writers, and the creators of ideal commonwealths, ancient or Renaissance, tend to agree on certain permissible causes: self-defence, protecting an ally, liberating the unjustly oppressed. Even More's Utopians concur that war is sometimes necessary. Where does Crusoe stand?

Since the 'enemy' is ignorant of Crusoe's existence, self-defence is hardly tenable – indeed self-preservation would dictate that he refrain from action. More interestingly, he also rejects the ideological justification of war against 'Idolaters and Barbarians'.[57] In fact, he gropes towards a kind of cultural relativism in his self-debate:

> How do I know what God himself judges in this particular Case; it is certain these People either do not commit this as a Crime; it is not against their own Consciences reproving, or their Light reproaching them. They do not know it be an Offence, and then commit it in Defiance of Divine Justice, as we do in almost all the Sins we commit; They think it no more a Crime to kill a Captive taken in War, than we do to kill an Ox; nor to eat humane Flesh, than we do to eat Mutton.[58]

It requires an effort of imagination on Crusoe's part to get this far. Nevertheless, he stops short of Montaigne's tolerance of difference, and the French writer's willingness to fit cannibalism into his world map as part of utopia.[59] In spite of occasional satiric parallels between 'civilised' and 'barbaric' behaviour, Crusoe remains generally convinced of the superiority of his own cultural norms. He cannot remain emotionally neutral on the subject of cannibalism, even if he argues himself into a temporary armed neutrality. Logically, what impels him to take action at last is the liberation of a victim. Ironically, the first victim he rescues – and therefore the first human subject of Crusoe's utopia – is himself a cannibal.

The coming of Friday begins as a dream. Like Adam, in Keats's wonderful phrase, Crusoe dreams and awakes to find it truth.[60] But the narrative truth is delayed, and doesn't exactly replicate the dream episode. Prior to the latter, Crusoe has been obsessed with a fresh project of escape to the mainland, and he interprets his imaginary encounter as a means to this end. On waking, he consciously resolves 'to get a Savage into [his] Possession':[61] the motive is self-interested, the terminology is reminiscent of the younger Crusoe who, in the case of Xury, had already once procured his own liberty through using, and afterwards selling on, another human being. Yet when the encounter with Friday actually happens, both the event and its aftermath turn out to be much more complicated than the premonition suggests.

The nature of the relationship between Crusoe and Friday inevitably raises disturbing and sensitive questions, particularly for a modern reader. Put harshly, is Crusoe's social utopia – like those of the ancient world – founded on slavery and racism? Both race and gender are implicated in the form their relationship takes, just as much as the circumstances in which it begins. For instance, the fact that Friday is male precludes any version of the biblical and political myths that locate the origins of society in the patriarchal family.[62] Crusoe clearly subscribes to the view that male companionship is superior to female on all grounds other than biological necessity. And he has his own view of Friday's providential role: 'It came now very warmly upon my Thoughts, and indeed irresistibly, that now was my Time to get me a Servant, and perhaps a Companion, or Assistant; and that I was call'd plainly by Providence to save this poor Creature's Life . . .'[63] 'Servant' precedes 'Companion, or Assistant', yet Crusoe's utopia has been functioning reasonably well for 25 years without any labour force except Crusoe himself, who does his own dirty work and betrays no sense of being demeaned by it (in contrast to his attitude in Brazil). True, he is restricted by the lack of extra hands, notably in his escape plans as the débâcle of the immovable boat proved. However, the existence of slavery is not essential to the island economy. Nor does Crusoe seize the opportunity to transfer the burden of manual work after Friday's arrival.[64] The work itself increases because the cultivated land now has to support two people. Crusoe shows certain management skills, if of a politically incorrect kind. ('Friday not only work'd very willingly, and very hard; but did it very chearfully, and I told him what it was for.')[65] Although he trains Friday so that he can take over, it is clear that they cooperate in skilled work, and that Crusoe continues to do his share. If Friday is a slave, as many readers assume, he is not condemned to the life of a slave in the plantations.

But is Friday a slave?[66] The criteria to apply aren't modern ones, but rather the theories of slavery from Aristotle to Locke. This line of enquiry incidentally demonstrates how problematic utopian ideas become when, as in eighteenth-century fiction, they are realised through persons rather than institutions: when the relationship is that of Crusoe and Friday instead of masters and slaves as separate classes. In *The Politics*, Aristotle regards the master/slave relationship as elemental: 'the first and fewest possible parts of a family [i.e. household] are master and slave, husband and wife, father and children'. He defines a slave in terms which Crusoe would recognise: 'a living possession', 'the minister of action'.[67] Slaves are excluded from citizenship, but essential to the ideal state. However, they do not all belong to the same category, for there are slaves by nature and slaves by 'convention' such as the fortunes of war.[68] Aristotle distinguishes the relations of master and slave accordingly, and also distinguishes between the areas of knowledge proper to each: the master's sphere is theoretic – he 'need only know how to order that which the slave must know how to execute' – whereas the slave's sphere is practical, including such skills as 'cookery and similar menial arts'.[69] Although Crusoe is Friday's master by convention, and although he comes from a culture which, by eighteenth-century standards, might make him Friday's 'natural' superior, their relationship so far as work is concerned is far more flexible and brings them much closer than Aristotle's rigid differentiation. Even the natural superiority of western civilisation is called into question, when Crusoe begins to reflect that it may rather be the result of divine inscrutability in vouchsafing revelation to a section of humanity perhaps less intrinsically worthy than 'this poor Savage' and his kind.[70] Indeed he entertains the utopian 'noble savage' concept to the point of confessing that Friday, as a Christian convert, is his spiritual superior – an observation that assimilates Friday's status to the biblical context of the good and faithful servant rather than the classical context of slavery. The difficulty is to decide which, if either, is the true perception: Friday as affectionate subordinate and 'grateful Friend',[71] or Friday as exploited slave, stripped of his very identity.

If the enquiry shifts to the more recent theories of slavery which would have been familiar to Defoe, Friday's status remains controversial. This is where the origin of the relationship becomes as important as its subjective quality. The word 'slave' is first used in interpreting Friday's own action:

> I beckon'd him again to come to me, and gave him all the Signs
> of Encouragement that I could think of, and he came nearer and
> nearer, kneeling down every Ten or Twelve steps in token of

acknowledgement for my saving his Life: I smil'd at him, and look'd pleasantly, and beckon'd to him to come still nearer; at length he came close to me, and then he kneel'd down again, kiss'd the Ground, and laid his Head upon the Ground, and taking me by the Foot, set my Foot upon his Head; this it seems was in token of swearing to be my Slave for ever; I took him up, and made much of him, and encourag'd him all I could.[72]

This ritual gives Crusoe the right of dominion over Friday as a result of vanquishing their mutual enemies (an important detail missing from the dream) and saving Friday's life, which Friday now puts at his disposal. According to Hobbes, this voluntary ratification is crucial; but Hobbes defines the dominion as that of master over servant, not slave:

> . . . after such Covenant made, the Vanquished is a SERVANT, and not before: for by the word *Servant* . . . is not meant a Captive, which is kept in prison, or bonds, till the owner of him that took him, or bought him of one that did, shall consider what to do with him: (for such men, (commonly called Slaves,) have no obligation at all; but may break their bonds, or the prison; and kill, or carry away captive their Master, justly:) but one, that being taken, hath corporall liberty allowed him; and upon promise not to run away, nor to do violence to his Master, is trusted by him.
>
> It is not therefore the Victory, that giveth the right of Dominion over the Vanquished, but his own Covenant.[73]

Unless Crusoe's account is entirely discredited, Friday's 'own Covenant' stands, and is reinforced. As for the basis of trust separating servants from slaves, it is true that Crusoe takes precautions against violence and is anxious that Friday may not only escape, but return to feast on him with his compatriots. However, he admits that he is wrong, and ends by entrusting Friday with arms in addition to corporal liberty.

Locke, however, draws up different guidelines from Hobbes. His definition of servant applies primarily to a wage economy: a servant is someone who sells his labour:

> But there is another sort of Servants, which by a peculiar Name we call *Slaves*, who being Captives taken in a just War, are by the Right of Nature subjected to the Absolute Dominion and Arbitrary Power of their Masters.[74]

Where Locke contradicts Hobbes is in arguing that 'a Man, not having the Power of his own Life, *cannot*, by Compact, or his own Consent, *enslave himself* to any one . . . .' Master and slave are *ipso facto* in a state of war. If a compact is made 'the State of War and *Slavery* ceases, as long as the Compact endures'.[75] Friday's case may be a special one, but it hardly seems to fit the received definitions of slavery in contemporary terms. Where the real problems arise are less with theory than with literary representation.

Even though Crusoe's utopia resembles modern rather than ancient utopias in being based on work-sharing, not a slave economy, many readers feel that Friday is reduced to a slave mentality by Crusoe's treatment of him. Crusoe's attitude is regarded as at best paternalistic, at worst an appalling example of imperialist culture-stripping. He fails, it is said, to enter into or value Friday's experience or point of view. This criticism, however, may be partly conditioned by our expectation of *novels*. In utopian fiction before the eighteenth century, it is unusual to present anything that might be called a personal relationship between individuals of different races and cultures: the genre doesn't normally operate on this level.[76] In addition, the historical divide between the early eighteenth century and the present obstructs our assessment of such a relationship; we are unavoidably conscious of the legacy of colonialism. However, if the context adopted is utopianism rather than colonialism, then two crucial factors governing the relationship between Crusoe and Friday can be approached from a slightly different direction. These interrelated factors – often the target of justifiable criticism – are language and education.

It is customary for the traveller to a utopia to acquire a knowledge of the host language, no matter how bizarre (as Godwin's Gonsales does, for example, on the moon). Obviously this is necessary for communication. However, the exchange can be two-way, as when Raphael Hythlodaeus brings Greek studies to the Utopians.[77] When Friday comes to the island, although his people are indigenous to the region, he comes as an outsider into Crusoe's territory, where Crusoe has already established his own way of life, and in which his is the dominant culture. Moreover, as already noted, they do not meet on an equal footing since Friday owes his life to Crusoe. Gratitude on one side, responsibility on the other: in the circumstances, it is scarcely surprising that Crusoe should consider Friday entirely as a beneficiary, a surrogate son to be given a new name and taught the language of the country. What is disquieting of course is how badly he is taught. This was to offer a hostage to Defoe's critics from the outset. In Charles Gildon's contemporary satire, *The Life and Strange Surprizing Adventures of Mr D... De F... of London, Hosier*, 1719, Gildon has Friday complain against his creator – 'Have injure me, to make me such Blockhead, so much contradiction, as to be able to speak *English tolerably well* in a Month or two, and not to speak it better in twelve Years after . . . .'[78] Gildon's Friday is right in supposing that he is linguistically deprived, made to represent himself as a childlike primitive unable to develop to the level of the native English speaker. His own tongue silenced, he acquires only the rudiments of another. Although permitted arms, he is apparently denied access to a more potent weapon. He does not 'know how to curse' like Caliban; neither can he articulate his sense of the island like Caliban.[79] The most powerful image of this loss is, fittingly, the mutilated tongueless Friday created by the twentieth-century South African novelist, J.M. Coetzee, in *Foe*.

And yet: there is another side of the story in the original text, which shouldn't be suppressed. When the company of two expands to include Friday's father and the Spaniard, also rescued from the cannibals, it is Crusoe, not Friday, who has the problem of communication. Friday acts as Crusoe's interpreter, not just (obviously) to his father but, ironically, to the Spaniard, who unlike Crusoe himself has learned to speak 'the Language of the *Savages* pretty well'.[80] In other words, Friday's mediating role is central to the initial harmonising of relations among men of different races and cultures.

Nevertheless, this role is only possible because Friday has made the transition to what, in eighteenth-century eyes, is civilised living. Crusoe re-educates him in fundamental habits and attitudes, beginning the acclimatisation with clothes and diet (although Friday never really acquires a taste for salt, a symbolic item in the latter). As in all utopias, the most important purpose of education is induction into the ethos of a society, and this depends on inward as well as outward conformity. If Crusoe's island is to be a true Christian utopia, Friday's ethical and religious education is an essential part of the process. Crusoe does his best with this duty, and, despite his alleged lack of interest in Friday's inner life,[81] he does try to begin from what Friday already believes. Their discourse on theology may seem awkwardly naive, but it is not one-sided. As Locke suggests in *Some Thoughts concerning Education*, the process of question and answer is of mutual value.[82] And this brings them together in a Christian unity that Crusoe idealises in distinctly utopian terms: 'the Conversation which employ'd the Hours between *Friday* and I, was such, as made the three Years which we liv'd there together perfectly and compleatly happy, *if any such Thing as compleat Happiness can be form'd in a sublunary State.*'[83] To emphasise the point, he introduces a standard anti-utopian contrast with the world outside: 'As to all the Disputes, Wranglings, Strife and Contention, which has happen'd in the World about Religion, whether Niceties in Doctrines, or Schemes of Church Government, they were all perfectly useless to us; as for ought I can yet see, they have been to all the rest of the World.'[84] (Possibly the parallel absence of women is also felt to contribute to this placid state of affairs.)

When the all-male utopian idyll extends beyond Crusoe and Friday, it has to be on very carefully controlled terms. Friday's own nation turns out to be 'good' hospitable savages who have succoured a group of shipwrecked Europeans, one source of future colonists for the island. The pattern of rescue from 'bad' hostile savages is repeated for Friday's father and the Spaniard, and it becomes immediately apparent that Crusoe is thinking like a utopian founder and ruler:

> My Island was now peopled, and I thought my self very rich in Subjects; and it was a merry Reflection which I frequently made, How like a King I look'd. First of all, the whole Country was my own meer Property; so that I had an undoubted Right of Dominion. Secondly, My People were perfectly subjected: I was absolute Lord and Lawgiver; they all owed their Lives to me, and were ready to lay down their Lives, *if there had been Occasion of it,* for me. It was remarkable too, we had but three Subjects, and they were of three different Religions. My man *Friday* was a Protestant, his Father was a *Pagan* and a *Cannibal,* and the *Spaniard* was a Papist: However, I allow'd Liberty of Conscience throughout my Dominions: But this is by the Way.[85]

Crusoe's 'merry Reflection' has been used in evidence for some decidedly unmerry political analysis.[86] And it is certainly sobering to realise that not long before he has been neatly itemising the deaths of twenty-one of the enemy, on whose blood his little empire is founded. Yet Crusoe's is not the first utopian state to be founded upon conquest (More's Utopia is another); and he has concerned himself with sparing life as well as taking it. The entire episode is emotionally coloured by Friday's tender reunion with his father. If Crusoe seems to relish his new status rather too blatantly, the phrase 'merry Reflection'

still signals that he is consciously indulging in a utopian fantasy, closer
to Shakespeare's Gonzalo or Cervantes's Sancho Panza than to an
historical empire-builder. If Crusoe is a despot in his own mind, he is
a benevolent despot. His subjects have chosen to give him power out
of gratitude, and his exercise of it corresponds to good utopian
practice. Notably, he makes the point that religious harmony is not to
be put at risk, but that different faiths can coexist – like More's
Utopus, he tolerates 'Liberty of Conscience throughout [his]
Dominions'.[87]

However, Crusoe puts little faith in gratitude as a binding political
motive. He believes 'that Gratitude [is] no inherent Virtue in the
Nature of Man' and that people are more likely to consider self-
interest, 'the Advantages they expected'.[88] This makes good sense of
his insistence, now and later, on formal contracts even with those
whose interests might be supposed to coincide with his. Nationality
doesn't enter into it. The English captain and his companions whom
Crusoe rescues from the mutineers – so opening the way at last to his
own deliverance – are required to accept Crusoe's terms just as the
Spaniards are, and to defer totally to his authority on the island. By
adding to his collection of those who owe their lives to him, Crusoe
is, so to speak, practising an alternative form of patriarchy which
contrasts ironically with George Pine's on *his* island (and is much less
fun).[89]

However, the growth in numbers does make a new range of
imaginative roles available to him. As he becomes a still more
virtuoso writer of utopian fiction, Crusoe reinvents himself as
'*Generalissimo*' of a 'whole Army' – a further requisite of most utopian
states – and as the final arbiter of justice, a fiction created for him by
the captain to impress the mutineers.[90] So powerful does this fiction of
'the Governour' become, that it reaches the point where it is
autonomous, separable from Crusoe's own physical identity. He adopts
the mystique of the absent ruler 'for Reasons of State', like
Shakespeare's Duke in *Measure for Measure*.[91] The clothes he receives
from the captain are the signifier of his new dignity as well as his
return to his old civilisation (although, to begin with, he finds the
change as uncomfortable as Friday had). On the point of leaving his
island utopia, he receives 'official' recognition as its governor.

The final ceremony is the handing over of the island economy to
the men who are to remain there as a punishment. In effect, utopia is
metamorphosed into a penal colony: but then, in a sense, Crusoe had

seen it as that from the beginning in his darkest moods, as the place of divine punishment for his original sin. From this point, there is the opportunity of separate development for the colony, a new utopian narrative, with the additional prospect that the group of mutineers will be augmented by 'the sixteen *Spaniards* that were to be expected'.[92] So one utopian fiction generates another, of a more conventional kind, in which Crusoe himself still has a part to play.

After the island

In the final stage of *The Life & Strange Surprizing Adventures of Robinson Crusoe*, Crusoe's return to his former existence turns out to be less traumatic than it is for most travellers returning from such literary voyages. This may seem anti-climactic. Coetzee rewrites that voyage home as Crusoe's own voyage into death: what survives of him is story.[93] But for Defoe's Crusoe, it feels almost as if he is returning *from* the dead: 'When I came to *England*, I was as perfect a Stranger to all the World, as if I had never been known there.'[94] Yet he isn't as isolated as that suggests, for he is able slowly to pick up the threads of social and economic continuity. If his own family have presumed his death, others have kept faith with him: indeed, on the evidence of their honest and generous behaviour, this is not the anti-utopian 'real' world we might have been led to expect.[95] And the only major narrative sequence in this part of the novel, the attack by wolves in the Pyrenees, hints that predatory violence is back where it belongs, in the animal not human species. It is the nature of wolves to devour human flesh, and the horror it excites is different in kind from the horror Crusoe experienced at the evidence of cannibalism.

From the viewpoint of utopian fiction, it would be far more interesting to have an account of Friday's reactions to the impact of European civilisation instead of Crusoe's comparatively staid ending. However, of course, for Crusoe it isn't an ending. His famously perfunctory marriage 'not either to my Disadvantage or Dissatisfaction'[96] is only an interlude, and the real 'to be continued' is the summary of the island's subsequent history. Yet the interlude also slots into a larger pattern, and it allows Defoe to begin his sequel – *The Farther Adventures of Robinson Crusoe* – with a formal parallel to his original. For Crusoe, the family man, tries to construct the Augustan ideal of moderation and independence. His small country estate reproduces a naturalised version of the island economy in the familiar English

Midlands. He has fled from the two extremes of indulgent excess and 'living but to work, and working but to live'[97] against which his father warned him: fled also from the siren voices of his island haunting him in dreams. However, his attempt to recreate the balanced simplicity of his former kingdom founders with his wife's death. Once more Crusoe is a stranger in the world, 'desolate and dislocated'.[98] Inevitably he is drawn back to the island utopia described by his nephew as 'your new Colony . . . where you once reigned with more Felicity, than most of your Brother Monarchs in the World'.[99]

Return to the island

The problems that the island community have encountered in Crusoe's absence are endemic in human society, the kind that utopian fictions are designed to resolve. In this case, the three malcontents that cause the trouble represent the anti-social face of the English abroad. From their angle, they have the misfortune to be stranded in the wrong kind of utopia – not a tropical paradise, a version of the land of Tenter–belly,[100] but a full-employment model founded on the work ethic. It is the Spaniards, in particular the Spaniard first rescued by Crusoe, who take on the burden of leadership and initially tackle the problem by accepting an unfair division of labour, running the two kinds of utopian life side by side, as it were: 'as for the *English* Men, they did nothing but ramble about the Island, shoot Parrots, and catch Tortoises, and when they came Home at Night, the *Spaniards* provided their Suppers for them.'[101]

This laissez-faire policy doesn't work. The island community breaks up into factions resulting in territorial disputes and vandalism, and although the Spaniards manage to contain the situation, there is little sense that a utopian society emerges. What unifies the community at last isn't its own institutions, but the threat from an external enemy. However, Defoe provides a shrewd fictional analysis of social evolution, which shows the problems of creating an ideal state.[102] Despite fleeting indications that the Spaniards might come to represent an idealised ruling élite on the lines of Plato's Guardians, with their classic virtues – 'Moderate, Temperate, Virtuous . . . no Inhumanity, no Barbarity, no outragious Passions, and yet all of them Men of great Courage and Spirit' – their moral superiority is not matched by 'Application or Ingenuity' or the mental toughness associated with the English character. Even before coming to the island, they had failed 'to civilize the Savages they were with' as Crusoe felt he had done with Friday.[103] But they do have a further claim to the self-discipline required of authority: their sexual restraint.

This is put to the test by the major new factor in this phase of the island's history, namely the introduction of women. It is a development that changes Crusoe's original unique utopia into a more orthodox kind of commonwealth, capable of perpetuating its own existence. Again, the change originates with rescued prisoners. However, when the captive women are shared out, the Spaniards hold aloof: 'Some of them said, they had Wives in *Spain*, and the others did not like Women that were not Christians; and all together declar'd, that they would not touch one of them; which was an Instance of such Virtue, as I have not met with in all my Travels.' The English, lacking such scruples, 'took them every one a Wife, that is to say, a temporary Wife'.[104] Given that the authorities regulate sex and reproduction in virtually all utopian states, it is interesting to watch the Spanish governor, Crusoe's surrogate, handle this sensitive issue. Diplomatically, he will not interfere with the men's intention of using the women for sexual as well as other services (needless to say, the women aren't consulted), but he proposes that, for politic reasons, they adopt a model of strict monogamy:

> But this I think is but just, for avoiding Disorders and Quarrels among you; and I desire it of you, for that Reason only, *viz.* That you will all engage, that if any of you take any of these Women, as a Woman or Wife, that he shall take but one; and that having taken one, none else should touch her; for tho' we cannot marry any of you, yet 'tis but reasonable, that while you stay here, the Woman any of you takes, should be maintain'd by the Man that takes her, and should be his Wife . . . All this appear'd so just, that every one agreed to it without any Difficulty.[105]

Therefore, neither women nor property are held in common, and the former are treated pragmatically as part of the latter. No romantic consideration enters into choosing a wife: the first man successful in the drawing of lots picks the plainest and oldest woman, as most fitted for hard work 'and she prov'd the best Wife of all the Parcel'. Women are graded on their capacity for domestic management, their female submissiveness ('rather like Slaves than Wives') and, ultimately, their fertility – 'these five Savage Ladies . . . had all been pretty fruitful.'[106] After the practicalities are catered for, all that is lacking is religious instruction coupled with legal marriage, 'both which', says Crusoe, 'were happily brought about afterwards by my Means, or, at least, in Consequence of my coming among them.'[107]

When Crusoe revisits his utopia, he resumes responsibility for its well-being. He finds it flourishing and peaceable after its recent vicissitudes. For example, Will Atkins, the former mutineer, has turned into a more or less model citizen, expending his energies on basketry not mayhem, and creating a beehive dwelling for a family commune. It has even acquired a 'capital City' of sorts, the ultimate badge of utopian status: Crusoe's 'old Habitation under the Hill' transformed into a hidden 'little City in a Wood'.[108] To this community, Crusoe brings a material and human cargo to boost its economy. And among the various survivors acquired during the adventures at sea en route for the island is someone whose professional services fill a gap Crusoe has overlooked. His original utopia was anti-clerical and tolerant. With the advent of the French priest, institutional religion comes for the first time to the island. The *de facto* marriages are regularised, removing Crusoe's island still further from the polygamous Isle of Pines, or any other utopia where sexual liberty is the norm. And the priest also sets in motion a campaign for the mass conversion of the captured savages.

Significantly, this idea had not struck Crusoe himself, not had he conceived it as part of his responsibility as a utopian ruler. For all its cultural representativeness, his conversion of Friday is rooted in an individual relationship. He cannot relate to the group on the island in the same way, or see them as a spiritual mission, because he does not in fact see them as human beings with any rights – as he himself acknowledges: 'I had not so much as entertain'd a Thought of this in my Heart before, and I believe should not have thought of it; for I look'd upon these Savages as Slaves, and People, who, had we had any Work for them to do, we would ha' used as such, or would ha' been glad to have transported them to any other Part of the World.'[109] Moreover, he would not be Crusoe if he didn't also think of the personal inconvenience and economic cost of staying on the island for longer than the stop-off he had planned. The priest asks him 'whether the Blessing of saving seven and thirty Souls, was not worth my venturing all I had in the World for? I was not so sensible of that *as he was*' Crusoe remarks dryly.[110]

The religious issue is intertwined with the racial one. In the event, by the time Crusoe leaves the island, a political solution has been found to the ethnic problem. Although it perpetuates inequality, it at least reinstates the distinction between servants and slaves which Crusoe's earlier attitude had starkly disregarded. He proposes that the governor should offer the Indians an alternative 'to remove, and either plant for themselves, or take them into their several Families as Servants to be maintain'd for their Labour, but without being absolute Slaves, for I would not admit them to make them Slaves by Force by any Means, because they had their Liberty given them by Capitulation, and as it were Articles of Surrender, which they ought not to break.'[111] He has returned to first principles. With the absorption of this group into the island economy, by their own consent, the community is on the way to becoming, not an egalitarian common-wealth,[112] but one which has stabilised and learnt to live with its divisions. Even the cannibals are left with an uninhabited zone, where there is space 'for their usual customary Barbarities . . . if they disturb'd no Body, no Body would disturb them'.[113]

Legally, the island remains Crusoe's: the inhabitants are his tenants in perpetuity. How does his departure fit in with his responsibility to the state he has founded? More than one critic has accused him of abandoning the colony he calls his, of failing to follow through his paternalistic policies.[114] Yet if the paternal analogy is adopted, it might be argued that the crucial test of a father figure is whether or not he is capable of letting go, of granting independence when maturity is reached. Although Crusoe hangs on to his property rights, he hands over political rights. Granted that he is partly driven, as of old, by his own restless temperament, this still isn't the action of a diehard imperialist. Is it the action of a good utopian ruler? He articulates an important political ideal when he records: 'As to the Government and Laws among them, I told them I was not capable of giving them better Rules, than they were able to give themselves' – the principle of self-determination – '*only made them promise me to live in Love and good Neighbourhood with one another*; and so I prepared to leave them'.[115] Crusoe's farewell to his people is, *mutatis mutandis*, like that of Lycurgus, who bound the Spartans by their own oath to keep faith until he returned from Delphi, and then, having ascertained that his laws were good, submitted himself to a voluntary death in exile so that they would have to abide by their promise.[116] Of course, Crusoe does not contemplate going to such lengths: but he does exact not only the promise quoted above, but also the further promise – in a spirit of true utopian optimism – 'that they would never have any

Differences or Disputes one with another about Religion'.[117] Incidentally, like Lycurgus, he has tried to ensure that his islanders shouldn't be tempted to leave their state: he decides not to let them have the DIY sloop he has brought with him, in case they opt for a life of piracy and make 'the Island a Den of Thieves, instead of a Plantation of sober and religious People as I intended it'.[118] He does, however, send the sloop back to the island from Brazil, with supplies, stock, and Portuguese wives for the unmarried Spaniards.

Twice Crusoe tells the reader that he has finished with his island. On the first occasion, he is on the point of departure: 'I left them all in good Circumstances, and in a flourishing Condition.' On the second occasion, he has heard of the sloop's safe arrival, which marks the discharge of his final responsibility to the colonists: 'I have now done with my Island, and all Manner of Discourse about it . . . '[119] It may be worth noting that between these two narrative moments, very different from each other in tone, Crusoe has lost his last human link with his island experience, through Friday's death. Yet the second relinquishment shouldn't be taken literally. It's followed almost immediately by a reflective passage, in which Crusoe seems half to blame himself for being a utopian dreamer instead of a sensible English coloniser. Again he is seduced by 'if only': 'but I was possest with a wandring Spirit, scorn'd all Advantages, I pleased my self with being the Patron of those People I placed there, and doing for them in a kind of haughty majestick Way, like an old Patriarchal Monarch . . .' Much later, in a long Russian winter, he will indulge in nostalgia for his lost domain, like an ancient king in exile. However, he did not follow the path of history, taking instead the path of myth:

> I never so much as pretended to plant in the Name of any
> Government or Nation, or to acknowledge any Prince, or to call
> my People Subjects to any one Nation more than another; nay, I
> never so much as gave the Place a Name; but left it as I found it,
> belonging to no Man; and the People under no Discipline or
> Government but my own; who, tho' I had Influence over them
> as Father and Benefactor, had no Authority or Power, to Act or
> Command one way or other, farther than voluntary Consent
> mov'd them to comply.[120]

In another age, that would be seen as a political strength, not a weakness. But this is Crusoe's renunciation of the utopian imagination in favour of the 'real' world.

Crusoe's self-accusation leads up to the last word we have of the island: that the community is crumbling, and that the colonists have succumbed to an older, deeper loyalty, the yearning to 'see their own Country again before they dy'd'.[121] Still, there is no reason to believe that Crusoe's continued presence would have made any difference to the outcome. Even Lycurgus' Sparta came to dust. Crusoe's island survives as a nameless fiction, a no-place, a utopia on the world map at which humanity is always landing.

Libertalia

If the attribution to Defoe of A General History of the Pyrates is correct,[122] then Defoe himself landed at least once more on the shores of an island utopia, this time with a generic name: Libertalia. Here Crusoe's fear that his island colony could easily end up as 'a Den of Thieves' is vividly realised. Libertalia is founded by Captain Misson, an aristocratic and well-educated Frenchman who has taken to piracy. His evil or good genius, depending on viewpoint, is a renegade priest, Caraccioli, who demythologises religion in the name of reason and has persuaded Misson 'that all Religion was no other than human Policy'.[123] Caraccioli's political philosophy is equally anti-authoritarian, at least so far as traditional authority is concerned. Adopting the principle 'that every Man was born free, and had as much Right to what would support him, as to the Air he respired',[124] he runs through a gamut of radical commonplaces relating to the origins of government and the law of nature. He preaches egalitarianism of the variety found amongst the felons in Gay's The Beggar's Opera – 'We are for a just partition of the world, for every man hath a right to enjoy life.'[125] Similarly, Caraccioli twists the law of self-preservation to justify piracy. But his basic creed is that might is right, and he urges Misson to 'reign Sovereign of the Southern Seas, and lawfully make War on all the World'.[126]

For his part, Misson is a genuine idealist. He emerges as a natural leader, while enjoining the practice of democracy and communism: he preaches brotherly love, and is extraordinarily humane for a pirate, preferring moral suasion to force. Unlike Crusoe, he opposes slavery and the slave trade on principle:

> the Captain . . . told his Men, that the Trading for those of
> our own Species, cou'd never be agreeable to the Eyes of divine

Justice: That no Man had Power of the Liberty of another; and while those who profess'd a more enlightened Knowledge of the Deity, sold Men like Beasts; they prov'd that their Religion was no more than Grimace, and that they differ'd from the *Barbarians* in Name only, since their Practice was in nothing more humane: For his Part . . . he had not . . . asserted his own Liberty, to enslave others [contrast Crusoe's treatment of Xury].[127]

Misson refuses to accept racial difference as fundamental to the question: 'That however, these Men were distinguish'd from the *Europeans* by their Colour, Customs, or religious Rites, they were the Work of the same omnipotent Being, and endued with equal Reason: Wherefore he desired they might be treated like Freemen (for he wou'd banish even the Name of Slavery from among them)'.[128]

Not surprisingly, when Misson establishes his utopian settlement in a conventionally fertile and healthy location, he calls it Libertalia and its people Liberi, 'desiring in that might be drown'd the distinguish'd Names of *French, English, Dutch, Africans*, &c.'[129] This in itself points a contrast with Crusoe's island and its differentiated ethnic groups.

Moreover, to begin with, the colony practises the common sharing of wealth and land: prize money is put 'into the common Treasury, Money being of no Use where every Thing was in common, and no Hedge bounded any particular Man's Property'.[130] Yet, as Libertalia develops and becomes politically more sophisticated, it evidently reverts to a degree of privatisation side by side with equal distribution, making laws 'That the Treasure and Cattle they were Masters of should be equally divided, and such Lands as any particular Man would enclose, should, for the future, be deem'd his Property, which no other should lay any Claim to, if not alienated by a Sale.'[131] The irony that clearly differentiates Libertalia from a humanist utopia like More's arises of course from the fact that its economy prospers as a result of alienating the property of outsiders, through piracy on the high seas.

From a modern point of view, this society's most enlightened attitude to human relations is demonstrated by the emancipation of slaves. Conversely, its least enlightened attitude is demonstrated in the treatment of women, who are acquired – like other wealth – from the capture of a ship carrying pilgrims to Mecca. Misson's crew abduct '100 Girls, from twelve to eighteen Years old' who had been travelling with their parents: 'The Lamentations this Separation caused among the Prisoners, had such effect on *Misson*, that he was for letting them go, but every one of his Men were against him.'[132] And, according to democratic principle, the majority prevail.

After another captain and crew, Captain Tew and his men, arrive in Libertalia, a constitutional structure becomes necessary to defuse potential conflict. They formalise the kind of organisation most in keeping with the original ethos of the colony, 'a Democratical Form, where the People were themselves the Makers and Judges of their own Laws'.[133] The constitutional machinery, with its arrangements for various offices, a system of rotation, and so on, is procedurally much more elaborate than anything in Crusoe's utopia: if the original sharing philosophy of the colony recalls Winstanley, its political arrangements recall Harrington.[134]

Even so, its appeal is not universal. The inhabitants of a parallel separate colony, founded by Tew's quarter-master, decline an invitation to join Libertalia: they already have their own democratic system up and running, and they prefer to wait for an amnesty from England, and recognised colonial status. Had Crusoe chosen to develop his island into a regular colony under English authority and protection, this might have been its destiny also. Crusoe, like Misson, opts for his independent utopian dream instead of colonial reality. Yet it is too simple to contrast Misson's idealism with *realpolitik*, and to attribute the failure of Libertalia to the former.[135] In practice, there is surprisingly little difference between Libertalia and the quarter-master's colony: its government is also by consent and the ballot-box, and the governor's powers and term of office are limited. Both colonies practise the policy of good relations with the indigenous population, although the quarter-master uses language suggesting a greater wariness – 'The Natives are, or seem to be, very humane.'[136]

What destroys Libertalia is an unanticipated and inexplicable attack: 'without the least Provocation given, in the Dead of the Night, the Natives came down upon them in two great Bodies, and made a great Slaughter, without Distinction of Age or Sex, before they could put themselves in a Posture of Defence'.[137] However, this massacre by an external enemy isn't directly linked to the political, economic and social experiment that Libertalia represents. Misson's utopia doesn't collapse under internal strain: after all, it has already survived treachery from two former prisoners who had broken their oath of never serving against Misson. If anything dooms it from the outset, it is the illegitimacy of its origins. One reason for the colony's failure to defend itself is the absence of men at sea. An orderly

Harringtonian republic cannot be built by Hobbesian predators, and those who start out by making 'War on all the World' will sooner or later encounter greater savagery and force than their own. But it remains an interesting and bizarre attempt to put a radical political philosophy into practice, far from the ideological constraints of the mother country. Regarded in the light of utopian fiction, this narrative from A General History of the Pyrates both contrasts with and complements The Farther Adventures of Robinson Crusoe. It belongs as of right to the category of eighteenth-century writing that imaginatively recreates utopia in the unclaimed territory beyond seas.

Interestingly, the same literary territory is still being colonised by twentieth-century writers, such as Barry Unsworth in Sacred Hunger (1992).[138] Unsworth's novel projects a similar ideologically-driven venture, created from necessity in the Florida swamps by the remnant of the crew and human cargo of a slave-ship. This colony evolves in ways comparable to earlier fictional utopias, and is finally destroyed, like Captain Misson's, by an enemy from without – but, ironically, an enemy from the 'civilised' world. To make a utopia from the scarred survivors and outcasts of that world is a difficult and doomed, but also beautiful, enterprise. To discover a utopia, as opposed to making one, is the easier option.

Gaudentio di Lucca and Peter Wilkins

If Defoe's characters achieve utopia by their own creative agency, other fictional travellers, like Simon Berington's eponymous hero in The Memoirs of Signior Gaudentio di Lucca, 1737,[139] have utopia thrust upon them in the classic voyage imaginaire tradition. (Another example of this pattern is Prevost's The Life And entertaining Adventures of Mr Cleveland, Natural Son of Oliver Cromwell, Written by Himself, the title given to the English translation of 1734.) As writers find ways of grafting the old utopian stock upon the novel, attractive new hybrids begin to appear. Robert Paltock's The Life and Adventures of Peter Wilkins (1750) manages to combine both options, creation and discovery. And, as often in utopian fiction, both Berington and Paltock sustain the illusion of historicity by devising elaborate framing devices to explain the transmission of their texts.

In the case of Gaudentio di Lucca, the provenance is alleged to be a document 'Taken from his Confession and Examination before the

Fathers of the *Inquisition* at *Bologna* in *Italy*' and preserved in the Venetian library at St Mark's.[140] These circumstances not only intrigue the reader, but are a pointer to the writer's agenda. Simon Berington was an English Catholic priest: his protagonist, Gaudentio, a physician and polymath, is defending himself against suspicions of heterodoxy roused by his claim to have 'met with a Nation in one of the remotest Parts of the World, who, tho' they were *Heathens*, had more Knowledge of the Law of Nature and common Morality, than the most civiliz'd *Christians*.'[141] Although there is a strong continental lineage for such a utopia, for English readers the most distinguished precedent for this paradox is the original Utopia of Thomas More. However, whatever our specific expectations, anyone familiar with the genre will recognise the basic components in Berington's fiction. The title-page fashionably alludes to China as a cultural equivalent – 'an unknown Country in the midst of the vast Deserts of *Africa*, as Ancient, Populous, and Civilized, as the *Chinese*' – but there are parallels everywhere in utopian writing.

Yet Berington handles his derivative material well, and with some sense of its novelistic possibilities. He achieves a mythic glamour in the account of the origin and migration of the Mezzoranians, their quest for the waters of the south, the legendary location of the rains feeding the Nile, which leads them to the unknown and paradisal heart of Africa. Gaudentio's first impression is of 'an immense Garden [rather] than a Country',[142] an impression that springs partly from illusion since, like most utopias, it is essentially a city state. What creates the illusion is an abundance of trees and roof gardens. The principal city, Phor, is a city of waterways like Amsterdam or Venice, and is designed on a solar plan, like a number of ancient utopias, reflecting the religion of the people. Men worship the sun, women the moon, recognising a single divine principle behind these entities. Although Gaudentio confesses that this religion 'is really Idolatry in the main',[143] the effect of his eloquent exposition is to reinforce the idea of a people with a highly developed sense of reverence, like More's Utopians. Also like More's Utopians, the Mezzoranians have a cult of the family. However, in their case, respect for parents and ancestors is used to explain both their political system, which is patriarchal, and the absence of war: 'there has been no War for near Three Thousand Years; there being indeed no Enemies but the inhospitable Sands around them, and they all consider themselves as Brothers of the same Stock, and living under one common Father'.[144]

In accordance with utopian theory, laws are very few but rigorously obeyed. Such is their innocence and well-being that the consequences of the Fall of Adam seem scarcely to impinge on this happy people.

The Fall of Eve is perhaps a different matter. If there is a serpent in this Eden, it takes the old form of sexual temptation, which has in the past threatened to destabilise their society. The way that the Mezzoranians express any kind of moral vulnerability is through a quasi-Platonic theory that 'the Souls of Brutes' are continually attempting to take over human bodies,[145] particularly female bodies. This requires constant vigilance in relation to the young and to women, since if that vigilance lapses the result is decadence, gender confusion, and marriage breakdown. In order to maintain their utopia, therefore, the Mezzoranian construction of sexuality is as central to their culture as their religion and politics. It is also central to the fiction. If Berington is to enliven the catalogue of perfections, and transform utopian description into novel, this is the area he has to work on in relation to his narrator's consciousness.

At the crucial point where utopia and *roman* intersect is Gaudentio's own emotional involvement with the Mezzoranians. In pre-eighteenth-century utopian fiction it is unusual to establish sexual contact, let alone a committed sexual relationship, between the traveller-observer and a member of the observed civilisation. In part this may be because the otherness of that civilisation itself precludes the imagining of such a thing: in part it may be because of the formal requirement to exclude romantic distractions from analytical discourse. (Suggestively, an exception is the female traveller to Margaret Cavendish's New Blazing World, who becomes its all-powerful Empress through marriage to the Emperor.[146]) Even Gabriel de Foigny's Jacques Sadeur, who is spared by the hermaphroditic Australians because luckily he himself was born a hermaphrodite, turns out to differ sharply from them in his sexual proclivities.[147] Gaudentio, in contrast, discovers a family romance which gives him a bloodlink with the Mezzoranians through his mother. Instead of being a complete alien among his utopians, he contains their otherness within himself, and narrative contingency predisposes him to form an emotional attachment to a Mezzoranian woman. Even so, the utopian ideal doesn't readily accommodate the individuality associated with sexual attraction in novels. Confronted with uniformly beautiful people in a ready-made paradise, Gaudentio hints more than once that it is possible to tire of physical perfection: lacking any racial mixture, the Mezzoranian features also lack variety. However, in a world of Platonic beauty and chastity, this is a minor quibble.

What he does admire is the Mezzoranian sexual ethos, which reflects the standards professed by his own Christian culture. As already observed, they guard against any form of promiscuity or deviance. More explicitly, like many utopians, the Mezzoranians perceive the issue as primarily related to the role of women: in the section *The Education of their Women, and Marriages*, the psychology of females is defined as irrational, 'yet they are so far from being an indifferent Thing in the Common-wealth, that much more depends on the right Management of them than People imagine'.[148] Their ancestors debated how to control women's sexuality, some favouring the 'despotick' rule of husbands (as 'in other Nations'), others objecting that this would turn women into 'mere Slaves, or at least mere Properties' and (a suggestion of male self-interest here) 'deprive the Husband of the voluntary Love of his moiety, and take away the most endearing part of conjugal Happiness'.[149] The upshot is a utopian compromise. The Mezzoranians implement harsh and ignominious penalties for adultery, and rigorously supervise the young; but they encourage women's participation in education and public recreation, and promote companionate marriage as 'the Happiest State that can be wish'd for in this Life.'[150] Interestingly, this means giving the woman's choice and happiness priority, though both partners are encouraged to marry for love alone. They are sufficiently sophisticated psychologists not to make romance too easy: difficulties are deliberately put in the way of lovers to test their commitment. Consequently, according to Gaudentio's own experience, 'one may say they are a Nation of faithful Lovers, the longer they live together the more their Friendship encreases . . .'[151] And Berington, who was after all a priest, devises a beautiful wedding rite to signify precisely the movement from passion to friendship which is the mark of companionate marriage.

There is nothing new, of course, in a utopian fiction that posits faithful monogamy as the best foundation for the commonwealth. But if Berington's imaginary state is set beside More's, the distance between early-sixteenth-century assumptions and those of the eighteenth century immediately becomes apparent. Although successful personal relationships serve the interests of the state, in *Gaudentio di Lucca* they also represent emotional fulfilment for individuals and the question of how to maximise that fulfilment is taken seriously as an end in itself. Mezzoranian theory and practice bear directly on major concerns of the eighteenth-century novel. It is not that Berington is particularly enlightened when dealing with gender, as some of the attitudes to gender difference demonstrate, but at least he uses his utopian fiction to question current ideology. What is more, he attempts to integrate his protagonist's experience into a utopian structure as a novelist would. If the dominant strain in this hybrid is still the utopian one, the narrative requirements of the novel modify it in imaginative directions.

The process is further refined in Robert Paltock's mid-century novel, *The Life and Adventures of Peter Wilkins, A Cornish Man*, and again the catalyst is a central relationship. Peter Wilkins's history begins in the naturalistic mode of eighteenth-century fiction, concentrating in detail on his family circumstances and misfortunes. He is a posthumous only child, a stepson deprived of his inheritance, and a husband and father when still in his teens. As a result, he is estranged from his own background and emotionally predisposed to search for an alternative, an ideal family as the paradigm of happiness. Without knowing it, he is in quest of a personal utopia. His African adventures further prepare him for his destiny, by expanding his religious capacity and his human sympathies through his friendship with his companion in slavery and escape, the African Glanlepze. Unlike Crusoe or Gulliver, Peter (it seems natural to use the Christian name in this case) is continually attracted to the idea of married life: the 'moving Scene' of Glanlepze reunited with his loving wife and children imprints his own loss 'deeply on [his] Imagination'.[152]

In other respects, however, comparisons with Crusoe and Gulliver are hard to resist. The association is a contemporary one, slightingly summed up in a reviewer's genealogical reference to 'the illegitimate offspring of no very natural conjunction betwixt *Gulliver's* travels and *Robinson Crusoe*'.[153] To change the metaphor, in the world map of utopias Peter's 'arkoe' – lake surrounded by woods – and his second wife's country lie somewhere between Crusoe's desert island and Gulliver's fantastic countries. In effect, Paltock amalgamates different varieties of utopian fiction. This would be less remarkable if he had simply juxtaposed the two main forms, the individual creation and the discovery of a pre-existing society. Instead he dovetails them through an imaginative act of miscegenation which is both literary – in the hostile reviewer's sense – and literal, the marriage of Peter and Youwarkee. The resulting offspring may be illegitimate, but it is one of the few eighteenth-century English texts that can accurately be described as a utopian novel.

For a time during his solitude, after he has been cast away on his magnetic rock, Peter does behave very much like a clone of Crusoe: curious, resourceful, fearful, intermittently reflecting on the state of his soul and perpetually preoccupied with the state of his stomach. He shares Crusoe's sense of unique status – 'I now began to enjoy myself in my new Habitation, like the absolute and sole Lord of the Country'[154] – as well as his creative triumphs and disappointments, and his dread of the unknown. However, Peter's unknown reaches out to touch him in a different way from Crusoe's. In place of the famous footprint in the sand, he hears the sound of aerial voices in the dark time of the year, which he interprets first as imagination and later as the presence of spirits. Again like Crusoe, he has a premonitory dream: but Peter's dream has deep psychological and mystical roots, since he receives an intimation of his wife's death, and of his reunion with her: 'Methought I did not know her, she was so altered; but observing her Voice, and looking more wistfully at her, she appeared to me, as the most beautiful Creature I ever beheld.'[155]

With the coming of Youwarkee, Peter's life is completed and transformed far more radically and inwardly than Crusoe's could be by the coming of Friday. It would be too crude to say that *Peter Wilkins* is *Robinson Crusoe* with sex, for sex is only part, although a vital part, of Peter's encounter with another race. It is another race, not a different species: the children born to Peter and Youwarkee share characteristics of both parents in varying degrees. Youwarkee's race is distinguished from the rest of humanity solely because they have wings, integral wings of bone and membrane that fulfil the ancient human dream of unaided flight. In imagining their physiology, Paltock inventively threads together two strands of utopian fantasy, anatomical variations (which tend to occur more in satiric writers like Lucian) and the recurrent technical images of flying. However, because this is also a love story, wings and the absence of wings are a metaphor for difference.[156] Throughout the scene following Peter's rescue of the beautiful woman who falls like a wounded bird outside his door, that difference is gradually bridged by a mutual desire to communicate, a genuine effort of interpretation, and gestures of respect and tenderness. If, as Peter says, 'she endeavoured all in her Power to learn to talk like me', unlike Crusoe with Friday 'I was not behind Hand with her in that Respect, striving all I could to imitate her.'[157] Admittedly, he takes precautions for fear of losing her. However, their sexual union grows out of a relationship marked by deliberate restraint, and is accompanied by 'mutual solemn Engagements to each other: which are, in truth, the Essence of Marriage, and all that was there and then in our Power'.[158]

It is in the intimate treatment of 'the Essence of Marriage', in all its senses, that the novelist improves upon the skills of the utopist. Beside Paltock's account of the wedding night – which is beautifully handled, erotic, but not prurient, and enhanced by a hint of comedy – the approach to sex by most early utopian writers appears clinical or crass. In antiquity, the favoured analogy is with the breeding of animals; in the Christian era, the insistence on morality and mono-gamy can turn wife and children into what Bacon calls 'a kind of discipline of humanity';[159] but once utopian fiction opens up to the personalising influence of the novel, and the cultural influence of the ideal of companionate marriage,[160] then *Gaudentio di Lucca* and *Peter Wilkins* become possible. Peter and Youwarkee ceremoniously exchange personal names as the seal of intimacy. Although their relationship is traditional in certain respects – Peter takes his place as the patriarch of a growing family – it is far removed from the opportunistic polygamy of *The Isle of Pines*.[161] It is represented as a true partnership, sharing work and child-rearing. Even more important, Peter and Youwarkee compensate for each other's deficiencies. Peter invents spectacles to aid the weak sight which is Youwarkee's racial inheritance; whereas she accomplishes successive flights to the ship, and contrives a method of packing and securing the various cargoes. In terms of gender, there can be no simple demarcation between superior and inferior, as Peter himself realises:

> . . . what could I, or almost any of us Master-pieces of the Creation (as we think ourselves) and Heavens peculiar Favourites have done, in this present Case, that has been omitted by this Woman, (for I may justly stile her so in an eminent Degree) and that in a way to which she was bred an utter Stranger.[162]

The same question of whether to see difference in terms of superiority and inferiority arises in relation to the two civilisations that Peter and Youwarkee represent. As in the more subtle utopian fictions, it is interestingly poised. In their ability to fly, the Swangeantines are biologically better equipped than Peter, but they are not technologically more advanced. It would have been possible for Paltock to follow seventeenth-century speculative writers like Bacon, Wilkins, and Godwin, in hypothesizing scientific developments that would make mechanical flight feasible, and so create a utopian civilisation that had already invented flying machines. Conversely, he could have reverted to the totally fantastic, like Lucian's Volplaneurs (Lucian, incidentally, has a race of men who convert themselves into ships by hoisting their genitals as masts – a less polite equivalent of the alternative function of Swangeantine wings).[163] Instead, Paltock balances the 'scientific' – signified by the anatomical plates – and the imaginative wonder of a different mode of being, like birds or angels. The elegant structure and soft silky texture of the *graundee* make a powerful aesthetic appeal. However, it is left to Peter to solve the engineering problem of how to harness this natural flying power for the use of flightless humans like himself.

The description of the *graundee* allows Paltock to make another utopian point. Like Swift's Houyhnhnms, Youwarkee's people have no need or comprehension of other clothing. A Swiftian conversation, softened by its context, takes place between Youwarkee and Peter before their marriage, when Youwarkee is puzzled and a little anxious about what might be concealed under Peter's clothes: she says 'indeed I was afraid something was the Matter, by that nasty Covering you wear, that you might not be seen', and concludes 'you would not wear this nasty cumbersome Coat . . . if you were not afraid of shewing the Signs of a bad Life upon your natural Cloathing.'[164] However, it is ultimately Youwarkee who is changed by the impact of Western artifice, to the point where she can completely transform herself into a fashionable English lady and be unrecognisable to her own kin. Peter's attempts to impress his in-laws by sartorial splendour provide more ammunition for sub-Swiftian satire. Yet his anguished dithering over whether or not to shave betrays an insecurity that goes deeper than social comedy: he hesitates similarly between cultures, wanting to look up to the utopian qualities in his wife's civilisation, but at the same time to assert his own values and change that which he admires.

The desire to turn difference to advantage extends to other familiar topics. For instance, food, as always, is tremendously important. In his Robinson Crusoe incarnation, Peter has experimented with all the natural resources he can find, and is invariably excited by the prospect of 'several new Sorts of Eatables'.[165] When Youwarkee comes, he shares this pleasure with her and acclimatises her to the variety of his table, with delicacies ranging from preserved pears to fresh or dried fish 'and a biting Herb, I had found, for Pepper': 'so there was no want', he adds proudly. 'There's no want' in Youwarkee's country either,[166] but their diet is salt-free and entirely vegetarian. A vegetarian utopia is not unique, but in this instance they can eat their meat without having it, as it were, since the fruits of that country taste exactly like fish or fowl. Youwarkee's people aren't familiar with the practice of killing for food, still less with the use of a gun. However, when Peter persuades them to try his offerings when they visit his utopia – he hospitably lays on a successful if somewhat disorderly fish barbecue – they relish his provisions immensely. Paradoxically, something that might have divided the two cultures becomes a means of bringing them together. The shared feast performs its traditional function of cementing trust and friendship.

Utopian language, the other fundamental mode of communication, is one of the few areas where Paltock's touch seems to falter. Although Peter is prepared to learn, even he balks at the tongue-twister *Normbdsgrsutt*, proposing a substitute. For the reader, the problem is more that of farcical incongruity, from the Wodehousian name of Peter's father-in-law Pendlehamby to the heavy muddy syllables Glumms (males) and Gawreys (females), with which Paltock burdens his wonderful winged beings. Unusually, this utopia is not a literate culture: whereas Raphael Hythlodaeus introduces printing to More's Utopians, Peter introduces the far more basic transformational skills of reading and writing. This raises the question of how his entire 'civilising' mission is to be regarded.

The impact that this emissary of eighteenth-century English civilisation has on his discovered utopia far surpasses that of most of his fictional predecessors, and defines the problem of the legitimacy of such interference in particularly acute form. Peter himself, in an extraordinary moment placed proleptically in the narrative, questions the term 'civilising':

> *Pendlehamby* could not well understand all I said; and I found by him, that all the Riches they possessed were only Food and Slaves; and, as I found afterwards when amongst them, they know the want of nothing else: But, I am afraid, I have put them upon another way of thinking, tho' I aimed at what we call civilizing of them.[167]

Peter's ambivalence is understandable, when the effects of this aim are analysed. In his own setting, his use of the gun alters their perception of food sources. After he enters their country, like Gulliver offering the invention of gunpowder as proof of higher civilisation to the King of Brobdingnag, Peter brings the knowledge of sophisticated artillery for use in war. Yet if this is corruption of innocence – as it undoubtedly is – it is also the means of salvation. He fulfils the legendary role waiting for him as the saviour of the Swangeantine people from destruction by their enemy; and his power to do so takes the significant (and ominous) form of harnessing their natural flying skills to his technological expertise.

Peter – named for the apostle who is the rock of the Church – conceives his mission to be also that of the saving of souls. From his viewpoint, he 'came hither [not] to possess, but redress a Kingdom',[168] and that includes its spiritual state. His propagation of Christianity in his own patriarchal utopia and correction of his wife's faulty ideas expands into a full-scale campaign to convert her people from idolatry (an expansion that Crusoe had been less willing to contemplate).

Nor does it stop there: Peter sets out to change the basis of their economy as well. The remark 'all the Riches they possessed were only Food and Slaves' sounds very like ancient utopianism, where a slave-based economy tends to be taken for granted. Peter crusades against slavery on religious and humanitarian grounds, articulating principles that echo Captain Misson's, although he makes it clear that he doesn't envisage social egalitarianism. However, emancipation is a shrewd move for other reasons. Politically, it strengthens the state, since former slaves 'may by Industry gain Property: and then their own Interest engages then to defend the State' (a Lockean observation).[169] Economically, freedom advances the 'civilising' process since it increases incentives: 'my Meaning in giving Liberty', explains Peter, 'is, in order for what is to follow, that is, for the Introduction of Arts amongst you.'[170]

The kind of utopia he has in mind for the Swangeantines is not the one they already have, based on the perfect match of needs and resources, but one driven by economic incentives and market forces, the opposite of Socrates' simple state or More's Utopia. To that end, he is prepared to introduce luxury trades such as watchmaking – characteristic of eighteenth-century civilisation – notwithstanding the fact that Swangeantines already have a high standard of beauty and comfort: beautiful and spacious buildings, lit by gentle living lights, hot and cold springs, abundant delicious food, music and the visual arts. In political structure the country closely resembles the European norm, but Peter adds the dimension of imperialism, with the annexation of Mount Alkoe and its industrial and trading potential, under the dominion of King Georigetti. The new imperial power is united, in exemplary British fashion, by a sporting event, the flight-race organised by Peter. As a crowning coup, he arranges a royal marriage, so bringing together and consolidating the personal and political ideals that run through the fiction.

The possible faultlines reappear in the penultimate chapter, where Peter attempts to assess the gains and losses he has brought to his chosen people. He starts with the progressive view, the Mandevillian argument for the effects of luxury:

> I have often reflected with myself, and have been amazed to think, that so ingenious and industrious a People, as the *Swangeantines* have since appeared to be; and who till I came amongst them, had nothing more than bare Food, and a Hole to lie in, in a barren rocky Country, and then seemed to desire only what they had; should in ten Years time, be supplied not only with the Conveniencies, but Superfluities of Life; and that they should then become so fond of them, as rather willingly to part with Life itself, than be reduced to the State I found them in.[171]

In fact, he rewrites the record to fit his thesis. He then reverses the image to that of the 'natural' utopia, in which Providence itself supplies all that is necessary, a kind of golden age with a perfect compensatory balance: no tools, but the means to shape rock into dwellings; no meat or fish, but fruit 'of the same Relish, and as wholesome without shedding Blood'; no fire, but constant hot water; no clothes, but the beautifully adapted *graundee*.[172]

In a couple of pages, Paltock through his narrator articulates the classic dilemma of the utopian ideal. Is it better to discipline needs and desires to an environment that is perceived to be natural, or to adapt the environment to the human pursuit of unlimited happiness? Should change be welcomed or resisted, and is it in any case irreversible? One fact that is certainly irreversible is that of personal mortality, and here the novelist rather than the utopian theorist comes into his own. For Peter Wilkins, the fictional character, the utopian dream ends with the death of his beloved Youwarkee who was its true embodiment; and, as an old man, his desires turn towards home. So it is that in all these texts the overseas utopia remains tantalisingly beyond the horizon.

Notes and references

1. Samuel Wesley A Letter from a Country Divine to his Friend in London 1703 cit L. Girdler 1953 p. 574

2. D. Defoe 1697/1969 p. 25.

3. D. Defoe 1705 pp. 34, 61.

4. L. Girdler 1953 pp. 587, 590.

5. v H. Heidenreich 1970.

6. D. Defoe 1697/1969 p. 3.

7. cf D. Defoe 1726.

8. D. Defoe 1697/1969 p. 123.

9. D. Defoe 1697/1969 p. 171.

10. Verses on the Death of Dr Swift 1731 11 479–80. In J. Swift 1726/1960 p. 473. D. Defoe 1697/1969 p. 181.

11. D. Defoe 1697/1969 pp. 282–304.

12. v M. E. Novak 1962 p. 49.

13. D. Defoe 1719/1927 vol. 1 p. 3.

14. D. Defoe 1719/1927 vol. 1 pp. 3–4: for Crusoe's response to his father's ideal v E. H. Pearlman 1976 pp. 41–2.

15. D. Defoe 1719/1927 vol. 1 p. 20.

16. D. Defoe 1719/1927 vol. 1 p. 39.

17. cf C. Kay 1988 pp. 82–4.

18. D. Defoe 1719/1927 vol. 1 p. 41.

19. D. Defoe 1719/1927 vol. 1 p. 42.

20 D. Defoe 1719/1927 vol. 1 p. 50.

21. For Robinson Crusoe and the Hobbesian state of nature v M. E. Novak 1963 ch. 2 (Aristotle cit p. 25): I. Kramnick 1968 p. 191: H. O. Brown 1971 pp. 565–6: P. Rogers 1979 pp. 74–5: cf C. Kay 1988 pp. 66–75.

22. T. Hobbes 1651/1968 p. 186.

23. D. Defoe 1719/1927 vol. 1 p. 53.

24. D. Defoe 1719/1927 vol. 1 pp. 150–1.

25. cf J. J. Richetti 1975 pp. 49–50.

26. D. Defoe 1719/1927 vol. 1 p. 171.

27. D. Defoe 1719/1927 vol. 1 p. 60: cf M. Schonhorn 1991 p. 157.

28. D. Defoe 1719/1927 vol. 2 p. 32: cf vol. 2 p. 59.

29. D. Defoe 1719/1927 vol. 1 p. 114.

30. D. Defoe 1719/1927 vol. 1 p. 114.

31. e.g. M. E. Novak 1962 pp. 49–66: I. Kramnick 1968 pp. 188–200: E. Tavor 1987 pp. 16–20. Schonhorn modifies the Lockean reading: v M. Schonhorn 1991 pp. 154–7.

32. J. Locke 1690/1988 p. 288.

33. J. Locke 1690/1988 p. 290.

34. cf J. J. Richetti 1975 pp. 46–7.

35. D. Defoe 1719/1927 vol. 1 p. 149: cf J. Locke 1690/1988 p. 300.

36. cf I. Watt 1951/1959. In J. L. Clifford (ed) pp. 169–70.

37. D. Defoe 1719/1927 vol. 1 p. 116.

38. D. Defoe 1719/1927 vol. 1 p. 116.

39. For Crusoe as *homo domesticus* v P. Rogers 1974: for his reaction to the 'delicious Vale' v pp. 380–1.

40. For Defoe on luxury v J. Sekora 1977 pp. 115–18: C. H. Flynn 1990 pp. 46–50: also cf P. Hulme 1986 pp. 213–14.

41. W. Shakespeare 1623/1985 p. 93 II:iv:264–5.

42. v M. de Montaigne 1580–1588/1991 pp. 253–6.

43. D. Defoe 1719/1927 vol. 1 p. 154.

44. D. Defoe 1719/1927 vol. 1 p. 64: among the many commentators on this passage v P. Rogers 1979 pp. 80–2. I. A. Bell 1985 pp. 90–1. Cf C. Watts 1990 pp. 81–94.

45. S. Johnson 1753–60/1963 p. 387.

46. D. Defoe 1720/1895 vol. 3 pp. 11–12.

47. D. Defoe 1719/1927 vol. 1 p. 62: for commentary on this development v C. H. Flynn 1990 pp. 152–9.

48. v P. Rogers 1979 p. 158. Cf I. Watt 1951/1959. In J. L. Clifford (ed) p. 174.

49. D. Defoe 1719/1927 vol. 1 p. 167.

50. D. Defoe 1719/1927 vol. 1 p. 73.

51. v H. O. Brown 1971 p. 573: P. Hulme 1986 p. 197.

52. D. Defoe 1719/1927 vol. 1 pp. 171–2: for commentary v M. Schonhorn 1991 pp. 147–8.

53. D. Defoe 1719/1927 vol. 1 p. 181.

54. eg G. A. Starr 1965: J. P. Hunter 1966: L. Damrosch 1985.

55. D. Defoe 1719/1927 vol. 1 p. 218: cf vol. 1 p. 148.

56. D. Defoe 1719/1927 vol. 1 p. 191.

57. D. Defoe 1719/1927 vol. 1 p. 199: compare Crusoe's attitude here with *Serious Reflections* iv and vi. In D. Defoe 1720/1895 vol. 3. Also v M. E. Novak 1963 pp. 44–7: P. Hulme 1986 pp. 199–200.

58. D. Defoe 1719/1927 vol. 1 p. 198.

59. v M. de Montaigne 1580–1588/1991 pp. 228–41: cf Novak's comparison with Montaigne (M. E. Novak 1963 p. 38).

60. J. Keats 1954 Letter 31 p. 49.

61 D. Defoe 1719/1927 vol. 1 p. 231.

62. For the philosophical and political context of the Crusoe/Friday relationship v M. E. Novak 1963 pp. 50–2: C. Kay 1988 pp. 86–7: M. Schonhorn 1991 pp. 158–60.

63. D. Defoe 1719/1927 vol. 1 p. 235.

64 The point is made by I. Watt 1951/1959. In J. L. Clifford (ed) p. 166.

65. D. Defoe 1719/1927 vol. 1 p. 247.

66. v I. Watt 1951/1959. In J. L. Clifford (ed) p. 172. Also v P. Hulme 1986 pp. 205–6: C. Kay 1988 p. 82: M. Schonhorn 1991 pp. 151–2, 159–60.

67. Aristotle 1988 pp. 4, 5.

68. v Aristotle 1988 pp. 6–9.

69. Aristotle 1988 p. 9.

70. D. Defoe 1719/1927 vol. 1. p. 243: cf vol. 2 p. 6.

71. D. Defoe 1719/1927 vol. 2 p. 10.

72. D. Defoe 1719/1927 vol. 1 p. 236.

73. T. Hobbes 1651/1968 pp. 255–6.

74. J. Locke 1690/1988 pp. 322–3.

75. J. Locke 1690/1988 pp. 284, 285.

76. Bell makes a parallel point in relation to the conventions of travel writing: v I. A. Bell 1985 pp. 104–5.

77. v F. Godwin 1638 pp. 93–6: T. More 1516/1989 Book II pp. 77–8.

78. P. Rogers 1972 (ed) p. 42.

79. W. Shakespeare 1623/1961 p. 33 I:ii:365–6. Novak also alludes to *The Tempest*: v M. E. Novak 1963 p. 50.

80. D. Defoe 1719/1927 vol. 2 p. 31: cf J. H. Maddox 1984 pp. 38–9.

81. v I. Watt 1951/1959. In J. L. Clifford (ed) pp. 172–3.

82. J. Locke 1693/1989 pp. 184–5: cf J. P. Hunter 1966 pp. 184–8.

83. D. Defoe 1719/1927 vol. 2 p. 6.

84. D. Defoe 1719/1927 vol. 2 p. 7.

85. D. Defoe 1719/1927 vol. 2 pp. 30–1.

86. e.g. in M. Schonhorn 1991 p. 147.

87. cf T. More 1516/1989 Book II pp. 97–8: for a connection with Hobbesian sovereignty v C. Kay 1988 pp. 87–8. Also v M. E. Novak 1974 pp. 69–70.

88. D. Defoe 1719/1927 vol. 2 p. 34.

89. v H. Neville 1668/1930: for *Robinson Crusoe* and *The Isle of Pines* v M. E. Novak 1963 pp. 58–9: for Crusoe as patriarch v M. Schonhorn 1991 pp. 160–1.

90. D. Defoe 1719/1927 vol. 2 pp. 60, 62.

91. D. Defoe 1719/1927 vol. 2 pp. 62–5: for commentary v D. Trotter 1988 p. 36: M. Schonhorn 1991 p. 145.

92. D. Defoe 1719/1927 vol. 2 p. 72: for the significance of the island as penal colony v J. Bender 1987/1994. In D. Defoe 1719/1994 pp. 390–402.

93. v J. M. Coetzee 1986/1987 pp. 44–5.

94. D. Defoe 1719/1927 vol. 2 p. 74.

95. v McKeon's suggestion that Crusoe's internal utopia is externalised (M. McKeon 1987 p. 335).

96. D. Defoe 1719/1927 vol. 2 p. 105.

97. D. Defoe 1719/1927 vol. 2 p. 118.

98. D. Defoe 1719/1927 vol. 2 p. 117.

99. D. Defoe 1719/1927 vol. 2 p. 120.

100. v J. Hall 1605/1981 Book I.

101. D. Defoe 1719/1927 vol. 2 p. 152.

102.   cf M. E. Novak 1963 pp. 51–9.

103.   D. Defoe 1719/1927 vol. 2 p. 195: vol. 3 pp. 1, 3.

104.   D. Defoe 1719/1927 vol. 2 p. 189.

105.   D. Defoe 1719/1927 vol. 2 pp. 188–9.

106.   D. Defoe 1719/1927 vol. 2 pp. 190, 191, 221.

107.   D. Defoe 1719/1927 vol. 2 p. 222.

108.   D. Defoe 1719/1927 vol. 3 p. 12.

109.   D. Defoe 1719/1927 vol. 3 pp. 24–5.

110.   D. Defoe 1719/1927 vol. 3 pp. 25–6.

111.   D. Defoe 1719/1927 vol. 3 p. 59.

112.   Contrast E. Tavor 1987 p. 20 where the sequel doesn't appear to be taken into account.

113.   D. Defoe 1719/1927 vol. 3 p. 60.

114.   e.g. M. E. Novak 1962 pp. 65–6, 143–4: D. Trotter 1988 p. 37.

115.   D. Defoe 1719/1927 vol. 3 p. 59.

116.   v Plutarch 1914 vol. 1 pp. 293, 295, 297.

117.   D. Defoe 1719/1927 vol. 3 p. 61.

118.   D. Defoe 1719/1927 vol. 3 p. 69.

119.   D. Defoe 1719/1927 vol. 3 pp. 70, 79.

120.   D. Defoe 1719/1927 vol. 3. p. 80: cf vol. 3 pp. 199–200: also v D. Trotter 1988 p. 37: M. Schonhorn 1991 pp. 163–4.

121.   D. Defoe 1719/1927 vol. 3 p. 81.

122.   v Schonhorn's intro to D. Defoe 1728/1972 p. xxiii: also v P. N. Furbank, W. R. Owens 1988 pp. 100–14.

123.   D. Defoe 1728/1972 p. 388.

124.   D. Defoe 1728/1972 p. 389.

125.   J. Gay 1728/1986 p. 69 II:i.

126.   D. Defoe 1728/1972 p. 391.

127.   D. Defoe 1728/1972 p. 403.

128.   D. Defoe 1728/1972 pp. 403–4.

129.   D. Defoe 1728/1972 p. 417.

130.   D. Defoe 1728/1972 p. 427.

131. D. Defoe 1728/1972 pp. 432–3.

132. D. Defoe 1728/1972 p. 428.

133. D. Defoe 1728/1972 p. 432.

134. cf G. Winstanley 1651/1983: J. Harrington 1656/1977. v above pp. 44–7.

135. cf M. E. Novak 1962 p. 145.

136. D. Defoe 1728/1972 p. 436.

137. D. Defoe 1728/1972 p. 437.

138. B. Unsworth 1992 Book 2.

139. For information about author and context v L. M. Ellison 1935.

140. v titlepage of 1737 edn.

141. S. Berington 1737 p. 8.

142. S. Berington 1737 p. 161.

143. S. Berington 1737 p. 187.

144. S. Berington 1737 p. 172.

145. S. Berington 1737 p. 196.

146. v M. Cavendish Duchess of Newcastle 1666 pp. 13–14.

147. v G. de Foigny 1676/1693 pp. 85, 164–6.

148. S. Berington 1737 pp. 223–4.

149. S. Berington 1737 pp. 226–7.

150. S. Berington 1737 p. 224.

151. S. Berington 1737 p. 228.

152. R. Paltock 1750/1990 p. 55.

153. *Monthly Review* Dec 1750 cit Turner in R. Paltock 1750/1990 intro p. vii.

154. R. Paltock 1750/1990 p. 84.

155. R. Paltock 1750/1990 p. 104: for the dream's significance v Turner's intro to Paltock 1750/1990 p. xxviii.

156. For flight symbolism v Turner's intro to Paltock 1750/1990 pp. xx–xxiv.

157. R. Paltock 1750/1990 p. 108.

158. R. Paltock 1750/1990 p. 116.

159. F. Bacon 1597–1625/1985 p. 82.

160. For different theories of the historical evolution of marriage v L. Stone 1977: A. Macfarlane 1986.

161. cf H. Neville 1668/1930: v above pp. 57–9.

162. R. Paltock 1750/1990 p. 151.

163. v Lucian 1913 vol. 1 pp. 265, 353: the Swangeantines can also transform themselves into boats.

164. R. Paltock 1750/1990 p. 111.

165. R. Paltock 1750/1990 p. 129.

166. R. Paltock 1750/1990 pp. 126–7.

167. R. Paltock 1750/1990 p. 215.

168. R. Paltock 1750/1990 p. 283.

169. R. Paltock 1750/1990 pp. 301–2.

170. R. Paltock 1750/1990 pp. 324–5.

171. R. Paltock 1750/1990 p. 372.

172 R. Paltock 1750/1990 p. 373.

CHAPTER 5

Utopia and satire:
the Travels *of* Gulliver *and others*

Utopia and satire have always had a natural affinity. Writing utopian fiction is a subversive act. Even (or especially) where the writer is committed to a conservative or nostalgic view of how human affairs should be conducted, by constructing an imaginary alternative, he or she implies that whatever is, is *not* right. Like satire, the utopian mirror forces us to see in close-up features of human behaviour and society that may be swollen or shrunk or contorted, but are still all too recognisable. However, which is the monster, the reflection or what is reflected? Just because it professes rationality and order, while being a product of the distrusted imagination, the authority of the utopian discourse is suspect and unstable. The utopian satire is doubly insecure, peculiarly vulnerable to overthrow from within. In this looking-glass world, more than the reader's illusions are shattered.

No-one knows this better than Swift, himself an informed reader of utopian texts. The classical sources can be taken as read: his library contained two editions each of Plato and Aristotle, as well as Xenophon, Herodotus, Plutarch, Cicero, Tacitus, and, of course, Lucian, alternative comedian of ancient utopianism.[1] Among Renaissance and post-Renaissance writers with some sort of utopian angle on the universe, Swift evidently admired and relished those whose genius was for comic irony – More, Rabelais, Cervantes – all expert narrators and exquisite philosophers. Swift also possessed Montaigne's essays, Bacon's works, Hobbes's *Leviathan*, Harrington's *Oceana*, Henry Neville's *Plato Redivivus*, and other works of political theory and historiography, the compost in which utopian ideas grow. Although to document an author's reading is not to explain the origins of his writing in any simplistic way, nevertheless, the author of *Gulliver's Travels* benefits from as rich a grounding as any of his contemporaries. In Swift's case, there are other texts which he cannot be proved to have read, but which are contextually interesting (and which could conceivably have been among the 'diverting books' or 'abundance of

Trash' he soaked up when working on his own fiction).[2] Swift, like Defoe, was in a number of respects the product of the later seventeenth century, and that century had been fertile in utopian fictions on both sides of the Channel. These include the moon voyages of Francis Godwin and Cyrano de Bergerac, and the literary explorations of a fantasised Australia by Gabriel de Foigny and of a mythical country called Severambia by Denis Vairasse d'Allais.[3]

The significance of any or all of the above texts has caused controversy. In his preface to the French translation of *Gulliver's Travels* (1757), Desfontaines simultaneously asserts Swift's originality and sets out a checklist of the genre, with which, he remarks, his book could, but shouldn't, be classified:

> Sans parler de la *République* de Platon, de l'*Histoire véritable* de Lucien, & du *Supplément* . . . on connoît l'*Utopie* . . . la *Nouvelle Atlantis* . . . l'*Histoire des Sevarambes*, les *Voyages de Sadeur*, & *de Jacques Maçé* & enfin le *Voyage* . . . de Cyrano de Bergerac. Mais tous ces Ouvrages sont d'un goût fort différent, & ceux qui voudront les comparer à celui-ci, trouveront qu'ils n'ont rien de commun avec lui, que l'idée d'un voyage imaginaire, & d'un pays supposé.[4]

A number of Swift's readers, including myself, would want to take issue with him, though each might want to qualify the sense of Swift's parallels with his predecessors in different ways. For instance, a contemporary Englishman, Abel Boyer, accepts a range of influences, while regretting that of Rabelais: 'Gulliver's Travels, are an ingenious romantick satyr, in imitation of Plato's *Commonwealth*, Moor's [sic] *Utopia*, Bacon's *New Atlantis*, Rabelais and *The History of the Severambi*: but it were to be wish'd the author had not follow'd Rabelais so close, in some filthy, and obscene descriptions . . .'[5] In reply to Desfontaines, it could be argued that it is not only an imaginary voyage and country that structure these texts, but the utopian imagination itself, that relocates familiar philosophical questions in the *terra incognita* of fiction – and that Swift's work is both a brilliant demonstration and a critique of utopian imagination. In reply to Boyer, one could say that the human body, its needs and limitations, are fundamental to utopian satire, often indeed its starting point, and that the Rabelaisian treatment makes more impact than any other. Whatever the influences claimed or rejected for *Gulliver's Travels*, in this single text Swift offers the reader a portfolio of different kinds of utopian writing, bound together by strong threads of theory as well as narrative. In Gulliver, he creates the archetypal utopian traveller for the eighteenth century, with his prejudices and projects, sophistication and naïveté. The result is the most comprehensive, the most dazzling, and the most self-deconstructive utopian fiction of the period.

Of course, the starting point of *Gulliver's Travels* can be looked for in a variety of places, including Swift's correspondence and biography. Other texts are only one kind of context. Dr Johnson supposed that Swift began by thinking of big men and little men.[6] And, however reductive, this observation does make the familiar and essential point that Swift, like other utopian satirists such as Lucian and Joseph Hall, begins from the physical, from the body as well as books. In a sense, the body *is* his book.[7] Gulliver himself, the ship's surgeon, knows about bodies, and is notoriously conscious of the functioning of his own; he too is a reader – 'My Hours of Leisure I spent in reading the best Authors, ancient and modern; being always provided with a good Number of Books'[8] – and something of an anthropologist and linguist. Thus equipped, he sets sail unwittingly for utopia (in the plural): and when he gets back, he writes a book about them.

In the editions of *Gulliver's Travels* published after 1735 when Swift added the prefatory 'Letter from Capt. Gulliver to His Cousin Sympson', the conscientious reader first encounters Gulliver in the persona of utopian writer. However, paradoxically, he refuses to recognise himself as such. We have a *cri de coeur*, not simply of the thwarted idealist for whom the rest of the world is out of kilter, but of the writer for whom the medium of communication has irretrievably broken down. Gulliver blames the failure of his reforming vision entirely upon the recalcitrant nature of his Yahoo readership, but his complaints make it clear that there is a problem with the identity and status of the text, not just with its reception by readers. The issues of language and genre displace – or become part of – the moral issue. In the first place, the text is at the publisher's mercy, and Gulliver's outrage at the mutilation of his work erupts against editorial interference: '. . . you have either omitted some material Circumstances, or minced or changed them in such a Manner, that I do hardly know mine own Work.'[9] Post-publication, the proliferating 'Libels, and Keys, and Reflections, and Memoirs, and Second Parts' further erode any illusion of authorial control or even existence – 'some of them will not allow me to be Author of mine own Travels'.[10] The printer is unreliable, and the original manuscript – that mainstay of so much fictional authentication of utopian fiction – is allegedly destroyed.

In the second place, language itself is crumbling (a characteristic Swiftian anxiety transferred to Gulliver: Swift had flirted with a utopian project in A Proposal for Correcting, Improving and Ascertaining the English Tongue, 1712). Gulliver remarks apropos of rapid linguistic shifts, 'I remember upon each Return to mine own Country, their old Dialect was so altered, that I could hardly understand the new.'[11]

In the third place, the genre of Gulliver's Travels is no more fixed than the medium of language. The putative author waxes particularly splenetic against readers who dare to take his Travels as fiction 'and have gone so far as to drop Hints, that the Houyhnhnms and Yahoos have no more Existence than the Inhabitants of Utopia' – a strong signal, in this ironic context, the code we're expected to use.[12] The disclaimer of fiction is, of course, a standard ploy, but this is unmistakably specific. Although Gulliver ends by renouncing 'all such visionary Schemes for ever',[13] the schemes to which he refers concern the dream of reforming his fellow human beings. He continues to assert the truth of his utopian experience, refusing to see it as chimerical. The reader, thoroughly unsettled, is left to embark on the uncertain text of Travels into Several Remote Nations of the World, better known – since even the title isn't fixed – as Gulliver's Travels.

The utopian traveller and utopian institutions: Lilliput and Brobdingnag

Swift's experiments with utopian fiction are complicated constructions, designed to accommodate intricate cross-reference. Each of his inventions is a fully functioning society put together from a sophisticated literary kit. Almost every topos known to the genre is in there somewhere: parodies of political and scientific utopias, simple-life versus progressive utopian societies, the idea of the moral commonwealth. Each society has its own manners, dispositions and language, the objects of Gulliver's fascinated attention, which compare and contrast with each other and with his original standard of measurement, his own dear native country. To begin at the beginning, with Lilliput, is to watch the experiment build and diversify from what is a relatively simple narrative structure.

The form of the imaginary voyage is particularly adapted to a first-person narrator, absorbing and interpreting his or her impressions.

Even before his initial encounter and negotiation with this new culture, Gulliver is given topographical clues: unlike Crusoe he paddles ashore, and the grass where he sleeps is 'very short and soft'.[14] It is he that is out of scale in this landscape – a point to bear in mind when, at the beginning of the second chapter, he records a prospect analogous to that of many utopian travellers: 'the Country round appeared like a continued Garden; and the enclosed Fields, which were generally Forty Foot square, resembled so many Beds of Flowers.'[15] What puts this lyricism in perspective is, first, the angle of vision – Gulliver is short-sighted[16] and in Lilliput small is beautiful – and, second, Swift's technique of ironic juxtaposition. The next paragraph is the famous extended passage documenting Gulliver's defecation and the Lilliputian answer to the problem of sewage disposal, a problem that early utopias tend to pass over discreetly, even when it is on a less massive scale.[17] Although the reader isn't told what the servants actually do with 'the offensive Matter' it is entirely characteristic of Swift that thoughts of flowers and thoughts of dung should go together.

Gulliver presents a philosophical and physical problem to the Lilliputians, as they do to him. From their point of view he is the (possibly extra-terrestrial) alien: 'For as to what we have heard you affirm, that there are other Kingdoms and States in the World, inhabited by human Creatures as large as your self, our Philosophers are in much Doubt: and would rather conjecture that you dropt from the Moon, or one of the Stars . . .'[18] However, what strikes the reader, and slowly dawns on Gulliver, is that the institutions of Lilliput represent his own culture, shrunk in the negative mirror, but reproducing all the adverse effects of party politics and court life. Gulliver hasn't previously experienced these at first hand, but only vicariously: 'I had indeed heard and read enough of the Dispositions of great Princes and Ministers; but never expected to have found such terrible Effects of them in so remote a Country, governed, as I thought, by very different Maxims from those in *Europe*.'[19] There is some excuse for Gulliver's belief in those 'very different Maxims', for Lilliput is a degenerate utopia, a fractured ideal. Its present, shadowed by intrigue and malice, is backlit by a golden past, an alternative culture corresponding to an alternative text, the utopia that Gulliver – or Swift – didn't write. Gulliver inserts an advertisement for this hypothetical treatise in the fourth chapter:

> But I shall not anticipate the Reader with farther Descriptions of
> this Kind, because I reserve them for a greater Work, which is
> now almost ready for the Press; containing a general Description
> of this Empire, from its first Erection, through a long Series of
> Princes, with a particular Account of their Wars and Politicks,
> Laws, Learning, and Religion; their Plants and Animals, their
> peculiar Manners and Customs, with other Matters very curious
> and useful . . .[20]

Again the reader is teased with the notion that what he or she is
reading is not the definitive text: that remains a work-in-progress, a
utopian dream, just as the Lilliputian empire itself is, so to speak, a
work-in-regress. However, the narrator generously gives us a précis of
its contents: 'although I intend to leave the Description of this Empire
to a particular Treatise, yet in the mean time I am content to gratify
the curious Reader with some general Ideas.'[21]

Apart from some good Swiftian jokes on Lilliputian handwriting
and burial practice, these 'general Ideas' include principles of justice
and government that recall the moral commonwealths of More[22] and
the ancients. Honesty and plain-dealing are the bedrock of social
virtue, reinforced by law; the legal system rewards the upright as well
as punishing the guilty, and the non-hereditary honours system is
based on merit. 'In choosing Persons for all Employments, they have
more Regard to good Morals than to great Abilities'[23] – a concept
which, together with the animus against political professionalism, is
by no means universal among utopian theorists. Indeed the policy has
radical implications, since moral qualifications unlike intellectual ones
are assumed 'to be in every Man's Power'. It isn't altogether easy to
imagine Swift subscribing to the notion of ignorant and well-disposed
amateurs as the best people to run the country, but the distrust of
professionalism – especially cleverness divorced from conscience – is
to be expected of a satirist. The religious stipulation is also pre-
dictable: in the great majority of early utopias, atheism fundamentally
disqualifies anyone from participation in public life, since it
undermines the very basis of political authority. However, by making
these theories a fiction within a fiction (rather as 'real' Christianity is
displaced from the *Argument* defending 'nominal' Christianity[24]) their
credibility is even more ironically compromised. 'In relating these and
the following Laws, I would only be understood to mean the original
Institutions'[25] says Gulliver.

In fact, 'the following Laws' relating to parents and children reflect the less acceptable face of utopian authoritarianism. From an idealistic emphasis on the moral capacity of ordinary human beings, the discourse swings abruptly to a cynical view of their emotional capacities. Like Socrates in Plato's *Republic*, the Lilliputians adopt an animal paradigm for the regulation of sex and reproduction, denying that any emotional bond between parents and offspring is either necessary or desirable: 'Men and Women are joined together like other Animals, by the Motives of Concupiscence' and 'their Tenderness towards their Young' is likewise biological. This is also the view taken by the freethinkers in Cyrano de Bergerac's lunar society. From this premise they deduce 'that Parents are the last of all others to be trusted with the Education of their own Children' – a conclusion in sharp contrast to Locke's argument in *Some Thoughts concerning Education* (1693), although Locke shares the opinion that servants are a bad influence.[26] The Lilliputian educational system is Spartan in the exact sense of the term, based on separating young children from parents (parental visits are severely rationed and supervised) and inculcating austerity, morality, and self-reliance. Although the sexes are segregated, there is an approximation to Spartan equality in the standards set for girls and boys, if only for the benefit of the latter: 'a Wife should be always a reasonable and agreeable Companion, because she cannot always be young.' As for financing the system, parents are to pay for the privilege of having their children educated in this fashion, on the grounds that 'nothing can be more unjust, than that People, in subservience to their own Appetites, should bring Children into the World, and leave the Burthen of supporting them on the Publick.'[27] The Lilliputians run counter to most utopians, who regard education as the financial as well as moral responsibility of the state. In any case, in contrast to More's Utopia, education doesn't include all social classes: the children of 'Cottagers and Labourers' escape the system because their destiny is to labour like their parents. Yet – a final gesture to a utopian ideal – society does accept responsibility for the old and ill, and as a result Lilliput, unlike Brobdingnag we might note, has no beggars.

However this synopsis is assessed, in context it represents the gold standard that present-day Lilliput has abandoned – in Gulliver's estimation at least. It confirms the theory of degeneracy inscribed in all four voyages. Unlike More, Swift doesn't invent a new political and social structure for the Lilliput that Gulliver actually encounters.

He doesn't have to. Instead, using the device of physical scale, he ironically investigates the basis and workings of political power in a 'modern' state.

If power derives from brute strength, then Gulliver is evidently superior. Though the narrative shows that the Lilliputians can take initial advantage of the physical vulnerability of their giant, Gulliver quickly realises that, given certain precautions, he could be a match for them and regain his freedom. However, Gulliver feels bound in more senses than one. The crucial factor is not force but implicit consent, the civilised man's adherence to contract that removes him from the state of nature. When the Lilliputians try diplomacy in place of force, despite the fact that neither party can understand a syllable of the other's language, Gulliver makes signs of submission in return for food. Afterwards, his reasons for not displaying aggression combine prudence with the code of honour:

> I confess I was often tempted, while they were passing backwards and forwards on my Body, to seize Forty or Fifty of the first that came in my Reach, and dash them against the Ground. But the Remembrance of what I had felt, which probably might not be the worst they could do; and the Promise of Honour I made them, for so I interpreted my submissive Behaviour, soon drove out those Imaginations. Besides, I now considered my self as bound by the Laws of Hospitality to a People who had treated me with so much Expence and Magnificence.[28]

Gulliver is absurdly dazzled by the magnificence of Lilliput's ruling hierarchy and the authority of its emperor. The point is that he believes in that authority, and, whatever his protests when the tyranny of absolute power turns against him, he does not withdraw his assent to the legitimate rights of the sovereign. Although he is forced into awareness that the emperor is a less enlightened despot than he at first imagines ('nor did any thing terrify the People so much as those Encomiums on his Majesty's Mercy; because it was observed, that the more these Praises were enlarged and insisted on, the more *inhuman* was the Punishment, and the *Sufferer more innocent*'),[29] Gulliver is not the stuff of which revolutionaries are made:

> Once I was strongly bent upon Resistance: for while I had Liberty, the whole Strength of that Empire could hardly subdue me, and I might easily with Stones pelt the Metropolis to Pieces:

But I soon rejected that Project with Horror, by remembering the
Oath I had made to the Emperor, the Favours I received from
him, and the high title of *Nardac* he conferred upon me. Neither
had I so soon learned the Gratitude of Courtiers, to persuade
myself that his Majesty's *present Severities acquitted me of all past
Obligations.*[30]

This suggests that Gulliver unconsciously constructs Lilliput as a
Hobbesian state, in which he has forfeited his rights by submitting
himself to the sovereign power: he 'hath his life and corporall Libertie
given him, on condition to be Subject to the Victor, he hath Libertie
to accept the condition; and having accepted it, is the subject of him
that took him; because he had no other way to preserve himselfe'
(*Leviathan*).[31] Hobbes adds, 'The case is the same, if he be deteined on
the same termes, in a forreign country.' However, even Hobbes allows
for the right of self-preservation: a man cannot be forced to acquiesce
in destroying himself. In taking steps, as he says, to save 'mine Eyes,
and consequently my Liberty', Gulliver might be said to act upon this
principle. His only fear is of being accused of naïveté, for 'if I had
then known the Nature of Princes and Ministers, which I have since
observed in many other Courts, and their Methods of treating
Criminals less obnoxious than myself; I should with great Alacrity and
Readiness have submitted to so *easy* a Punishment.'[32] Utopian satire
depends on where you're standing: alternatives can be worse as well as
better, estimates can go down as well as up. Lilliput confuses Gulliver,
because his basis of comparison keeps shifting. What he gains from it
is a political education, of a kind, and a capacity to assimilate to life
on a different scale which will be put to the test in his next voyage.

If Lilliput past is an institutional utopia and Lilliput present is an
institutional anti-utopia, what is Brobdingnag? Swift pitchforks
Gulliver into a land of giants where he is only a fraction of the
normal size, but to deduce that this is therefore the obverse of Lilliput
is misleading. Gulliver himself falls into the trap of making
assumptions from size. Although he reflects sagely that 'nothing is
great or little otherwise than by Comparison', his first terrified
reaction is that big people are bullies and barbarians and the bigger
they are the more dangerous they are.[33] He expects, like Crusoe, to be
eaten. Readers might equally draw the opposite conclusion, that 'these
enormous Barbarians' will be gentle giants, more truly civilised than
the ultra-polite Lilliputians. Both generalisations are flawed. In
narrative terms, Gulliver's early experiences in bucolic Brobdingnag

are as mixed as those in sophisticated Lilliput. Like Cyrano on the moon, he is exhibited as a freak,[34] and the many kindnesses he receives never cancel out the continuing element of exploitation in the Brobdingnagians' treatment of him, though it becomes less overt. He is consistently exposed to emotions of fear, humiliation and disgust associated with his extreme physical inferiority. However, because many episodes are funny as well as cruel, and because he brings many of his misfortunes upon himself, readers may be less inclined to find fault with Brobdingnag. Indeed there is a prevalent belief that, if not an ideal state, it comes closer to Swift's own pragmatic standard of a decent society more decently governed than any other. This view supports Gulliver's own summing up of his verdict at the end of the fourth voyage: 'the least corrupted [among human societies] are the *Brobdingnagians*, whose wise Maxims in Morality and Government, it would be our Happiness to observe.'[35] How does this judgment (given by a narrator whose reliability is certainly not beyond question) stand up to examination with the evidence actually available in Book II?

If Brobdingnagian institutions are compared with the present state of Lilliput, it becomes clear that the characters of the respective rulers are the main key to the image of each government. Swift was acutely aware of the problem involved in idealising a monarchical state: he notes succinctly in his copy of Bodin, 'His Royall Monarchy, which he proposeth as the most perfect Government is visionary unless every Country were sure to have always a good King.'[36] Yet the nature of the society also counts for a great deal. The reader in fact learns relatively little about how Brobdingnag is actually run, as opposed to the principles of its king. The rural economy is obviously important. As if to signal the point, Gulliver's story begins among country people harvesting the crop – a cue, one might think, for an idyll of productive pastoral harmony anticipating William Morris. However, none of Swift's imaginary countries is especially favoured by nature – the earthly paradise is not his style – and Brobdingnag is no exception. Nor does he idealise the rustic way of life. Gulliver encounters the usual vagaries of human nature, such as curiosity, generosity, greed, self-interest, and the maternal instinct, among the ordinary country-dwellers of Brobdingnag.

After he reaches the metropolis, it too seems neither better nor worse than life in eighteenth-century London: only blown up to grotesque proportions which ensure that the negative sights make most impact. It's impossible to forget the beggars, lice-ridden, diseased and deformed, thrusting round the privileged occupants of the coach. Certainly this is a very un-utopian spectacle, which would not be paralleled in either 'realistic' utopias like More's or fantasy utopias like Severambia, where facial wens are the result not of natural disease, but of unnatural behaviour.[37] Indeed, most utopias design their institutions to deal with avoidable and unavoidable suffering (including Lilliput). Similarly, the necessity of capital punishment for the crime of murder is accepted by a number of utopian writers, though certain races in utopian fiction, like Godwin's lunar people and Berington's Mezzoranians, refuse to shed blood. However, that acceptance does not lead to such descriptions of a public execution as Gulliver provides, complete with fountain of blood and bouncing head.[38] In terms of physical daily experience, Brobdingnag often seems closer to nightmare than to a simple-life utopia or a moral commonwealth. This in itself makes a point about the inadequacy of abstract theory confronted with the human waste which clogs the best-planned system. The pragmatic approach recognises that it is pointless to be discontented and repine over 'the Quarrels we raise with Nature' – an aspect of moral philosophy that the Brobdingnagians leave to women and the lower orders.[39]

At the core of Book II, however, Swift places a collision of ideas that bears centrally on the definition and aims of a moral commonwealth. This is the important dialogue between Gulliver and the King of Brobdingnag. Dialogue as a formal structure is central to utopian writing as well as satire, and Swift uses it here to combine and complicate both genres. Whatever else is happening in the satire at this stage, it is certainly working to incriminate Gulliver. He has become a very different kind of utopian traveller from the one in the first voyage. In Book II, he edits his account of his 'own beloved Country' to represent Britain as, in effect, a utopian fiction, even to the point of beginning with a generic cliché: 'I dwelt long upon the Fertility of our Soil, and the Temperature of our Climate.'[40] He describes Britain's constitution, government and legal system as it ought to be in an ideal world where, for example, MPs are 'principal Gentlemen, *freely* picked and culled out by the People themselves, for their great Abilities, and Love of their Country, to represent the Wisdom of the whole Nation'.[41] The king, already established as a man of clear apprehension, exact judgement and wise reflection, systematically dismantles Gulliver's discourse by the Socratic method of asking awkward questions. It is a familiar technique in utopian writing, and it works, devastatingly. Like Gulliver himself in Lilliput, he applies the theory of degeneration: 'I observe among you some Lines of an Institution, which in its Original might have been tolerable . . .' but the present state of Britain elicits a notorious verdict, which has often been identified with Swift, simply because of the intense emotional. charge it carries: 'I cannot but conclude the Bulk of your Natives, to be the most pernicious Race of little odious Vermin that Nature ever suffered to crawl upon the Surface of the Earth.'[42]

Perversely, as it seems, Gulliver goes on virtually to prove the point. He is trapped into offering the indisputable sign of superior 'civilised' power that from the fifteenth to the eighteenth centuries had starkly differentiated Europe from the New World: the use of gunpowder. Swift's satire ironically revises all those encounters, in fact and in fiction, between 'advanced' old-world and 'primitive' new-world cultures where the gun signifies power, fear, and desire (compare *Robinson Crusoe* and *Peter Wilkins*).[43] When Gulliver patronises this unambitious and isolated monarch of an under-developed country, the king's response goes to the heart of the matter, the question of government priorities. 'Wise Maxims in Morality and Government' or '*narrow Principles* and *short Views*'?[44] The right definition is not in much doubt. Again, as in the utopian version of Lilliput, political science is demystified and reduced to the simplicity which is the hallmark of one kind of utopian thinking:

> He confined the Knowledge of Governing within very narrow Bounds; to common Sense and Reason, to Justice and Lenity, to the speedy Determination of civil and criminal Causes; with some other obvious Topics which are not worth considering. And he gave it for his Opinion; that whoever could make two Ears of Corn, or two Blades of Grass to grow upon a Spot of Ground where only one grew before; would deserve better of Mankind, and do more essential Service to his Country, than the whole Race of Politicians put together.[45]

Refreshing as the sentiments may be, however, they leave unanswered the genuine questions that a number of utopian writers struggle to answer. How can these ends best be achieved? More, who is no less conscious of the importance of agriculture, for instance, also tackles the question of who is to grow the food, and how it is to be fairly distributed. Brobdingnag's traditional class-structure, from king to beggars, doesn't really suggest any attempt to put the royal principles into practice: it is at a far remove from, say, Winstanley's concept of an England dug over by and for the people.

It is, however, closer to Winstanley's contemporary, James Harrington, in one respect at least.[46] Ironically, the one Brobdingnagian institution we hear much about is its well-disciplined citizen army (in satiric contrast to the English political bogey, a standing army in peacetime): 'every Farmer is under the Command of his own Landlord, and every Citizen under that of the Principal Men in his own City, chosen after the Manner of Venice by Ballot'.[47] Swift, who possessed a copy of Oceana, would be familiar with Harrington's fixation on the ballot; and the conjecture that he had seventeenth-century English history in mind at this point seems to be confirmed when he has Gulliver raise the question relevant to any self-contained moral commonwealth, namely how military training comes to be a requisite at all. As far as Brobdingnag is concerned, the answer lies in the past, in the conflict of the three political estates, which had led to civil war, but which is now 'happily put an End to by this Prince's Grandfather in a general Composition'. If Lilliput was a Hobbesian state, Brobdingnag it seems is a Lockean one, where the demands of 'the Nobility . . . for Power, the People for Liberty, and the King for absolute Dominion' have been constitutionally resolved.[48] The king of Brobdingnag governs by love, that is, consent, not fear: he is 'almost adored by his Subjects'.[49]

And yet: how free are those adoring subjects? Again there is little evidence apart from the treatment of Gulliver himself, but that is significant enough. Although the king is benevolent, the court hierarchy as such generates a degree of malice and envy as it did in Lilliput, although in this instance – the episode of the Queen's dwarf – it is unsuccessful. There is always the fear of losing the royal favour, which certainly affects Glumdalclitch.[50] Kindness cannot mask the reality of power – a power that the King of Brobdingnag, no less than the Emperor of Lilliput, assumes as his right. This emerges most sharply at the beginning of the final chapter, just before Gulliver accidentally obtains his freedom. He remarks of the king's orders to capture any other specimens of Gulliver's race that might sail into Brobdingnagian waters, 'He was strongly bent to get me a Woman of my own Size, by whom I might propagate the Breed: But I think I should rather have died than undergone the Disgrace of leaving a Posterity to be kept in Cages like tame Canary Birds; and perhaps in time sold about the Kingdom to Persons of Quality for Curiosities.'[51] Control of propagation, human and other, is nothing new in utopian fiction. There is a comic precedent for Swift's scenario in Cyrano de Bergerac's moon voyage, where the king and queen, mistaking the narrator's gender, try hopefully to mate him with an earlier moon traveller, Godwin's Gonsales (since both are males the scheme founders).[52] The initial confusion is also one of species, and in Gulliver's case the pet animal/bird analogy has run continuously through Book II. Because of his size, he is threatened not only by the animals and insects of Brobdingnag, but also by human attitudes, of which this is a chillingly well-intentioned example. Of course, Gulliver's frequent attempts to assert his dignity are usually funny, reflecting an incongruous self-consequence. He is dismayed by the liberties taken with his person by the Maids of Honour, who certainly display none of the sexual modesty prized among such legendary peoples as de Foigny's Australians, or the Severambians. However, the humour shouldn't allow his claim to human dignity to be discounted altogether. In certain contexts, such as this one, the reader might infer a failure of imagination, or at least of subtlety, on the part of Brobdingnagian royalty: as Gulliver observes, 'I was indeed treated with much Kindness; I was the Favourite of a great King and Queen, and the Delight of the whole Court; but it was upon such a Foot as ill became the Dignity of human Kind.' He adds, 'I could never forget those domestick Pledges I had left behind me.'[53] True, Gulliver has given little sign that his 'domestick Pledges' have been weighing on his mind, but his freedom has been no greater in Brobdingnag than in Lilliput. For the twentieth-century reader, there is an element of cruelty and exploitation of the individual in both books. Gulliver's escape, fittingly after all his quarrels with nature, is by courtesy of an eagle that carries off his box – a nice variation on similar devices in utopian fantasies like Godwin's and de Foigny's.

Any final judgment on Brobdingnagian institutions must take into account Gulliver's severely compromised position as utopian traveller in Book II. His naïveté has taken a new and dangerous turn, into pseudo-sophistication. For all their lack of imagination, the Brobdingnagians have turned limitation into a moral strength. Perhaps their height of wisdom is indicated by Gulliver's complaint that when it comes to 'Ideas, Entities, Abstractions and Transcendentals, [he] could never drive the least Conception into their Heads' – not unlike More's Utopians, who can't grasp the meaning of 'man-in-general'.[54] However, in Book III Gulliver is about to encounter a breed of utopians who are the diametric opposites of the practical Brobdingnagians and whose institutions embody theory taken to extremes.

The composite utopia: Laputa, etc.

If *Gulliver's Travels* as a whole offers a compendium of different kinds of utopian writing, the third book is itself a compendium of what one might term *utopoi*. Much scholarly work has been done on the scientific or 'modern' satire, but that is only one element, although a very important one.[55] More precisely, the third voyage is an amalgam of ancient topics updated to the modern context that Swift is attacking. For example, while the Academy of Lagado is the obvious instance of a would-be scientific attempt to realise utopian projects, in the island of Glubbdubdrib Swift abandons state-of-the-art technology and reverts to old-fashioned necromancy. To sustain this shape-shifting narrative, he opts formally for the Lucianic type of marvellous voyage which in turn had satirised precedents such as the collection of travellers' tales in Diodorus Siculus. The title of Book III (last of the voyages to be written) also signals diversification. In the first two voyages, a single basic premiss – Johnson's big men and little men – controls the ramifications of the marvellous, but in the third voyage Swift uses a variety of locations and devices to represent a variety of utopian dreams. The one thing they have in common is the desire of human beings to liberate themselves from the limits of the possible, and the sensible.

In Swift's first choice of utopian vehicle in Book III, the flying island, political satire (which has also been subjected to expert decoding)[56] combines with the scientific. In terms of utopian fiction, this is yet another variant on the recurrent fantasy of flight; but Swift makes it collective, not individual, to represent an aerial élite, dangerously cut off politically and intellectually from the concerns of others – like the English from the Irish, or a certain type of specialist from the general public. These inhabitants of the flying island, the equivalent of an ivory tower, pride themselves on the mental attitude that is literalised in the function of the flappers: 'the Minds of these People are so taken up with intense Speculations, that they neither can speak, nor attend to the Discourses of others, without being rouzed by some external Taction upon the Organs of Speech and Hearing.'[57] Far from finding peace of mind in contemplation, however, they are terrified, like Johnson's astronomer in *Rasselas*, with the expectation of cosmic disaster and the annihilation of the solar system: 'they are so perpetually alarmed with the Apprehensions of these and the like impending Dangers, that they can neither sleep quietly in their Beds, nor have any Relish for the common Pleasures or Amusements of Life.'[58] That goes for the pleasures of the body as well, for the Laputans have the worst of both worlds. They are so wedded to abstractions that their efforts at applied technology go ludicrously wrong, resulting in uninhabitable houses and unwearable clothes. The presentation of food takes precedence over taste. Ordinary skills are totally beyond them ('I have not seen a more clumsy, awkward, and unhandy People' remarks Gulliver).[59] Significantly, it is the women who 'lament their Confinement to the Island, although', adds Gulliver, 'I think it the most delicious Spot of Ground in the World; and although they live here in the greatest Plenty and Magnificence and are allowed to do whatever they please . . .'[60] Like the occupants of the Happy Valley in *Rasselas*, they are discontented because their every wish is granted. The Laputan women express that discontent by sexual rebellion, which takes a typically Swiftian form in the tale of the 'great Court Lady' who escapes from wealth, status, loving husband and children to the world below, to cohabit in squalor with 'an old deformed Footman, who beats her every Day.'[61] None of Swift's utopias – unlike Lucian's or Rabelais' – equates sex with happiness. The unsatisfactory sex lives of the Laputans sour his anti-utopian satire still further.

If Swift had come across any version of Campanella's *City of the Sun*, he might be suspected of parodying certain features of that learned community. Certainly the Laputans share the same transcendental hobbies as their predecessors. Campanella's scientists had 'discovered the art of flying . . . and they are expecting to obtain an eye-glass with which to see the hidden stars, and a hearing instrument with which to listen to the harmony of the motions of the planets'.[62] The Laputans not only have their flying island, but they also go one better than these earlier utopians 'in observing the celestial Bodies . . . by the Assistance of Glasses' and cataloguing 'ten Thousand fixed Stars' of which only a third are known to European astronomers.[63] Moreover, when Gulliver is deafened by a three-hour musical performance, he is informed 'that the People of their Island had their

Ears adapted to hear the Musick of the Spheres, which always played at certain Periods'.[64] Curiously, even the sexual mésalliances between Laputan women, with their 'Abundance of Vivacity', and their complaisant husbands 'always so rapt in Speculation' and not noticing anything, are foreshadowed in the City of the Sun: there, intellectuals are mated with 'lively, vigorous and beautiful women' on the principle that the ideal alliance is that between brains and beauty. It only needs a simple satiric twist to turn these intellectuals into Laputans: 'on account of their strenuous speculative activity, they have weak animal spirits and they do not pass on their mental worth, because they are always thinking about something' (Campanella).[65] Of course, Swift's point in all this is the reverse of Campanella's. In the utopian City of the Sun, speculative learning isn't divorced from practical capacity, but on the contrary enhances all aspects of human life. In Laputa, the thinker is not just accident-prone himself – 'in manifest Danger of falling down every Precipice, and bouncing his Head against every Post'[66] – but a walking disaster area so far as others are concerned, creating a political and matrimonial wasteland. Finally, whereas Campanella's happy people honour the Sun as an image of God, Swift's 'scientific' Laputans inhabit a mechanistic and decaying universe where the Sun is the focus of dread and doom-laden futurology.

These apparent parallels between *The City of the Sun* and Swift's satire in the third voyage are probably pure coincidence. All that is necessary to explain them is the fact that Swift is mocking the ideal embodied in the 'pansophia' type of utopia. Whether or not Swift knew Campanella's work, he certainly knew Bacon's *New Atlantis*, and the section of Book III dealing with Lagado and its Academy has been directly and plausibly linked with the fictional House of Salomon as well as the historical Royal Society.[67] He successfully degrades the image of privilege and power created by Bacon (excremental yellow instead of peach-coloured velvet shoes). The aim is to strip the mystique from institutions investigating the secrets of nature, and to question not only their utility but their ideology.

Before Gulliver's guided tour of the grand Academy of Lagado itself, Lord Munodi tells him about the imitations it has spawned, the provincial academies which spread the 'Schemes of putting all Arts, Sciences, Languages, and Mechanicks upon a new Foot' emanating from Laputa:

there is not a Town of any Consequence in the Kingdom without such an Academy. In these Colleges, the Professors contrive new Rules and Methods of Agriculture and Building, and new Instruments and Tools for all Trades and Manufactures, whereby, as they undertake, one Man shall do the Work of Ten; a Palace may be built in a Week, of Materials so durable as to last for ever without repairing. All the Fruits of the Earth shall come to Maturity at whatever Season we think fit to chuse, and increase an Hundred Fold more than they do at present; with innumerable other happy Proposals. The only inconvenience is, that none of these Projects are yet brought to Perfection; and in the mean time, the whole Country lies miserably waste, the Houses in Ruins, and the People without Food or Cloaths.[68]

If the grand Academy caricatures Bacon's temple of science, this rather brings to mind Abraham Cowley's more mundane version of the Baconian dream. Cowley too envisages a centre of research and teaching devoted to the natural sciences, with an adulation of human achievement which cries out for Swiftian parody – as when he proposes 'Pictures and Statues of all the Inventors of any thing useful to Humane Life; as Printing, Guns, *America*, &.' However, Cowley disclaims utopian fantasising: 'we do not design this after the Model of *Solomon's* House in my Lord *Bacon* (which is a Project for Experiments that can never be Experimented) . . .'[69]

Swift doesn't seem to discriminate between science fiction and practical science in his satire, but he does contrast two kinds of ideal, corresponding in his view to Ancient and Modern. On the one hand, Lord Munodi's beautifully run and flourishing rural estate corresponds to the Augustan aspiration to the good life centred on country house and landscaped gardens (an aspiration which itself takes on utopian overtones in the novel); on the other hand, the Academy of Lagado is associated with everything that Swift detests about the Moderns.[70] Yet the distinction isn't altogether clear-cut. If Munoni's estate imitates one classical paradigm, the dreams derided by Swift also have classical roots, in fiction at least. Although specific details of his satire are prompted by experiments recorded in *The Philosophical Transactions of the Royal Society*,[71] the utopian imagination that fantasises about fruit available in all seasons, perpetual sunshine, miracle cures, labour-saving natural products, is far from a purely modern phenomenon. In a sense, the Royal Society was trying to turn the wildest dreams of antiquity into the facts of Augustan England. Healing by the application of animal blood features in the utopia of Iambulus; in Virgil's Golden Age, lambs grow scarlet wool; in Lucian's Isle of the Blest, people wear purple spider-silk; eternal spring is commonplace.[72] The tradition continues up till Swift's own time. For instance, the 'Device of plowing the Ground with Hogs' attributed to one of Swift's projectors has an earlier parallel in de Foigny. In the 1693 translation of *A New Discovery of Terra Incognita Australis*, there is a species of animals called Hums (yes, really) which are rather like swine and very good at working the earth: with a twist that would have pleased Swift, the Australians find the Hums more trouble than they are worth 'because of the nastiness they fill all places with, and because they are useful but seven or eight days in a year'.[73] The desire to mould the natural world closer to human convenience is timeless, even if it is only in modern times that the scientific means to do so have become more feasible. Swift targets means and ends equally, so straddling the boundary between ancient and modern world. Instead of creating a no-place full of marvellous mutated flora and fauna, as some utopists do, he creates a grotesque not-quite-reality, where human beings attempt to use scientific methods to interfere physically with nature. Unlike the reverend fathers of Salomon's House, they fail ignominiously; it seems highly probable that Swift is accusing Bacon of the intellectual hubris that underlies both success and failure.[74]

Nor do the projectors meddle only in the physical sphere of cucumbers and excrement. The old humanist domains – rhetoric, the arts, 'the whole Nature and System of Government'[75] – are ripe for invasion by the new brutalism. With the invention of a kind of primitive computer, one professor prides himself on a truly utopian breakthrough to the ultimate academic shortcut: substituting a little manual effort (not even artificial intelligence) for the mental application required in all disciplines: 'every one knew how laborious the usual Method is of attaining to Arts and Sciences; whereas by his Contrivance, the most ignorant Person at a reasonable Charge, and with a little bodily Labour, may write Books in Philosophy, Poetry, Politicks, Law, Mathematicks and Theology, without the least Assistance from Genius or Study.'[76] The same reductive approach manifests itself in the school of languages, where Swift's own pet scheme for improving language is turned on its head. It's much simpler to abolish language altogether and substitute things for words. Again, this solution parodies the old utopian dream of a universal language combined with the newer scientific tendency to mechanise language by some means.[77] In an earlier utopian fiction, Cyrano de Bergerac offers variations on both. During his voyage to the Sun, the narrator discovers the secret of the original language spoken by Adam and intelligible to every creature in the universe. In the moon world, he comes across a device which sounds more like the kind of invention popular in Lagado, except that it works (in fact it anticipates twentieth-century technology): this is the book substitute which on being wound up produces speech/music and can be carried in the pocket or belt, or attached 'in the form of ear pendants'. Cyrano praises this wonderful aid to learning, which explains why lunar youth are more educationally advanced than the ancients of our world.[78] However, in the Lagadian school of humanities, the proposed shortcuts unfortunately bypass the brain as well, making not only words but meaning redundant. Interestingly, it is the political scientists of Lagado who alone subscribe to a kind of moral utopianism comparable to the original institutions of Lilliput and those of Brobdingnag – 'wild impossible Chimaeras' – and Gulliver thinks they're mad. Nevertheless, as he ironically observes, 'all of them were not so visionary'.[79]

When Gulliver leaves Lagado, he exchanges the travesty of a 'scientific' utopia for one that lapses into ancient superstition and offers him a form of other-worldly journey that is as old as Homer. His diversion to the island of Glubbdubdrib – the name 'signifies the Island of *Sorcerers* or *Magicians*' – brings him into direct communication with the supernatural, something that Bacon was careful to exclude from New Atlantis.[80] For the purposes of satire, Swift adopts Lucian's tactic of integrating illustrious classical ghosts into a less than reverent context. It's impossible to feel awe or fear at an island where the first function of the summoned spirits is to solve the servant problem: 'the Governor and his Family are served and attended by Domesticks of a Kind somewhat unusual . . .'[81]

Having become acclimatised in this way 'to the Sight of Spirits', Gulliver wants to satisfy his curiosity by calling up and interrogating an array of ancient notables, as Lucian had done before him.[82] Strikingly, Swift includes among those heroes of European civilisation one Renaissance humanist, the founder of post-classical utopianism, Thomas More himself: 'I had the Honour to have much Conversation with *Brutus*; and was told that his Ancestor *Junius*, Socrates, *Epaminondas*, *Cato* the Younger, Sir *Thomas More* and himself, were perpetually together: A *Sextumvirate* to which all the Ages of the

World cannot add a Seventh.'[83] The extended contrast between the ancient world and the modern operates, not surprisingly, almost entirely in favour of the former, reinforcing a sense that Swift's preferred form of utopianism is the nostalgic. With the celebrated comparison of the Roman Senate and a modern parliament – 'the first seemed to be an Assembly of Heroes and Demy-Gods; the other a Knot of Pedlars, Pick-pockets, Highwaymen and Bullies' – Gulliver as commentator seems scarcely distinguishable from his creator. However, Swift does make one joke that casts doubt on Gulliver's taste for the austerities of the best-known ancient utopian state, Sparta – 'A *Helot* of *Agesilaus* made us a Dish of *Spartan* Broth, but I was not able to get down a second *Spoonful*.'[84] In general, this sequence supports both the theory of human degeneracy and the unreliability of historical interpretation. Spirits, like the Houyhnhnms, can only tell the truth.

After his contact with one kind of immortality in Glubbdubdrib, Gulliver encounters another in Luggnagg, that of the Struldbruggs who are condemned to eternal life on Earth. Initially, Gulliver the utopian dreamer is caught out by failing to recognise the snag in this particular dream of personal immortality: that it carries no guarantee of 'a Perpetuity of Youth, Health, and Vigour' but the reverse.[85] He makes a fool of himself by elaborating a scenario based on the apparent 'good Fortune' of being born a Struldbrugg. He imagines not only the accumulation of riches, learning and power, but also the quasi-utopian idea of the Struldbruggs as a race of supermen, a ruling élite who, however benevolent their intentions, come to regard mortals as a separate inferior species, no more emotionally significant than seasonal flowers.[86] The reformist project of trying to prevent the degeneracy of this species by superior knowledge, instruction, warning, and example, coexists with an inevitable disregard of ephemeral individuals. In fact, Gulliver attempts to combine a vision of human progress, masterminded by the Struldbruggs, with a cyclic theory of history. His system isn't logically consistent, although (or because) he has had a great deal of practice in such imaginings:

> . . . it was easy to be eloquent on so copious and delightful a Subject, especially to me who have been often apt to amuse myself with Visions of what I should do if I were a King, a General, or a great Lord: And upon this very Case I had frequently run over the whole System how I should employ myself, and pass the Time if I were sure to live for ever.[87]

In point of fact, few utopian writers entertain this specific fantasy. Apart from specialised myths like the Islands of the Blest or lands of immortal youth, their ideal states are intended to accommodate and alleviate the realities of old age and death. Immortality is for the other side of the grave. The horror of 'a perpetual Life under all the usual Disadvantages which old Age brings along with it' intensifies the insight attributed to another utopian legislator, Solon, 'Call no man happy until he dies' or the myth of the Sybil who answers the children's question 'What do you want?' with 'I want to die.'[88] The Struldbruggs are Swift's version of that myth. And what gives the myth its power is that human beings do *not* want to die. As Gulliver's interpreter remarks, in countries other than his own 'he observed long Life to be the universal Desire and Wish of Mankind.'

Swift is writing satire, and so subverts the usual utopian assumptions about old age and death. In almost all ideal states, old age brings honour, authority, universal respect: longevity is very much a utopian ideal, provided that good health – another utopian priority – accompanies it. Significantly, in utopias ancient and modern, where longevity and good health are taken as the norm, it is common to find the practice of euthanasia as well: Iambulus, More and de Foigny all describe methods of easing the passage from this world to the next when the appropriate time comes.[89] Of course, for Swift's Struldbruggs there is no such option and they live on in the worst of all possible worlds.

That world ironically redefines and subverts Gulliver's vision. Instead of accumulating the wisdom of centuries, as Gulliver had fondly imagined, the failing memory of senility deprives them of all the pleasures of the mind, including reading. They are indeed set apart from the rest of humanity, not because they are superior, but because their company is intolerable. Far from having to harden themselves against loving the passing generations, they become 'uncapable of Friendship, and dead to all natural Affection'.[90] Gulliver had smugly asserted that as a Struldbrugg he 'would never marry after Threescore, but live in an hospitable Manner, yet still on the saving Side'. The state doesn't give the Struldbruggs a choice in the matter, dissolving any inter-marriages when the younger reaches 80, on humanitarian grounds ('those who are condemned without any Fault of their own to a perpetual Continuance in the World, should not have their Misery doubled by the Load of a Wife').[91] However, the state is perfectly prepared to increase their misery by simultaneously regarding them as legally dead and stripping them of all assets except the barest subsistence – so much for Gulliver's dream of riches. Yet Gulliver ends by acquiescing in these draconian measures, because he recognises their political justification. A gerontocracy is one thing; an immortal gerontocracy is quite another. It is scarcely to be wondered at that the spectre of Grey Power haunts the Luggnaggians.

There is ample evidence that Swift himself was haunted by the spectre of old age he conjures up in Book III. Of all his anti-utopian satires, this is also one that cuts close to the bone for a future age which has realised the utopian dream of increased longevity, but fails to confront some of the associated implications. Gulliver reports, 'They were the most mortifying Sight I ever beheld; and the Women more horrible than the Men.'[92] But this is not after all the worst that Swift can do by way of mortifying sights. Ahead of Gulliver and the reader is that *tour de force* of utopian fiction, the fourth voyage, which the Struldbrugg episode in some ways adumbrates.

The simple utopia: 'the Country of Horses'

To use the word 'simple' in the context of the fourth voyage might be seen as provocative. No other book of *Gulliver's Travels* has caused such difficulty to readers, or such acrimony among critics. Yet, considered as a utopia,[93] Book IV might be called simple in at least two senses. First (as with big men and little men) the organising principle of a role-reversal between species is brilliantly simple. Second, the society of Houyhnhnms is closer than any other of Swift's imaginary societies to the classical simple-life utopia. However, if Book IV remodels the archetypal utopian state, given form by Plato in antiquity and More in the Renaissance, it also challenges the very basis of that fictional state. Not content with questioning the nature of man as a political animal, Swift questions the definition of man as a rational animal, seeking, in his own well-known words 'to show it should be only *rationis capax*', capable of reason.[94] Throughout the first three voyages Gulliver and the reader are driven to revalue all sorts of human activities and attitudes: now, confronted with a country in which the horse is the rational species and the Yahoo the irrational, we are forced to revise the most basic assumption of all – the answer to the question, what makes us human?

Book IV registers a profound mental disorientation, and the

utopian method is the paramount one that Swift uses. He reworks certain techniques still more exhaustively than he did in the earlier books: the extended inset dialogue, the unreliable narrator, even, as it were, the final debriefing. It doesn't matter that the modern reader is not likely to be versed in the kind of textbook definitions of man that Swift learnt when studying logic at Trinity College Dublin,[95] nor that the horse isn't an indispensable adjunct to daily life as it was in earlier periods. The distinction between Yahoo, Houyhnhnm, and, crucially, Gulliver, structures the narrative in such a way as to force contrast and interrogation on us, as the most demanding utopian fiction always does. To estimate how deeply Book IV draws on the tradition, it is easier to divide this complicated material into different but related categories: first, the basic necessities that divide species and are the building blocks of any utopia (food, clothes – if any – and so on); second, the politics of utopia, which in this case might be termed the politics of species; and third, the attitudes governing the organisation of life from birth to death.

To begin with the basics: by making his master-race horses, Swift immediately takes advantage of certain physical characteristics that fit the primitivist ideal. He might have chosen a republic of dogs (there is a precedent in Segrais' *L'Isle Imaginaire* and Socrates makes analogies between Guardians and watch-dogs in the *Republic*); or birds, as in one of Cyrano's countries of the sun.[96] But the choice of horses, even if originally prompted by a logic textbook, has certain practical advantages as well. Since diet counts for a great deal in utopia, it's important that horses are not carnivores, but that they possess formidable dignity and power not usually associated with herbivores. Early in Book IV Houyhnhnms and Yahoos are sharply distinguished by their eating habits. The Yahoos, who are omnivorous, rip apart rotting carrion as well as feeding on roots. Later in the narrative the Houyhnhnm goes into more detail about their 'undistinguishing Appetite' and their uncouth behaviour – their junk diet, their propensity to fight over food, and their preference for food that is stolen, even when it is inferior to what is provided (a curious distorted echo of Spartan training).[97] The Houyhnhnms, on the other hand, don't feed like horses in the natural state though their staple diet is similar to that given to horses. Instead they behave like rational utopians. They milk cows (how?) and boil oats; when they entertain, everything is done in orderly fashion:

They dined in the best Room . . . . Their Mangers were placed
circular in the Middle of the Room, and divided into several
Partitions, round which they sat on their Haunches upon Bosses
of Straw. In the Middle was a large Rack with Angles answering
to every Partition of the Manger. So that each Horse and Mare
eat their own Hay, and their own Mash of Oats and Milk, with
much Decency and Regularity. The Behaviour of the young Colt
and Fole appeared very modest; and that of the Master and
Mistress extremely chearful and complaisant to their Guest.[98]

Although this may look like an illustration for a child's story, it
represents the characteristic image of the shared feast, with the
younger generation knowing its place, which signifies ideal social
relationships from ancient Sparta to More's Utopia. Admittedly it is
more of a household group than a fully communal one, but the
principle is the same, and contrasts strongly with the Yahoos who
'instead of eating peaceably, fall together by the Ears'.[99]

The Yahoos' diet explains some of their most rebarbative traits. For
instance, their excremental feats – they relieve the effects of over-
eating with a root purgative – become less astonishing. Conversely, in
utopias where the diet is pure instead of gross, more than one narrator
notes the hygienic result. The Australian infant, according to de
Foigny's Jacques Sadeur, is nourished entirely on mother's milk so that
'the Excrements it voids are in so small a quantity, that it may almost
be said, it makes none' – an attractive and convenient phenomenon.
Similarly, Cyrano's moon people, who live entirely on vapours,
produce 'hardly any excrement, which is the origin of almost all
diseases'.[100] That, of course, is the clue. The link between diet and
disease, so generally accepted and so easily moralised, is a
commonplace of utopian writing from Plato onwards.[101] When waste
products are added into the equation, it lends itself to satire like
Swift's. Utopian populations such as de Foigny's Australians also avoid
meat on high moral grounds: 'it were better for a Man not to be at all,
than to debase his noble nature, so far as to adulterate it with the
mixture of that of a Beast, by making it his Food.' Berington's
Mezzoranians are another race who consider meat as 'too gross a Food'
and prefer to eat a great deal of fish instead.[102]

When Gulliver is put to a dietary test in his new cultural
environment, it signals clearly his in-between status. The sorrel nag
offers Yahoo food – a root and a piece of stinking ass's meat – which
he rejects: 'he afterwards shewed me a Wisp of Hay, and a Fetlock full

of Oats; but I shook my Head, to signify, that neither of these were Food for me.' Nevertheless, it is the horse-diet that Gulliver manages to modify to suit his needs, and he comments 'it was at first a very insipid Diet, although common enough in many Parts of *Europe*' – Johnson's definition of oats as food for men in Scotland, horses in England, comes to mind – 'but grew tolerable by Time . . . And I cannot but observe, that I never had one Hour's Sickness, while I staid in this Island.' Yet he falls short of complete assimilation of the vegetarian (and Houyhnhnm) ideal, varying his meals with the occasional fowl or rabbit.[103]

As Gulliver describes more of the culture of the Houyhnhnms, the similarities to the simple-life utopia grow stronger. Although they use tools, have a very basic form of transport, and practise agriculture, they are still in the stone age technologically. Lacking iron, they are less advanced than Lycurgus' Sparta. What Gulliver has to offer – the trinkets he carries with him – are useless and patronising. Since the Houyhnhnms neither adorn themselves nor wear clothes, the needle that he lends the mare is singularly and comically inappropriate. However, of course, the matter of clothes is itself a major utopian topic that Swift exploits in its most fundamental form in Book IV.

How essential are clothes to civilisation? Is nakedness more natural, more innocent – more utopian? The questions that begin with the Fall from Eden receive fresh impetus with the encounters between 'civilised' and 'primitive' people that inspire so much utopian fiction and accustom Europeans to the idea of cultures where nakedness, or near-nakedness, is the norm. Earlier travellers put on record their naive amazement that this state of affairs doesn't result in priapism, though they rarely put it so bluntly, preferring to stress the extraordinary modesty of these children of nature in fact or fiction.[104] Swift produces a new variation on the confrontation of the naked and the clothed, by diversifying it: Gulliver is faced with two species to whom nakedness is natural, the Houyhnhnms and the Yahoos, and again he is the odd man out. So far as sex is concerned, the Houyhnhnms pose no problem to him (the Yahoos are a different story – of which more later) since they have the bodies of horses. However, his dress poses a considerable problem to them ('they were under great perplexity about my Shoes and Stockings . . .').[105] When his secret comes out, Gulliver tries to explain the custom of wearing clothes in terms reminiscent of Montaigne and indeed Crusoe. But he slips inadvertently into a revealing euphemism when he asks to be excused from exposing 'those Parts that Nature taught us to conceal'. The Houyhnhnm finds this most peculiar 'for he could not understand why Nature should teach us to conceal what Nature had given . . . neither himself nor Family were ashamed of any Parts of their Bodies'.[106] That this perfectly rational position is compatible with human sexual modesty seems to be demonstrated by de Foigny's hermaphrodite Australians, who 'are so accustomed to go naked, that they think they cannot speak of covering themselves without being declared Enemies to Nature, and deprived of Reason'.[107]

The Yahoos, however, are naked and shameless in a different sense. It is to preserve his fragile sense of distinction from them that Gulliver clings so tenaciously to his garments. Seen through his eyes, the first impact of their naked bodies is one of literally horrid fascination. He notes their distribution of body hair, dwelling particularly on 'those Parts that Nature taught us to conceal'. Both Houyhnhnms and Yahoos are 'natural', but Gulliver's reactions discriminate totally between them – at first. The narrative forces him into admitting the anatomical likeness between the Yahoo body and his own; and with that recognition he and the reader have to take full account of judgments based on what I have called the politics of species.

In the French rationalist utopias of the seventeenth century, the rethinking of classification by species plays an important part.[108] The question of what it means to be human, and how we earn that status relative to other species, is one that Swift has in common with these earlier writers. And this in turn links up with the debate over what is, or isn't, 'natural' or 'rational' behaviour. Perhaps the closest analogue to Swift's 'Country of Horses' in this respect is the bird utopia of Cyrano de Bergerac already mentioned. Cyrano's birds, like Swift's Houyhnhnms, find it almost if not altogether impossible to accept the human claim to rationality. What especially arouses their indignation is the way this upstart species arrogates the right to dominate and destroy other species, and indeed their own. If only because of his cruelty and intolerance, man does not deserve his privileged position; and one effective way of making that clear is to thrust him, in imagination at least, into the bestial state he despises, to strip him of power and status. So, the moon people decide to classify Cyrano as a bald parrot, and among the birds he's advised to pretend to be an ape (he accepts the theory, but fails the practical).[109] Likewise the Houyhnhnms end by treating Gulliver as a rather less hairy Yahoo. It should be said, however, that utopian writers can and do take the opposite line, using the ideal state to assert the innate superiority of humanity to animals. Even then it is humanity as it ought to be, rather than as it is, a point exemplified by de Foigny's Australians. Their spokesman, criticising all of the species who aren't hermaphroditic Australians, sounds rather like Gulliver's Houyhnhnm, though he's arguing from the assumption that hermaphrodites not horses are 'the Perfection of Nature': 'thou canst never reconcile the use of Reason with the exclusion of both Sexes in one person'.[110]

What these fictional examples draw attention to is that we're all guilty of species snobbery (and inverted snobbery). In Gulliver's fourth voyage, Swift gleefully exposes our bias both in favour of *and* against our own humanity. Any attempt at so-called political correctness founders on the fact that we, and Gulliver, cannot even verify our judgments, let alone rectify them. If the reader intellectually accepts the premiss that the Houyhnhnms are the rational species, the Yahoos an irrational species, and that anyway both are hypothetical, the former still continue to look and in some respects behave like horses, and the latter like humans. The fiction is further complicated by the existence of other familiar species in the same frame of reference: the Yahoos aren't the only animals around, only the most difficult to ignore. Indeed the casual allusions block in the picture of a working rural economy, an Animal Farm of sorts. The Houyhnhnms keep cows, as previously noticed; they also keep cats (presumably for rodent control, with all that grain in store); and they contemplate regretfully the failure 'to cultivate the breed of *Asses*' as a cleaner and more tractable substitute for Yahoos.[111] The latter detail comes up in the course of the debate about exterminating the Yahoos as a species, which – like Gulliver's use of their skins for shoe-leather – creates uneasiness even in readers determined to keep their non-human status firmly in mind. When it comes to the relation between Houyhnhnms and Yahoos, this is not a utopia with a ruling class and an underclass, citizens and non-citizens, freemen and slaves. The Yahoos are outside the political system. If they have any rights – and it is not clear that they have – the analogy would be with animal rights, not human.

That said, there *are* two separate political structures within this framework, that of the Houyhnhnms and that imputed to the Yahoos. The latter is a more savagely anti-utopian satire on British political life than anything in Lilliput or Laputa. The Yahoo equivalent has its leader and sycophant, its power struggles and sexual favours, dismissals and public disgrace of an all too literal kind. Its internal relations are self-interested, competitive, and in continual conflicts over territory, sex, possessions, or for no 'visible Cause'.[112] As an attack on human pride, this delivers a double blow: first it strips human behaviour of the pretence of high-mindedness or rationality, reducing it to the basest instincts; then it restores the claim to reason as the ultimate perversion. The Houyhnhnm reacts in just this way to Gulliver's account of warfare in his own culture, saying that 'although he hated the *Yahoos* of this Country, yet he no more blamed them for their odious Qualities, than he did a *Gnnayh* (a Bird of Prey) for its Cruelty, or a sharp Stone for cutting his Hoof. But, when a Creature pretending to Reason, could be capable of such Enormities, he dreaded lest the Corruption of that Faculty might be worse than Brutality itself.'[113] Gulliver's defence of his species crumbles altogether under the weight of adverse evidence. The only vindication he can even think of, that human beings are no dirtier than pigs (an animal unfortunately unknown to the Houyhnhnms), again falls back on the comparison of species. In fact, he improves on the Houyhnhnm's hint: 'I expected every Moment, that my Master would accuse the *Yahoos* of those unnatural Appetites in both Sexes, so common among us. But Nature it seems hath not been so expert a Schoolmistress; and these politer Pleasures are entirely the Productions of Art and Reason, on our Side of the Globe.'[114] The Yahoos at their worst have a kind of innocence which goes with their animal lack of sophistication and inhibition. It is only when their behaviour is decoded and attributed to human motives by a far from impartial observer that it becomes degraded as well as irrational. From a Yahoo viewpoint – which of course we never have – the degradation might arise from being thought to ape the social and political system of eighteenth-century Britain.

The Houyhnhnms, in contrast, have developed a social and political structure on a classical model. Again the keynote is simplicity. Their economy is entirely functional, and isn't based on money: not only do they have no concept of luxury, but like Plato's Guardians or More's Utopians they appear to have all material things in common. Gulliver's Houyhnhnm master is baffled by the division between rich and poor, 'for he went upon a Supposition that all Animals had a Title to their Share in the Productions of the Earth' – a creed which might align him with seventeenth-century radicals like Winstanley, were it not for the oddly ambiguous rider – 'and especially those who presided over the rest'.[115] A rigid class system does exist among the Houyhnhnms, based on colour and fixed from birth:

> He made me observe, that among the *Houyhnhnms*, the *White*, the *Sorrell* and the *Iron-grey*, were not so exactly shaped as the *Bay*, the *Dapple-grey*, and the *Black*; nor born with equal Talents of Mind, or a Capacity to improve them; and therefore continued always in the Condition of Servants, without ever aspiring to match out of their own Race, which in that Country would be reckoned monstrous and unnatural.[116]

This clearly recalls Plato's *Republic* with its graded gold, silver, iron and brass for the different classes, though it is more inflexible even than Plato and certainly more so than More. However, Swift seems to borrow from both Plato and More for aspects of Houyhnhnm ideology. Since 'Friendship and *Benevolence* are the two principal Virtues among the *Houyhnhnms*; and these not confined to particular Objects, but universal to the whole Race', the ethos of sharing spreads beyond the ruling class and isn't confined to the equivalent of Plato's Guardians. As in More's Utopia, hospitality is universal and a Houyhnhnm is at home everywhere.[117]

One important consequence of a rational utopia is that it minimises the need for institutions, especially the much loathed institution of the legal profession. As the Houyhnhnm puts it, reflecting on human society's over-endowment in this respect, 'Institutions of *Government* and *Law* were plainly owing to . . . gross Defects in *Reason*, and by consequence, in *Virtue*; because *Reason* alone is sufficient to govern a *Rational* Creature'.[118] Never- theless, in spite of the expectation that rational creatures will agree, the Houyhnhnms do have one political institution which acts as a forum for discussion. This is 'a Representative Council of the whole Nation' – the Houyhnhnm state is a classical republic – which meets for 'about five or six Days' every four years (minimalist government indeed).[119] Swift is unlike the classical republican theorist James Harrington in showing very little interest in the constitution of this body and giving practically no information about how it is set up. 'Representative' might signify either an oligarchy or democracy, more likely the former. Outside utopia, a representative system would presumably involve some form of election or vote, but in an entirely rational utopia which doesn't comprehend the meaning of the word 'opinion' would that be necessary? All that we're told is that

Houyhnhnm politics, like Parliament, is based on locality ('my Master
went as the Representative of our District').[120]

The ensuing debate on the Yahoos shows that even if rational
creatures concur on ends, they may disagree over means. Further,
when Gulliver's own case is discussed, it becomes plain that in this
utopia, like most others, the interest of the state will always override
the interest of the individual. Here, in fact, it is worse than that, for
reason is elevated to a totalitarian concept against which there is no
appeal. A dissenter is trapped in a Catch-22; dissent is itself a proof of
unreason. Exhortation is therefore more powerful than compulsion:

> I should here observe to the Reader, that a Decree of the general
> Assembly in this Country, is expressed by the Word *Hnhloayn*,
> which signifies an *Exhortation* . . . For they have no Conception
> how a rational Creature can be *compelled*, but only advised, or
> *exhorted*; because no Person can disobey Reason, without giving
> up his Claim to be a rational Creature.[121]

But how rational is the political decision to expel Gulliver? (Strictly
speaking, if the majority view is purely rational, then Gulliver's master
is behaving irrationally in his own attitude to Gulliver.) Since the
Houyhnhnms practise discrimination even amongst themselves, they
are unlikely to display tolerance to a being who has been designated
as a Yahoo, however 'wonderful'. Yet Gulliver poses no very evident
threat to them or their culture, although they are afraid that he may
revert to type and prove especially dangerous because of his tincture
of reason. He is only too willing to turn traitor to his humanity, which
he learns to see through Houyhnhnm eyes. 'At first, indeed,' he
admits, 'I did not feel that natural Awe which the *Yahoos* and all
other Animals bear towards them: but it grew upon me by Degrees . . .
and was mingled with a respectful Love and Gratitude, that they
would condescend to distinguish me from the rest of my Species.'[122]
However, the upperclass Houyhnhnms aren't very good at respecting
or loving individuals regardless of species. They believe cultural
assimilation to be irrational and unnatural. Gulliver's master summarises the case against him:

> . . . the Representatives had taken Offence at his keeping a
> *Yahoo* (meaning my self) in his Family more like a *Houyhnhnm*
> than a Brute Animal. That, he was known frequently to converse
> with me, as if he could receive some Advantage or Pleasure in

my Company: That, such a Practice was not agreeable to Reason or Nature, nor a thing ever heard of before among them.[123]

Arguably, emotion as much as logic is at work here. It is characteristic of the utopian mentality to fear change and nonconformity, and the argument that the situation is unprecedented carries as much weight as the appeal to reason and nature. Unlike More's Utopians, who *are* receptive to new ideas while maintaining their belief in their own way of doing things, the Houyhnhnms correspond to the closed, or arrested, society that Karl Popper accuses Plato of creating.[124] Much of what Gulliver tells the reader about their attitudes and society reinforces this deduction. Their politics of species is a natural extension of their social organisation, which starts like Plato's from the beginning of life, and which can now be looked at in more detail.

For example, the prohibition against the inter-marriage of horses of different colours is consistent with the regulation of sex and reproduction often found in utopias. Although the Houyhnhnms don't have mares and foals in common as Plato's Guardians have wives and children in common, the intention of their arranged marriages and impartial parenting is exactly the same: to eliminate individual attachments. A rational utopia regards with deep suspicion any move to privatise emotions, preferring to nationalise, and so neutralise, them in the public interest. 'They have no Fondness for their Colts or Foles . . .' notes Gulliver: 'I observed my Master to shew the same Affection to his Neighbour's Issue that he had for his own. They will have it that *Nature* teaches them to love the whole Species, and it is *Reason* only that maketh a Distinction of Persons, where there is a superior Degree of Virtue.'[125] Anything so contrary to human experience can only belong in a utopia. And utopian theorists suggest various means to bring it about, ranging from total control (the eugenic approach) to total freedom (the romantic approach). Swift combines the methods of Plato and More, by making faithful marriage compatible with genetic engineering – but the only way this can work is by making the choice of partners entirely dependent on the 'Parents and Friends' of the couple, and considering their compatibility on purely reproductive grounds.[126] Predictably, sex is for procreation only, to replace the population. All marriages are happy and chaste. Behind all this is the pressure of much utopian thinking on the topic: given the individual and anarchic nature of the sexual impulse, the question of how to control it challenges most writers of utopian fiction. Some, like Aldous Huxley in the twentieth century, hypothesise scientific or psychoanalytic methods of coping with sex and reproduction.[127] Swift takes to an ironic and logical conclusion Socrates' original equation of human and animal breeding (Plato does mention horses in this connection).[128] However, by applying it to rational horses, he makes the reader confront culturally conditioned ideas about the association of sex with animal instinct and with the irrational. Is it possible to be completely rational about sex? Or is it literally inhuman? Creators of rationalist utopias can't agree, but come up with some ingenious answers. To return for a moment to de Foigny's hermaphrodite Australians as a case in point: in spite of what might be considered a biological advantage, they suppress anything connected with sexuality as far as possible, maintaining a conspiracy of silence about how they actually do it, much to the narrator's frustration. They are much offended by their visitor's persistent curiosity and occasional levity on the topic (and, even worse, by his own propensity to unseemly arousal – 'the extraordinary Caresses of the Brethren, caused some unruly motions in me, which some of them perceiving, were . . . very much scandaliz'd at it . . . Wherefore I soon became odious to them all').[129]

Not being a horse, Gulliver doesn't fall foul of the Houyhnhnms in this way, but he has his own problems with the Yahoos. Naturally, as the opposite of the Houyhnhnms, their sexual and reproductive processes are a rationalist utopian's nightmare. That is, they are irrepressibly natural and abundantly fertile, inconveniently so from the viewpoint of the Houyhnhnms, who keep their own numbers under such careful population control. When the Yahoos 'in a short time grew so numerous as to over-run and infest the whole Nation',[130] the Houyhnhnms proceed to cull them; but it is Gulliver (himself a father, and a husband who left behind a pregnant wife) who inadvertently puts into their heads the notion of castrating the younger males, a policy not just of fertility control, but ultimate extermination. Yet Gulliver is not as immune as he would like to believe from the powerful instincts represented by the Yahoos. It isn't accidental that whereas his relationships with Houyhnhnms belong to the masculine world, the life of instinct reaches out to him through a child and a female. Perhaps with some suppressed memory of his own children, he tries on one occasion to quieten 'by all marks of Tenderness' a Yahoo three-year-old whom he has caught. Refusing to be pacified, it escapes, but not before 'it voided its filthy Excrements of a yellow liquid Substance, all over my Cloaths'.[131] Gulliver, of course, uses this incident to justify further his revulsion from the Yahoos, but it has another, and recognisably human, side.

The next encounter he relates seems comic even to the Houyhnhnm household. The young female Yahoo who leaps on Gulliver as he bathes naked doesn't just embarrass but also terrifies him: 'she embraced me after a most fulsome Manner; I roared as loud as I could, and the Nag came galloping towards me, whereupon she quitted her Grasp, with the utmost Reluctancy, and leaped upon the opposite Bank, where she stood gazing and howling all the time I was putting on my Cloaths.'[132] This incident finally removes Gulliver's figleaf of civilisation and, as he confesses, proves him 'a real Yahoo'. In addition, it reveals that his objectivity as utopian traveller is an illusion. When an individual of the species he has been observing takes the initiative, a hint of unconscious susceptibility comes to light. She isn't red-haired (so confuting his generalisation about red hair and libido) 'and her Countenance did not make an Appearance altogether so hideous as the rest of the Kind; for, I think, she could not be above Eleven Years old'.

If the Yahoo young are primitive little brutes, recalling the image of the child as unruly animal in Plato's *Laws*,[133] the Houyhnhnm young are educated in a manner entirely in keeping with the parental code of reason not fondness. Since reason, for the Houyhnhnms, is a matter of ascertainable truth, they see no point in useless learning, 'wherein' says Gulliver of his master 'he agreed entirely with the Sentiments of *Socrates*, as *Plato* delivers them; which I mention as the highest Honour I can do that Prince of Philosophers.'[134] Tongue-in-cheek as it may be, the allusion fits the priorities of the Houyhnhnm educational system:

> Temperance, *Industry*, *Exercise* and *Cleanliness*, are the Lessons equally enjoyed to the young ones of both Sexes: And my Master thought it monstrous in us to give the Females a different Kind of Education from the Males, except in some Articles of Domestick Management; whereby, as he truly observed, one Half of our Natives were good for nothing but bringing Children into the World: And to trust the Care of their Children to such useless Animals, he said was yet a greater Instance of Brutality.[135]

The reader has heard Swift pontificating on this subject before, in Book I. The inclusion of both sexes is part of the standard utopian manifesto from *The Republic* onwards (and still utopian in the

eighteenth century), often with the proviso, as here, that domestic
and maternal functions are not neglected, but improved. However,
the Houyhnhnms' emphasis on body rather than mind is closer to the
Spartans than the Athenians, with the obvious difference that the
aim is not military proficiency as it was in ancient Sparta.[136]

Indeed the strongest anti-war satire – stronger even than in
peaceable Brobdingnag – is found in Book IV. Although war is a
recurring phenomenon in the imaginary history of utopia, as it is in
the real world, the Houyhnhnms fall into that rare category of a
people virtually without a history.[137] However, the anti-war propaganda has plenty of scope in Gulliver's account of the irrational causes
that ignite European wars, and the horrific carnage that weapons of
war inflict. It is not until after he returns home that Gulliver reflects
that the Houyhnhnms do have the potential for heroic resistance that
characterises   almost   all   ancient   and   Renaissance   ideal
commonwealths: 'The Houyhnhnms, indeed, appear not to be so well
prepared for War, a Science to which they are perfect Strangers, and
especially against missive Weapons. However, . . . Their Prudence,
Unanimity, Unacquaintedness with Fear, and their Love of their
Country would amply supply all Defects in the military Art.' In this
respect, as in others, the Houyhnhnms represent a hard rather than a
soft utopian ideal.[138]

The same hardness has seemed particularly evident to readers in
the description of the Houyhnhnms' attitude to death:

> If they can avoid Casualties, they die only of old Age, and are
> buried in the obscurest Places that can be found, their Friends
> and Relations expressing neither Joy nor Grief at their Departure;
> nor does the dying Person discover the least Regret that he is
> leaving the World, any more than if he were upon returning
> home from a visit to one of his Neighbours. . . .

Gulliver illustrates this with the story of the mare whose husband has
just died, but who keeps her engagement and behaves 'as chearfully as
the rest' (though 'she died about Three Months after').[139] Whatever
his personal feelings about death, here too Swift is very much in the
utopian tradition of 'the good death'. In Plato's Republic, men do not
mourn excessively for the loss of a friend, and in Lycurgus' Sparta the
actual period of mourning is restricted. However, although stoicism in
the bereaved is admired, some utopian writers, including More, go
beyond stoicism to positive rejoicing at the passage of a soul into

eternity.[140] Swift cannot go so far and is perhaps too honest to do so. Belief in an afterlife isn't, of course, confined to Christian utopias, but Swift's avoidance of any religious dimension in Book IV restricts him to the purely rational responses: dignified acceptance, consideration for others, refusal on the part of either the departing or the bereft to rage against the inevitable . . . it can seem noble rather than unfeeling. Moreover, the Houyhnhnm term for 'die' is more resonant and more emotive than might be expected: 'the Word', says Gulliver, 'is strongly expressive in their Language, but not easily rendered into English; it signifies, *to retire to his first Mother*'.[141] For a race distinguished, again like the Spartans, for their laconic and practical language, this recourse to deep metaphor is particularly eloquent.

In fact it is language – not politics or sex or education or philosophy – that is at the heart of Swift's utopian enterprise. A final retrospect from Book IV brings out the degree to which each imaginary society has language as the measure of its value and literature (or its lack) as the measure of its culture.[142] By their discourse you shall know them. Thomas More had preceded Swift in this respect, playing language games with a serious purpose; Orwell was to follow him in *Nineteen Eighty-Four*. And like other travellers to utopia, such as Godwin's Domingo Gonsales who reproduces the musical notation of lunar language, Gulliver relies heavily on his language-learning skills and parades his credentials as a linguist, a reminder to the reader that he acts as interpreter in more senses than one.

In the first three books language relates directly to institutions. The language of Lilliput is an inflated currency, the medium of official documents that combine the jargon of civil servants and lawyers with the purple prose of privilege. To communicate the plain sense of imperial decrees is not a priority. What this style is used for is to enact power over people's lives, to impress with the actuality behind the formal surface which contradicts its ostensible meaning – 'nor did any thing terrify the People so much as those Encomiums on his Majesty's Mercy'.[143] From its bureaucratic language alone, one could diagnose the political diseases of Lilliput: the comic mismatch between the size of the inhabitants and their grandiose phrases gilds the satire further. In a utopia of more style than substance, it is also appropriate that naming should be so important: proper names and titles proliferate more than in any other book.

As might be expected, the Brobdingnagian style reverses Lilliput's.

Gulliver describes it as 'clear, masculine, and smooth, but not Florid; for they avoid nothing more than multiplying unnecessary Words, or using various Expressions'. However, if Lilliput inflates the verbal currency, in a sense Brobdingnag devalues it as a literary medium. It is very utopian to have laws 'expressed in the most plain and simple Terms, wherein these People are not Mercurial enough to discover above one Interpretation'; less so to have (relatively) small libraries.[144] Nevertheless, the accessible Brobdingnagian discourse seems clearly intended to represent a golden mean between the mandarin mode of Lilliput and the scientific brutalism of Lagado (which was discussed earlier).

When, finally, the land of the Houyhnhnms is reached, the linguistic and literary range shrinks still further. Purification or impoverishment? The Houyhnhnms 'have no Word in their Language to express Lying or Falshood',[145] but their linguistic philosophy appears to exclude fiction as well as falsehood: 'For he argued thus; That the Use of Speech was to make us understand one another, and to receive Information of Facts; now if any one *said the Thing which was not*, these Ends were defeated. . . .' Ironically, the Houyhnhnm experiences great difficulty in understanding Gulliver's 'Information of Facts', precisely because of the conceptual limitations of his own discourse. Instead of being able to speak more plainly, Gulliver has to devise indirect verbal substitutes to convey any meaning at all: 'it put me to the Pains of many Circumlocutions to give my Master a right Idea of what I spoke; for their Language doth not abound in Variety of Words, because their Wants and Passions are fewer than among us.' Incidentally, this may modify his first impression 'that their Language expressed the Passions very well'. The one principle of word formation that the reader is given does, however, suggest that this language is far from being value-free – quite the opposite in fact. Anything unpleasant or evil is designated by having 'Yahoo' affixed to it.

According to Gulliver, the Houyhnhnm tongue isn't only functional in the Baconian sense, but also pleasing to the ear with its nasal intonation rather like High Dutch or German.[146] Sceptical readers, many of whom balk at the orthography and pronunciation of 'Houyhnhnm' itself, may regard Swift's linguistic wit somewhat sourly. This rational utopia may be felt to carry the philistinism of Laputa and even Brobdingnag to a satirical extreme. Considering their rejection of academic controversy, Gulliver reflects upon 'what Destruction such a Doctrine would make in the Libraries of *Europe*;

and how many Paths to Fame would be then shut up in the Learned World'.[147] We might expect a similar exclusion of imaginative literature, following Platonic doctrine in his *Republic*. Instead poetry is central, and highly praised: 'In *Poetry* they must be allowed to excel all other Mortals; wherein the Justness of their Similes, and the Minuteness, as well as Exactness of their Descriptions, are indeed inimitable.'[148] Of course, Gulliver may be totally deluded. Yet it seems possible that Swift isn't inclined to imagine a civilisation without poetry, however simple a utopia it may be (the Brobdingnagians have it too). This is an oral culture: the account of the style and subject-matter of Houyhnhm verse strongly suggests that Swift has in mind an early golden age of Greece, and Greek lyric praising heroism, not in battle, but in athletic contests. Certainly there is no sign here of the dangers that prompted Plato to exclude artists from his ideal state. Houyhnhnm poets confine themselves to the safe subjects, such as friendship and benevolence – no hint of love or death or religion to disturb the just similes and minute description.[149]

If the land of the Houyhnhnms is the most 'classical' and the most anti-individualistic utopia in *Gulliver's Travels*, its language matches it perfectly. Unlike the others, but like More's *Utopia*, it has no mention of individual proper names: even the sorrel nag is nameless, although he is an all-important exception to the rule that Houyhnhnms don't feel any distinguishing affection for individuals. It is both touching and wonderfully inconsistent, in true Swiftian style, that the final example of Houyhnhnm speech recorded in Book IV is the sorrel nag's emotional farewell: 'My Master and his Friends continued on the Shoar, till I was almost out of Sight; and I often heard the Sorrel Nag (who always loved me) crying out, *Hnuy illa nyha maiah Yahoo*, Take Care of thy self, gentle *Yahoo*.'[150]

The utopian traveller returns

It is with this friendly whinny in his ears that Gulliver sails away, contemplating with horror his return to his own world. Indeed his initial objective is to exchange his lost rational utopia for an isolated utilitarian utopia like Crusoe's, which seems infinitely preferable to the society and government of Yahoos: 'my Design was, if possible, to discover some small Island uninhabited, yet sufficient by my Labour to furnish me with Necessaries of Life, which I would have thought a greater Happiness than to be first Minister in the politest Court of

Europe . . . .' His first encounter with his own species – the 'stark naked' savages – apparently justifies this sense of alienation, since he is scarred for life by a hostile arrow ('I shall carry the Mark to my Grave').[151] However, the physical scar is negligible compared to the psychological scars he already bears. He exhibits these in the second much-discussed encounter with the human race, in the person of the kind and wise Portuguese sea-captain, Pedro de Mendez, and his honest crew who speak to Gulliver 'with great Humanity'.[152] In the space of a few pages, primitive and civilised behaviour, violence and compassion, are juxtaposed; but Gulliver has lost his sense of balance. He responds not only ungraciously, but obtusely to the latter, preferring his utopian diet and clothes to the 'Chicken and some excellent Wine' and the proffered 'best Suit' which are the signs of the captain's hospitality. His extreme reluctance 'to cover [himself] with any thing that had been on the Back of a *Yahoo*' is in particularly ironic contrast to his unperturbed use of genuine Yahoo products. Moreover, he crudely equates the captain's wondering reaction to his tale 'as if it were a Dream or a Vision' with an accusation of lying.

How does Gulliver compare with other travellers in utopian fiction who leave their legendary countries and rehabilitate themselves in the known world? He is certainly not the first of these to be unwillingly expelled, on the grounds that, even after a prolonged stay, he is deemed not to have been successfully integrated into the host culture. For example, it is recounted in Diodorus Siculus that after seven years 'Iambulus and his companion were ejected against their will, as being malefactors and as having been educated to evil habits'; similarly, Jacques Sadeur is condemned to death by the Australians for his un-utopian sexual impulses and fraternisation with the enemy, and contrives to escape on a huge bird. Others, in contrast, like moon voyager Domingo Gonsales, feel the pull of home ties and depart voluntarily. Not all are governed by selfish considerations: Raphael Hythlodaeus lives for over five years in Utopia, 'and would never have left, if it had not been to make that new world known to others'. Gulliver expresses a similar altruism, but he adopts it only when he has to.[153]

Apart from the circumstances of their departure, the reception of utopian travellers on their return is also of particular interest. Many of them come back to an uncomprehending world: some are badly treated, some are well treated, and for some, life and adventures simply continue. The difficulties of readjustment may be relatively trivial: Sadeur struggles to acclimatise himself again to 'European meats', Crusoe to European clothes.[154] However, the major problems are predictably with human relationships, especially if the transition is from an ideal or isolated situation. For Crusoe, Gulliver's fellow-countryman, the experience of re-entry to civilisation is generally positive. Everyone behaves extraordinarily well to him, as Pedro de Mendez does to Swift's hero. Yet, unlike Gulliver, Crusoe has no wife or children to welcome him home. It is Gulliver's revulsion from his family – who, he says, 'received me with great Surprise and Joy'[155] – that provides the most damning evidence in the critical debate over how certifiable he is by the end of the fourth voyage.

In almost all the utopian societies he visits, Gulliver manages to form satisfying if inconclusive individual relationships under often unpromising circumstances. Yet when he finally returns to his own species he cannot tolerate the presence of the individuals who were dearest to him – a response that makes nonsense in this instance of Swift's claim that it is possible to 'hate and detest that animal called man' but at the same time 'hartily love' individual persons.[156] If this is the effect of experiencing utopia, then it can seriously damage your mental health. Gulliver locates his particular horror in sex and procreation: 'when I began to consider, that by copulating with one of the *Yahoo* Species, I had become a Parent of more; it struck me with the utmost Shame, Confusion and Horror.' The word 'copulating' is carefully chosen. So is the language describing the impact on his raw sensibility of any close contact:

> As soon as I entered the House, my Wife took me in her Arms, and kissed me; at which, having not been used to the Touch of that odious Animal for so many Years, I fell in a Swoon for almost an Hour. At the Time I am writing, it is five Years since my last Return to *England*: During the first Year I could not endure my Wife or Children in my Presence, the very Smell of them was intolerable; much less could I suffer them to eat in the same Room.[157]

When he returns to the topic, it is to report that communication is barely restored, and then only with the aid of keeping his 'Nose well stopt with Rue, Lavender, or Tobacco-Leaves'.[158] But who or what is responsible for this darkly satiric outcome? Does it discredit the utopian ideal represented by the Houyhnhnms, or only Gulliver's misinterpretation and misapplication of that ideal? He thinks he is following reason, but he is doing so irrationally by concentrating on accidentals not essentials. Trotting like a horse, he has allowed his imagination to get the upper hand. Only by imagination can the individual make the doomed attempt to opt out of his species.

It is above all the utopian imagination that is on trial in these last chapters of *Gulliver's Travels*. Gulliver himself observes, 'my Memory and Imaginations were perpetually filled with the Virtues and Ideas of those exalted Houyhnhnms'.[159] He becomes the utopian writer who is convinced and obsessed by his own ideal. Characteristically utopian fiction represents the interest of the species rather than the individual, though with the development of the novel that begins to change. Gulliver takes upon himself the mantle of Socrates and Raphael Hythlodaeus,[160] in the belief that all that is required is to confront humanity with its own image for the monstrous delusion of human pride to be exposed. Like Hythlodaeus, he is disillusioned. Yet his message about the evils of supposedly civilised humanity cannot be easily ignored, even if we would prefer to shoot the messenger.[161] In a postscript, as it were, to the *Travels*, Gulliver also assesses the damage his own country has the power to inflict on other cultures through its belief in its own civilising mission. The satire on colonialism is a reminder of the complexities of the real world, in which the imperial dream is no more to be trusted than the utopian one.

Finally, the literary verdict: although *Gulliver's Travels*, Book IV in particular, is a more devastating satire on the utopian imagination than any preceding text, it is also one of its most powerful creations. To travel with Gulliver to utopia is hardly to travel hopefully; but it is better to travel – *and* arrive – than never to set out.

Gulliver's fellow-travellers

For the reader interested in eighteenth-century English utopian satire, *Gulliver's Travels* must be the unrivalled centre of attraction. However, it pulls a number of lesser works into its orbit, enough to fill several volumes of *Gulliveriana*.[162] Questions of influence can, to adapt Sterne's words, '[lead] us a vagary some millions of miles into the very heart of the planetary system', so I set them aside.[163] But to make a brief voyage around a few English examples of the type will lead us a vagary in another sense, and help to map the area dominated by Swift's text, but long-established in its own right. The common factor is the journey to another world. This is the blueprint for the sometimes clanking literary machinery of Defoe's *The Consolidator* and *A Vision of the Angelic World*; Samuel Brunt's *A Voyage to Cacklogallinia*; and Fielding's *A Journey from this World to the Next*.

The Consolidator is the earliest of them (published in 1705, the year after Swift's *Tale of a Tub* and 21 years before *Gulliver's Travels*) and actually derives its title from an imaginary machine. The eponymous consolidator is Defoe's version of a space shuttle, complicated in construction, since it requires both feathered wings and fuel tanks for rocket propulsion. It is complicated in another way as well, since it turns out to be an allegorical vehicle for, among other things, the House of Commons. At one level of meaning, the feathers represent MPs, who are by no means reliable and who cause at least one historic disaster by bringing down a British monarch in midflight (he 'struck himself against his own Palace, and beat his Head off').[164] As a political allegory, *The Consolidator* wobbles violently but keeps more or less on course. As a utopian fiction, it can only be regarded as something of a wasted opportunity, with unfulfilled possibilities suggested by the narrator's dark hints and name-dropping:

> No Man need Wonder at my exceeding desire to go up to the World in the *Moon*, having heard of such extraordinary Knowledge to be obtained there, since in the search of Knowledge and Truth, wiser Men than I have taken as unwarrantable Flights, and gone a great deal higher than the Moon, into a strange Abbyss of dark *Phaenomena*, which they neither could make other People understand, nor ever rightly understood themselves, witness *Malbranch*, Mr. *Lock*, *Hobbs*, the Honourable *Boyle*, and a great many others . . . .[165]

Another machine that might have a future in utopian fiction, but isn't fully exploited here, is Defoe's thinking machine 'call'd *The Cogitator, or the Chair of Reflection*', described as 'an Engine *to screw a Man into himself*'.[166] Neither the consolidator nor the cogitator, however, function efficiently enough for the satire to do more than splutter spasmodically. In fact the opening section of the narrative, on China, presents a more effective alternative for the purposes of utopian satire than the disappointing so-called 'enlightned Country' of the moon.[167]

A somewhat similar disappointment awaits the reader who travels with Crusoe in imagination to see *A Vision of the Angelic World*. The journey is sparked off by a discussion on that popular topic, the plurality of worlds, but in the event it explodes 'our modern notions that the planets were habitable worlds' in the sense of supporting human or animal life: 'you may depend upon it that none of the planets, except the moon, are in this sense habitable: and the moon, a poor, little, watery, damp thing, not above as big as Yorkshire, neither worth being called a world, nor capable of rendering life comfortable to mankind, if indeed supportable . . . .'[168] So much for fantasies of lunar utopias, shrinking before our gaze to the dimensions of a sodden Yorkshire. Yet, despite the bathos, Defoe through Crusoe identifies the true purpose of contemplative voyagers: 'the soul being gone of this errand had quite different notices of the whole state of life, and was neither influenced by passions or affections, as it was before.'[169] However, one of Crusoe's passions remains. Having had a vision of the aerial region as Satan's domain, he judges the nations of this world to be divided between the barbarians who are totally under Satanic rule, and the civilised societies where the devil's power is at least restricted in its operation. As so often, the view from the moon is of the dark side of the earth.

Samuel Brunt (unidentified: presumably a pseudonym) offers the best of both worlds in A Voyage to Cacklogallinia (1727), which both imitates Gulliver's Travels and incorporates a voyage to the moon.[170] From its conception, this narrative is a hybrid: the utopian element is closely associated with satire, and the creation of Cacklogallinia itself slots so neatly into the Gulliver pattern that only familiarity with the original can bring out the full relevance of certain details. However, Brunt starts off in the style of Defoe, with pseudo-historical material including piratical adventure and an account of escaped slaves in Jamaica. When he arrives in Cacklogallinia, the narrator's discourse switches into Swiftian mode, in a skilful mix-and-match blend of the four voyages. However, since this is a bird utopia, the first comparison a reader is likely to make is with Book IV of Gulliver's Travels.

Cacklogallinia (the name is partly onomatopoeic like Houyhnhnm-land) is inhabited by giant barnyard fowl, whose stature varies in accordance with their place in the socio-economic pecking order. As the dominant rational species, they 'have . . . a Notion, that no Creatures are endued with Reason like themselves',[171] but they have a quite different function in the satire from Swift's rational horses. Indeed Brunt takes pains to emphasis the basic contrasts in their attitude to clothes and food. He recapitulates episodes in Gulliver's

Travels to make the point: 'the pulling off my Cloaths he did not wonder at, for the Rich and Great among 'em wear Mantles, and cover their Legs with fine Cloath'; and when the offer of corn is rejected 'one of them went out, and fetch'd me a Piece of boil'd Mutton; for these *Cacklogallinians*, contrary to the Nature of *European* Cocks, live mostly on Flesh, except the poorer Sort, who feed on Grain.'[172] We discover later that 'the poorer Sort' actually form part of the diet of the rich: 'and not one . . . is in any Security of their Lives, in case a hungry Grandee sets his Eyes on, and has a Mind to him' – a fate for which there is no shortage of volunteers however.[173] Clearly Brunt was an apt pupil of Swift's when it came to political satire. Yet his use of a utopian structure for his satiric strategy is less sophisticated than Swift's, depending as it does on a relatively straightforward application of the bird fable to contemporary Britain. In the customary exchange of information between visitor and host, the former represents England as an absurdly idealised state, whereas the latter's Cacklogallinian account represents the 'true' version of a corrupt social and political system. Besides being highly specific in its strong anti-Walpole line, this satiric description targets a number of familiar anxieties such as excessive expenditure on luxuries, female domination, laxity in sexual conduct and religion, and the decline of education for political reasons ('there were publick Colleges erected for the Education and Provision of poor Chickens; but as there is a strong Party, which takes them to be of ill Consequence; they are discountenanc'd so much, that it is thought they must fall some time or other').[174] Plus ça change . . . . As with Lilliput, and by extension Britain itself, this state of affairs marks a degeneration from a supposedly utopian past. In the case of Cacklogallinia, the cause is given as the contamination of the race by intermarriage with inferior birds like owls and magpies – an explanation which recalls the ideology of other utopian states, such as Plato's Republic. Immigrants are not welcome in Cacklogallinia.

The narrator, a tolerated outsider, becomes caught up in the first Minister's grandiose scheme for financial speculation in shares (a satiric equivalent of the South Sea Bubble),[175] raised on the project of a gold-hunting expedition to the moon. So a second utopian fiction is introduced, reverting to another traditional type: the idealised moon world of the beautiful Selenites. If Brunt, like Defoe, chooses to create a vision of the angelic world, his creation is more in keeping with such a title. Instead of Defoe's Satan-dominated region of the air,

Brunt offers the lunar dwelling of the blessed spirits, waiting to cast off their last vestiges of humanity and to be translated into the presence of God. Even so, this is a utopian rather than a mystical vision. The evidence is in the details of the fiction.

To begin with, the moon landscape corresponds to the paradisal image discovered by Cyrano (it's certainly not the damp and gloomy invention of Crusoe): it's filled with the traditional delights of 'everlasting Spring' with its flowers and fruits. This leads to a utopian disquisition on the Selenite outlook and way of life: devout, hospitable, eating only fruit – 'since the eating any thing that has had Life, is look'd upon with Abhorrence, and never known in this World' – they lead an utterly tranquil existence. Among their perceived advantages is that of no 'Distinction of Sexes', as a Selenite explains: 'for know, all Souls are masculine'. Sensing a contradiction here, he adds parenthetically '(if I may be allowed that Term, after what I've said)'.[176] What strikes the narrator is the contrast between the beauty of the Selenites and himself – 'I seem'd . . . something of the same Species, but frightfully ugly' – and the equally ugly projections of mortal humanity who enact their dream lives on the moon.[177] This opens a crack in the fiction into which satire can again insert itself. It's observed that the moon's population has been shrinking recently, since the supply of virtuous souls ('especially of the *European* Quarter') has decreased. In particular, few of the earth's aristocracy find their way to the moon, which is an egalitarian utopia: 'we have no Occasion for Servants; we are all Artificers, and none where Help is necessary, but offers his with Alacrity.'[178]

By mixing his utopian models in this part of the narrative, Brunt produces an oddly incongruous effect of the transcendental superimposed on the absurd. After all, the abortive expedition has been mounted and financed by the Cacklogallinians, who also provide the means of transport; and the reader remains conscious of those ungainly fowls from a different kind of utopia hanging about uncomfortably in this rarified atmosphere. At one point they become understandably upset by the discovery that their species appears to be, theologically speaking, *persona non grata*. The Selenites, also understandably, are baffled by this clash of generic types, and their spokesman enquires of the narrator, 'by what Art have you taught Fowls articulate Sounds? and where could you possibly find them of that Size?' To which the narrator hastily replies that 'they were rational Beings, but that the Story was now too long to tell him'.[179]

At the end of his stay, it is hardly astonishing that he elects not to return to Cacklogallinia, but to the human world like other moon voyagers before him. Of course, in terms of the satiric fiction, it amounts to the same thing. He is going back from a gentle ideal existence to avarice, corruption, and all kinds of vice. However, through the Selenites' example he has learned to value the true Christian treasure, which is not transitory but eternal. It is this perspective of the next world – conspicuously absent from *Gulliver's Travels* – that finally places this entertaining utopian satire in context.

By way of a postscript, it is an easy leap from Samuel Brunt's moon to Henry Fielding's *Journey from this World to the Next* (1743), which also views the frivolity, selfishness, and short-term aims of human existence *sub specie aeternitatis*. Although Fielding doesn't set out to describe an other-worldly utopia as such, his fiction shares with his mentor, Lucian, a satiric dislocation of the reader's perceptions, and a vivid appreciation of detail, that allies it with the utopian tradition.[180] His traveller embarks on his journey to eternity as a passenger in a stage-coach full of fellow-spirits and drawn by a team of equally ghostly horses who 'had, indeed, all died in the Service of a certain Post-Master'.[181] Their first staging-post is the City of Diseases, where they are to pay their respects to their deliverers from earthly life. In this urbane, darkly comic allegory, Fielding drives home the connection between social behaviour and physical consequences as cogently as any utopian manifesto. When 'the *Maladie Alamode*, a *French* Lady' speaks 'greatly in approbation of the Method so generally used by Parents, of marrying Children very young, and without the least affection between the Parties'; and concludes 'by saying, that if these Fashions continued to spread, she doubted not, but she should shortly be the only Disease who would ever receive a Visit from any Person of considerable Rank',[182] it is clear how much the skills of the satirist and the skills of the utopian writer converge. If the inspiration for utopian fiction is supposed to weaken in the eighteenth century, compared to its vitality in other periods, then satire must take much of the credit for providing a support machine to keep life in the invalid genre.

Notes and references

1.   v H. Williams 1932: for Plato v I. Samuel 1976.

2.   J. Swift 1726/1965 intro p. xv.

3. For a checklist and survey of utopian works that Swift *might* have known v W. A. Eddy 1923/1963: also v M. Voight 1968. In F. Brady (ed) pp. 13–22. Turner's annotation in J. Swift 1726/1986 cites many parallels.

4. cit P. B. Gove 1941/1961 pp. 20–1.

5. *Political State of Great Britain* Jan 1727 cit I. Ehrenpreis 1962–83 vol. 3 p. 503.

6. J. Boswell 1791, 1799/1934–50 vol. 2 p. 319.

7. cf Flynn's extensive analysis (C. H. Flynn 1990).

8. J. Swift 1726/1965 Part I ch. i p. 20.

9. J. Swift 1726/1965 A Letter from Capt Gulliver to his Cousin Sympson p. 5: as the textual history of *Gulliver's Travels* makes clear, the 'author's' complaints have a basis in fact: v William's intro to J Swift 1726/1965 pp. xxiv–xxviii.

10. J. Swift 1726/1965 A Letter p. 7: the subtleties of Swift's devices in manipulating the categories of 'author' and 'reader' are admirably dealt with in C. J. Rawson 1973 ch. 1: also cf F. N. Smith 1984.

11. J. Swift 1726/1965 A Letter p. 7.

12. J. Swift 1726/1965 A Letter p. 8: cf J. Traugott 1961 p. 536.

13. J. Swift 1726/1965 A Letter p. 8.

14. J. Swift 1726/1965 Part I ch. i p. 21.

15. J. Swift 1726/1965 Part I ch. ii p. 29.

16. For the importance of Gulliver's sight v P. Rogers 1978. In C. T. Probyn (ed) pp. 179–88.

17. cf M. Eliav-Feldon 1982 pp. 37–8: C. Fabricant 1982 pp. 40–2.

18. J. Swift 1726/1965 Part I ch. iv p. 49.

19. J. Swift 1726/1965 Part I ch. vii p. 67.

20. J. Swift 1726/1965 Part I ch. iv p. 47: cf Gulliver's similar intention in Part IV ch. ix p. 275.

21. J. Swift 1726/1965 Part I ch. vi p. 57.

22. Among critics who consider the relation between *Gulliver's Travels* and *Utopia* v B. Vickers 1968a. In B. Vickers (ed) pp. 233–57: F. P. Lock 1980 pp. 20–3: C. T. Probyn 1987/1989 pp. 66–8: also v Turner's annotation on Part I ch. vi in J. Swift 1726/1986.

23. J. Swift 1726/1965 Part I ch. vi p. 59.

24. v J. Swift 1939–68 vol. 2 pp. 26–39.

25. J. Swift 1726/1965 Part I ch. vi p. 60.

26. J. Swift 1726/1965 Part I ch. vi p. 60: cf Plato 1955/1987 pp. 236–43: Cyrano de Bergerac 1657/1965 p. 66: J. Locke 1693/1989 pp. 117, 126–7, 196–7.

27. J. Swift 1726/1965 Part I ch. vi pp. 62–3: cf Xenophon 1925 pp. 141–9: Plutarch 1914 vol. 1 pp. 255–65. For Swift and Sparta v W. H. Halewood 1965: I. Higgins 1983.

28. J. Swift 1726/1965 Part I ch. i p. 24.

29. J. Swift 1726/1965 Part I ch. vii p. 72.

30. J. Swift 1726/1965 Part I ch. vii p. 73.

31. T. Hobbes 1651/1968 p. 273: for Swift and Hobbes v P. Rogers 1968 in B. Vickers 1968a (ed) p. 33: F. P. Lock 1980 pp. 10–11: J. A. Downie 1984 p. 39.

32. J. Swift 1726/1965 Part I ch. vii p. 73.

33. J. Swift 1726/1965 Part II ch. i p. 87.

34. v Cyrano de Bergerac 1657/1965 pp. 30–1: for Cyrano/Swift parallels v Strachan's intro pp. xiv–xvi: W. A. Eddy 1923/1963 pp. 21–2, 61–4.

35. J. Swift 1726/1965 Part IV ch. xii p. 292.

36. cit H. Williams 1932 pp. 51–2: for kingship in *Gulliver's Travels* v F. P. Lock 1980 pp. 127–8.

37. v [D. d'A Vairasse] 1727 vol. 3 part 2 pp. 5, 55.

38. v F. Godwin 1638 p. 103: S. Berington 1737 p. 204. For the significance of execution as public spectacle v M. Foucault 1975/1977 Part I ch. 2: C. H. Flynn 1990 pp. 26–9.

39. J. Swift 1726/1965 Part II ch. vii p. 137.

40. J. Swift 1726/1965 Part II ch. vi p. 127.

41. J. Swift 1726/1965 Part II ch. vi p. 128.

42. J. Swift 1726/1965 Part II ch. vi p. 132.

43. cf S. Greenblatt 1985 pp. 21–8. In J. Dollimore, A. Sinfield (eds).

44. J. Swift 1726/1965 Part IV ch. xii p. 292: Part II ch. vii p. 135.

45. J. Swift 1726/1965 Part II ch. vii pp. 135–6.

46. For parallels between Brobdingnag and Oceana v M. Jones 1974 pp. 66–70: for Swift and Harrington also v F. P. Lock 1980 pp. 42–3, 138–9, 148.

47. J. Swift 1726/1965 Part II ch. vii p. 138: for the link between Harrington

and the standing army debate v J. Harrington 1656/1977 intro pp. 138–41.

48. J. Swift 1726/1965 Part II ch. vii p. 138: cf J. Locke 1690/1988 pp. 354–74: for discussion of the issues involved v F. P. Lock 1980 ch. 5: J. A. Downie 1984 pp. 279–80.

49. J. Swift 1726/1965 Part II ch. vii p. 135.

50. v J. Swift 1726/1965 Part II ch. viii pp. 141–2.

51. J. Swift 1726/1965 Part II ch. viii p. 139.

52. v Cyrano de Bergerac 1657/1965 pp. 44–5: the parallel is noted in W. A. Eddy 1923/1963 pp. 21, 128.

53. J. Swift 1726/1965 Part II ch. viii p. 139.

54. J. Swift 1726/1965 Part II ch. vii p. 136: Turner notes the parallel with More in J. Swift 1726/1986 p. 335 n. 9.

55. v M. H. Nicolson, N. M. Mohler in M. H. Nicolson 1956/1976 pp. 110–54: P. J. Korshin 1971: F. N. Smith 1990 in F. N. Smith (ed) pp. 139–62. A most valuable discussion of the utopianism of Part III which connects both Ancients and Moderns is J. Mezciems 1977.

56. cf A. E. Case 1945 pp. 80–94: Lock challenges this extreme type of allegorical reading (v F. P. Lock 1980 pp. 101–4)

57. J. Swift 1726/1965 Part III ch. ii p. 159: for the 'ivory tower' aspect of Laputa v B. Hammond 1988 pp. 50–2: cf C. H. Flynn 1990 pp. 183–7.

58. J. Swift 1726/1965 Part III ch. ii p. 165.

59. J. Swift 1726/1965 Part III ch. ii p. 163.

60. J. Swift 1726/1965 Part III ch. ii p. 165.

61. J. Swift 1726/1965 Part III ch. ii p. 166.

62. T. Campanella 1602, 1637/1981 p. 62.

63. J. Swift 1726/1965 Part III ch. iii p. 170.

64. J. Swift 1726/1965 Part III ch. ii p. 162.

65. J. Swift 1726/1965 Part III ch. ii p. 165: T. Campanella 1602, 1637/1981 p. 30.

66. J. Swift 1726/1965 Part III ch. ii p. 160.

67. v J. Mezciems 1977.

68. J. Swift 1726/1965 Part III ch. iv pp. 176–7.

69. A. Cowley 1906 pp. 205–1: Cowley entitles his scheme A Proposition For the Advancement of Experimental Philosophy (1661).

70. cf J. A. Downie 1984 pp. 280–1: for Munodi and utopian ideology v M. McKeon 1987 p. 344.

71. v M. H. Nicolson, N. M. Mohler, in M. H. Nicolson 1956/1976 pp. 110–54.

72. v Diodorus Siculus 1933–67 vol. 2 pp. 75–7: Virgil 1980/1984 Eclogue IV p. 59: Lucian 1913 vol. 1 p. 315.

73. G. de Foigny 1676/1693 p. 125: Turner notes a Rabelaisian parallel in Swift 1726/1986 p. 348 n 11.

74. cf J. Mezciems 1977 pp. 9–10.

75. J. Swift 1726/1965 Part III ch. vi p. 187.

76. J. Swift 1726/1965 Part III ch. v pp. 183–4.

77. For language theory in relation to utopian fiction v E. D. Seeber 1945: P. Cornelius 1965: for Swift and language reform v A *Proposal for Correcting, Improving and Ascertaining the English Tongue* (1712) in J. Swift 1939–68 vol. 4 pp. 1–21: for language in *Gulliver's Travels* v A. C. Kelly 1978: cf Swift 1726/1986 pp. 350–1 ns 29, 32.

78. v Cyrano de Bergerac 1657/1965 pp. 144–5, 88–9.

79. J. Swift 1726/1965 Part III ch. vi p. 187.

80. J. Swift 1726/1965 Part III ch. vii p. 193: contrast F. Bacon 1605–1627/ 1906 p. 270. For the archetype cf Homer *Odyssey* XI: Virgil *Aeneid* VI.

81. Swift 1726/1965 Part III ch. vii p. 194.

82. J. Swift 1726/1965 Part III ch. vii p. 195: cf Lucian 1913 vol. 1 pp. 319– 21: the Lucian parallel is noted in W. A. Eddy 1923/1963 pp. 55, 164–5: J. Swift 1726/1986 p. 354 n. 8.

83. J. Swift 1726/1965 Part III ch. vii p. 196: v M. M. Kelsall 1969.

84. J. Swift 1726/1965 Part III ch. viii p. 198: Higgins notes the link with Martin Scriblerus (I. Higgins 1983 p. 528).

85. J. Swift 1726/1965 Part III ch. x p. 211.

86. J. Swift 1726/1965 Part III ch. x pp. 209–10.

87. J. Swift 1726/1965 Part III ch. x p. 209.

88. J. Swift 1726/1965 Part III ch. x p. 211: cf Herodotus 1954/1972 p. 53: Petronius 1965/1986 p. 67. Eddy compares the Tithonus myth and Lucian (W. A. Eddy 1923/1963 pp. 165, 167–8): Turner compares Juvenal's tenth Satire (J. Swift 1726/1986 pp. 358–9 ns 1, 7).

89. v Diodorus Siculus 1933–67 vol. 2 pp. 73–5: T. More 1516/1989 Book II p. 81: G. de Foigny 1676/1693 pp. 58–9, 104–6.

90. J. Swift 1726/1965 Part III ch. x p. 212.

91. J. Swift 1726/1965 Part III ch. x pp. 209, 212.

92. J. Swift 1726/1965 Part III ch. x p. 214: cf C. T. Probyn 1987/1989 pp. 48–9: for Swift's attitude to old age v J. Swift 1963–5 vol. 3 pp. 254–5 cit. D. Nokes 1985 p. 334.

93. Various critics observe general and specific resemblances between Part IV and ancient and Renaissance utopias e.g. W. H. Halewood 1965: J. F. Reichert 1968: B. Vickers 1968a in B. Vickers (ed) pp. 233–57. For a summary of utopian genealogy v M. M. Kelsall 1969 p. 36. Hammond queries the utopian claim (B. Hammond 1988 pp. 95–6).

94. Letter to Pope in J. Swift 1963–5 vol. 3 p. 103.

95. R. S. Crane performs an invaluable service to Swift's readers by explaining how these definitions apply to Part IV: v R. S. Crane 1959/1962: also v C. T. Probyn 1978. In C. T. Probyn (ed) pp. 57–80.

96. Eddy cites Segrais and also d'Ablancourt's Isle des animaux (v W. A. Eddy 1923/1963 pp. 182–5. cf Plato 1955/1987 pp. 125–8: Cyrano de Bergerac 1657/1965 pp. 167–87.

97. J. Swift 1726/1965 Part IV ch. ii p. 229: ch. vii p. 261: cf Xenophon 1925 p. 145. Also v Swift 1726/1986 p. 364 n 3.

98. J. Swift 1726/1965 Part IV ch. ii p. 231.

99. J. Swift 1726/1965 Part IV ch. vii p. 260.

100. v G. de Foigny 1676/1693 p. 86: Cyrano de Bergerac 1657/1965 p. 40.

101. For eighteenth-century views on this topic v C. H. Flynn 1990 pp. 42–6.

102. v G. de Foigny 1676/1693 p. 129: S. Berington 1737 p. 184.

103. J. Swift 1726/1965 Part IV ch. ii pp. 230, 232: cf J. Swift 1726/1960 p. 516 n 188. 19–20: C. H. Flynn 1990 p. 97.

104. cf R. Burton 1621/1972 Pt 3 Sec 2 Mem 2 Subs 3 pp. 88–9: A. Behn 1688/1992 p. 76.

105. J. Swift 1726/1965 Part IV ch. i p. 226.

106. J. Swift 1726/1965 Part IV ch. iii pp. 236–7: cf M. de Montaigne 1580–1588/1991 pp. 253–6: D. Defoe 1719/1927 vol. 1 p. 154: G. de Foigny 1676/1693 pp. 74–5.

107. G. de Foigny 1676/1693 p. 63.

108. For theriophily and Gulliver's Travels IV v J. E. Gill 1970: for Swift's French predecessors also v K. Williams 1958 pp. 179–88.

109.   v Cyrano de Bergerac 1657/1965 pp. 54, 171–3.

110.   J. Swift 1726/1965 Part IV ch. iii p. 235: G. de Foigny 1676/1693 p. 67.

111.   J. Swift 1726/1965 Part IV ch. ii p. 231: ch. ix pp. 271, 272.

112.   J. Swift 1726/1965 Part IV ch. vii pp. 260–4.

113.   J. Swift 1726/1965 Part IV ch. v p. 248.

114.   J. Swift 1726/1965 Part IV ch. vii p. 264.

115.   J. Swift 1726/1965 Part IV ch. v p. 250: v A. E. Case cit. by Landa in Swift 1726/1960 p. 517 n 203. 14–15: cf M. McKeon 1987 p. 347.

116.   J. Swift 1726/1965 Part IV ch. vi p. 256: the parallels with *The Republic* are noted in J. F. Reichert 1968 p. 182: cf I. Samuel 1976 p. 459.

117.   J. Swift 1726/1965 Part IV ch. viii p. 268: for parallels with Plato and More v J. F. Reichert 1968 pp. 188–9: J. Swift 1726/1986 p. 372 n 13: B. Vickers 1968a in B. Vickers (ed.) pp. 245–50.

118.   J. Swift 1726/1965 Part IV ch. vii p. 259: cf W. H. Halewood 1965 p. 187.

119.   J. Swift 1726/1965 Part IV ch. viii p. 270.

120.   J. Swift 1726/1965 Part IV ch. ix p. 271.

121.   J. Swift 1726/1965 Part IV ch. x p. 280.

122.   J. Swift 1726/1965 Part IV ch. x p. 278: for Swift's famous distinction between hating the species and loving the individual v letter to Pope in J. Swift 1963–5 vol. 3 p. 103.

123.   J. Swift 1726/1965 Part IV ch. x p. 279: for illumination on 'the nature-reason dialectic' v C. J. Rawson 1973 pp. 24–7.

124.   v T. More 1516/1989 p. 106: K. R. Popper 1945/1966 vol. 1 chs. 3–4.

125.   J. Swift 1726/1965 Part IV ch. viii p. 268.

126.   J. Swift 1726/1965 Part IV ch. vi p. 126: for utopian parallels v W. H. Halewood 1965 pp. 189–90: I. Higgins 1983 p. 529.

127.   cf A. Huxley 1932/1950 and 1962.

128.   v Plato 1955/1987 p. 239.

129.   G. de Foigny 1676/1693 p. 85: cf p. 64.

130.   J. Swift 1726/1965 Part IV ch. ix p. 271.

131.   J. Swift 1726/1965 Part IV ch viii p. 266.

132.   J. Swift 1726/1965 Part IV ch. viii p. 267.

133.   v Plato 1970/1988 p. 298.

134. J. Swift 1726/1965 Part IV ch. viii p. 268.

135. J. Swift 1726/1965 Part IV ch. viii p. 269.

136. cf I. Higgins 1983 p. 529.

137. J. Swift 1726/1965 Part IV ch. ix p. 273.

138. J. Swift 1726/1965 Part IV ch. xii p. 293: for application of the terms 'hard' and 'soft' more generally in the context of interpreting Part IV v J. L. Clifford 1974. In L. S. Champion (ed) pp. 33–49.

139. J. Swift 1726/1965 Part IV ch. ix pp. 274–5: v J. A. Downie 1984 p. 286.

140. Turner compares More in Swift 1726/1986 p. 374 n 13.

141. J. Swift 1726/1965 Part IV ch. ix pp. 274–5.

142. v above n 77: for a stimulating comparison of Swift's imaginary societies located within a theory of grammaphobia v T. Castle 1980: also cf A. C. Kelly 1978. Spadafora discusses eighteenth-century views of the interrelation of language and society: v D. Spadafora 1990 Part 2 ch. 5 pp. 194–202. For comparisons between Swift's utopian language and Orwell's v R. M. Philmus 1973.

143. Swift 1726/1965 Part I ch. vii p. 72: cf Kelly's description (A. C. Kelly 1978 p. 39).

144. J. Swift 1726/1965 Part II ch. vii pp. 136–7.

145. J. Swift 1726/1965 Part IV ch. iii p. 235: subsequent quotations are from ch. iv pp. 240, 242: ch. i p. 226. Kelly comments on the Yahoo formation: she takes a severe view of Houyhnhnm linguistics (v A. C. Kelly 1978 pp. 45–6): cf R. M. Philmus 1973 pp. 69–74.

146. J. Swift 1726/1965 Part IV ch. iii p. 234.

147. J. Swift 1726/1965 Part IV ch. viii p. 268.

148. J. Swift 1726/1965 Part IV ch. ix p. 273.

149. J. Swift 1726/1965 Part IV ch. ix p. 274: cf Plato 1955/1987 Parts 3, 10. Castle takes a somewhat different approach to the significance of this oral culture and its relation to a Platonic utopia (v T. Castle 1980 pp. 33, 41).

150. J. Swift 1726/1965 Part IV ch. xi p. 283.

151. J. Swift 1726/1965 Part IV ch. xi pp. 283–4.

152. J. Swift 1726/1965 Part IV ch. xi p. 286: subsequent quotations from Part IV ch. xi pp. 286–8.

153. v Diodorus Siculus 1933–67 vol. 2 p. 81: G. de Foigny 1676/1693 pp. 166–72: F. Godwin 1638 p. 111: T. More 1516/1989 p. 40: J. Swift 1726/1965 Part IV ch. x pp. 280–1.

154. v G. de Foigny 1676/1693 pp. 178–9: D. Defoe 1719/1927 vol. 2 p. 69.

155. J. Swift 1726/1965 Part IV ch. xi p. 289.

156. Letter to Pope. In J. Swift 1963–5 vol. 3 p. 103. cf C. T. Probyn 1987/1989 p. 51.

157. J. Swift 1726/1965 Part IV ch. xi p. 289.

158. J. Swift 1726/1965 Part IV ch. xii p. 295.

159. J. Swift 1726/1965 Part IV ch. xi p. 289.

160. cf J. Traugott 1961 pp. 558–64: for further comparisons between Gulliver and Hythlodaeus v B. Vickers 1968a in B. Vickers (ed) pp. 250–6: J. Swift 1726/1986 p. 378 ns 3, 5: p. 379 ns 18, 24.

161. cf C. J. Rawson 1973 pp. 27–9.

162. v J. K. Welcher, G. E. Bush 1970–6: J. K. Welcher 1988.

163. L. Sterne 1759–1767/1967 p. 94: for examples of possible cross-fertilisation v J. F. Ross 1941 section 3: J. K. Welcher, G. E. Bush 1970–6 vol. 4 pp. ix–xiii.

164. D. Defoe 1705 p. 39: for interpretation v C. Kay 1988 p. 60.

165. D. Defoe 1705 p. 33.

166. D. Defoe 1705 pp. 96–7.

167. D. Defoe 1705 p. 359.

168. D. Defoe 1720/1895 vol. 3 p. 263.

169. D. Defoe 1720/1895 vol. 3 p. 262.

170. Nicolson points out that earlier attributions include Defoe and Swift: v S. Brunt 1727/1940 intro p.v.

171. S. Brunt 1727/1973 p. 62.

172. S. Brunt 1727/1973 pp. 35–6.

173. S. Brunt 1727/1973 pp. 41–2.

174. S. Brunt 1727/1973 pp. 95–6.

175. v Nicolson's intro to S. Brunt 1727/1940 pp. viii–x: cf M. H. Nicolson 1948 pp. 99–104.

176. S. Brunt 1727/1973 pp. 135–8, 147–8, 150–1.

177. S. Brunt 1727/1973 pp. 140–3.

178. S. Brunt 1727/1973 p. 152.

179. S. Brunt 1727/1973 p. 144.

180. Goldgar highlights a Platonic source rather than Lucian, suggesting a connection with the myth of Er in *The Republic* X: v H. Fielding 1743/1993 intro pp. xxviii–xxx.

181. H. Fielding 1743/1993 Book I ch. i p. 9.

182. H. Fielding 1743/1993 Book I ch. iii pp. 17, 20.

CHAPTER 6

Domestic utopias: Joseph Andrews; Tom Jones; Clarissa; Sir Charles Grandison

Whether writing novels or satire, the writers so far considered have located their fictional utopias ostentatiously outside their own dear country, the better to comment on it. They may not need to go as far as the moon, but most opt for the southern hemisphere at least. Remoteness is a prerequisite. The reasons for this are formally related to genre, but also perhaps reveal something about eighteenth-century British culture. For this is a culture that is simultaneously sceptical about any sign of utopian thinking in domestic politics and starry-eyed about imperialist expansion. Eighteenth-century Britain tends to export its ideals.

However, there is another kind of utopia which comes into its own with the growth of the novel. As interest in the quality of 'private' life intensifies, and, concomitantly, its resistance to and effect upon society at large, so writers begin to investigate the possibility of utopian experiments existing within the dominant society and presenting an alternative to it. They experience imaginatively a form of internal exile, which had been taken to an extreme by the returned utopian travellers, Crusoe and Gulliver. To put it another way, inside the hospitable bounds of the novel, they domesticise utopia. In applying the term 'domestic' to these versions of utopia, I'm using it in two senses: first, in the sense of being located in Britain and explicitly related to contemporary (or near-contemporary) ways of life; second, in the sense of belonging to a household, the family or extended communal circle that people create for themselves, rather than have created for them. Personal relationships count more than public roles in such a context.

It is possible, in practice, to see this embryonic development embedded in some of the fictions already discussed. Not only do a number of utopian travellers recreate a domestic environment elsewhere – Crusoe's cave and 'country house', Will Atkins's beehive commune, Peter Wilkins's cosy grotto, even Gulliver's tastefully fitted

178

out box in Brobdingnag – but the ideal of domestic self-sufficiency also crops up in narrative interludes. For example, Crusoe tries to establish a country estate, the Augustan paradigm of the good life, during his family-man period at home in England, just as Lord Munodi does in Laputa. It could be objected that this familiar model shouldn't be called utopian and that it belongs to a separate literary lineage going back through Renaissance country-house poems to its true Augustan roots in Virgil and Horace – which is accurate enough. However, equally it could be argued that this is another example of genre convergence, an indicator of the open boundaries of utopian fiction. Eighteenth-century writers are developing the conceptual strain in utopian literature which represents the family unit both as political paradigm and as a structure for social well-being, the growing-point of the moral commonwealth. In doing so, they often merge this concept with the Horatian ideal: the satisfactions of an independent country property, large enough to be self-sufficient, but small enough to be under the proprietor's eye. Where better to experiment with new and socially beneficial methods of handling communal relationships and directing personal energy to good works and self-improvement? For any writer concerned with how men and women actually live, and how their lives might benefit from changes in social structure, fragments of utopian speculation will tend to adhere to the novel form, and utopian ideas – satiric or serious – can infiltrate their fiction. This is certainly the case with Fielding, whose interest in political and moral philosophy leads him to take a stand on such issues in both fiction and non-fiction; and with Richardson, whose interest in female experience makes him a natural investigator of the domestic utopia.

Fielding: a 'chimerical system'

Given his educational background, and the easy allusiveness of his writings, it is obvious that Fielding, like Swift, moves with utmost confidence and pleasure among the writers of the past.[1] Indeed he compliments Swift himself by his classification of 'the great Triumvirate, Lucian, Cervantes, and Swift' (The Covent-Garden Journal, 1752);[2] he admires and quotes writers connected with the utopian genre, and the constantly bubbling spring of his irony is fed from many texts. However, the sophisticated intertextuality of his own work doesn't preclude satire at the expense of those who simple-mindedly assume that their reading enables them to peddle utopian solutions to complicated problems in the real world. Fielding has little time for revolutionary fanatics. Yet he reveres the simple-hearted, if not the simple-minded, which causes complications in his own intelligent fiction.

His choice of targets in *The Covent-Garden Journal* gives short shrift to modern utopianism, which he blames partly on historical fallacy: 'Gentlemen who obtain an early Acquaintance with the Manners and Customs of the Antients, are too apt to form their Ideas of their own Times, on the Patterns of Ages which bear not the least Resemblance to them.'[3] Although tongue-in-cheek, the parallel between the university scholar and the moon voyager of utopian fiction scores a point: the scholar is as much at a loss in the metropolis as 'if he was to be at once translated into one of the Planets; *the World* in the Town and that *in the Moon* being equally strange to him, and equally unintelligible'.[4] An example of the utopian imagination at work takes the form of a letter dated 1 April from Bedlam, which purports to be a proposal for the abolition of money – an idea, as Fielding well knows, common to a number of ideal states. The supposed correspondent acknowledges its unoriginality, 'To the Philosophers among the Antients, and to some of their Poets, . . . this invaluable Secret was well known,' but he proceeds to spell out the advantages of a moneyless society.[5] The ends in view – the removal of corruption, luxury, theft, poverty – sound like Thomas More. But the argument reduces the means to absurdity (it's tricky to bribe people secretly when the backhander consists of a flock of sheep). Significantly, the assertion which starts by sounding like Raphael Hythlodaeus closes in the authentic accents of Fielding's own Peter Pounce: 'my Scheme would most certainly provide for the Poor, and that by an infallible (perhaps the only infallible) Method, by removing the Rich. Where there are no Rich, there will of Consequence be found no Poor: for Providence hath in a wonderful Manner provided in every Country, a plentiful Subsistence for all its Inhabitants . . . .'[6]

These are ironic fictions. However, Fielding is painfully conscious of the real social evils that utopian theory aims to redress. In *An Enquiry into the Causes of the Late Increase of Robbers, &c. with Some Proposals for Remedying this Growing Evil* (1751), his own handling of the crime problem reveals in a much more sombre context the limits that he sets on utopian idealism. Throughout, the legal mind curbs the liberal imagination: he recommends the more effective enforcement of existing laws, rather than radical rethinking of the penal system. Ironically, a point that he does have in common with the constructors of utopias is his approval of the extent to which the civil authorities can and should control the personal lives of the poor in the interests of society at large (witness his discussion of the laws concerning vagrancy).[7] It isn't that Fielding lacks compassion, but he opposes its misdirection towards thieves rather than victims.

Perhpas the most illuminating passage in *An Enquiry* for Fielding's sense of the chasm between utopia and reality is his analysis of the conflict between private virtue and public benefit:

> Indeed the Passion of Love or Benevolence . . . seems to be the only human Passion that is in itself simply and absolutely good; and in *Plato's* Commonwealth or (which is more) in a Society acting up to the Rules of *Christianity*, no Danger could arise from the highest Excess of this Virtue; nay the more liberally it was indulged, and the more extensively it was expanded, the more would it contribute to the Honour of the Individual, and to the Happiness of the whole.
>
> But as it hath pleased God to permit human Societies to be constituted in a different Manner, and Knaves to form a Part, (a very considerable one, I am afraid) of every Community, who are ever lying in wait to destroy and ensnare the honest Part of Mankind, and to betray them by means of their own Goodness, it becomes the good-natured and tender-hearted Man to be watchful over his own Temper; to restrain the Impetuosity of his Benevolence, carefully to select the Objects of this Passion, and not by too unbounded and indiscriminate an Indulgence to give the Reins to a Courser, which will infallibly carry him into the Ambuscade of the Enemy.[8]

This is a bitter lesson for an instinctive benevolist like Fielding. He applies it in different ways in the novels, although fiction does allow him the option of evading consequences that he sees as inevitable in society as it is actually constituted.[9] He is no Hobbesian or Mandevillian,[10] but neither does he subscribe uncritically to Shaftesburian optimism. Indeed, he attacks both extremes of philosophical dogma. It follows that social utopia or dystopia are unlikely fictional models for Fielding, except as an object of satire.[11] His scepticism about institutional reform is particularly evident in his last and darkest novel, *Amelia*, but there are signs of it even in *Joseph Andrews*.

What *is* open for negotiation is the domestic utopia. Fielding's characters can build a heaven in hell's despite, because of the passion – human love – that Mandeville is accused of leaving out of his calculations. In all his major fiction, Fielding endorses the happy-ever-after closure that centres firmly on family life, its nucleus the happy couple with their children surrounded by some form of extended family embracing the generations, its guarantee financial security and healthy country living. It might seem yawningly conventional, but it's hard-earned: not simply by the usual tribulations of epic romance, but by an intellectual testing through discussion of the alternatives. Structurally, the learning process is handled through continuous debate and the technique of inset narratives. No less than any utopian theorist, Fielding writes unashamedly about values and uses fiction to illustrate his points. If the reader experiences his values vicariously, so too do the protagonists from time to time, as an internal audience.

The first example in Fielding's novels of what might be called a domestic utopia occurs not at the end, but in the middle of *Joseph Andrews*: the Wilsons' tale. In his rake's progress, Wilson has run through the gamut of eighteenth-century urban society. His account of it, interspersed with comments from the sometimes uncomprehending, sometimes horrified Parson Adams, isn't altogether unlike the interlocutory sessions in utopian fiction where an entire culture is put on trial before an innocent auditor. Fielding even includes a satire on current philosophical fashions in the description of the Freethinkers' club, which, as a modern editor points out, manages to target Hobbes and Mandeville as well as Shaftesbury.[12] When the Wilsons choose a life of rural retirement, it represents a conscious rejection of a society driven by the profit motive; yet the choice is made possible – a standard feature of eighteenth-century domestic utopias – by the windfall of unearned money (inherited, won in a lottery, acquired through marriage) which they are able to invest in their country idyll. To earn money in society as it is constituted requires an ethical or social compromise.

However, country society can also require social compromises, which Wilson is unwilling to make. In effect, the Wilson household becomes a separate entity within the community: 'we have here liv'd almost twenty Years, with little other Conversation than our own, most of the Neighbourhood taking us for very strange People; the Squire of the Parish representing me as a Madman, and the Parson as a Presbyterian; because I will not hunt with the one, nor drink with the other.'[13] Obviously this doesn't prevent the exercise of charity and hospitality to those in need, as the narrative context makes plain. However, charity is possible because of their self-sufficiency, in line with classical and utopian precept. Mr Wilson's garden is not for display but use – 'here was variety of Fruit and every thing useful for the Kitchin' – and he himself does all the necessary manual labour, and is rewarded by good health 'without Assistance from Physick'.[14] This is, so to speak, the eighteenth-century equivalent of a late-twentieth-century 'green' lifestyle, based on the efficient small-scale use of natural resources. In his valuing of family above any other social bonds – he declares 'I am neither ashamed of conversing with my Wife, nor of playing with my Children' – and his refusal to regard women as inferior, Wilson himself might seem like a precursor of the New Man. Certainly his internal exile contrasts sharply with Gulliver's: a closer parallel in eighteenth-century utopian fiction would be Peter Wilkins in his very different circumstances. Yet, consistently with Fielding's own views, Wilson's high valuation of female understanding doesn't extend to the idea that wives or daughters should be educated like men: 'he would not be apprehended to insinuate that his own [wife] had an understanding above the Care of her Family' – a knowledge of Greek, for instance.[15] Essentially the ideal remains conservative and patriarchal.

Nor, for all its independence, is the ideal way of life immune to the abuses of power that society at large sanctions. The local squire's authority, brutally and senselessly enforced in his slaughter of the child's pet spaniel, is a reminder of an anti-utopian political alternative: 'his Father had too great a Fortune to contend with . . . he was as absolute as any Tyrant in the Universe'. When Adams asserts on departing 'that this was the Manner in which the People had lived in the Golden Age', the comparison has to be severely qualified.[16] If this is in some respects a simple-life utopia, it is in other respects far removed from the manners of the classical Golden Age. However, like many utopias, it serves as a model to which to aspire. When Joseph, true son of Mr Wilson, and Fanny finally achieve their destiny, they are naturally absorbed into the same patriarchal family unit, even repeating the pattern of the financial windfall which makes it feasible (it's a nice irony that the source is another country squire, Fanny's brother-in-law, Booby). Literally, at the end, *il faut cultiver notre jardin* – in the immortal words of Candide.[17]

Apart from the Wilson episode, Fielding inserts another exchange in *Joseph Andrews* which bears upon the primitivist ideal. In this instance, however, the purpose is to satirise its misapplication. Peter Pounce tries to wriggle out of the duty of practical charity by arguing that the sufferings of the poor are largely illusory: "How can any Man complain of Hunger," said *Peter*, "in a Country where such excellent Salads are to be gathered in almost every Field?" Let them eat grass? The same goes for thirst: there is no shortage of rivers and streams. 'And as for Cold and Nakedness, they are Evils introduced by Luxury and Custom. A Man naturally wants Clothes no more than a Horse or any other Animal, and there are whole Nations who go without them . . . '[18] Clearly this touches satirically on a familiar utopian debate about the usefulness and significance of wearing clothes (the mention of the horse in particular invokes Gulliver's fourth voyage). Pounce's theory of luxury recalls Mandeville, who also robustly declares that meat and clothing postdate the Golden Age. On the subject of diet, Mandeville turns the point to moral advantage: 'I have often thought, if it was not for this Tyranny which Custom usurps over us, that Men of any tolerable Good-nature could never be reconcil'd to the killing of so many Animals for their daily Food, as long as the bountiful Earth so plentifully provides them with Varieties of vegetable Dainties.'[19] For Pounce and his ilk, Mandeville's solution to the problem of the poor – cutting back their needs, so that less provision has to be made for them – satisfactorily refutes the case for increased charitable giving, while allowing the luxury of a good conscience. England, in Pounce's view, is already too utopian in its social attitudes. In the Mandevillian spirit of *An Essay on Charity, and Charity-Schools* ('Charity, where it is too extensive, seldom fails of promoting Sloth and Idleness') he claims that 'the greatest Fault in our Constitution is the Provision made for the Poor'.[20] Parson Adams, despite having 'read of the Gymnosophists', will have no truck with this sham Golden Age primitivism: he may sentimentalise the Wilsons' way of life to some extent, but he doesn't sentimentalise the real 'Distresses which attend the Poor'.[21] And it is Adams's Christian and classical philosophy that triumphs in *Joseph Andrews*.

The techniques of inset narrative and debate offer a mainstream novelist the means of admitting utopian discourse into his or her fiction, but also cordoning it off at the same time. While invoking an alternative standard of comparison, the writer registers its alternative status through form. Even when its importance to the main narrative is unquestionable – as with the Wilsons' domestic utopia – it is still encapsulated within a secondary narrative, or, in the case of all Fielding's happy endings, projected beyond the time scheme of the novel itself. In *Tom Jones* Fielding uses the same technical method to present political as well as domestic utopian constructions.

One of these is the Man of the Hill's history, an even darker variation on Wilson's tale, with a pessimistic outcome. At the beginning of the episode, it looks as if Fielding is reworking his earlier material – benighted travellers, supernatural fears, nocturnal lawlessness, the need for shelter. However, the open charity of the Wilson household is set against the defensive solitariness of the recluse and his housekeeper, in what emerges as a crucial contrast for readers of both novels. Before the Man of the Hill embarks on his history, he is given the reputation of a great traveller, and appears like an aged Crusoe or Gulliver, clad in animal skins.[22] The tale itself, however, concentrates in much more detail on his experiences at home than abroad; and it is clear that his resemblance to Gulliver in particular arises from how he interprets those experiences. Just like Gulliver's creator, he has gathered materials for building a treatise upon a 'great foundation of Misanthropy', which, in a paradox that Swift should have appreciated, he calls philanthropy – 'for however it may seem a Paradox . . . certain it is that great Philanthropy chiefly inclines us to avoid and detest Mankind'.[23] All his philosophy (and he has studied Plato and Aristotle), his Christian theology (which he prizes far beyond the ancients) and his cosmology (including the idea of the plurality of worlds) lead him, like his travels, to only one conclusion: 'Human Nature is every where the same, every where the Object of Detestation and Avoidance.'[24] Logically, therefore, he chooses to go into an internal exile like Gulliver's, but even more intensely solitary. The result is to close down all possibility of change, as in the most absolute form of utopia: he puts it succcinctly, 'from that Day to this my History is little better than a Blank.'[25] In effect, he aspires to the condition of Swift's Houyhnhnms, a race happy in having no history. However, he has a function in the history of Tom Jones, namely to contribute to the hero's further education. Tom resists the Swiftian verdict on the human species, arguing (after Cicero) that the characteristics of a species should be derived from the best, not the worst, individual members. In the broader canvas of Fielding's novel, the Man of the Hill's choice of life also supplies a deliberate contrast to the domestic values that the narrative finally endorses. Within limits, he can be read as Fielding's comment on the utopian traveller who ends by despising and rejecting humanity: a salutary warning.

Between solitude and domesticity there is a third utopian option in the world of *Tom Jones*: the self-governing society existing on the margin of society at large. Fielding depicts this phenomenon in the shape of the kingdom of the gipsies. Like the Man of the Hill sequence, this curious episode slots yet another building block into the edifice of Tom's social education; and it too has highly specific political connotations. As Martin Battestin has argued, these connotations are inseparable from its utopian form: in his view, Fielding derives an image of ancient Egypt from such sources as Herodotus and Diodorus Siculus, and uses it to discredit the political illusion of benevolent despotism: 'the Tory dream of utopia is made to appear foolish through its association with an exotic band of thieves and fortune-tellers adrift in the heart of England.'[26] However, if this makes a plausible case for reading the episode in the light of Fielding's politics, as a brief foray into utopian fiction it also connects with the social concerns of the novel as a whole. Politically, the kingdom of the gipsies may be the kind of constitution – absolute sovereignty vested in one person – that can only work in the Golden Age (as the authorial commentary takes pains to point out). However, socially, the mores of this community offer an example of utopian attitudes relevant to contemporary behaviour: attitudes to sexual relations, the code of honour, and fitting the punishment to the crime.

The cultural practice of basing punishments primarily on shame isn't unique to ancient Egypt. In particular, sexual misdemeanours are punished by public shaming in all kinds of societies, historical and fictional, including, *a fortiori*, those that are regarded as utopian in their strictness. Tacitus in his *Germania* writes approvingly of the brutal Germanic punishment of wives guilty of adultery, which involves stripping and public flogging; centuries later, Berington goes into similar detail about his legendary Mezzoranians, and their method of exposing the naked corpses of adulterous couples (at least they wait till after death, and don't exclude the male partner entirely, though the female is treated more ignominiously).[27] Fielding chooses to show his king of the gipsies, who plays the familiar utopian role of 'naive' foreign monarch ready to ask awkward questions, as he exercises his authority on a domestic issue rather than a political one.

The occasion arises from Partridge's roll in the hay with the young wife of one of the gipsies. When Tom Jones agrees to compensate the

husband financially, the royal judge ascertains the facts of the case –
that the husband is prepared to barter his wife's honour for money –
and rules that both husband and wife should suffer a period of public
infamy. Adultery is an important subject in *Tom Jones*, and both the
reader and ultimately the hero are required to discriminate according
to the circumstances and motives of the adulterous act. The punishment of shame is clearly approved of; but Tom's education has still to
pass through several stages before this part of the gipsies' utopian
lesson will be fully brought home to him.

Infidelity in any circumstances poses a threat to the domestic
utopia, yet it carries different degrees of risk. In Tom's case, he learns
the true meaning of honour through theory and experience. Fielding
uses the gipsy episode to question the public as well as the sexual
meaning of the word. When the king asks 'Are your Rewards and
Punishments den de same Ting?'[28] the question anticipates the final
moral drawn by the narrator, which is in a recognisable vein of
utopian satire. We cannot hope to take the gipsies as a political
examplar, precisely because their social utopianism ensures their
political stability, not vice versa: 'we must remember the very material
Respect in which they differ from all other People, and to which
perhaps this their Happiness is entirely owing, namely, that they have
no false Honours among them; and that they look on Shame as the
most grievous Punishment in the World.'[29]

In *Amelia*, the most philosophical and yet the most domesticated of
Fielding's novels, social utopianism breaks down altogether. Even the
domestic utopia comes under severer strain than ever before. Technically, Fielding retains the function of inset narrative and debate: but
whereas in *Joseph Andrews* and *Tom Jones* the inexperienced heroes
listen to the tales related by Mr Wilson and the Man of the Hill, in
the early stages of *Amelia*, Booth is both auditor and narrator of his
history to date. That history contains a recognisable version of a
domestic utopia now lost, the conditions for which were originally
created by the benevolent patriarchal figure, Dr Harrison. It is an
'earthly Paradise' – Dr Harrison's own term – centred on a plain house
in a pleasant pastoral landscape. Under his patriarchal scrutiny, the
community enjoys all the social harmony requisite for a utopia
conducted on a Christian model: 'all his Parishioners, whom he treats
as his Children, regard him as their common Father' and he
disciplines them accordingly. Booth adds, 'so good an Effect is
produced by this . . . Care, that no Quarrels ever proceed either to

Blows or Law-suits; no Beggar is to be found in the whole Parish; nor did I ever hear a very profane Oath all the Time I lived in it.'[30]

Here the Booths settle, as tenant farmers of the doctor's, to engage in a brief idyll of family life comparable to that of the Wilsons ('the whole was one continued Series of Love, Health, and Tranquillity').[31] However, unlike the Wilsons, they do not own their property; and, also unlike the Wilsons, in the doctor's absence Booth ceases to observe the utopian rule of sticking to one's station, the idea of justice that goes back to Socrates. Beginning with a bad economic invest-ment, he is then unwise enough to indulge in the 'childish Vanity' of a second-hand equipage, which ruptures the fiction of social harmony and lets loose the baser emotions of class conflict: as Booth tells it:

> Before this, as my Wife and myself had very little distinguished ourselves from the other Farmers and their Wives, either in our Dress, or our Way of Living, they treated us as their Equals; but now they began to consider us as elevating ourselves into a State of Superiority, and immediately began to envy, hate, and declare War against us. The neighbouring little Squires too were uneasy to see a poor Renter become their Equal in a Matter in which they placed so much Dignity . . .[32]

This is a shrewd analysis on Fielding's part of how little it takes to disturb the delicate equilibrium, the checks and balances of a social mechanism, once its breakdown is triggered by the absence of the authority figure. But, in its origins, this utopian community was a compromise in any case, created not by any kind of radical reform of social relations or institutions, but by the constant vigilance of its 'ruler' and his subordinate (the curate). The Booths will regain their domestic utopia at the end of the novel, but only after prolonged exposure to a complicated experience of social and economic failure and powerlessness.

Fielding uses his last novel to test a variety of theses about human behaviour and, as formerly, focuses these through discussion as well as action. Theories are matched to their proponents: it should come as no surprise that the calculating and self-interested Miss Matthews, who seduces Booth, has been impressed by 'that charming Fellow Mandevil' though her reading of him appears hazy.[33] Booth, in arguing against Mandeville's doctrines, asserts the faith in the reality and power of love that will ultimately be his salvation. However, not all the debates are so comparatively clear-cut. In fact, a particularly problematic chapter is the one that bears most explicitly on attitudes to utopian ideology, the discussion between Dr Harrison and a certain nobleman, headed 'Matters Political'.[34] In this connection, it is worth looking at in some detail.

Since the doctor is attempting to interest the nobleman in Booth's case, and the nobleman is proposing that the *quid pro quo* should be the doctor's political support for the nobleman's preferred candidate in an election, the scene serves as a neat example of eighteenth-century wheeling and dealing. It also generates discussion of the root causes underlying the specific situation, namely the expectations of a society in which career structures and politics alike are distorted by the exercise of undue influence. Such a society is self-evidently the opposite of the just society that is the ideal of most political utopists. Naturally, one might think, the doctor is allotted the moral or utopian argument; yet he is ready to justify it pragmatically as well as on principle. When the peer demands how promotion on merit can possibly work, since all who deserved it would need to be provided for, the doctor retorts:

> "Only by not providing for those who have none [i.e. merit] – The Men of Merit in any Capacity are not I am afraid so extremely numerous, that we need starve any of them, unless we wickedly suffer a Set of worthless Fellows to eat their Bread."
>
> "This is all mere *Utopia*," cries his Lordship; "the Chimerical System of *Plato's* Commonwealth with which we amused ourselves at the University; Politics which are inconsistent with the State of Human Affairs."
>
> "Sure, my Lord," cries the Doctor, "we have read of States where such Doctrines have been put in Practice. What is your Lordship's Opinion of *Rome* in the earlier Ages of the Commonwealth, of *Sparta*, and even of *Athens* itself, in some periods of its History?"
>
> "Indeed, Doctor," cries the Lord, "all these Notions are obsolete and long since exploded. To apply Maxims of Government drawn from the *Greek* and *Roman* Histories, to this Nation, is absurd and impossible. But if you will have *Roman* Examples, fetch them from those Times of the Republic that were most like our own. Do you not know, Doctor, that this is as corrupt a Nation as ever existed under the Sun? And would you think of governing such a People by the strict Principles of Honesty and Morality?"

"If it be so corrupt," said the Doctor, "I think it is high Time to amend it . . . "[35]

The question is, how? Here if anywhere in Fielding's fiction the reader might legitimately expect the utopian imagination, in its political aspect, to come into play. Moreover, Dr Harrison does have a programme of a kind. He accepts that, if the nobleman's dystopian picture of national decline is accurate, then the only remedy for despair is religious rather than political. However, religion apart, it's still possible to make a rationalist case for a just society on the grounds that it's in the best interests of the commonwealth to adopt the utopian principle of promoting men on ability and integrity. Even a minister of state might discover that the moral course is also the politically popular one: a utopian notion indeed. The nobleman, however, almost corners the doctor with his two final questions: is anyone 'ever a Rogue out of Choice?' and would the public ever believe in the morality of a minister of state, even if it were entirely genuine?[36] The doctor retreats from the first with the Socratic argument that men may be deluded into evil, or else that they may feel inadequate to the task of clearing the Augean stables of public life; to the second he replies not directly but in metaphor. In purely debating terms, it is hard to believe that either side scores decisively on points. The reason for this seems to me to go to the heart of Fielding's problem with the utopian imagination.

Regarded objectively, it is the nobleman's case which represents most nearly Fielding's own political realism (compare, for instance, the satire in *The Covent-Garden Journal*). While subscribing to Dr Harrison's ideal, he is deeply sceptical about its efficacy, and offers no detailed suggestion as to how it might be institutionalised. Fielding's editor offers an explanation of this paradoxical discussion in biographical terms, citing for instance Fielding's friendship with Bubb Dodington to account for the doctor's side of the argument.[37] It might be as true to say that Fielding is here arguing against himself, that this chapter is the site of an ideological conflict which is also a conflict within his own psyche between optimism and pessimism. It is noticeable that in *Amelia* he can only define theoretic social reform, and that in the most general terms. There's no suggestion of social change worked into the fiction itself: moral man and immoral society are two halves of an insoluble equation. As in his earliest novel, so in his latest, the utopian imagination effectively begins and ends with the family.

Yet with one vital difference: the family's survival, its final achievement of a domestic utopia, depends more crucially than ever upon the woman who holds it together through all vicissitudes. It's no accident that this is the only one of Fielding's novels to have an eponymous heroine instead of hero. However, it must be added that this shift of centre doesn't mean that Fielding intends to renege on the principle of patriarchy. Amelia sees her own role as loving, honouring *and obeying* Booth, upholding his authority in the family and, even more, to the outside world.[38] Cracks do become visible in the edifice, as Booth's authority is continually compromised by his own flawed behaviour. Even Amelia is prepared to question his ruling in private; and at one point, the severest test of her loyalty, she momentarily breaks down in front of her children – 'your Papa is – indeed he is a wicked Man – he cares not for any of us'.[39] Although this indictment is neither wholly deserved nor final, it damages Booth's status, perhaps irreparably. To ensure the stability of the utopian ending, Booth has to be summarily redeemed, and the patriarchal principle soldered back into place.[40] Yet the balance of power, emotional power at least, has shifted towards matriarchal influence, the strength of the weak. Fielding may have chosen his title for sentimental reasons,[41] but in terms of his fiction it is potentially subversive.

Richardson: 'agreeable schemes'

Richardson moves in the opposite direction from Fielding: starting with eponymous heroines, *Pamela* and *Clarissa*, he ends with an eponymous hero, *Sir Charles Grandison*. Titles may be only a crude indicator of priorities, but they count for something. In a sense, his fiction becomes more utopian, as Fielding's becomes less so.[42] In all his novels, Richardson investigates, with considerable subtlety, the tensions and conflicts involved in gender difference, and this applies equally to the workings of the utopian imagination which is shaped by the contrasting experiences of men and women. In *Clarissa*, for example, Lovelace attempts to appropriate utopia as a male prerogative. However, as in other areas of this novel, the reader is actually confronted with competing interpretations, Lovelace's and Clarissa's, of the utopian alternatives. For Lovelace this is not a simple proposition, since his own instincts are competing and contradictory, requiring to be rationalised. If he were to construct a utopian fiction among his many other fictions, what form would it take? Its ideology isn't much in doubt: Lovelace has only to apply the principle of his 'worthy friend' Mandeville – private vices, public benefits – to the sexual economy to find his answer.[43]

Lovelace does in fact produce a utopian scheme of a specialised sort at a fairly advanced stage of the narrative. By this point, the reader has had the chance to sift through a considerable quantity of evidence about his mode of thought. Even taking into account the male swagger of his style, it is clear that as Richardson's creation he can think intelligently about the historical relation between sex and power: in fantasy, he scales down the struggles for world power to the domination of a man over a woman. His conceptual weakness lies not so much in his strategy as in his assessment of the enemy, his essentialist view of the nature of women which leads to his fatal miscalculation of his opponent.[44] However, in a sense he also miscalculates the problem of male sexuality, in which he might be supposed to be an expert; and this explains his need for a utopian solution.

In certain obvious ways, Lovelace subscribes to patriarchy. He wants, and assumes as his right, an absolute authority over women; he regards women as a form of property; and he wants to assert his rights and prove his virility by fathering children (a recurrent fantasy is Clarissa as mother, suckling the Lovelace twins, producing 'every year a charming boy').[45] Nor does he consider that one to one should be cursedly confined. A curious offshoot of his imaginings is the idea of having a boy by Clarissa and a girl by Anna Howe, who, in ignorance of their parentage, will marry in adult life: a highly personalised variation on the Platonic suggestion that wives and children should be in common.[46] As a practising libertine, Lovelace reserves the right to enjoy as many women as he chooses. As a patriarch in theory, he might be expected to find the notion of polygamy attractive, as indeed did a number of male contemporaries. In the popular view, polygamy ratifies male sovereignty, inviting men to behave like masters and tyrants: which is one of Hume's arguments against it when writing 'Of Polygamy and Divorces'.[47] In this essay, Hume cites utopian as well as historical precedents, for example, the *History of the Severambians* (he could also have mentioned Neville's *The Isle of Pines* as a parallel instance). However, what lent respectability to polygamy, at least in the abstract, was its association with Old Testament patriarchy, an association that Lovelace doesn't hesitate to invoke, though respectability is scarcely his aim: 'Thus of old did the contending wives of the honest patriarchs; each recommending her handmaid to her lord, as she thought it would oblige him, and looking upon the genial product as her own' (shades of a very different modern utopian fiction *The Handmaid's Tale*).[48] Yet the patriarch and the libertine are incompatible role models, differentiated by the concept of paternal responsibility – a subject on which Lovelace is deeply ambivalent. Although he professes to believe that his desire for a child by Clarissa sets him apart from other libertines – incidentally, in a context where he reiterates the phrase 'genial product' – his fear that the patriarchal role will deprive him of liberty surfaces in an image of the drudgery of procreation, worthy of Rochester: 'what a couple of old patriarchs shall we become, going on in the mill-horse round; getting sons and daughters . . . .' sons and daughters who, inescapably slaves to gender, will repeat their parents' mistakes.[49] As a libertine thinker, Lovelace patronises patriarchs: as a patriarchal thinker, he looks down on libertines. No existing system can offer an answer to his dilemma, so he devises his own.

From his utopian scheme he wants not just sexual freedom *per se*, but a social structure that will solve at a stroke the problems arising from the drives of sex and procreation. In this respect, he shows himself a true utopist. His basic idea is to legalise annual marriage, or, looked at from another angle, annual divorce (the political analogy is with annual Parliaments, another prevalent utopian idea). Remarriage to the same person is permissible, but the primary object is to promote change and, so he claims, improve relationships. Lovelace lists the evils that would be removed (including the appeal of polygamy):

> *rapes*, vulgarly so called; adultery, and fornication; nor would *polygamy* be panted after. Frequently would it prevent *murders* and *duelling*: hardly any such thing as *jealousy* (the cause of shocking violences) would be heard of: and hypocrisy between man and wife be banished the bosoms of each. Nor, probably, would the reproach of *barrenness* rest, as now it too often does, where it is least deserved – Nor would there possibly be such a person as a barren woman.[50]

He goes on to point out the benefits to physical and mental health, observing in a finely ironic aside, 'But, that no body of men might suffer, the *physicians*, I thought, might turn *parsons*, as there would be a great demand for parsons.'[51] In other words, the scheme entails a reorganising of institutions, like all utopias of its kind.

Obviously there's a strong element of *épater les bourgeois* in all this, but at the same time it sounds like a surprisingly workable set of proposals by utopian standards, with a number of possible objections skilfully as well as wittily covered. It's also revealing to consider the utopian options that aren't taken up: why *not* polygamy, for instance? or the Platonic community of shared sexual partners and offspring? Either would satisfy the unrestrained male sexual appetite that Lovelace is sometimes supposed to epitomise. In William James's immortal formulation – 'Hogamus higamus, man is polygamous;/ Higamus hogamus, woman monogamous.' However, Lovelace's problem with patriarchal polygamy has already been noted; and the Platonic alternative isn't altogether satisfactory either (he *wants* property rights, in all senses). Besides, this isn't the kind of wish-fulfilment that produced the libertine utopias of the previous century, whether Golden Age or tropical paradise. What is most striking here is the prescient insistence on legal and political validity, sexual revolution by Act of Parliament.[52] By design or by accident, Richardson has made Lovelace the mouthpiece of an extremely inventive utopian fiction, which is a strange but effective amalgam of bourgeois convention and aristocratic freethinking. It even addresses the financing of such a scheme, and the provision made for children – a point on which Lovelace openly compares himself to one of the best-known classical precedents: 'those children which the parents could not agree about maintaining might be considered as the *children of the public,* and provided for like the children of the ancient Spartans; who were (as ours would in this case be) a nation of heroes. How, Jack, could I have improved upon Lycurgus's institutions, had I been a lawgiver?'[53] It isn't an altogether idle boast. Later he also boasts of the superiority of his system to the alternative already considered: 'how infinitely more preferable this my scheme, than the polygamy one of the old patriarchs; who had wives and concubines without number! I believe David and Solomon had their hundreds *at at time.*'[54]

The culminating irony is Lovelace's argument that (like Milton's divorce pamphlets) these arrangements are intended for the good of both sexes, that 'the women will have equal reason with the men to be pleased with it'.[55] In addition, the charge often levelled against Milton – that he ignores the interests of children – can't be brought here. And, moral considerations aside, Lovelace might be felt to have a point. Under his scheme, a pregnant woman's rights would be protected: her husband could not remarry without her consent until she had had the child, 'and till it was agreed upon between them, whether the child should be *his*, *hers*, or the *public's*. The women, in this case, to have . . . the *coercive option*'.[56] It's an option that might have seemed a genuinely utopian privilege to many eighteenth-century women, inside or outside fiction.

However, certainly not to a Clarissa: for, of course, in context Lovelace's utopia is meant to damn him further, to mark out the gulf between his thinking and hers, the gulf between the godless and the Godfearing, the reprobate and the elect. Clarissa's asceticism and self-discipline set her at variance with a secular and materialistic society. Given the social responsibility of wealth, she feels accountable for its use. If Clarissa were to envisage a utopian way of life, it would be based squarely on Christian principles. There is evidence that under more propitious circumstances than those of the narrative she has tried to establish a form of domestic utopia corresponding to this ideal.

Clarissa's scheme of living is described in Anna Howe's lengthy hagiographic letter towards the end of the novel, setting out in detail her education and accomplishments, her organisation of her day, and her good works.[57] In certain respects, this image of exemplary female pursuits anticipates Sarah Scott's utopian fiction, *Millenium Hall*. However, not only does Clarissa's present tragedy suspend it in an idealised past, so reversing the narrative structure of Scott's novel; in Clarissa's case, there are also painful constraints on her freedom of action, which are apparent from the outset. To a large extent, these are constraints imposed by gender, and by her own sense of her position. When Lovelace comments sarcastically that 'she never was in a state of *independency*; nor is it fit a woman should, of any age, or in any state of life',[58] he defines an oppression which is psychological as much as social or economic. Clarissa herself had been all too aware of the pitfalls of independence and power in relation to her age and sex. It was these considerations that prompted her to give up her grandfather's estate, and so leave herself vulnerable: ironically, she proves her fitness for power by her willingness to sacrifice it – in effect, she renounces utopia:

> All young creatures, thought I, more or less covet independency, but those who wish most for it are seldom the fittest to be trusted either with the government of themselves or with power over others . . . We should not aim at *all* we have power to do . . . .

(Plato and Aristotle had made a similar observation about political ambition.)

> It is true, thought I, that I have formed agreeable schemes of making others as happy as myself by the proper discharge of the stewardship entrusted to me (*are not all estates stewardships, my dear?*) But let me examine myself . . . Ought I not to suspect my own heart?[59]

'Let me examine myself': Clarissa's imaginative strengths are those that create a spiritual life, not a utopia. For someone in her situation, the utopian ideal even on a modest scale must generate deep tensions, since it requires incompatible commitments: self versus society, independence versus submissiveness, power versus powerlessness. She does achieve independence and power, but as inner resources gained through outward loss. Other fictional ways of resolving or escaping from Clarissa's conflict have to wait for women writers: Sarah Scott, Mary Hamilton, Frances Burney. Clarissa may dream of just such a way of life as the ladies of Millenium Hall practise, but she has to suppress her dream; and for her there can be no domestic utopia of the patriarchal kind either – the reward of Richardson's first heroine, Pamela. However, Richardson himself has not given up his interest in the domestic utopia as a force for social and individual good; and he returns to and develops this concept to its fullest extent in his final novel, *Sir Charles Grandison*.

His hero Grandison, as much concept as character, is a kind of utopian model: perhaps not the Platonic philosopher-king, but the eighteenth-century equivalent, the idealised Christian gentleman who has at his disposal the raw material of many lives and livelihoods to shape into a work of art. Were it not for his (heroically controlled) susceptibility to romantic passion,[60] Sir Charles might be regarded as the Houyhnhnm of the eighteenth-century novel, consistently rational and benevolent. He thinks just as he ought – or as Richardson thinks he ought – on all social topics.[61] The reader is as fully informed as he or she wants to be, if not more so, on Sir Charles's views: on women, on servants, on the poor, on dress, on religion, on education. His utopian credentials are not in doubt, and he is in a position to put them into practice, most strikingly on his country estate, Grandison-Hall.

Seen through the eyes of his new bride, Harriet, Grandison-Hall represents the country-house ideal in its most paternal form: 'the very servants live in paradise. There is room for every thing to be in order: Every-thing *is* in order . . . . It is a house of harmony, to my hand . . . . Every one knowing and doing his and her duty; and having, by means of their own diligence, time for themselves.'[62] Some of the arrangements resemble a microcosmic welfare state. For instance, a servants' library, carefully chosen and classified and complete with a system of fines, is provided to improve the mind; to take care of the body, there is a comprehensive health service, free to those unable to pay. As for the economy of the estate, Sir Charles, the ideal landlord, runs it with exemplary efficiency like Swift's Lord Munodi.[63] Everything prospers under his regime. However, like many utopias, this is first and foremost a moral commonwealth, dependent on self-regulation as well as supervision. It isn't such a paradise for servants that it can dispense with methods used in the real world – the servant's hall has its own codified laws and penalties – but compared to the domestic dystopia revealed in, say, Swift's *Directions to Servants*, it is at least an improvement on current conditions.

Sir Charles's ideology, and the benevolent officiousness it engenders, are particularly evident in his attitudes to his social inferiors, and to women. In spite of occasional disclaimers, he doesn't seem to regard people of a different class or sex as being entirely the same species as himself. In this he is being perfectly orthodox, but it is an orthodoxy that the author of *Clarissa* had shown himself capable of transcending. If education is taken as a test of utopian standing, Sir Charles's rating is somewhere between Plato and More. It is the *deserving* poor, in all senses, that he is prepared to benefit academically: but he does show a willingness to rescue any mute inglorious Miltons, and his scheme for selection according to aptitude is common to a number of utopias. If he sounds intolerably patronising, it's a function of style as much as substance:

> . . . I could be glad, that only such children of the poor, as shew a peculiar ingenuity, have any great pains taken with them in their *books*. Husbandry and labour are what are most wanting to be encouraged among the lower class of people. Providence has given to men different genius's and capacities, for different ends . . . Let us apply those talents to Labour, those to Learning, those to Trade, to Mechanics, in their different branches, which point out the different pursuits, and then no person will be unuseful; on the contrary, every one may be eminent in some way or other.[64]

Yet, although the principle would be recognised in More's *Utopia*, the initiative doesn't belong to the people most concerned as it does in More's commonwealth. When Sir Charles proceeds to assert that 'Learning, of itself, never made any man happy', then concedes 'but if a genius arises, let us encourage it', he is assuming a superior judgment as of right – a right which is also the right of control over other lives. He may be enlightened in supplying books for his household, but their reading is chosen for them. Sir Charles Grandison is certainly not the kind of gentleman who would permit his wife or his servants to read *Lady Chatterley's Lover*.

Not surprisingly, the extended discussion of the status and capacities of women requires more difficult negotiation, and is generally more problematic.[65] As always, Richardson's ability to imagine and feel, as well as to argue, from a woman's point of view, enables a powerful and disturbing case to be made (if not answered). It is spearheaded by two strong characters, Harriet's grandmother, vastly experienced and respected, and Sir Charles's sister, Charlotte, intelligent, rebellious, witty, and one of the most attractive people in the novel (it is she who writes the letter recording this conversation). The older woman opens first, with the proposition that 'women are generally too much considered as a species apart' – a point which is well substantiated and partly accepted. However, the language of species and individual gives the male opposition, in the person of Sir Charles, the chance to make its own case and to evade genuine confrontation of the female challenge. While allowing for individual exceptions, he believes in essential gender difference, without, however, letting himself be pinned down by Charlotte's shrewd question about natural inferiority and superiority. 'There is a difference, pardon me, Ladies, we are speaking *generally*, in the *constitution*, in the *temperament*, of the two Sexes, that gives to the one advantages which it denies to the other' – a maxim illustrated by the customary animal analogy, 'the surly bull, the meek, the beneficent cow'.[66] So far as Sir Charles is concerned, it is a case of *vive la différence*: 'Can there be characters more odious than those of a masculine woman, and an effeminate man?' he asks rhetorically. He goes on to explain that the differences are providentially arranged to fit the sexes for their different roles in life – 'Were it not so, their offices would be confounded, and the women would not perhaps so readily submit to those domestic ones in which it is their province to shine, and the men would be allotted the distaff or the needle.'[67] The argument from biology to social roles is wearily familiar, though as Aristotle pointed out it isn't altogether consistent with the animal analogy 'for animals have not to manage a household'.[68]

In many cultures, the educational arrangements reinforce the distinction: in the utopian tradition, however, equalising the sexes through education is at least an imagined possibility. This is the nettle that Sir Charles does *not* grasp. Although he holds forth on the benefits of academic learning, they are benefits that – as with the poor – he appears reluctant to extend to women. He refuses indeed to commit himself on the educational limits for women; but he concludes, again as he did in the discussion of working-class education, by making an exception only for the exceptional – 'genius, whether in man or woman, will push itself into light.'[69] It is a comfortable doctrine, requiring no true utopian alternative to the status quo. The one point on which Grandison and Lovelace agree – though for very different reasons – is that (as in Samuel Brunt's moon) souls have no sex:[70] so women have the dubious consolation of full equality with men in heaven.

Meanwhile on earth they have the domestic utopia of the patriarchal system. Compared to his male characters (Lovelace excepted) Richardson's women may – to adapt Leavis's well-known comment on Swift's Yahoos – 'have all the life'.[71] However, Harriet and even Charlotte end by conforming to their biological and social destiny, though with Charlotte it is motherhood rather than marriage itself that tames a free spirit. The female character for whom there is no such 'satisfactory' outcome is the prior claimant to Sir Charles's heart, the Italian heroine, Clementina, who can't bring herself to compromise her Catholic allegiance and marry him.[72] In collaboration with her family, he tries very hard to construct an acceptable future for her, with 'Articles' set out in detail,[73] and to frustrate her own choice which is to take the veil. Although this apparently succeeds, the question of how women can fulfil themselves outside marriage is left awkwardly open. Interestingly, this issue is one that prompts a general as well as a specific solution within the fiction, one that exercises Sir Charles's utopian imagination, as his libertine proclivities had exercised Lovelace's. Lovelace had come up with the utopian scheme of annual marriage; Sir Charles comes up with not one but two schemes for taking care of surplus women – Protestant nunneries and a hospital for female penitents. Both seem entirely in character.

The idea of an institution on the pattern of a Protestant nunnery isn't original (Mary Astell had developed it),[74] but it's worked out in sufficient detail to make an independent utopian statement in Richardson's fiction. 'Tho' the name of it would make many a Lady start', as Sir Charles explains, it's designed to improve women's lives:

> We want to see established in every county, *Protestant Nunneries*; in which single women of small or no fortunes might live with all manner of freedom, under such regulations as it would be a disgrace for a modest or good woman not to comply with, were she absolutely on her own hands; and to be allowed to quit it whenever they pleased.[75]

Sir Charles, accustomed to thinking in categories, scrupulously preserves social distinctions – 'the governesses or matrons of the society I would have to be women of family. The attendants, for the slighter services, should be the hopeful female children of the industrious poor.' He considers the financing as well as the membership of 'this well-regulated society': they could contribute to their own support by what they make. Not everything would be in common, however. 'Yet', he adds, 'I would have a number of hours in each day, for the encouragement of industry, that should be called their own; and what was produced in them, to be solely appropriated to their own use.'[76] So inspired is he by this utopian vision, that he matches it with the self-explanatory 'Hospital for Female Penitents'. Together they present rather a bleak view of female prospects, which might strike readers as a dreary contrast to Lovelace's scheme (which at least removed the stigma of being either a fallen woman or an old maid). Yet, for eighteenth-century women writers, it is the relative independence of the 'Protestant nunnery' that appeals most to the utopian imagination, as a prototype waiting to be transformed into a Millenium Hall. From a woman's viewpoint, the trouble with the domestic utopia of fiction is that it is rarely experimental enough. For male writers, the nucleus continues to be the patriarchal family, and it is mainly in women's novels that some sense of true utopian possibilities begins to break through. More than their masculine equivalents, novels such as *Millenium Hall* and *Munster Village* can be described as utopian in the strict paradigmatic meaning of the term, offering a programme for social living, an alternative which cannot yet free itself from its parent ideology, but which stimulates opposition to what Richardson and Fielding take for granted.

Notes and references

1. For Fielding's classical education v M.C. Battestin, R.R. Battestin 1989 Part I sec ix pp. 38–44.

2. H. Fielding 1752/1988 no 10 Tuesday 4 February p. 74.

3. H. Fielding 1752/1988 no 42 Tuesday 26 May p. 239.

4. H. Fielding 1752/1988 no 42 Tuesday 26 May p. 241.

5. H. Fielding 1752/1988 no 35 Saturday 2 May p. 211. cf Pope's 'bulky Bribes' passage in *Epistle to Bathurst* 11 35–64 (I am grateful to David Nokes for drawing attention to this parallel): also v C. Watts 1990 pp. 95–6.

6. H. Fielding 1752/1988 no 35 Saturday 2 May p. 213: cf H. Fielding 1742/1967 Book III ch. xiii p. 275.

7. v H. Fielding 1751/1988 Sec vi *Of Laws relating to VAGABONDS* pp. 130–44: for Fielding's social conservatism in this pamphlet v Zirker's intro pp. lx–lxiv. Also cf B. Mandeville 1705–1725/1989. *An Essay on Charity, and Charity-Schools* 1723: J. Swift 1939–68 vol. 13 *A Proposal to Give Badges to the Beggars* 1737: and v I.A. Bell 1991 pp. 190–7.

8. H. Fielding 1751/1988 p. 155.

9. v H. Fielding 1751/1988 p. 156 n 1: for problems in establishing ideology in Fielding's writing v I.A. Bell 1991 ch. 5.

10. But cf Zirker's comment on shared ground between Fielding and Mandeville despite Fielding's antagonism: H. Fielding 1751/1988 p. 71 n 2.

11. For interesting comments on Fielding and utopianism v M. McKeon 1987 pp. 388, 392, 408.

12. v H. Fielding 1742/1967 Book III ch. iii p. 212 n 1.

13. H. Fielding 1742/1967 Book III ch. iii p. 224.

14. H. Fielding 1742/1967 Book III ch. iv p. 226.

15. H. Fielding 1742/1967 Book III ch. iv p. 227.

16. H. Fielding 1742/1967 Book III ch. iv pp. 228, 229.

17. 'We must go and work in the garden': Voltaire 1759/1968 p. 144.

18. H. Fielding 1742/1967 Book III ch. xiii p. 275.

19. B. Mandeville 1705–1725/1924 vol. 1 p. 173 (Remark P).

20. B. Mandeville 1705–1725/1924 vol. 1 *An Essay on Charity, and Charity-Schools* p. 267: H. Fielding 1742/1967 Book III ch. xiii p. 275.

21. H. Fielding 1742/1967 Book III ch. xiii p. 275: Battestin notes on Gymnosophists, 'A sect of ascetic Hindu philosophers who wore little clothing and ate no meat' (p. 275 n 1).

22. H. Fielding 1749/1974 vol. 1 Book VIII ch. x p. 448: Battestin compares Lucian's Timon (n 1).

23. J. Swift 1963–5 vol. 3 p. 103: H. Fielding 1749/1974 vol. 1 Book VIII ch. x p. 450.

24. H. Fielding 1749/1974 vol. 1 Book VIII ch. xv p. 482.

25. H. Fielding 1749/1974 vol. 1 Book VIII ch. xiv p. 480.

26. M.C. Battestin 1967 p. 73: Battestin's article is a closely documented investigation of the utopian credentials of this episode in *Tom Jones* (Book XII ch xii).

27. v Tacitus 1948/1970 p. 117: S. Berington 1737 p. 205.

28. H. Fielding 1749/1974 vol. 2 Book XII ch. xii p. 669.

29. H. Fielding 1749/1974 vol. 2 Book XII ch. xii p. 673.

30. H. Fielding 1751/1983 Book III ch. xii p. 145.

31. H. Fielding 1751/1983 Book III ch. xii p. 147.

32. H. Fielding 1751/1983 Book III ch. xii p. 149.

33. H. Fielding 1751/1983 Book III ch. 1 v p. 114: v the exchange between Miss Matthews and Booth pp. 114–15 and editor's note (1).

34. H. Fielding 1751/1983 Book XI ch. ii pp. 456–65.

35. H. Fielding 1751/1983 Book XI ch. ii pp. 459–60.

36. H. Fielding 1751/1983 Book XI ch. ii pp. 464, 465.

37. v Battestin's intro pp. xxxvii–xxxix and notes to Book XI ch. ii (H. Fielding 1751/1983 pp. 456–65).

38. v H. Fielding 1751/1983 Book VI ch. v pp. 247–9: cf the private conversation between husband and wife in the following chapter (ch. vi pp. 249–53).

39. H. Fielding 1751/1983 Book XI ch. ix p. 491.

40. v H. Fielding 1751/1983 Book XII ch. v pp. 510–12: ch. ix pp. 532–3.

41. v Battestin's intro in H. Fielding 1751/1983 pp. xvi–xxi.

42. But for the suggestion of 'a utopian parable' in *Pamela* v M. McKeon 1987 pp. 373, 375, 380–1.

43. S. Richardson 1747–8/1985 Letter 246 p. 847.

44. For Lovelace's heroic analogies v S. Richardson 1747–8/1985 Letter 223 p. 718: Letter 232 p. 762. For a persuasive account of his psychology v M. Kinkead-Weekes 1973 chs 6, 7 (eg pp. 174–82, 186–7, 226–31): cf J.G. Turner 1989. In M.A. Doody, P. Sabor (eds) pp. 70–8.

45. S. Richardson 1747–8/1985 Letter 223 p. 720: cf Letter 220 p. 706.

46. v S. Richardson 1747–8/1985 Letter 271 p. 922.

47. v D. Hume 1882/1964 vol. 3 pp. 231–9: for contemporary interest in polygamy v A. Macfarlane 1986 pp. 218–22: for polygamy in fiction v A. O. Aldridge 1950. For polygamy in relation to Richardson's fiction v I. Watt 1957/1968 pp. 152–4: M.A. Doody 1989 in M.A. Doody, P. Sabor (eds) pp. 128–9. A utopian spouse-sharing scheme appears as a momentary possibility in drama: v J. Dryden 1673/1991 p. 110 V: i: 353–6.

48. S. Richardson 1747–8/1985 Letter 207 p. 670: cf M. Atwood 1985.

49. S. Richardson 1751/1962 vol. 3 Letter cxiii p. 474: this passage was added later than the first edn, and therefore appears in the modern Everyman edn (based on the original 3rd edn) but not in Ross's edn (based on 1747–8). For Richardson's textual revisions and their effects v M. Kinkead-Weekes 1959: S. Van Marter 1973, 1975.

50. S. Richardson 1747–8/1985 Letter 254 p. 872.

51. S. Richardson 1747–8/1985 Letter 254 p. 873.

52. Kinkead-Weekes sees the scheme as representing Lovelace's 'full aversion to marriage' but it could equally signify an involuntary fascination: v M. Kinkead-Weekes 1973 p. 227.

53. S. Richardson 1747–8/1985 Letter 254 p. 872.

54. S. Richardson 1747–8/1985 Letter 254 p. 874.

55. S. Richardson 1747–8/1985 Letter 254 p. 873: cf J. Milton 1953–82 vol. 2 pp. 220, 221.

56. S. Richardson 1747–8/1985 Letter 254 p. 874.

57. S. Richardson 1747–8/1985 Letter 529 pp. 1465–72: this letter is extended in later edns: cf S. Richardson 1751/1962 vol. 4 Letter clxviii pp. 490–510.

58. S. Richardson 1747–8/1985 Letter 231 p. 760.

59. S. Richardson 1747–8/1985 Letter 19 p. 104 (italics in parenthesis are a later addition).

60. cf M.A. Doody 1974 p. 264.

61. For analysis of the problems incurred in so representing the hero v M. Kinkead-Weekes 1973 pp. 279–95.

62. S. Richardson 1751/1972 Part 3 vol. VII Letter viii pp. 285–6.

63. v S. Richardson 1751/1972 Part 3 vol. VII Letter viii pp. 287–8.

64. S. Richardson 1751/1972 Part 2 vol. V Letter ii pp. 477–8.

65. v S. Richardson 1751/1972 Part 3 vol. VI Letter lv pp. 242–51.

66. S. Richardson 1751/1972 Part 3 vol. VI Letter lv p. 247: this appears to contradict Brophy's view: v E.B. Brophy 1991 p. 237.

67. S. Richardson 1751/1972 Part 3 vol. VI Letter lv p. 248.

68. Aristotle 1988 Book II p. 29.

69. S. Richardson 1751/1972 Part 3 vol. VI Letter lv p. 251.

70. cf S. Richardson 1747–8/1985 Letter 219 p. 704: S. Richardson 1751/1972 Part 3 vol. VI Letter lv p. 250: S. Brunt 1727/1973 pp. 150–1.

71. F.R. Leavis 1952/1962 p. 84.

72. v Harris's intro in S. Richardson 1751/1972 p. xx.

73. v S. Richardson 1751/1972 Part 3 vol. VII Letter xxxvi pp. 374–5: cf Doody's comments on his attitude (M. A. Doody 1974 p. 26).

74. v I. Watt 1757/1968 pp. 150–2: editor's note in S. Richardson 1951/1972 Part 2 p. 676: J. Harris 1989 in M.A. Doody, P. Sabor (eds) pp. 193–4. Upham proposes a connection between Astell and *Clarissa*: v A.H. Upham 1913. Also v ch. 7 below.

75. S. Richardson 1751/1972 Part 2 vol. IV Letter xviii p. 355: cf Part 3 Vol. VI Letter iv p. 9.

76. S. Richardson 1751/1972 Part 2 vol. IV Letter xviii p. 356.

CHAPTER 7

Women's utopias: New Atalantis; A Serious Proposal to the Ladies and Reflections upon Marriage; Millenium Hall; Munster Village

If the creation of utopia represents a chance for any writer to escape intellectually from the limitations of an actual society and way of life, it is women writers who arguably stand in most need of such liberation. Yet, almost inevitably, women's utopian fiction in this period has to define itself against precedents established by male writers. In considering the relation of their utopian writing to that of men, it's necessary to ask how far it is feasible for eighteenth-century women to see themselves as founding and sustaining any politicised utopian scheme, inside or outside fiction. Imaginary worlds are certainly available to the aspiring woman reformer, experimenter, or ruler, as Margaret Cavendish, writing in the seventeenth century, had flamboyantly demonstrated.[1] However, given the all too evident constraints on women in the 'real' world, what does the utopian tradition have to offer beyond fantasy and wish-fulfilment? Even for male writers, to account plausibly for the origins of a political and social utopia (as opposed to a purely domestic one) presents certain difficulties. The power to create an ideal state presupposes just that: *power*, the power to acquire territory and economic resources through discovery, conquest, or inheritance.

Yet the eighteenth-century domestic utopia also requires resources, usually in the form of inherited property (even Crusoe starts from a kind of legacy, the legacy of his drowned shipmates). Normally its origins are legitimised by marriage, the equivalent of conquest. For women, there is virtually no opportunity to exercise power that doesn't derive from property and privilege, and, unsurprisingly, their utopian fictions reflect this fact of life. But for women the accompanying condition – marriage – tends to be regarded as the problem, not the answer. In a depressing equation, man's domestic utopia turns out to equal woman's dystopia. Freedom becomes a personal and social rather than a political objective, and women writers at this stage don't waste their time focusing their utopian dreams on unthinkable futuristic forms of emancipation, such as the vote. What they focus on instead is the attainable: above all, better education, seen as the key to inner freedom, and also capable of being institutionalised in utopian structures.

In this context, the traditional utopian texts transmit very mixed messages, holding out uncertain promises and not keeping them. By and large, they assume that women benefit from the same institutional arrangements that benefit men. Before the advent of the novel, the writers of utopias are in any case unaccustomed to entertaining the idea of the individual point of view, let alone identifying a distinctive female viewpoint: consequently, they are prone to generalise too readily on the basis of gender. Woman's place in the classical utopia is dictated by function (as indeed is man's). On the one hand, she is seen as a set of reproductive organs, guaranteeing the production of future citizens; but on the other hand, that in itself makes her of central rather than marginal importance in the ideal state, and utopists can and do promote the belief that mothers should not only be physically healthy, but well educated, capable of participating in the responsibilities of citizenship to the extent (in Plato's Laws and More's Utopia) of being allowed to fight and be killed for their country.[2] Nevertheless, old habits of thought die hard. The argument over whether or not Plato was a feminist perhaps begs too many questions, not least of definition, but it serves to highlight a continuing problem. Although classical and Renaissance utopian writers may devise possible methods of giving women more of a stake in the political community, they can't make sexual functions truly interchangeable, and they find it very hard to imagine genuine power-sharing (which Plato, for one, doesn't believe women want anyway).[3] Even in imaginary societies based on having everything in common, there is some division of labour; and, particularly if sexual relationships and reproduction aren't based on the same principle, but on some form of marriage system, then subordination of women appears unavoidable – as More's Utopia graphically shows.[4] Where the state and its needs take priority, men's liberties are curtailed, sometimes drastically: women's much more so. Although some early utopian writers may be very willing to give women equal educational opportunities, they don't necessarily appreciate what all the consequences might be and how it might affect their reproductive policies, or the attitudes to marriage where that applies. It is precisely the effects of education and marriage in women's experience that are of most pressing concern to a number of eighteenth-century women writers.

However, the utopian tradition does offer some specific models which can prove attractive on other than political grounds. One such model, which relates to the hunger for more and better education, is the 'pansophist' utopia of the seventeenth century.[5] For avid minds, denied the chance of recognised professional careers, the utopia devoted to the advancement of learning and equipped like a glorified university with everything required for the study of arts and sciences must hold irresistible appeal. So, from Margaret Cavendish in the 1660s, creating her philosophical dream-world ablaze with speculative rage, to Mary Hamilton in the 1770s, creating her vision of an academy to rival Athens and Renaissance Florence, women imaginatively appropriate an inspiration associated with masculine learning and culture. However, by its nature, this is for the chosen few: the pansophist utopia tends, paradoxically, to be an élitist concept for either sex. Women can claim the right as scholars and scientists to enter the male preserve of the House of Salomon, but that right doesn't emancipate their sex as a whole. Although this dream enhances women's fiction with a concept of an ideally academic world elsewhere, at a great remove from either the monotonous drudgery of domestic duties or the vacuous pastimes of bored leisure, it doesn't replace the more general concern with how to improve women's lives within the domestic sphere.

Another option for those wishing to escape the domestic utopia altogether is a remaking of the political utopia, to centre on female power rather than male. The classical republic is displaced by romance. Again, Margaret Cavendish might be considered to set a precedent, with her female utopian travellers and exotic empire dominated by an empress. The allocating of such dazzling roles to the allegedly weaker sex is of course commonplace in the romance genre.[6] However, in the utopian tradition, female domination normally functions as a focus of fear and satire. From Lucian's vine-women and women with asses' legs who prey on men, to Joseph Hall's Shee-landt with its caricatured female traits, male writers attempt by parody to exorcise the perceived threat, not just of women's sexuality, but of their capacity for collective organisation.[7] If women writers want to reclaim a defiantly independent and aggressive image of female utopia, they have to negotiate between romance and satire, with the risk of stabbing their own sex in the back under cover of the confusion generated. The politicised writing of those who accept this challenge contrasts vividly with the work of women novelists who prefer to reclaim the domestic utopia as a centre of matriarchal rather than patriarchal influence. What both camps share is an interest in the very different ways that women can, as it were, take over and occupy a distinctively utopian space within eighteenth-century fiction, and reinvent their lives accordingly.

Delarivier Manley and Mary Astell: cabal and convent

In the case of women's writing, any chronological divide between seventeenth and eighteenth centuries is particularly arbitrary. It so happens that the examples which show writers using utopian fiction as a coded form combining politics, satire, and erotic romance tend to come from the earlier period, whereas examples of the treatment of 'realistic' utopias by women writers are a later development. But while Delarivier Manley and Eliza Haywood seem much closer to Aphra Behn, and to the sexual (and other) politics of the seventeenth century, than to Sarah Scott, Mary Hamilton, or Frances Burney, gender if not genre does form a link. Also, a non-fictional text like Mary Astell's *Serious Proposal* of the 1690s has clear implications for the novel using conventions of formal realism. Consequently it's necessary to backtrack and consider the utopian connections of works by Manley and Astell, before turning to the women novelists who postdate Richardson and Fielding.

Manley, followed by Eliza Haywood, gestures towards utopian allegory in her choice of title, which runs in full *Secret Memoirs and Manners of several Persons of Quality of Both Sexes, From the New Atalantis, an Island in the Mediterranean*, 1709 (Haywood's equivalent is *Memoirs of a Certain Island Adjacent to the Kingdom of Utopia*, 1725). Manley's titillating title combines the allusion to Plato's lost city-state and Bacon's island with a verbal echo recalling the virgin Atalanta – she who outstripped all her male pursuers until seduced by the golden apples thrown in her path. If to go naked is the best disguise, Manley's scandalous *roman-à-clef* certainly does the next best thing, by adopting the most outrageously transparent of veils. Seduction narratives, of one kind and another, form the bulk of the work. In claiming, however, to write Varronian satire 'after the manner of Lucian', she invites the reader to place the material in a particular literary context, which invokes an anti-romantic response.[8]

When Manley invents a female utopia within the New Atalantean framework, she incorporates serious political comment, but handles her subject with a mixture of mockery and envy. The ladies of the female Cabal drive through the scene in coachloads, laughing 'loud and incessantly' and apparently without a care in the world: 'Can any persons be more at their ease? Sure these seem to unknow that there is a certain portion of misery and disappointments allotted to all men, which one time or other will assuredly overtake 'em.'[9] The explanation for this apparent immunity is simple: they exclude 'that rapacious sex', men. But the price they incur is to be the target of social censure, which concentrates on unremitting speculation about their erotic activities. Whenever the Cabal appears, it is in a cloud of sexual innuendo. As the personified Intelligence points out, women can't win: 'if they seek their diversion out of themselves and include the other sex, they must be criminal? If in themselves (as those of the new Cabal), still they are criminal?'[10] In fact, as the later story of the widow and the actress seems to bear out, members of the Cabal can be as sexually predatory and possessive as Lucian's terrifying females, only they turn their predatoriness against their own sex: 'they do not in reality love men, but dote of the representation of men in women.'[11] In this utopia, it is cross-dressing that makes a cultural statement. Insofar as they rebel against their conventional sexual roles, aspiring to masculine freedom, and, if required to marry, dominate and shut out their husbands, the Cabalists exemplify the same attitudes that are satirised and feared in Hall's Shee-landt or Womandeçoia.[12] At their most extreme, they exclude not only men, but heterosexual women from their inner circle.

However, their solidarity rests also on principles that are more generally utopian than that of sexual proclivity, principles derived from the classic ideal society:

> In this little commonwealth is no property: whatever a lady possesses is, *sans ceremone*, at the service and for the use of her fair friend, without the vain nice scruple of being obliged. 'Tis her right; the other disputes it not, no, not so much as in thought. They have no reserve; mutual love bestows all things in common. . . .[13]

Astrea, however, goddess of justice, draws attention to the difficulty of discriminating between utopian motives:

> If only tender friendship, inviolable and sincere, be the regard, what can be more meritorious or a truer emblem of their happiness above? 'Tis by imitation, the nearest approach they can make, a feint, a distant landshape [sic] of immortal joys. But if they carry it a length beyond what nature designed and fortify themselves by these new-formed amities against the hymenial union, or give their husbands but a second place in their affections and cares, 'tis wrong and to be blamed.

The line drawn is a fine one, and she warns ironically against the consequences of being perceived to cross it:

> . . . obscene laughter, new invented satire, fanciful jealousies and impure distrusts in that nice, unforgiving sex who arbitrarily decide that woman was only created (with all her beauty, softness, passions and complete tenderness) to adorn the husband's reign, perfect his happiness, and propagate the kind.

And there's the rub. No eighteenth-century female utopia can totally ignore the biological and social pressures exerted on women, no matter how much they lament 'the custom of the world, that has made it convenient (nay, almost indispensable) for all ladies once to marry'.[14] The strategies of withdrawal, mutual vows, communal solidarity: all end by testifying to the entrenched power of the host society on which they are effectively parasitic. Manley includes a version of a country retreat that parodies the moral idealism later embodied in Millenium Hall by hinting at the less licit pleasures available in this 'bower of bliss': 'the Lady L- and her daughters make four of the cabal. They have taken a little lodging . . . in a place obscure and pleasant with a magazine of good wine and necessary conveniences as to chambers of repose, a tolerable garden and the country in prospect. They wear away the indulgent happy hours according to their own taste' – and in the absence of men.[15] The bower of bliss subverts the domestic utopia. But the Cabal is itself subverted by anti-utopian tensions and conspiracy, something tainted in the air. For example, the exercise of power by older women over younger is intolerant and open to abuse (recalling Joseph Hall's satire against female political arrangements that result in the dominance of 'the most aged matrons').[16] In assuming male prerogatives, the Cabal also assume the violence, exploitation and secrecy of male-dominated society. In the end they imitate, rather than creating a true alternative.

Yet the germ of an alternative exists. The idea of a women's community, developing, enriching and fulfilling the lives of its individual members, has recognisable potential for writers of the period. Manley's hybrid – and lurid – utopian fiction is only one way of formally articulating problems addressed in women's writing before and after. She herself recognises the limits of law in regulating and punishing the sexual behaviour of men towards women. However, utopian structures don't have to have a legal framework. If, without more enlightened legislation, the institution of marriage presents an intractable problem, then why not approach the situation from another direction? Either educate women to give them greater inner resources to endure marriage, if it can't be enjoyed; or provide a haven for the unmarried and for refugees from marriage: or do both.

Such is the thrust of the arguments in Mary Astell's *A Serious Proposal to the Ladies*, first published in 1694, fifteen years before Manley's *New Atalantis*. One of the early proponents of advanced education for women, Astell in some respects makes a piquant contrast with Manley – a contrast between the austere and the rackety, which seems to be reflected in their choice of respective literary forms. Yet biography throws up the irony that it was Astell whose emotional drives were apparently closer to those satirised in the female Cabal, not the erotically adventurous Manley's.[17] In any case, the differences between their experiences and their literary responses don't preclude a shared perception of how and why women are shackled and frustrated in their society (nor indeed a shared allegiance to Tory politics). However, although Astell isn't a stranger to emotional needs that can be satisfied in female friendship, her idea of a community founded on that friendship differs essentially in its priorities from the Cabal. She takes an idealistic view of the recip- rocal connection between good personal relations and a good society – 'were the World better there wou'd be more Friendship, and were there more Friendship we shou'd have a better World'[18] – and clearly thinks that women are more fitted to put such a utopian ideal into practice. In her proposed community 'there are no Interests . . . to serve, no contrivances for another to be a stale to; the Souls of all the *Religious* will be open and free, and . . . particular Friendships must be no prejudice to the general Amity.'[19] The tone of this statement sufficiently measures the distance between this separatist movement and that of the worldly, intriguing, and basically self-gratifying Cabal. Astell envisages a religious foundation with educational aims, not a sophisticated social clique. Yet, in its way, her proposal of 'a *Monastery*, or if you will . . . *Religious Retirement*'[20] (in effect a Protestant convent) is potentially more revolutionary and more influential than the utopia of sexual freedom.

Although specialised in its aims and exclusively for women, this scheme has more generalised utopian features as well. For example, discipline is compatible with the pleasure principle: 'happy Retreat! which will be the introducing you into such a *Paradise* as your Mother *Eve* forfeited. . . . Here are no Serpents to deceive you, whilst you entertain your selves in these delicious Gardens.'[21] The earthly paradise topos is familiar, but the upper-class women to whom Astell addresses her prospectus might be less than entertained to discover that the pleasures on offer are those of the spirit, not the body. Temperance is nothing new in utopias, but the proposer shows less interest than most devisers of such schemes in organising the physical necessities: 'as to *Lodging, Habit* and *Diet*, they may be quickly resolv'd on by the Ladies who shall subscribe'.[22] That 'quickly' is a giveaway, a sign of how, in this instance at least, Astell underestimates the realities of institutional life. However, she has no doubts that they 'will make choice of what is most plain and decent, what Nature not Luxury requires': a sound principle of the simple-life utopia. Incidentally, she doesn't overlook the costing of her proposal, arguing persuasively that it would be a good investment for those with superfluous daughters.[23]

If diet and dress don't interest her, education certainly does; though here again she puts perhaps surprisingly meagre flesh on the bones of her syllabus. She has a very clear idea in general of the *kind* of education she wants for women, emphasising pragmatism, quality control, and accessibility more than range and erudition:

> Such a course of Study will neither be too troublesome nor out of the reach of a Female Virtuoso; for it is not intended she shou'd spend her hours in learning *words* but *things*, and therefore no more Languages than are necessary to acquaint her with useful Authors. Nor need she trouble her self in turning over a great number of Books, but take care to understand and digest a few well-chosen and good ones.[24]

This subscribes to the Baconian standard rather than to earlier Renaissance humanism. It's in keeping with Astell's insistence that her institution should not be an ivory tower, but contribute something useful, combining good works and contemplation.[25] From one angle, it looks like the best of both worlds for women: from another, it might be viewed as curtailing their academic freedom in a way that doesn't apply to men. Not that Astell admires the products of the male system: she can be superbly scathing about their claims to achievement, as when she remarks in her later work 'all famous Arts have their Original from Men, even from the Invention of Guns to the Mystery of good Eating.'[26] However, whether from conviction or as a defensive strategy, she acknowledges limitations on female activity and intellect. Unlike Margaret Cavendish, for instance, who endows her utopian empress with 'an excellent gift of Preaching', Astell states firmly, 'we pretend not that Women shou'd teach in the Church'.[27] What women *can* do, however, she wants to be done well.

This, of course, raises the question of the fundamental purpose of women's education. Here too Astell takes what might be called a utopian perspective. Although she argues from first principles of natural justice – 'since GOD has given Women as well as Men intelligent Souls, why should they be forbidden to improve them?'[28] – she is keenly aware of the utilitarian argument. The education of women has social value, even if public office isn't open to them. In particular, she writes, 'to give a Specimen how useful they will be to the World, I am now inclin'd to declare, that it is design'd a part of their business shall be to give the best Education to the Children of Persons of Quality'.[29] In both the *Proposal* and its *Second Part*, Astell points out that it is in the interests of the patriarchal family for the mother to be equipped to teach her young children.[30] Given the interest in educational psychology from the 1690s onwards, the point is well taken, and is relevant to the idea of the domestic utopia. In *Some Thoughts concerning Education* (1693), Locke had consciously excluded girls, confining his discourse by gender and class to the 'Gentleman's Son';[31] but he emphasises the importance of the mother in the early stages, particularly in teaching the child to read (she can help him with his Latin, Locke suggests, even though ignorant of it herself).[32] Locke is partly responsible for the eighteenth-century mother's sense of mission.

Characteristically, Astell isn't prepared to limit this capacity only to women destined for marriage and maternity, but foreshadows the alternative eighteenth-century ideal of the purposeful single life (at least for those with sufficient means and status, like some later heroines of the novel):

> Nor will Knowledge lie dead upoñ their hands who have no Children to Instruct; the whole World is a single Lady's Family, her opportunities of doing good are not lessen'd but encreas'd by her being unconfin'd. Particular Obligations do not contract her Mind, but her Beneficence moves in the largest Sphere. And perhaps the Glory of Reforming this Prophane and Profligate Age is reserv'd for you Ladies. . . .[33]

Brave words: but the vision of utopian reform has more to contend with than profanity and profligacy. Marriage would still claim many of Astell's prospective students, and the aims of her original proposal for a female 'monastery' were, as the second part shows, misinterpreted: 'it is not my intention', she explains, 'that you shou'd exclude yourselves from the World. I know it is necessary that a great number of you shou'd live in it . . . '[34]

In her *Reflections upon Marriage* (1700), Astell goes on to dissect the problems of those who must live in it as married women. In the process, she delivers a devastating critique of the actuality that is to form so much of the raw material of the novel. Her preface, added later 'in Answer to Some Objections', demolishes the theory of women's innate inferiority on both theological and political grounds. As a result of concentrating on marriage, and what is, rather than on education, and what might be, she has become even more militant and much less hopeful. Yet, in keeping with her religious convictions, she is not against marriage as an institution – on the contrary:

> The Christian Institution of Marriage provides the best that may be for Domestic Quiet and Content, and for the Education of Children; so that if we were not under the tye of Religion, even the Good of Society and civil Duty would oblige us to what that requires at our Hands.
> . . . There may indeed be inconveniences in a Married Life; but is there any Condition without them?[35]

That Johnsonian observation leads into a sharp denunciation of promiscuous bachelorhood. In fact, the women writers who advocate the founding of female utopias won't admit to being against marriage *as such.* But Astell pithily articulates the paradox faced by all of them: 'but if Marriage be such a blessed State, how comes it, may you say, that there are so few happy Marriages?' She has her own answer to the conundrum: 'it is not to be wonder'd that so few succeed, we should rather be surpriz'd to find so many do, considering how imprudently Men engage, the Motives they act by, and the very strange Conduct they observe throughout.'[36]

Much of the *Reflections* is occupied with shrewd analysis of the causes of unhappy marriage according to this formula. Astell recognises that both sexes can be at fault; but she also recognises that the social system stacks the odds very heavily against the woman, that 'if the Matrimonial Yoke be grievous, neither Law nor Custom afford her that redress which a Man obtains.'[37] Here and in the preface she introduces very effectively the analogy with political relations so prominent in this period. In the preface, this reaches a climax with the question *'If all Men are born free,* how is it that all Women are born slaves?'[38] Like the classical city-state, the domestic utopia of the eighteenth century is essentially based on the principle of slavery. But, however powerful her intellectual challenge, Astell has no utopian alternative to offer as she had with her *Proposal,* because she doesn't seriously entertain the possibility of legal or constitutional change. Instead, in answer to the crucial question 'What then is to be done?' she can only offer guidance to those choosing a partner, that they should base their relationship on the compatibility of minds and 'as much equality as may be'.[39] For those who have already made their choice and live to regret it, she has recourse – like Milton, another failed revolutionary – to what Milton calls in another context 'the better fortitude / Of patience and heroic martyrdom'.[40] She uses this kind of language to describe not a utopian, but an otherworldly ideal: 'she who Marries purely to do Good, to Educate Souls for Heaven . . . does certainly perform a more Heroic Action than all the famous Masculine Heroes can boast of, she suffers a continual Martyrdom to bring Glory to GOD and Benefit to Mankind, which consideration indeed may carry her through all Difficulties, I know not what else can. . . .'[41] Evidently a case of lie back, close your eyes, and think of Heaven rather than England; the laws of England certainly hold out little hope for her.

The century just opening will prove no more utopian for women, despite Astell's efforts, but will tend to confirm her dystopian diagnosis. Yet she might have derived some satisfaction from knowing that her ideas would find support among both men and women writers, and that the distinctively utopian strain of imagination wouldn't die out. Both Defoe, in his proposal of 'An Academy for Women' and Richardson in *Sir Charles Grandison* take up the concept of an institution designed to improve the quality and purpose of women's lives.[42] However, it is women writers who *imagine* what this kind of utopia would be like in fictional experience. Whereas Defoe includes his scheme in *An Essay upon Projects* and Richardson assigns it to a male character as a discourse within a novel, Sarah Scott in *Millenium Hall* and Mary Hamilton in *Munster Village* work versions of utopia created by women into the fabric of their own imaginative creations. Of the two, it is Sarah Scott who is the more obvious successor to Mary Astell, since her utopia is created not only *by* women, but to a very large extent *for* women: it is the culmination of the ideal of domestic and communal life which in one sense parallels, in another sense displaces, the patriarchal ideal.

Millenium Hall

Millenium Hall (1762) is a rarity, not just because it presents a separatist female utopia, but because it so thoroughly assimilates the utopian genre to the novel of formal realism: a familiar combination in nineteenth- and twentieth-century fiction, but less frequent in the eighteenth century. Had it been a satire or romance, it would have been less remarkable. Scott, like many novelists, is adapting auto-biographical material. In her case she adapts the convent-like mode of life that she and Lady Barbara Montagu shared in Bath.[43] However, she cuts and shapes this material to fit a traditional utopian frame-work. For example, she chooses to mediate the description through a male narrator, who with his younger companion, also male, enacts the role of the utopian traveller. This function is signalled at the outset by his emphasis on the salutary effect on human vanity of learning to make comparisons – a mild form of the Gulliver syndrome: he remarks 'my vanity must rather be mortified than flattered in the description of such virtues as will continually accuse me of my own deficiencies, and lead me to make a humiliating comparison between these excellent ladies and myself.'[44] These are, as it were, travellers from another culture, reporting an experience that has changed their perceptions radically: only in this instance the alien culture from which they come is defined by gender. They inhabit the culture of masculinity, and they need to reexamine the assumptions they have constructed on that basis. Like other such travellers, the younger man in particular is required to undergo a conversion. The older (who, like Gaudentio di Lucca, finds that he can claim a blood relationship with the utopian community) ends with the intention of 'a scheme to imitate them on a smaller scale'[45] – a familiar response to being initiated into a utopian experience.

What he intends to imitate is itself a literary imitation, at least in certain aspects. From the semi-mythical title, the reader is led to expect the symbolism attached to the religious ideal community, the kingdom of Christ on Earth. However, the country-estate location means that the discourse also ranges over familiar secular ground: social and economic relations, education, work and leisure, regulations for daily life, and personal relationships. The setting is central, ensuring continuity and stability as well as a standard of reference for the successive narratives recounting the life histories of members of the group. Instead of focusing her novel on a person, or persons, in the first instance, or on the imaginary voyage format, Scott chooses to make her utopian place the main structural principle of her fiction.

Her full title advertises her priorities: A Description of Millenium Hall and the Country Adjacent Together with the Characters of the Inhabitants And such Historical Anecdotes and Reflections As May excite in the Reader proper Sentiments of Humanity, and lead the Mind to the Love of Virtue. Unlike Richardson and Fielding, who insert utopian descriptions and episodes into an extended narrative, Scott subordinates her narratives to her utopian description. First impressions of place are correspondingly heightened. If the blasé reader feels that having seen one earthly paradise one has more or less seen them all, this writer nevertheless manages to execute some elegant variations on a literary cliché which she doesn't scorn to use.[46] There are all the signs of a golden age type of utopian setting: the pastoral idyll reminiscent of Theocritus; a 'profusion of flowers'; healthy and happy women and children engaged in haymaking.[47] This scene has the kind of nostalgia and romanticising of agricultural labour later associated with William Morris and his News from Nowhere. When it moves to the cultivated interior, with its posed female figures absorbed in a variety of intellectual and creative pursuits, the same sense of pleasurable activity persists, but at a perceptibly higher social level. (Morris would no doubt approve the emphasis on arts and crafts.) The narrator reiterates the Greek motif with his allusion to 'the Attic school',[48] though this merges with the Christian associations of sacred music – 'the sight of so many little innocents joining in the most sublime harmony made me almost think myself already amongst the heavenly choir,' he records.[49]

However, Millenium Hall is not heaven. What is more interesting than the conventionally harmonious picture is the way in which the writer paints in apparently jarring details, inconspicuously at first with the physically impaired musicians, but later foregrounding the evidence of earthly imperfection so that it can scarcely be overlooked. This isn't, like some utopias, a golden world of uniformly strong beautiful bodies; nor is it a Spartan regime, contemptuous of physical infirmity. (Plato gives authority in the *Republic* to the argument that prolonged medical treatment is wasted on the chronically sick.[50]) Possibly because this is a women's utopia, Scott devotes considerable thought to the practical question of how to create a sense of self-respect and a role within the wider community for those suffering from 'the churlishness wherewith they had been treated by nature'[51] – nature not being by any means as benign as the original golden age myth assumes. Of course, there are precedents in earlier realistic utopias such as More's and Campanella's for humanitarian attitudes to the physically or mentally disadvantaged members of society. In fact, Campanella's idea of employing those with disabilities according to their capacities, and locating them in villages rather than the city, is close to Scott's scheme.[52] However, Scott develops in greater detail her rationale for a protected community within the utopian society, which attempts to give those formerly exploited as public spectacles – like Gulliver in Brobdingnag – a measure of personal dignity and independence. Defoe's projected 'Fool-house' enshrined the same principle.[53] Nor are they segregated to spare the sensibilities of others, but to spare their own (they are encouraged, by gentle degrees, to entertain visitors).

Indeed the household itself is run by people considered unemployable elsewhere. The housekeeper with the deformed hand points out that 'few of [her] fellow-servants are better qualified; the cook cannot walk without crutches, the kitchen maid has but one eye, the dairy maid is almost stone deaf, and the housemaid has but one hand'.[54] Scott is perfectly aware that this catalogue of misfortunes is a hairsbreadth away from comic satire; and she contains the reaction with a smile shared by the housekeeper and narrator, and the latter's comment on 'something so whimsically good in the conduct of the ladies' which he later perceives to be 'entirely rational'.[55] Modern readers might perhaps be more inclined to wince at the housekeeper's corollary, 'and yet, perhaps, there is no family where the business is better done; for gratitude, and a conviction that this is the only house into which we can be received, makes us exert ourselves to the utmost'. Gratitude is no longer a fashionable emotion. However, seen in another light, this bears out the utopian assumption that human behaviour, even under the best conditions, is produced by two kinds of social pressure, carrot and stick. And if Millenium Hall requires grateful recipients of its bounties, at least it offers them a genuine refuge from the harsher world outside. As befits a Christian community, its social relations are predicated on respect for others and a sense of reciprocity of rights and obligations.

This sense of respect also applies to the relation between the community and the natural environment, which shifts from the aesthetic to the ethical. Here again, Scott shows sensitivity to a relatively new way of thinking about humanity's responsibility to other species. Traditional 'dominion' is displaced by a more protective and millennial – even egalitarian – vision:

> The wood is well peopled with pheasants, wild turkeys, squirrels and hares, who live so unmolested, that they seem to have forgot all fear, and rather to welcome than flee from those who come among them. Man never appears there as a merciless destroyer; but as the preserver, instead of the tyrant, of the inferior part of the creation . . . . We there walked 'joint tenant of the shade' with the animal race; and a perfect equality in nature's bounty seems enjoyed by the whole creation. One could scarcely forbear thinking those happy times were come, when 'The wolf shall dwell with the lamb, and the leopard shall lie down with the kid . . . .'[56]

In this challenge to the eighteenth-century hunting squirearchy, it is tempting to read 'man' as gender-specific rather than universal. But it would be unfair not to recognise that male utopian writers can and do share these sentiments (More's Utopians, for instance, are against hunting[57]), although not many go to such an extreme. Shortly after this commentary in *Millenium Hall*, Scott uses the presumed contrast between male and female values to make a strongly political point. Lamont, the more unsympathetic of the two male visitors, mentions a collection of exotic wild animals, particularly big cats, belonging to one Lord Lamore: to the speaker, the display of 'those beautiful wild beasts, brought out of their native woods, where they had reigned as kings, and here tamed and subjected by the superior art of man' constitutes 'a triumph of human reason, which could not fail to afford great pleasure'.[58] Miss Mancel takes eloquent exception to this definition of reason, distinguishing between the necessary discipline used to tame horses and oxen for the mutual benefit of both human and animal species, and unnecessary cruelty to animals whose natural habitat is the wild: 'to see a man, from a vain desire to have in his possession the native of another climate and another country, reduce a fine and noble creature to misery, and confine him within narrow inclosures whose happiness consisted in unbounded liberty, shocks my nature.' She adds, 'I imagine man has a right to use the animal race for his own preservation, perhaps for his convenience, but certainly not to treat them with wanton cruelty . . .'[59] The discrimination is necessary, if the female utopians are to avoid the charge of inconsistency. For, though they reserve one wood as an animal sanctuary, nevertheless this is very much a working estate, and they cannot afford to redress the balance too far. The later account of its economy reverts to the familiar standard of self-sufficiency: pigeons, rabbits, fish, deer, hares, and other game are listed among its resources for human consumption, apparently without a qualm. However, the language used by Miss Mancel carries more disturbing implications. What is immediately striking about her shocked reaction is how applicable her terms are to other kinds of domination: out of context, they might equally allude to the power lust of empire and slavery, or even to sexual possessiveness. At the very least, her speech provides not merely the intended contrast between male and female sensibilities, but also an insight into women's attitude to, and exercise of, power – something that is central to the utopian structure of the novel.

For all the emphasis on harmony with nature and the Arcadian setting, it's clear from the outset that this is not a simple-life utopia, but a highly cultivated version of simple living. Although the ladies shun the perilous frivolity later exemplified by Marie Antoinette and her model farm,[60] and conduct their social experiment with high seriousness, they do not renounce their status, or the property and privilege that enable their good works in the first place. Millenium Hall is not an egalitarian utopia in the economic sense. If they all invest their capital in the project, nevertheless, the notion of 'all

property laid in one undistinguished common'[61] is confined to the
ideal of perfect friendship between equals, and not universalised as in
some utopias. Nor is Millenium Hall egalitarian in the social sense. If
all are equal in the sight of God, all are certainly not equal in the
sight of society. However, the ladies are deeply interested in using
their power to enable others, especially through education and work,
to achieve what would otherwise be impossible. Their efforts are
particularly directed to members of their own sex; and perhaps
because, as women, they have all experienced what it is like to be on
the receiving end of arbitrarily exercised power, they at least attempt
to exercise their own power with sensitivity.[62] If readers from another
age are inclined to view with suspicion social relations based on
gracious giving and grateful receiving, it is only fair to acknowledge
that the women in Scott's fiction have thought clearly and rigorously
about the religious principles that inform their efficient economic
management. Almost at the end of the novel, Miss Mancel articulates
their creed of accountability, derived from the parable of the talents:

> How we ought to use them he has likewise told us; as to our
> fortunes in the most express terms, when he commands us to feed
> the hungry, to clothe the naked, to relieve the prisoner, and to
> take care of the sick. Those who have not an inheritance that
> enables them to do this are commanded to labour in order to
> obtain means to relieve those who are incapable of gaining the
> necessaries of life. Can we then imagine that every one is not
> required to assist others to the utmost of his power, since we are
> commanded even to work for the means of doing so?[63]

Her conclusion that 'each state [wealth or poverty] has its trials',
ending with a tentative speculation 'as for the future, there may
probably be no inequality',[64] accepts inequality as a fact even of
utopian life. However, the response to that fact, if hardly revolutionary, is far from passive. People are to be helped to help
themselves *and* others: like the old village women, organised within
an inch of their lives, but given purpose and a sense of community.

   Indeed the enterprise of Millenium Hall in all its aspects – social
work, schools, institute, factory, farm – triumphantly vindicates the
organisational skills of women. Although they do not totally dispense
with male staff, their financial affairs are under their own control.[65]
Morality and profit go together. The 'manufacture of carpets and rugs'
started with Miss Trentham's capital prospers for the benefit of the

workers as well as the directors. A policy of positive discrimination ensures that children and the elderly are paid proportionately more. [66] What is novel is not the social or economic thinking as such, but the fact that they put it into practice – and they claim no more – and, of course, the fact that they are women. 'If any people', comments Lamont, 'have a right to turn reformers, you ladies are best qualified, since you begin by reforming yourselves; you practise more than you preach . . . '[67] To which Miss Mancel retorts, 'we do not set up for reformers . . . we wish to regulate ourselves by the laws laid down to us, and as far as our influence can extend, endeavour to enforce them; beyond that small circle all is foreign to us; we have sufficient employment in improving ourselves; to mend the world requires much abler hands.' (Mary Astell might have considered this defeatist.) The laws, she goes on to explain, are those of Scripture: 'there, independent of the political regulations of particular communities, is to be found the law of the supreme Legislator . . . the true and invariable law of nations'.[68]

Although this exchange might appear to justify a narrowly isolationist and fundamentalist concept of utopia, both the narrative flow of the novel and its broader context of ideas suggest otherwise. These are educated women, cognisant of secular philosophy as well as the Bible. In an earlier conversation, apropos of the dangers of self-sufficiency, Mrs Morgan cites (without attributing it) a version of Aristotle's dictum that anyone able to live outside human society must be, as she phrases it, 'more than a God, or less than a man': indeed she argues that all species are social by nature 'except we allow the existence of that exploded and unsociable bird the Phoenix'.[69] The ladies show no desire to emulate 'that exploded and unsociable bird', for all their idealism. What justifies their separatist stance is the belief that society at large has reverted to a Hobbesian state of nature, as Miss Mancel asserts in her turn:

> How little society is there to be found in what you call the world? It might more properly be compared to that state of war, which Hobbes supposes the first condition of mankind . . . a constant desire to supplant, and a continual fear of being supplanted, keep the minds of those who have any views at all in a state of unremitted tumult and envy . . . What I understand by society is a state of mutual confidence, reciprocal services, and correspondent affections; where numbers are thus united, there will be a free communication of sentiments. . . .[70]

This alternative definition, to which Millenium Hall conforms, stresses the opposite characteristics from the Hobbesian pre-social state or Mandeville's prosperous society. With its openness, altruism, and freedom from competitive aggression, it seems, in Scott's view, to be a more likely outcome in a community where power is in the hands of women rather than men.[71]

In accordance with this line of thought, there are hints early in the novel that she is substituting a matriarchal model of a domestic utopia for a patriarchal one: of Mrs Morgan, the dignified elder stateswoman of the group, it is said, 'one would almost think nature had formed her for a common parent, such universal and tender benevolence beams from every glance she casts around her.'[72] She is a female counterpart of Fielding's Dr Harrison. Another pointer towards the importance of maternal responsibility is the way that poor children are provided for. As was proposed for Plato's 'second-best' society in the Laws, the authorities compensate for the awkward fact that nature doesn't distribute children equally, or with regard to parental circumstances, by systematically redistributing them with a view to social welfare.[73] In Plato's ideal society, of course, the logical solution is to make responsibility for children entirely collective and erase individual relationships altogether (though even Plato confines this to the ruling class);[74] but this is too extreme for the majority of utopian writers in the Christian era. Instead, they compromise. In the case of Millenium Hall, the 'good ladies . . . take every child after the fifth of every poor person, as soon as it can walk' (having provided financial support to nursing mothers) and, until it reaches school age, put it in the care of the elderly village women – an arrangement that results in making the latter 'mothers again, as it were, in [their] old age'.[75] This is presented as a benign dispensation, welcomed by all concerned. What is perhaps most significant is the symbolism of motherly care that softens the institutionalism of Millenium Hall: the matriarchal utopia counterpoints the loss and absence of mothers which recurs so conspicuously as a motif in the inset narratives recounting the past histories of the characters.

Conversely, the persons very much present in these histories and conspicuous by their absence from the community itself are husbands and fathers. Mary Astell would have recognised the coded message, that so far from marriage being the foundation of the domestic utopia, it is actually a threat to it from the eighteenth-century woman's point of view. The same goes for fatherhood. The narratives of the women characters rehearse time and again the painful and often futile sacrifices made by women, in the name of duty and against feeling, to uphold male authority. Mrs Morgan's domestic dystopia is reflected graphically in the landscape surrounding her marital home, 'the situation dreary, the roads everywhere bad, the soil a stiff clay. . . . Nature nowhere appears graced with fewer charms' in all too pointed contrast to the 'female Arcadia'.[76] Certainly, as Astell also recognises, women can be to blame in misjudged marriages, and men can suffer from unhappy relationships; but, in terms of her fiction, it is women for whom Scott constructs her utopian alternative. Indeed she provides an alternative within the alternative, so to speak, in the society for 'indigent gentlewomen' with its scrupulously catalogued provisions and rules.[77] This is a kind of daughter community of Millenium Hall and embodies much in the proposals of Astell, and Richardson's proxy, Sir Charles Grandison.

Although some of the gentlewomen embrace the prospect of matrimony, the ladies of Millenium Hall don't entertain the same prospect themselves. For them, there is to be no triumph of hope over experience.[78] They aren't against marriage in principle, but in this area they decline to practise what they preach. Marrying? The servants will do that for us.[79] Mrs Morgan defends this position, with an awareness of its irony that goes some way to deflate criticism:

> We consider matrimony as absolutely necessary to the good of society; it is a general duty; but as, according to all ancient tenures, those oblig'd to perform knight's service, might, if they chose to enjoy their own firesides, be excused by sending deputies to supply their places; so we, using the same privilege substitute many others, and certainly much more promote wedlock than we could do by entering into it ourselves.[80]

A similar wry comparison with the world of male heroics had occurred to Mary Astell.

The context of this discussion is the wedding of one of the Millenium Hall protégées, a young woman who has been in service with a local farmer. Again, it's impossible to ignore the class-consciousness that permeates the novel, and that is actually reinforced, not weakened, by the utopian structure. A modern reader might infer that social and economic power is being used – or abused – to control other people's lives even in their most personal aspects, and remember the later case of Jane Austen's Emma, and her nearly disastrous attempt to manage Harriet's affairs. However, this is precisely where Scott's utopianism does alter and generalise the particular situation. Virtually all utopian fictions, as opposed to other kinds of novel, tolerate a very high level of manipulation of individual private lives for the public good: what counts is whether authority is in the right hands or the wrong ones.

Scott's narrator picks up the point about class distinction, but sets the matter in a very different light: 'in this case . . . your example is somewhat contradictory, and should it be entirely followed, it would confine matrimony to the lower rank of people, among whom it seems going out of fashion, as well as with their superiors'.[81] His concern is with the power of example, and possibly – though he is too polite to hint this – with the procreation of the 'better' sort. At any rate, the discourse expands to consider the economic and psychological disincentives to marriage for both men and women; because, as Miss Trentham observes, 'the case is pretty equal as to both sexes, each can destroy the other's peace.'[82] Ironically, it is the misery of marriage more than anything else that guarantees a form of sexual equality in eighteenth-century life.

Scott links marriage not only with class, but with the subject of education. Of all the issues in *Millenium Hall* which relate the utopian community to experience in the world outside, the education of women is the most persistent and influential campaign. If the inset narratives draw the cautionary moral that marriage is best avoided, they also draw the moral that education is to be encouraged. Miss Mancel and Miss Melvyn (the future Mrs Morgan) cement their friendship at a girls' boarding school, where they also acquire the intellectual resources that they value beyond any material ones. In the story of Lady Mary Jones, deficiencies in moral education are held to account for faulty behaviour.[83] As for Miss Selvyn, 'bred a philosopher from her cradle',[84] her putative father gives her an excellent grounding in everything except religion, an omission later remedied. Harriot Trentham, last of the group to have her history narrated, is likewise distinguished from the more empty-headed members of her sex by her 'admirable understanding . . . great fund of knowledge . . . inexhaustible variety in her conversation'.[85] The message is clear: to educate women isn't necessarily to improve their chances of happiness (indeed it may be positively damaging if a woman marries her intellectual inferior), but it is far better for them to learn to think rationally, and above all religiously, than not to think at all.

In establishing their utopia, therefore, the group naturally give priority to schools. As with Astell, the immediate aims are practical; and they take account of the kind of lives the girls in their care can realistically aspire to, although, like Richardson's Grandison and earlier utopian writers, they consider the possibility of the rare exception: 'when, among the lower sort, they meet with an uncommon genius, they will admit her among the number'[86] – that is, among the number of their genteel female orphans. The latter 'are educated in such a manner as will render them acceptable where accomplished women of a humble rank are wanted, either for the care of a house or children'. In other words, these girls are being educated for domestic dependence, which is the only career open to them in an un-utopian world. That is why, in the opening scene inside Millenium Hall, refined accomplishments tend to predominate. In the village school for girls, on the other hand, the lessons are strictly vocational, with the exception of the all-important and universal religious education: we're shown 'some writing, others casting accounts, some learning lessons by heart, several employed in various sorts of needle-work, a few spinning and others knitting. . . .' They aren't limited to single skills, but practise each in turn 'that they may have various means of gaining their subsistence in case any accident should deprive them of the power of pursuing any particular part of their business'.[87] However, there is an element of selectivity, of matching particular talents to particular functions, which somewhat mitigates the narrow-ness of their actual options, and which would be recognised as good utopian practice by a host of predecessors. In short, this is a utopian education for the real world. Scott clearly enjoys filling in the details of this happy learning environment, with its clean scrubbed wood, shining pewter, and – a particularly attractive touch – samples of the children's own work on display. Moreover, the activity that seals the utopian charter of the school is the outlet for individual creativity and communal pleasure which the girls, like More's Utopians, find in their gardening.[88] In contrast to this lovingly detailed description is the mere paragraph devoted to the boys' school, with its grim reminder that working-class boys have, if anything, a more restricted prospect than their sisters. Not only is their school half the size, but the pupils are 'most of them small, as they are dismissed to labour as soon as they are able to perform any work, except incapacitated by ill health.'[89]

Sarah Scott has been categorised as not being sufficiently radical in her thinking, as though that compromised her utopian credentials.[90]

However, 'radical' is a relative term, and in any case utopian fictions need not be radical in any politicised sense of the word. Compared with, say, Mary Wollstonecraft,[91] or with much later writers of modern feminist utopias, Scott may seem to overvalue the qualities that her religion and culture demand of women – discipline, a sense of duty, elegance of mind – even while she protests against some of the consequences of the demand. However, she can be imaginative, she can be angry, and she can be ironic as well as morally uplifting. Perhaps it takes a woman writer to prise apart the consensus in the eighteenth-century novel that the domestic utopia must be identified with the orthodox family unit, inclusive of both sexes: all that's needed is a happy marriage in the first place. *Millenium Hall* achieves an unusual balance between utopian discourse and the novel of domesticity that challenges the work of better known authors of the period. In itself, it demonstrates the results of educating a woman and liberating her from an unhappy marriage as effectively as any of its fictional narratives.

Munster Village

Since *Millenium Hall* (1762) and *Munster Village* (1778) are both utopian novels and both by women writers, they invite comparison: even the titles, when the former is abbreviated, superficially parallel each other.[92] There are, however, significant differences between the texts, starting with the structure. Mary Hamilton plunges the reader straight into a drama of family relationships, told in the manner of tragic romance. That is, she doesn't employ the utopian framing device nor the retrospective technique in the same way as Scott, and is less innovative in relating her symbolic centre to its satellite narratives. In fact, there are some uncertainties of register in this opening sequence that can disconcert as well as amuse the reader. Like other writers of the later eighteenth century, Hamilton is addicted to moral sentiment, to the point of overdosing; but she also has a pragmatic streak. So the ill-fated marriage, against parental opposition, of Lord and Lady Finlay, results in Lady Finlay's becoming the family breadwinner by using her talent for painting. Her heavily symbolic masterpiece entitled *Arcadia* '(they had retired to Wales for cheapness)' is the first hint of a classical Golden Age motif;[93] but the romantic and unfortunate pair are killed off by their creator before they have a chance of constructing an authentic simple-life Welsh utopia. However, their 'melancholy catastrophe'[94] frees Lord Finlay's sister, Lady Frances, to take over their father's estate and to embark on utopia-building on the grand scale. If her sister-in-law had painted Arcadia, she intends to recreate Athens. Indeed 'she was advised to call her elegant village by the name of *Athens*; but this she declined, naming it *Munster Village*: but she justly thought it deserved it; with this difference, that the inhabitants are too well informed to give into such gross superstitions . . . as the Grecians did.'[95]

In other words, this is a modern Athens, enlightened by Christianity and science. Village it may be called, but its centre is a temple of learning dedicated to the arts and sciences, with a fine library offering all necessary facilities for scholars. As so often in utopian fiction, the contrast with existing institutions is marked, here explicitly by Hamilton's critical remarks about the British Museum: 'the British Museum is rich in manuscripts . . . but it is wretchedly poor in printed books: and it is not sufficiently accessible to the public; their revenue not being sufficient to enable them to pay a proper number of attendants.'[96] In a more general context, she invokes the standards of the classic utopian paradigms:

> The institutions of modern nations are not to be compared to those of the ancients, as almost all these had the advantage of being founded by philosophers. Athens and Sparta were the two first formed states of Greece. Solon and Lycurgus, who had seen the success of the plan conducted by Minos in Crete, and who partly copied after that wise prince, erected these two celebrated republics. The sagacious system of Egypt served as a model to all the east.[97]

If an original political state is beyond the scope of a female founder, she can at least aim at a philosophical and social ideal. Unlike Millenium Hall, Munster Village is very much a one-woman enterprise. Even though Lady Frances has a wise male counsellor in Mr Burt, the vision is hers.

Unable as a woman to be admitted to university, she creates her own in the pansophist tradition of Bacon and Campanella. Everything – paintings, architecture, the observatory, anatomy theatre, and Linnaean botanic garden – contributes to the cultivation of the mind. Lady Frances is collector, patroness, principal: 'and as the encouragement given was great, it is not surprising that her academy became a seat of the muses, and a place to which many resorted for the solution of literary doubts.'[98] We learn from the account of the

academy that the encouragement extends to members of her own sex,
although they are very much in the minority; also, she believes in the
humanist principle of selecting students according to talent, and, like
the ladies of Millenium Hall, she practises positive discrimination in
favour of 'those who labour under any imperfection of body'.[99] Nor is
encouragement limited to those with an academic vocation, wanting
to resolve literary doubts. Although Lady Frances, and her creator,
evidently believe in the value of learning for its own sake, accomplished idleness is deplored. The pragmatic streak surfaces again, when
she stresses the value of manual skills to produce basic necessities, in a
passage which cites the ancient authorities, but sounds very much like
Robinson Crusoe. Her system is designed to produce useful members
of society, both men and women (though it has to be said that
whereas men have vocations in their own right, the primary vocation
for women is to become 'useful and interesting companions . . .
whether in the character of wives or friends').[100] For all her scholarly
idealism, she doesn't neglect the practical talents.

The proof of this is in the experimental, Baconian side of Munster
Village, which allows Mary Hamilton happily to trot out a variety of
hobbyhorses, such as a disquisition on silk manufacture. Whereas
Millenium Hall basks in a golden haze of plenitude, Munster Village
promotes a closer and more inquisitive scrutiny of farming practices.
While echoing the idea that human beings should live in harmony
with nature and hold themselves responsible for animal welfare – an
idea rather endearingly embodied in this instance by 'a receptacle for all
sorts of animals to retire to in their old age' – Hamilton is struck by a
novel suggestion: 'Lady Frances makes use of buffaloes to draw her
ploughs. These animals are far stronger than oxen, and eat less. Why
have we not them in this country, and dromedaries and camels?'[101] If
the notion seems a trifle exotic for a country village, it is certainly in
keeping with the utopian quest for new and improved methods of
husbandry. At least Hamilton doesn't go as far as some writers of
utopian fiction in inventing totally new species. Again, as in *Millenium
Hall*, this tenderness towards the creatures stops short of privileging
them above human interests. Social considerations prevail in Lady
Frances's permission to farmers to shoot on her land, 'as none are
better entitled to game than those whose property is the support of
it'.[102]

The social philosophy that is the basis of *Munster Village* resembles
Sarah Scott's in being grounded on eighteenth-century benevolist

thinking. Instead of challenging social or economic inequality, these writers see it as a literally God-given opportunity for the exercise of mutual giving and receiving, 'a circulation of kindness' as Hamilton puts it: 'it is not to be supposed that Providence would have made such distinctions among men, such unequal distributions, but that they might endear themselves to one another by mutual helps and obligations. Gratitude is the surest bond of love, friendship, and society'.[103] Even the most powerless, 'the most slenderly endowed, aren't 'a mere burthen on the community', but have something positive to give – a belief especially attractive to women.[104] On this idea of reciprocity, in place of the Hobbesian struggle for survival, are women's utopias constructed. (It is interesting, incidentally, that the only direct mention of Hobbes's state of nature in Hamilton's novel connects it with the barbaric masculine code of honour that has 'civilized [us] into brutes'.[105]) So Lady Frances has her charities, like the hospital for incurables, 'a thing much wanted in this kingdom, without paying any regard to their country, religion, or disease, requiring no security in case of death'.[106] There follows the unsurprising contrast: 'the practice of most of the public hospitals in this country is widely different. . . .' From More's *Utopia* onwards, good hospitals feature in a number of 'realistic' utopian societies, so this can be seen as part of the tradition.[107] However, one consequence of Hamilton's benevolist mode of thinking is to make the exercise of personal charity seem more rewarding than any institutional welfare. Lady Frances, with the assistance of 'her secret almoner' Mr Burt, adopts families in need and enjoys 'the happiness arising from the consciousness of having maintained numerous families in decent plenty, who, without her well-timed and secret bounty, must have been a charge to the parish'.[108] The corollary is to devalue parish benefits in favour of private enterprise: 'she was a great enemy to poor-rates, judging . . . that they will be the bane of our manufactures.'

In a sense, this attitude runs counter to the collective spirit of utopianism, by making so much depend on one person's activity and subjective assessment. A few years later, in her novel *Cecilia* (1782) Frances Burney defines more acutely than Hamilton the potential problems arising from this kind of situation. She too has a wealthy heroine, with an almoner, who assumes personal responsibility for people in need, but, as *Cecilia* demonstrates, this creates a precarious dependency on the circumstances of one generous patron – and

circumstances may change. On the other hand, it's true to say that
both Lady Frances and Cecilia direct their charity towards helping
people to find and keep employment and so make themselves
independent. Lady Frances's stated objection to the poor-rates is
compatible with her encouragement and protection of local
manufactures. Hers is a full-employment as well as a scholarly utopia,
combining two earlier patterns found in the Renaissance. Towards the
end of the novel, when her achievements are being fêted in a suitably
erudite entertainment, the social consequences of her policy aren't
overlooked amongst the cultural junketings: 'a hangman from the
assizes told [her] that she had ruined his trade; for, all the poor of the
country-side being employed in manufactures, etc. they had no
inducement to steal, theft being the necessary consequence of
idleness.' Prostitutes too, finding their occupation gone because of the
promotion of industry and the pleasures of theatre and other innocent
recreations, decide to migrate to Birmingham to improve their career
prospects.[109]

However, if *Munster Village* manages to solve the problem of the
oldest profession by relocating it in the outside world, the position of
women in this novel remains at best ambivalent. As usual in
eighteenth-century families of standing, status and wealth derive from
a male line of inheritance: Lady Frances inherits because of her
brother's death, and in fact holds her estate in trust for her nephew.
As a result of this, she postpones for many years her own ideal match
with Lord Darnley, sacrificing their mutual love to family duty. It is
this delay, and her dedication 'to the improvement of that property
invested in her person',[110] that makes possible the creation of Munster
Village. Once more, in a woman writer's fiction, utopia and marriage
are represented as incompatible. However, this time, it is for different
reasons from those implied in *Millenium Hall*, which celebrates the
idea of women's separate development and achievement. Disappoint-
ingly, perhaps, Hamilton doesn't attribute that sense of truly
independent achievement to Lady Frances: on the contrary, when she
is at last in a position to contemplate marriage to the romantically
faithful Darnley, she observes that in spite of all the plaudits the final
credit is not hers:

> It is true, the great works I have carried on, the encouragement I
> have given to learning, the manufactories I have introduced into
> this kingdom, etc. etc. have procured me the suffrage of the

world, and may transmit my name down to posterity. But what flatters me most is, that if I have acquired any fame, it is derived from the man I love. My acquaintance with him, has been a happiness to my mind, because it has improved and exalted its powers.[111]

Wealth, it appears, is not the only power for which women feel indebted to men. This acknowledgement hardly detracts from her utopian creation, but it puts her in a different – and, to the eighteenth-century reader, more acceptably feminine – light.

If Lady Frances stands for the traditional view that the ultimate fulfilment for a woman is in happy marriage, there is still a wide enough spectrum of relationships in the novel to generate a lively debate, as well as much-needed fictional interest. The latter can be a problem for utopian writers, who become absorbed in description rather than narrative. Hamilton prefers not to develop the option of bringing outsiders into utopia, but rather moves in the opposite direction. Yet, whereas Sarah Scott had varied her account of Millenium Hall by giving the women contrasting personalities and interesting pasts, her successor is more haphazard in her method of connecting characters' histories with the concept of Munster Village. The exception is the character of Mrs Lee, who acts as a counterpoint to Lady Frances in expressing more radical attitudes, particularly to marriage.

Mrs Lee reacts to personal unhappiness by finally rebelling and leaving her husband. She takes refuge in rural retirement, to 'pass [her] days in sweet tranquillity and study',[112] and justifies her course of action in a letter to Lady Frances, which cites as authority Milton's arguments for divorce, and, like Mary Astell, makes subversive use of the political analogy for husbands' tyranny over wives (Astell, however, had pointed out the contradiction between Milton's revolutionary politics and his sexual politics).[113] Although Mrs Lee is not the only woman in Munster Village to attempt to salvage some alternative from marriage breakdown – there is an abandoned duchess who founds 'an institution for the provision of the infirm and destitute',[114] a more obviously utopian solution – she poses the most direct threat to the ideology of Lady Frances. Lady Frances believes in the ideal of the domestic utopia: 'domestic society is founded on the union betwixt husband and wife',[115] she declares in her reply to Mrs Lee's letter. However, even at the end of the novel, in the heart of

Munster Village and the wedding anniversary celebrations, Mrs Lee is still an eloquent dissenting voice. When, now widowed, she is addressed by a former lover, she speaks from bitter experience: '. . . I cannot help shuddering at a contract which nothing can dissolve but death. To me it is terrible to reflect, that it is a strangely unequal conflict, in which the man only ventures the loss of a few temporary pleasures, the woman the loss of liberty, and almost the privilege of opinion.'[116] Yet there is no narrative answer to this indictment. Her resistance abruptly collapses. Among all the ecstatic reunions, these lovers too, we are given to understand, settle their differences tamely, in accordance with 'their mutual wishes'. *Munster Village* is wound up in appropriately harmonious closure.

What has it contributed to eighteenth-century women's utopias? Clearly, in conception, Munster Village itself conforms to almost all that one could reasonably ask of a traditional utopian ideal of this particular kind. In the celebratory masquerade, its founder receives tribute from the great and good, representing the acme of European civilisation: ancient Athens, Augustan Rome, Renaissance Florence, and, more tendentiously but patriotically, Restoration London. The 'elegant harangue' of Demosthenes summarises the creation of this philosopher-queen: 'he . . . expatiated on the advantages she had procured to society – the influence of the philosophic spirit in humanizing the mind and preparing it for intellectual exertion and delicate pleasures – in exploring, by the help of geometry, the system of the universe – in promoting navigation, agriculture, medicine, and moral and political science.'[117] Yet the unstable mixture of erudition and romance seems a more volatile experiment than *Millenium Hall*, less under its author's control and closer to purely literary wish-fulfilment. Munster Village as utopian place is a hybrid showpiece, for which masquerade is the fitting medium. Hamilton's often professed admiration for the ancients leads to a strained attempt to process human material into art forms, with the effect of preciousness: 'she also took some pains in regulating the dress of the young women' – a utopian commonplace – 'a country girl returning from the spring with a pitcher of water on her head, perfectly resembles those figures which the most exquisite antiques represent in the same attitude.'[118] This, for all its intellectual intentions, is more of a feminised than a feminist utopia.

Still, if Hamilton is less original and less focused than Scott in her utopian fiction, if the big ideas are essentially derivative, her vitality and intellectual curiosity remain strongly appealing. She does have problems in integrating her more progressive utopian views with her conservative morality; that is why the flicker of intelligent rebellion in Mrs Lee fizzles out in the narrative, despite flaring up rhetorically at almost the last moment. And she seems to have difficulty in deciding what kind of fiction she is writing. From elevated utopian discourse she deviates into quasi-utopian satire, laced with an allusion to Gulliver's voyage to Laputa,[119] when she is describing the eccentricities of fine London ladies – like the anecdote of the lady addicted to cards, who gives up not because of her husband's disapproval, but because, having read that the passions are responsible for dental disease, she is afraid that she will damage her teeth.[120]

This sometimes incongruous combination of high principle and relish for social eccentricity is something that Mary Hamilton shares with her contemporary, Frances Burney. Burney, however, has much greater literary skills than Hamilton, and it seems appropriate to give her the last word on eighteenth-century women's utopias.[121] In fact, she is the woman writer who most decisively places the dreams of a female utopia in relation to the actual limits of even the most gifted and apparently fortunate eighteenth-century heiress. Were she a heroine of romance, Cecilia might have been another Lady Frances; but she is not. Nor has she the scope of the inhabitants of Millenium Hall. In both her biography of Frances Burney and her introduction to Cecilia, Margaret Anne Doody draws a telling contrast between Burney's novel and Scott's, and incisively analyses Cecilia's own utopian dream of power and benevolence.[122] It is doomed, if not to complete failure at least to major modification, largely by the familiar constraints of love and marriage. The disturbing and painful vicissitudes of Cecilia's life don't destroy her 'strong spirit of active benevolence', but it is subdued to an 'oeconomy' dictated both by prudence and by her love for her husband.[123] Cecilia has to learn the hardest of lessons for a utopian reformer, intensified by the disadvantage of being a woman: that idealistic endeavour has to accommodate itself to human society as it is actually constituted. In a sense we have come full circle, back to the domestic utopia as the centre of woman's existence. The novel's ending is grave, low-key, attuned to reason rather than emotion:

> The upright mind of Cecilia, her purity, her virtue, and the moderation of her wishes, gave to her in the warm affection of

Lady Delvile, and the unremitting fondness of Mortimer, all the
happiness human life seems capable of receiving: yet human it
was, and as such imperfect! . . . Rationally, however, she
surveyed the world at large, and finding that of the few who had
any happiness, there were none without some misery, she
checked the rising sigh of repining mortality, and, grateful with
general felicity, bore partial evil with chearfullest resignation.[124]

As often with Burney in her most serious mood, we catch the accents
of Johnson. It is with Johnson, whose *Rasselas* contains one of the
century's most philosophical reflections on the utopian dream, though
not its latest manifestation, that this study will conclude.

Notes and References

1. K. Lilley discusses similar general points in relation to seventeenth-
    century women's utopian writing. In C. Brant, D. Purkiss 1992 (eds) pp.
    102–33.

2. v Plato 1970/1988 pp. 322–3: T. More 1516/1989 Book II pp. 92–3.

3. At least if the Athenians' views on women's reluctance to participate in
    communal meals indicate a general principle: v Plato 1970/1988 pp. 262–3.
    Cf Sargent's survey of the topic (L. T. Sargent 1973).

4. e.g. T. More 1516/1989 Book II p. 104.

5. v F. E. Manuel, F. P. Manuel 1979 pp. 205–21.

6. cf J. Spencer 1986 pp. 181–7: for women as consumers of romance v
    H. Hackett 1992. In C. Brant, D. Purkiss (eds) pp. 39–68.

7. v Lucian 1913 vol. 1 pp. 257–9, 353–5: J. Hall 1605/?1608 Book II: cf
    F. Nussbaum 1984 ch. III pp. 43–8.

8. v R. Ballaster's comments on her claim. In C. Brant, D. Purkiss 1992
    (eds) pp. 217–41.

9. D. Manley 1709/1992 pp. 153–4.

10. D. Manley 1709/1992 p. 154.

11. D. Manley 1709/1992 p. 235: cf p. 157: also cf Ballaster's intro pp.
    xiii–xiv.

12. v J. Hall 1605/?1608 Book II: e.g. *Shrewes-bourg* (ch. 7)

13. D. Manley 1709/1992 p. 161.

14. D. Manley 1709/1992 p. 156.

236 UTOPIAN IMAGINATION AND EIGHTEENTH-CENTURY FICTION

15. D. Manley 1709/1992 p. 155.

16. J. Hall 1605/?1608 Book II ch. 3 p. 104: for the social and sexual impli-cations of Manley's fiction v J. Todd 1989 pp. 84–98: cf J. Todd 1980 p. 341.

17. v Hill's intro to M. Astell 1694–1706/1986 pp. 8–10, 12: Ballaster's intro to D. Manley 1709/1992 pp. viii–ix, xii: Todd also contrasts Manley's utopianism with Astell's and Scott's (J. Todd 1989 p. 92).

18. M. Astell 1694–1706/1986 p. 163.

19. M. Astell 1694–1706/1986 p. 164.

20. M. Astell 1694–1706/1986 p. 150.

21. M. Astell 1694–1706/1986 p. 151.

22. M. Astell 1694–1706/1986 p. 157.

23. v M. Astell 1694–1706/1986 pp. 168–9.

24. M. Astell 1694–1706/1986 pp. 152–3.

25. For this and other aspects of Astell's *Proposal* v K. Lilley 1992. In C. Brant, D. Purkiss (eds) pp. 114–18.

26. M. Astell 1694–1706/1986 *Some Reflections upon Marriage* p. 130.

27. M. Cavendish Duchess of Newcastle 1666 p. 60: M. Astell 1694–1706/1986 p. 154.

28. M. Astell 1694–1706/1986 p. 153.

29. M. Astell 1694–1706/1986 p. 165.

30. v M. Astell 1694–1706/1986 pp. 167–8, 177–8.

31. v J. Locke 1693/1989 pp. 80, 86, 265.

32. v J. Locke 1693/1989 pp. 208–9, 234.

33. M. Astell 1694–1706/1986 p. 178.

34. M. Astell 1694–1706/1986 p. 178: cf K. Lilley 1992. In C. Brant, D. Purkiss (eds) p. 114.

35. M. Astell 1694–1706/1986 pp. 93–4.

36. M. Astell 1694–1706/1986 p. 94.

37. M. Astell 1694–1706/1986 p. 101.

38. M. Astell 1694–1706/1986 p. 76: cf Hill's discussion of the political analogy (intro pp. 39–43). Also cf J. Todd 1989 pp. 27–8.

39. M. Astell 1694–1706/1986 p. 108.

40. *Paradise Lost* ix 31–2. In J. Milton 1674/1971 p. 437.

41. M. Astell 1694–1706/1986 pp. 130–1: cf C. Sharrock's analysis of the contradictions in Astell's ideology. In I. Grundy, S. Wiseman 1992 (eds) pp. 109–24.

42. v D. Defoe 1697/1969 pp. 282–304: S. Richardson 1751/1972 Part 2 Vol. IV Letter xviii pp. 355–6.

43. v R. S. Neale 1981 pp. 319–20: S. Scott 1762/1986 intro pp. viii–ix.

44. S. Scott 1762/1986 p. 2: for the significance of the male narrator and his companion v Spencer's intro pp. xi–xii, xiv–xv.

45. S. Scott 1762/1986 p. 207: cf S. Berington 1737 pp. 114–15.

46. For the actual phrase 'earthly paradise' v S. Scott 1762/1986 p. 6: cf 'a female Arcadia' p. 179.

47. S. Scott 1762/1986 pp. 4–5.

48. S. Scott 1762/1986 p. 6.

49. S. Scott 1762/1986 p. 11.

50. v Plato 1955/1987 pp. 168–71.

51. S. Scott 1762/1986 p. 21.

52. v T. Campanella 1602, 1637/1981 p. 35.

53. D. Defoe 1697/1969 p. 181.

54. S. Scott 1762/1986 pp. 120–1.

55. S. Scott 1762/1986 p. 121.

56. S. Scott 1762/1986 p. 17: the narrator is quoting Pope's *Essay on Man* Epistle iii l 152 (v A. Pope 1733–4/1950 p. 108) and Isaiah 11:6, 35:1. For shifting attitudes to the natural world v K. Thomas 1983 Part IV.

57. v T. More 1516/1989 Book II p. 73.

58. S. Scott 1762/1986 p. 18.

59. S. Scott 1762/1986 pp. 18–19: cf p. 59.

60. In legend at least: Marie Antoinette's reputation for frivolity is arguably more apocryphal than historical.

61. S. Scott 1762/1986 p. 41: the ideal is qualified, even in its schoolday context, by the discrepancy in age.

62. cf J. Todd 1980 p. 344.

63. S. Scott 1762/1986 p. 202.

64. S. Scott 1762/1986 p. 203.

65.   S. Scott 1762/1986 p. 121: cf their accounting system p. 205.

66.   S. Scott 1762/1986 pp. 201–2.

67.   S. Scott 1762/1986 pp. 117–18.

68.   S. Scott 1762/1986 p. 118.

69.   S. Scott 1762/1986 p. 60: cf Aristotle 1988 p. 4.

70.   S. Scott 1762/1986 p. 61: v T. Hobbes 1651/1968 p. 186.

71.   cf J. Todd 1980 p. 344.

72.   S. Scott 1762/1986 p. 8.

73.   v Plato 1970/1988 pp. 208–9.

74.   v Plato 1955/1987 p. 237.

75.   S. Scott 1762/1986 p. 14.

76.   S. Scott 1762/1986 pp. 82, 179.

77.   S. Scott 1762/1986 pp. 64–71.

78.   v Johnson on remarriage in J. Boswell 1791, 1799/1934–50 vol. II p. 128: 1770 Aetat.61.

79.   cf Philippe-Auguste Villiers de L'Isle-Adam: 'Vivre? les serviteurs feront cela pour nous' (Axël 1890 iv:2).

80.   S. Scott 1762/1986 p. 115: cf M. Astell 1694–1706/1986 pp. 130–1.

81.   S. Scott 1762/1986 p. 115.

82.   S. Scott 1762/1986 p. 116.

83.   v S. Scott 1762/1986 p. 125.

84.   S. Scott 1762/1986 p. 154.

85.   S. Scott 1762/1986 p. 194.

86.   S. Scott 1762/1986 p. 111.

87.   S. Scott 1762/1986 p. 150.

88.   v S. Scott 1762/1986 p. 151: cf T. More 1516/1989 Book II p. 47.

89.   S. Scott 1762/1986 p. 151.

90.   e.g. R. S. Neale 1981 pp. 319–20: but cf Todd's observation of the paradox that a work not 'politically radical' can have radical implications (J. Todd 1980 p. 344): also v Spencer's intro to S. Scott 1762/1986 p. xiii: E. B. Brophy 1991 p. 266.

91.   cf M. Wollstonecraft 1792/1989 vol. 5.

92. It is difficult to know if Hamilton intended any historical resonance in her choice of family name: the association between sixteenth-century Münster and religious/social utopianism seems too revolutionary for conscious allusion, but the unconscious undertone is interesting (I owe this suggestion to David Nokes).

93. M. Hamilton 1778/1987 pp. 16–17 Vol. I pp. 16–17.

94. M. Hamilton 1778/1987 Vol. I p. 17.

95. M. Hamilton 1778/1987 Vol. I p. 31.

96. M. Hamilton 1778/1987 Vol. I p. 23.

97. M. Hamilton 1778/1987 Vol. I p. 23.

98. M. Hamilton 1778/1987 Vol. I p. 27.

99. v M. Hamilton 1778/1987 Vol. I pp. 25–6.

100. M. Hamilton 1778/1987 Vol. I p. 26.

101. M. Hamilton 1778/1987 Vol. I p. 33: Baylis calls her attitude to animals and the environment 'a curiously female vision' (intro p. viii) but it could equally be described as a standard utopian vision.

102. M. Hamilton 1778/1987 Vol. I p. 35.

103. M. Hamilton 1778/1987 Vol. I pp. 20–1.

104. M. Hamilton 1778/1987 Vol. I p. 20.

105. M. Hamilton 1778/1987 Vol. II p. 75.

106. M. Hamilton 1778/1987 Vol. I p. 29.

107. v T. More 1516/1989 Book II pp. 57–8: cf M. Eliav-Feldon 1982 ch. 2 sec. B.

108. M. Hamilton 1778/1987 Vol. II p. 144.

109. M. Hamilton 1778/1987 Vol. II pp. 144–5.

110. M. Hamilton 1778/1987 Vol. I p. 20: cf p. 56.

111. M. Hamilton 1778/1987 Vol. I p. 57.

112. M. Hamilton 1778/1987 Vol. I p. 53.

113. v M. Hamilton 1778/1987 Vol. I pp. 50–2: cf M. Astell 1694–1706/1986 *Reflections upon Marriage* pp. 76, 101–2.

114. M. Hamilton 1778/1987 Vol. II p. 70.

115. M. Hamilton 1778/1987 Vol. I p. 55.

116. M. Hamilton 1778/1987 Vol. II p. 150.

117. M. Hamilton 1778/1987 Vol. II p. 130: the inclusion of the Restoration age (p. 133) is a suggestive link with the Stuart cult to which earlier women writers subscribed: v J. Todd 1989 pp. 15–17.

118. M. Hamilton 1778/1987 Vol. I p. 28.

119. v M. Hamilton 1778/1987 Vol. II p. 111.

120. M. Hamilton 1778/1987 Vol. II p. 114.

121. I include this only as a brief coda, since M. A. Doody has already dealt brilliantly with the utopian element in Burney's fiction (v n 122 below).

122. v M. A. Doody 1988 ch. 4: e.g. pp. 116–17 (Gulliver reference p. 117): 127–8: 137 (*Millenium Hall* reference). For the reception of *Cecilia*, including a reference to Wollstonecraft, v pp. 143–8. Cf F. Burney 1782/1988 intro pp. xxxiv–xxxvi.

123. F. Burney 1782/1988 p. 939.

124. F. Burney 1782/1988 p. 941.

CHAPTER 8

Utopia and the philosophical tale: Rasselas

Both the category of eighteenth-century fiction that scholars define as the 'philosophical tale' and its overlapping genre, the 'oriental tale', appear to be tailormade for the utopian imagination. In a number of French and English examples the vivid utopian motif is woven into the figurative carpet as part of the pattern: the account of the Troglodytes in Montesquieu's *Lettres Persanes* (1721), or Eldorado in Voltaire's *Candide* (1759), or Johnson's own Happy Valley in *Rasselas*, (also 1759).[1] Not all philosophical tales are oriental, but this particular vogue – which can be traced to the influence of the French translation of the *Arabian Nights* (1704–17) – adapts well to the taste for fictional theorising about other cultures in relation to one's own.[2] 'All judgment is comparative' is one of Imlac's aphorisms,[3] and this applies to utopian fiction and oriental tale alike. 'Oriental' becomes loosely synonymous with exotic (to Westerners) civilisations covering areas of three continents: Eastern Europe, Northern Africa, and the whole of Asia. As in many utopian fictions, distance evidently lends enchantment. Moreover, not only enchantment, but curiosity: Islam and China in particular represent imaginative structures alien and attractive to eighteenth-century Europeans. In more recent times, the cult of Orientalism has become a noted ideological battleground;[4] again, as with utopias, any resemblance to the real world is sensitive and problematic. Even in its earlier period, the excesses of the cult's devotees can excite derision not unlike that directed to utopian chimeras.

However, the convergence of the oriental and the philosophical tale meant that serious writers did find possibilities in the former, comparable with fictions set in randomly located imaginary cultures. What they wanted was a forum for discussion and illustration of topics already familiar in utopian discourse: the nature of happiness, the problems of power, differences in sexual practices, attitudes to mortality – in short, the philosophy of an entire society. All this comes giftwrapped in a powerful fantasy, permitting the reader to experience vicariously encounters with hermits in deserts and princesses in seraglios, and to savour the extremes of asceticism and luxury in a single journey. Alternatively, the reader can see western life through the eyes of travellers from the East, like Montesquieu's Usbek and Rica, or Goldsmith's Lien Chi Altangi.[5] Imagining the outsider's impressions is, of course, a basic utopian device. It's refreshed in these texts by the shift away from representatives of the New World (Montaigne's cannibals, Addison's Iroquois) to a different stereotype, representing an ancient and sophisticated culture. East judges West, and vice versa.[6]

Yet, if the oriental tale offers the same stimuli as utopian fiction, in certain respects it promotes a contrasting ethos. This is especially true of the first type, tales actually set in the Orient. The utopian urge towards activism, the conviction that human circumstances are subject to rational control, is reversed in the oriental tale, which usually – at least on the surface, which can be deceptive – teaches a fatalistic acceptance of circumstance, a reliance on virtuous submission to whatever supernatural powers rule the world. It is this supernatural, or magical, component that differentiates the majority of oriental tales from their utopian equivalents. Although utopian writers happily invent more things in heaven and earth than are dreamt of in the sceptic's philosophy, they are less inclined to negotiate with angels or demons. Whereas Gulliver holds his most important conversations with a talking horse, Voltaire's Zadig holds his with an angel.[7] Utopias are this-worldly in their dominant concerns; oriental tales tend to be other-worldly in their apparatus, however sceptical in intent.

However, the philosophical tale in general (and the second type of oriental tale) needn't emulate the more magical effects of the *Arabian Nights' Entertainments*. As attention focuses more on discourse than narrative, the mists of supernatural enchantments may disperse to give a clearer, less distracting view. Either the setting becomes an allegorical location in which ideas take centre stage, or, if the setting is realistic, travellers from the East become the medium through which the West learns to reappraise its own cultural norms. In Johnson's *Rasselas*, although the characters don't make a literal journey beyond the geographical limits of the Middle East, they figure in both kinds of context: from the Happy Valley – an overtly utopian setting – they make the transition to the outside world, where they

encounter the range of social experience that Johnson believes is
common to humanity everywhere, whether in the environs of Cairo
or eighteenth-century London.

Johnson and utopianism

Johnson would no doubt categorise utopian speculations as among the
vainer of human wishes. He gives famously short shrift to the cant
that accompanies unthinking idealism, whether it takes the form of
egalitarianism or primitivism. Confronted with a female republican,
he proposes that she put her principle of equality into practice and
allow her footman to join them at table ('I thus, Sir, shewed her the
absurdity of the levelling doctrine').[8] To the gentleman who rhap-
sodises about life in the American wilderness with an Indian woman
and a gun as the sum of happiness, he retorts, 'If a bull could speak,
he might as well exclaim, – Here am I with this cow and this grass;
what being can enjoy greater felicity?'[9] On the other hand, he is
equally prepared to detect and analyse fallacious reasoning – as he sees
it – in the anti-utopianism of a Mandeville.[10]

These are random examples from Boswell's *Life*: but they support a
more fundamental and general tendency on Johnson's part to distrust
a certain kind of discourse. Politically, he is very conscious of the
central utopian problem – how to translate planning into action: 'the
inseparable imperfection annexed to all human governments, consisted, he said, in not being able to create a sufficient fund of virtue
and principle to carry the laws into due and effectual execution.
Wisdom might plan, but virtue alone could execute. And where could
sufficient virtue be found?'[11] From Plato's Guardians onwards, utopian
philosophers had tried to find a guaranteed answer to this sharply
pertinent question. However, Johnson's 'inseparable imperfection'
preempts them all.

In any case, Johnson doubts not just the efficacy but the relevance
of political institutions, real or imaginary, when it comes to improving
the quality of human life. It isn't that he makes no distinction
between forms of government, or is indifferent to how the system is
run: he is known to have held strong political views.[12] However, at
the same time, he asserts in a number of contexts (including the
couplet he wrote for Goldsmith's *The Traveller*) that political systems
have very little impact on individual happiness or suffering, even
telling Sir Adam Fergusson in the heat of the moment that

Fergusson's political notions are 'all visionary' and that he himself 'would not give half a guinea to live under one form of government rather than another. It is of no moment to the happiness of an individual.'[13] Although extraordinarily sweeping, this comment identifies a real challenge to political utopianism: the challenge to imagine the ordinary human being's priorities and point of view. His riposte to Boswell, when discussing population and economics, makes his position still more explicit: **BOSWELL**: "So Sir, you laugh at schemes of political improvement." **JOHNSON**: "Why, Sir, most schemes of political improvement are very laughable things." As Donald J. Greene – who quotes this exchange with direct reference to modern utopianism – has pointed out in parenthesis, 'it should be noted that Johnson says "most" not "all"'.[14] Even so, there is an underlying consistency in Johnson's suspicion of such visionary schemes. His case against them rests on two simple observations: first, that they wouldn't work, and, second, that they're largely irrelevant to human wellbeing.

Apart from distrusting the political aspect of the utopian imagination, Johnson also distrusts it on psychological grounds. Perhaps no eighteenth-century writer has more acute insight into what it is in human psychology that impels us to invent utopia in the first place. As all his readers must be aware, the idea of imagination in itself fascinates Johnson. Throughout his work, he analyses its functions and power in ways relevant to the creation of fiction in general, and utopian fiction in particular. However, ironically, the very impulses that produce utopian constructs ensure that these constructs are unstable and unrealisable. According to Johnson 'the natural flights of the human mind are not from pleasure to pleasure, but from hope to hope.'[15] The need for variety, novelty, in a word, change, is deeply ingrained in the human psyche, so that a state of permanent happiness in this world is impossible: without anything to hope for, the 'happy' life stagnates into misery. However, the occupation and development of the mind is profoundly pleasurable, so that inventing utopia is far more satisfying than living in it would be. Of all utopian values, the one that Johnson seems to endorse most unreservedly is that of education.[16] Our psychology may make our species unfit to inhabit utopia, but the pursuit of happiness, justice, and knowledge in an imperfect world is still a legitimate aim – provided that we accept certain disillusion and consign the achievement of happiness to eternity.

If Johnson appears to disqualify himself as a utopian theorist because of his attitude to both politics and psychology, he has a further disqualification for the writing of utopian fiction: namely, that he firmly dissociates the state of happiness from place ('Happiness not local'). In the classic statement of this theme in a *Rambler* essay, he criticises the poet Cowley's scheme of escaping to an 'American elysium' as a futile kind of wishful thinking: there is no point in changing one's environment and not oneself.[17] For a number of utopian travellers, the former tends to precede the latter, but Johnson, for all his vast interest in travel literature, doesn't expect that locality or climate can radically alter the species or the individual. He constantly emphasises the fundamental sameness of human nature underlying superficial cultural difference. In his preface to his translation of Lobo's *Voyage to Abyssinia*, a precursor of *Rasselas*, he goes out of his way to recommend the work precisely because it is *not* a utopian fiction or imaginary voyage:

> The reader will here find no regions cursed with irremediable barrenness, or blessed with spontaneous fecundity, no perpetual gloom or unceasing sunshine; nor are the nations here described either devoid of all sense of humanity, or consummate in all private and social virtues, here are no Hottentots without religion, polity, or articulate language, no Chinese perfectly polite, and compleatly skill'd in all sciences: he will discover, what will always be discover'd by a diligent and impartial enquirer, that wherever human nature is to be found, there is a mixture of vice and virtue, a contest of passion and reason, and that the Creator doth not appear partial in his distributions, but has balanced in most countries their particular inconveniences by particular favours.[18]

Nevertheless, in spite of Johnson's disclaimers, A *Voyage to Abyssinia* carries traces of the ore which could be refined into golden utopian fiction. To take the incidental information about fertility and climate: at least one province of the country is described as being exceptionally beautiful, temperate, and fruitful all year round (and elsewhere the phrase 'perpetual spring'[19] makes its routine appearance). The locality praised in such terms – 'so great, so charming is the variety, that the whole region seems a garden, laid out and cultivated, only to please'[20] – isn't far distant from a fictional African utopia situated near the legendary source of the Nile, the land discovered by the migrant Mezzoranians in *Gaudentio di Lucca* – 'they wandered thus at Pleasure thro' those natural Gardens, where there was a perpetual Spring . . .' a land which 'look'd rather like an immense Garden than a Country'.[21] Indeed, the Catholic Berington might have known the Jesuit Father's description. Lobo's material also contains, as might be expected, a good deal about Abyssinian religion, which is a unique, separately evolved tradition of Christianity, and Abyssinian customs, including a form of marriage which sounds very utopian – 'marriages in this country are only for a term of years, and last no longer than both parties are pleased with each other'[22] (the Jesuit naturally disapproves). On this evidence it could be claimed that inside Johnson's translation of a soberly factual travel narrative a wilder utopian fantasy is struggling to get out.

Johnson himself isn't unaffected by this. As Boswell suggests in the *Life*, 'it is reasonable to suppose' that his work on the French version of Lobo's text is associated with his later composition of *Rasselas*[23]. Modern scholars continue to suppose it, and to investigate in depth Johnson's use of this and other sources, explaining for instance how the traditional mountain fastness in which the Abyssinian princes were confined evolves into the myth of the Happy Valley.[24] The point is that, for all his historical scepticism, it is Johnson's own utopian imagination that works upon this material to produce the text that is a gold standard for eighteenth-century utopian writing of the purest kind. As a 'philosophical tale' – Boswell's phrase – *Rasselas* is closer to myth (like Plato's myth of Er) than to either novel or satire.[25] Perhaps it is the sceptics who create the finest utopian fictions.[26] If so, Johnson is no exception. And his opening sentence addresses the kind of reader most imaginatively receptive to utopian illusion – that is, all readers in a certain frame of mind: 'Ye who listen with credulity to the whispers of fancy, and pursue with eagerness the phantoms of hope; who expect that age will perform the promises of youth, and that the deficiencies of the present day will be supplied by the morrow; attend to the history of Rasselas prince of Abissinia.'[27]

The Happy Valley

In a sense, the Happy Valley sequence of *Rasselas* extracts and purifies the utopian element that exists in a compound state in other fiction. Yet how complete is it *as* a utopia? By choosing an Abyssinian setting and an Abyssinian legend, Johnson isn't starting from a blank canvas like Plato's artist in the *Republic*. The forms of both government and religion are already established. Unlike other authors of oriental tales, Johnson selects a country with a Christian tradition of its own,[28] which disposes of one controversial variable. And although the political arrangements of Abyssinia are sufficiently complicated to give scope for analysis and argument, Johnson doesn't go into them in detail. In the fifth Dissertation of *A Voyage to Abyssinia*, it is made clear that one purpose of confining the princes of the blood was to assess their fitness to rule, since the succession depended on a combination of heredity and election.[29] Johnson makes little or nothing of this specific background, although Rasselas's education for an imperial destiny is important to his scheme. Unlike the overtly political thrust of John Hawkesworth's *Almoran and Hamet* (1761)[30] *Rasselas* pays comparatively slight attention to constitutional questions. This seems to bear out Johnson's feeling that politics aren't central to the quest for happiness. Even if the existence of the Happy Valley is the result of a constitutional arrangement, what makes it utopian is the quality of life available to its inhabitants.

Predictably, in view of its origins, the society of the Happy Valley is hierarchical. 'The sons and daughters of Abissinia' are at the centre of a system devoted to satisfying their every need or desire, for pleasure, education, and entertainment.[31] It elaborates the idea of a purpose-designed environment 'cultivated only for pleasure' which Johnson had already sketched in his tale of Seged in *The Rambler*.[32] Just as Seged devises a performers' competition (which defeats the object by stirring up emulation and envy), so entry to the Happy Valley is by competition, judged not only on artistic skill, but novelty of performance. Unlike Plato's Republic, the Happy Valley welcomes poets; and its preferred musical mode appears to be soft, rather than the rigorous mode recommended by Socrates: 'to heighten their opinion of their own felicity, they were daily entertained with songs, the subject of which was the Happy Valley.'[33] From first impressions, it sounds a little like Rabelais' Abbey of Thélème, a utopia for cultivated hedonistic leisure rather than a working community.[34] Part of Johnson's strategy, however, is to expose the discontents and tensions beneath this elegantly ordered social surface. The architecture, as so often in utopias, reveals the power structure, both openly and obliquely. If the Abbey of Thélème reflects Renaissance magnificence, the Abyssinian palace reflects Oriental magnificence. However, it also serves the secrecy and constant scrutiny endemic in a closed and tortuous society that keeps all its members under control. The subtext of this edifice 'built as if suspicion herself had dictated the plan' is certainly utopian, in the Benthamite or Orwellian sense.[35] When Imlac tells Rasselas about the true feelings of those trapped in the perpetual pleasures of the Happy Valley, it comes as no surprise to those who have read the signs.

Johnson uses Imlac's revelation to criticise another utopian assumption: that equal access to material goods, and complete economic security, will improve human relationships and subdue, if not eliminate, certain passions. Rasselas might be speaking for Plato or More when he advocates the idea that having everything in common can be an answer to the competitive and acquisitive instincts of humanity getting out of hand: ' "What passions can infest those", said the prince, "who have no rivals? We are in a place where impotence precludes malice, and where all envy is repressed by community of enjoyments." ' Imlac counters with the assertion 'There may be community . . . of material possessions, but there can never be community of love or of esteem. It must happen that one will please more than another . . . '[36] Again, the objection is rooted in a sense of the individual self which obstinately persists in the most collective of states.

Given Johnson's known views on the inevitability of political and social subordination, and his distrust of 'the levelling doctrine', it isn't to be expected that the Happy Valley would take the form of a successful egalitarian utopia in any case. Yet it is interesting that he seems to envisage a community which is radical in one respect at least: they don't value money. Admittedly, this is an ironic point made in passing at a later stage of the narrative, when the principal characters have left the Happy Valley behind them: 'the prince had, by frequent lectures, been taught the use and nature of money; but the ladies could not, for a long time, comprehend what the merchants did with small pieces of gold and silver, or why things of so little use should be received as equivalent to the necessaries of life.'[37] Although Johnson's editor traces this to A Voyage to Abyssinia, the notion of a society that has abolished money and exists in a kind of pre-monetary innocence is so ubiquitous in utopian writing that there is scarcely any need to identify a source. All that matters is to note that in the Happy Valley, money, like politics, is an irrelevance.[38]

The same is true, more astonishingly, of sex. This is where a comparison with other hedonistic utopias, like the Abbey of Thélème,

evidently breaks down. Although the atmosphere is conducive to a
romantic idyll – 'their appetites were excited by frequent enume-
rations of different enjoyments, and revelry and merriment was the
business of every hour from the dawn of morning to the close of
even'[39] – romance itself is absent, at least in any tangible form. An
original version of the Abyssinian legend had excluded women from
the princes' mountain:[40] clearly that isn't the case with the Happy
Valley, but the utopian discussion of love and marriage is postponed
until the travellers are experiencing the world outside. Even then,
neither the prince nor his sister become involved in love relationships, in marked contrast with the protagonists of some oriental tales.
Rasselas remains a detached observer both inside and outside the
Happy Valley. It is through his dissident consciousness that utopia is
primarily judged.

Significantly, the first indication of his discontent with the Happy
Valley is his failure to participate in the communal meal, symbolic
centre of so many ideal communities, and his withdrawal from
communal pleasures. He begins to prefer being on his own, an anti-
utopian trait. In solitude, he articulates a response to the natural
surroundings that make the Happy Valley the traditional earthly
paradise. Like most paradises, it is isolated and inaccessible, its
mountain barricade pierced only by an underground passage through a
cavern (a recurrent dream image). Within this seclusion every living
thing is safe, since no predator can enter. Apart from dangerous
beasts, it is as comprehensive as the first paradise: 'all the diversities of
the world were brought together, the blessings of nature were
collected, and its evils extracted and excluded.'[41]

In this setting, like another Adam, Rasselas enjoys and
meditates upon the life of the creatures and the distinction
between the human species and the rest (a familiar topic of
utopian fiction). He concludes with the conventional wisdom that
humanity possesses 'some latent sense' which requires more than
physical satisfaction, but he refutes the corollary that animals are
therefore happier than humans: 'surely the equity of providence has
ballanced peculiar sufferings with peculiar enjoyments.'[42] Among
these enjoyments are the aesthetic and the scientific; for Rasselas
has something of the Baconian utopian in him, as well as the moral
philosopher: 'he discerned the various instincts of animals, and
properties of plants, and found the place replete with wonders. . . .'[43]
Finally, this benign attention to the behaviour of other species is

rewarded when Imlac and the prince hit on a plan of escape by observing the rabbits of the Happy Valley.

However, before that happens, Rasselas has to learn to know himself better. His self-questioning is reinforced by the sage's question which strikes to the heart of the utopian fallacy: 'Look round and tell me which of your wants is without supply: if you want nothing, how are you unhappy?'[44] In Johnson's view, the perfect equation between want and supply, supposedly the aim of the ideal society, is a mirage which always vanishes because to want is to be human – I want, therefore I am. So far as Rasselas is concerned, he solves the dilemma elegantly and ironically by reversing the utopian dream. What utopia requires for its very existence is some standard of comparison: if that is not provided within the fiction, it has to rely on the reader's awareness of difference. As an inhabitant of the Happy Valley, Rasselas has to learn the opposite of imagining utopia, that is to 'long to see the miseries of the world, since the sight of them is necessary to happiness'.[45] Meanwhile, he uses his imagination and intellect to compensate for the tedium of his actual state.

As already observed, one utopian ideal to which Johnson does subscribe is that of education. However, unlike many utopian thinkers, he follows this through to a logical conclusion: teaching people to think actually makes them more unfit to live in an ideal state. Education disturbs and disillusions as well as empowers and enriches. There are no guarantees that increasing educational opportunity will increase social cohesion or even individual satisfaction. Yet Johnson was prepared to confront that risk, challenging contemporary attitudes with the words 'the privileges of education may, sometimes, be improperly bestowed, but I shall always fear to withhold them . . .'[46] In the case of Rasselas, the learning process will ultimately lead him out of the Happy Valley altogether, but that outcome can't be anything other than a *felix culpa*, a fortunate fall. In the Happy Valley sequence, Johnson demonstrates a central paradox of literary utopias: they grow out of imagination and the concept of change, but their internal arrangements have to be immune to change and resist the subversive power of imagination.

Most readers recognise that *Rasselas* is not only an imaginative fiction, but a self-referential one, questioning the creative faculty in a variety of contexts. Even, or especially, in the Happy Valley, Rasselas develops this ability to spin fictions to satisfy his longings. If the inhabitant of an imperfect world escapes by fantasising about utopia or an earthly paradise, the inhabitant of utopia escapes by fantasising about the world outside. The prince reveals a romantic disposition – his daydream of the 'orphan virgin' is the only hint, and a very innocent hint, of sexual interest in these chapters[47] – and also a benevolent one. However, at this stage, his 'visionary bustle' is self-indulgence, and it is a sign of growing maturity that he is able to smile at himself. It presumably isn't accidental that this chapter of introspective fancies is symmetrically balanced by the following one describing his Baconian enquiries into natural science: both engage the powers of the mind in different ways (or, as Bacon himself would have put it, they reflect the mind as 'enchanted glass' and as 'clear and equal glass').[48] Both are a necessary part of the education of Rasselas. However, if Johnson criticises the excesses to which the literary imagination is prone, he is no less ready to criticise the utopian dreams of the scientist. He does this most effectively in the episode of the 'man eminent for his knowledge of the mechanick powers'[49] who furthers the prince's education in the chapter entitled 'A dissertation on the art of flying'.

From antiquity, the dream of flying figures in utopian fiction as well as speculative science, and Johnson's debt to predecessors such as Bishop John Wilkins has been well documented.[50] Bacon had also included a suggestion in *New Atlantis* that the scientists of the House of Salomon had made progress in this direction (cautiously he doesn't specify how much).[51] However, Johnson considers moral education to take priority over scientific knowledge,[52] and, true to his creed, it is the moral meaning of 'A dissertation upon flying' that predominates. Not that he is uninterested in the technical feasibility of the project: although this is an oriental tale, he disdains any recourse to magical props, and uses terms derived from authentic scientific discourse. But the problem, as so often with scientific discovery, lies with the human factor. Who is to have access to scientific knowledge and the power it confers? Even in a utopia like Bacon's New Atlantis, something like an Official Secrets Act is deemed to be necessary.[53] Rasselas, instinctively and naively idealistic, argues against the inventor's condition of secrecy, on the utopian principle that 'all skill ought to be exerted for universal good; every man has owed much to others, and ought to repay the kindness that he has received.' However, the reply envisages the possible misuse of the science of flight: 'what would be the security of the good, if the bad could at pleasure invade them from the sky?'[54] The security of the Happy Valley itself would be shattered, like the prince's illusions.

Of course, the idea of assault from the air, or aerial battle, is as ancient as the dream of flying, but Johnson disentangles it from myth or satire to produce a chilling realism. We aren't in the world of Lucian's star wars or Swift's Laputa, but looking at a prescient glimpse of our own world. In the circumstances, the failure of the inventor's attempt comes as a welcome bathos: another utopian bubble bursts, as he falls ignominiously into the lake, parodying other more successful utopian flights.[55] Elsewhere, Johnson pricks the pretensions of earlier would-be moon voyagers: 'a voyage to the moon, however romantic and absurd the scheme may now appear, since the properties of air have been better understood, seemed highly probable to many of the aspiring wits in the last century, who began to doat upon their glossy plumes, and fluttered with impatience for the hour of their departure.'[56] However, this is harmless vanity, whereas the inventor's combination of cynicism about human nature and faith in scientific advance in the *Rasselas* episode is potentially far more damaging. Certainly it functions as a critique of science-based utopias, and possibly as a reflection upon Bacon who possessed both qualities in an eminent degree.

For a more balanced view of human life, Rasselas has to turn not to a single-minded specialist in 'mechanick powers', but to a poet-philosopher and traveller, Imlac. The history of Imlac utilises a double form familiar in utopian literature, the inset narrative and the dialogue.[57] Like Fielding's Mr Wilson or Man of the Hill,[58] he presents the story of his life in order that his young and inexperienced listener may learn from it. However, he has been first and foremost an observer rather than a participant, a wandering scholar who renounces material security for the sake of first-hand knowledge of people and places, his object being 'by drinking at the fountains of knowledge, to quench the thirst of curiosity'.[59] In his rejection of paternal values, he has a passing resemblance to Crusoe; there are even, it's been suggested, hints of a comparison and contrast with Gulliver.[60] In terms of philosophic dialogue, he plays Socrates to Rasselas's Glaucon. Most of all, perhaps, he inherits the cloak of Raphael Hythlodaeus, but a Hythlodaeus who has never found his utopia. Estimating the relative degrees of happiness in different parts of the world, his conclusion is firmly anti-utopian: 'human life is every where a state in which much is to be endured, and little to be enjoyed.'[61] Yet, like Hythlodaeus, his worldly wisdom has not eliminated a powerful commitment to an ideal, in Imlac's case the ideal of the poet. (And as with More, so with Johnson: critics debate how far this commitment represents the author's own view.)[62] If this ideal were capable of realisation – and for once it is Rasselas who brings his mentor down to earth by refusing to believe that it is[63] – then it would go a long way towards meeting Plato's objections to poetry in the *Republic*.

If Imlac is an impractical idealist with regard to the poet's profession, in other areas of human activity, such as politics, he is a pragmatist. He dampens the prince's ardour for redressing wrong, by pointing out the limitations even of good government – limitations which Johnson himself reiterates: 'oppression is, in the Abissinian dominions, neither frequent nor tolerated; but no form of government has been yet discovered, by which cruelty can be wholly prevented. Subordination supposes power on one part and subjection on the other; and if power be in the hands of men, it will sometimes be abused.'[64] He is also conscious of the imbalance of global power, which he attributes to the possession of superior knowledge by more advanced societies, but his ultimate explanation for European domination is not innate superiority but 'the unsearchable will of the Supreme Being'.[65] What Imlac has gained from his travels is the power of knowledge, but it is a power to be used intellectually, not politically, nor, as with the inventor, technologically (although he does claim some knowledge of applied engineering – 'I can burst the gate, but cannot do it secretly'[66]). As he began by pointing out, *c'est son métier*: the scholar 'wanders about the world without pomp or terrour, and is neither known nor valued but by men like himself.'[67] He himself learns to know and value. Only Imlac, of all its inhabitants, has the insight to judge the Happy Valley for what it is. Only Imlac can rehearse to Rasselas the cycle of illusion and disillusion experienced by the utopian traveller, which for him has already culminated in a homecoming to set beside that of Crusoe or Gulliver: his family dead or scattered, his friends of whom he relates 'the greater part was in the grave, of the rest some could with difficulty remember me, and some considered me as one corrupted by foreign manners.'[68] However, Rasselas, of course, is not deterred. When the opportunity presents itself, the prince, his sister, her attendant, and Imlac himself escape from utopia to the outside world.

Beyond the Happy Valley

Structurally, Johnson's narrative reverses the more usual procedure of leading up to utopia through a preliminary sequence set in the known world (though More's original order of composition in *Utopia* probably followed a similar pattern).[69] It is as if Johnson wanted to start by separating out and purifying the utopian element of his tale before testing it experimentally in the laboratory of universal human experience, to measure both its aspirations and its inadequacies. His travellers in quest of a choice of life have already experienced a supposedly idyllic existence and found it wanting. In a sense, Rasselas and Nekayah are already disillusioned with the utopian dream of happiness; but they don't know it. Their quest for utopia is over before it has begun. Nevertheless, they need to pursue their enquiries on an empirical basis, and to do this they have to become acclimatised to a world of which they are not the centre. Nekayah especially finds it hard to accept a temporary levelling with ordinary humanity,[70] often a side effect of leaving a utopian environment, even for those who are not royalty. They are literally displaced persons. On the other hand, the prince and princess are still privileged by wealth and birth, possessing what Rasselas perceives as an exceptional freedom of choice,[71] though he will learn that this freedom is circumscribed in a sense that he cannot yet discern.

The philosophical core of the tale follows a similar method to utopian fiction, in that it constantly tests theoretic assumptions against experience, trying out different models of how to live, and how to make sense of living. In the process, a number of ideologies upon which utopias have been constructed are set up to be broken down: the life of pleasure, the life of reason, the 'life led according to nature' whatever that may be.[72] The travellers also scrutinise several modes of living which have in the past been assimilated into a broadly defined utopian tradition: the simple life and its sophisticated pastoral imitation, the life of the wealthy landowner with his country estate, the solitary life and the life at the centre of political power.[73] However, what may engage most interest, particularly with the eighteenth-century novel in mind, is the extended discussion of private life.[74]

This is a stage in the narrative where differences between the sexes become more marked than previously. In the Happy Valley sequence this issue scarcely surfaced, but after Rasselas, Nekayah and Pekuah

enter the outside world the difference between the masculinity of
Rasselas and the femininity of his two companions becomes more
germane to their experience and attitudes, and remains so until the
conclusion. When the brother and sister 'divide between them the
work of observation',[75] it seems appropriate that Nekayah should
propose that Rasselas concentrate on life in the public domain, and
that she herself should take family life as her province. However, it
turns out that, like Pekuah later in the Arab's harem, she is too
well-educated and accustomed to intelligent (male) company to have
much in common with the domesticated female species or they with
her: 'with these girls she played as with inoffensive animals, and found
them proud of her countenance, and weary of her company.'[76] For the
lack of women's education, if for no other reason, the domestic utopia
appears to rest on shaky foundations. Deeper investigation into family
relationships reveals more cracking and warping of a would-be ideal
structure.

Nekayah begins from the familiar Aristotelian analogy between the
family and the political organism: but she reverses it pessimistically –
'if a kingdom be, as Imlac tells us, a great family, a family likewise is a
little kingdom, torn with factions and exposed to revolutions.'[77] Yet as
the debate develops, the political analogy is discarded, and indeed
appears largely irrelevant. The princess's 'dismal history of private
life'[78] is psychological rather than institutional. When she considers
the tensions and conflicts inherent in family relationships, either
between parents and children or between husbands and wives, she
attributes them not so much to social, economic or legal constraints as
to the difficulties that individuals of different ages, outlook and
temperaments have in living together in intimacy.[79] She heightens
awareness of the generation gap, so often complacently rationalised in
earlier utopian societies in terms of natural authority on one hand and
deference on the other (the same applies to the gender gap).

Where marriage is concerned, however, Nekayah is as firm as any
utopian in asserting that celibacy isn't a preferable alternative: 'it is
not retreat but exclusion from mankind. Marriage has many pains, but
celibacy has no pleasures.'[80] Rasselas attempts to resist the bleakness of
this viewpoint by arguing for marriage as an institution intended to
promote happiness: 'marriage is evidently the dictate of nature; men
and women were made to be companions of each other, and therefore
I cannot be persuaded but that marriage is one of the means of
happiness'[81] – a precarious premise and a still more precarious

conclusion. It is noticeable that he makes no appeal to divine as opposed to natural law, though he does later imply that marriage is a divine gift: noticeable, too, that it is the woman, Nekayah, who is more intensely conscious of the emotional cost that marriage can exact in personal unhappiness, and the man, Rasselas, who contends for its general benefits. The brother and sister between them articulate the paradox felt so keenly by women writers in particular: that marriage ought to be for the good of both sexes, for individuals and for society, but that all too often it is a site of conflicting interests. It is Rasselas, the potential ruler, who introduces the consequence of greatest concern to the state, the procreation of the next generation. Addressing his sister, he says:

> 'You surely conclude too hastily from the infelicity of marriage against its institution: will not the misery of life prove equally that life cannot be the gift of heaven? The world must be peopled by marriage, or peopled without it.'
>
> 'How the world is to be peopled,' returned Nekayah, 'is not my care, and needs not be yours. I see no danger that the present generation should omit to leave successors behind them: we are not now enquiring for the world, but for ourselves.'[82]

For Nekayah, the prince's argument is beside the point. In her dry retort, she decisively separates the two spheres, the public and the personal. Unless this separation is maintained, the demands of the political utopia will necessarily intrude into private lives. However, Rasselas, as a moral philosopher as well as political thinker, wants to maintain the utopian oneness between the good of the human community and the happiness of the individual – 'if marriage be best for mankind it must be evidently best for individuals, or a permanent and necessary duty must be the cause of evil, and some must be inevitably sacrificed to the convenience of others.'[83] Once more, Johnson disturbingly clarifies an unspoken assumption of utopian theorists, who keep trying with greater or lesser success to make us believe that they can square this particular circle. Rasselas himself refuses to abandon his faith in the possibility of a domestic utopia based on the characteristically eighteenth-century virtues of 'prudence and benevolence' (a creed borne out by Richardson and Fielding); and the discussion moves on to more circumstantial matters, which, however, tend to favour Nekayah's view.

All the precepts in these chapters of *Rasselas* could be amply illustrated from eighteenth-century novels. Johnson strips away the flesh of fiction to exhibit the bones of the marriage debate, and doesn't attempt to involve his principals in domestic narrative. However, the format of the oriental tale does allow him to explore one of the wilder byways of the same territory. In the story of Pekuah's abduction, and residence in the Arab's harem, he demystifies the fantasy of polygamy that tantalises the European imagination, and is sometimes presented as a utopian alternative to the problems of monogamy.[84] To judge the effect of Johnson's treatment of the harem, it's worth setting it against literary precedents. Montesquieu, in his *Lettres Persanes* (1721) had already played upon fascination with the subject by constructing an elaborately interwoven sequence of letters involving Usbek's efforts to retain and exercise his authority over his seraglio in Persia while he is far away in France.[85] However, the dark tangle of sexuality and intrigue resulting in murder and suicide within the harem isn't designed simply to titillate the reader: it is part of the intellectual design, not only ironically accentuating the cultural differences between East and West[86] but also contributing to a sophisticated analysis of sexual politics. Polygamy in this form, Usbek claims, increases men's control over their wives by decreasing the urgency of male desire.[87] Yet it demonstrably intensifies the passion of jealousy, which the women can manipulate in order to shift the balance of power.[88] That factor, together with the husband's inability to control the female imagination, is an essential flaw in a system of total male dominance, as the West perceives it. The European association between oriental polygamy and excessive jealousy is of long standing. Robert Burton, in *The Anatomy of Melancholy* published a century before *Lettres Persanes*, had written of wives in the Turkish seraglio 'which are so penned up they may not confer with any living man, or converse with younger women, have a cucumber or carrot sent into them for their diet, but sliced, for fear, etc., and so live and are left alone to their unchaste thoughts all the days of their lives.'[89] Burton, incidentally, considers Plato's utopian concept of having women and children in common to be one of the possible remedies for jealousy.[90]

Johnson, who is as interested in psychology as Burton (and who is recorded as saying that *The Anatomy of Melancholy* 'was the only book that ever took him out of bed two hours sooner than he wished to rise'[91]), nonetheless, deliberately refrains from using this material to speculate on different sexual practices. Just as he presents the effects of monogamy largely through Nekayah's eyes, so he presents the Arab's harem through Pekuah's eyes, from a social not erotic viewpoint.[92] The mode, however, changes from general discourse to specific fictional event. As a first-hand observer, Pekuah is in a more vividly realised situation than the princess among the daughters of Cairo. In her report she has, so to speak, scooped an exclusive. Yet the emphasis isn't on drama as in *Lettres Persanes*, but on dullness. The life of women in the harem stagnates in boredom and frivolity – so enhancing Pekuah's intellectual standing in contrast – and the point is forcefully made that this arrangement is unsatisfactory for both sexes. Rasselas asks Pekuah what pleasure an intelligent man can take in such company, assuming that they can have only one asset: 'Are they exquisitely beautiful?'[93] Pekuah's reply supports the case that Mary Astell, Defoe and others had been making for women's education: sexual attractiveness in itself does not compensate for the lack of 'friendship and society',[94] and is no basis for a deep or permanent relationship. The appeal to male self-interest is implicit. However, that isn't the only or even the main consideration: whatever his reservations about female bluestockings, in *Rasselas* Johnson adds his powerful weight to the argument that women should be treated as responsible adults, not pet animals.[95] Indeed, when Imlac later expresses doubts about Pekuah's capacity as a student seeking tuition from the astronomer, she proves him wrong.[96] While Johnson discriminates between characters according to gender, his primary concern is with what they have in common as human beings, rather than with what divides them. He sets as high standards for Nekayah and Pekuah as for Rasselas, standards that they all occasionally fail to attain: and the women are required to think as strenuously about the choice of life as the prince himself.

One such choice, the monastic life, fascinates the eighteenth-century Protestant public almost as much as the harem fantasy. In the chapter entitled 'The happiness of solitude. The hermit's history', the idea of retreat from the world has already been scrutinised under different conditions.[97] In her grief for the missing Pekuah, the princess revives it, but her purpose is deflected by the arguments of her brother, and of Imlac, who feels that time will cure her of the desire for a cloister (compare the attempts to dissuade Clementina from taking the veil in *Sir Charles Grandison*).[98] Nor is this the final word on the topic. When the monastery of St Anthony is fixed upon as the place of Pekuah's release in exchange for a ransom, the choice of location sows the seed of a future debate about the value of the monastic ideal. Rasselas later recalls this monastery, contrasting its ascetic way of life with the luxury of the Happy Valley.[99] If the Happy Valley represents a hedonistic utopia, the monastery of St Anthony represents the opposite kind of community (it may be remembered that More's Utopia is assumed to have been partly inspired by his attraction to monastic life[100]). Imlac goes so far as to assert that 'those men . . . are less wretched in their silent convent than the Abissinian princes in their prison of pleasure',[101] simply because of their motivated and regular labours. The hard monotony of their lives has as its goal 'endless felicity',[102] which makes them an exception to Johnson's thesis that there can be no happiness without variety and change. The upshot of the discussion is to reinforce an open-minded attitude: the monastic ideal is a valid choice for those with the right kind of temperament, or in a situation to benefit from it.

In general, however, Johnson is wary of any degree of isolation from active life, if only because it encourages the imagination to dominate the reason, 'by submitting the shows of things to the desires of the mind', as Bacon puts it, 'whereas reason doth buckle and bow the mind unto the nature of things.'[103] Yet it is hard for human beings to be satisfied with reality, 'the nature of things': that is why they build utopias in imagination, and pyramids in stone. Imlac's brilliant analysis of the hypothetical motives for the building of the pyramids demonstrates equally why utopias will never work and yet why people continue to create them: all such projects express the same 'hunger of imagination which preys incessantly upon life, and must be always appeased by some employment'.[104] Similarly, the astronomer's tale demonstrates the effects of a diseased imagination on a single individual.[105] It is perhaps Johnson's most powerful and melancholy fable on the dangers besetting the mind that dissociates itself from reality and exercises its faculties in an imaginary universe of its own making. That way madness lies.

Viewed from a satiric angle, Johnson's astronomer might well appear like a professional colleague of Swift's Laputans, with their advanced scientific theory and their dread of cosmic catastrophe that separates them from 'the common Pleasures or Amusements of Life'.[106] Or he might be taken as an exemplar of Dryden's couplet, 'Great Wits are sure to Madness near ally'd; / And thin Partitions do their Bounds divide'.[107] However, Johnson's own presentation is closer to tragic irony, which invites understanding and respect, and occasions relief and pleasure when the astronomer recovers from his delusion and the tragedy is averted.[108] What intensifies this response is the genuine altruism of the astronomer, who, unlike the Laputans, combines great learning with a benevolence exercised in charitable activity. Moreover, his sense of scientific responsibility is impeccable: he affirms 'integrity without knowledge is weak and useless, and knowledge without integrity is dangerous and dreadful.'[109] His delusion that he has mastered the Sun and controls the world's weather patterns takes a peculiarly utopian form, since he agonises over using his power for the maximum benefit of all humanity. In effect, he dreams of undoing the consequence of the Fall (a notion that floats in the background of certain Edenic utopias) by making an equitable distribution of sunshine and rain to all corners of the Earth. 'Exact justice' is his aim, like that of all the great utopian legislators: indeed at one point he compares his burden to that of a ruler of millions, only far more onerous.[110] However, even in his derangement, he is forced to recognise the inherent limitations of the physical world: he has 'formed innumerable schemes' but he has 'found it impossible to make a disposition by which the world may be advantaged; what one region gains, another loses by any imaginable alteration'[111] – an observation that might be taken to heart, and given a political application, by any utopian reformer. Subsequently, he counsels Imlac, his chosen successor, not to privilege his own country at the expense of others. The astronomer's madness starts with contemplating 'imaginary dominion,'[112] which grows into a global obsession. What cures him is human contact, the simple pleasures and distractions of ordinary social life (something in which Laputa is notoriously deficient).

The chapter on 'The dangerous prevalence of imagination',[113] which records a form of group therapy occasioned by the account of his malady, can stand as Johnson's finest direct critique not just of imagination in general, but of the utopian imagination in particular. It opens with Imlac's diagnosis of the stages of the disease which reaches its crisis when 'fictions begin to operate as realities, false opinions fasten upon the mind, and life passes in dreams of rapture or of anguish.'[114] In reaction to this, each of the other three confesses and renounces his or her secret fantasy. Nekayah reverts to her pastoral role-playing (which, unlike the ladies of Millenium Hall, does seem to anticipate Marie Antoinette).[115] Pekuah likewise dreams of changing her social station, but in the opposite direction: she wishes to become no less than the queen of Abyssinia. And she gives her aspiration a utopian colouring: 'I have repressed the pride of the powerful, and granted the petitions of the poor; I have built new palaces in more happy situations, planted groves upon the tops of mountains, and have exulted in the beneficence of royalty. . . .'[116] with the result that she neglects the very rituals that she prizes in her royal fantasy, and fails to repress her own pride.

Appropriately, however, it is the prince's vision which is most overtly utopian, in the precise definition of the term as applying to an ideal state. His fantasy centres not on role-playing as such, but on the structuring of a philosophical scheme analogous to Plato's *Republic*. Strictly speaking, it's not even pure fantasy in quite the same sense as the transparent fictions of the two women, since Rasselas has at least a distant prospect of succeeding to the throne, and is projecting a blueprint for a government that might be his:

> 'I will confess,' said the prince, 'an indulgence of fantastick delight more dangerous than yours. I have frequently endeavoured to image the possibility of a perfect government, by which all wrong should be restrained, all vice reformed, and all the subjects preserved in tranquility and innocence. This thought produced innumerable schemes of reformation, and dictated many useful regulations and salutary edicts.'[117]

One warning signal here is the use of the phrase 'innumerable schemes', which is identical to the astronomer's. Johnson found reassurance in the objective certainty of exact computation:[118] the failure to put number or limit on these schemes signifies their unsoundness. However, Rasselas reproaches himself less for the visionary and impracticable nature of his schemes than for their implications in the 'real' world. That is, he is shocked by recognising his disregard of the human lives – the lives of those closely related to him – that block his path to power: 'this has been the sport and sometimes the labour of my solitude; and I start, when I think with how little anguish I once supposed the death of my father and my brothers.'[119] It is a simple but profound comment on the greatest danger of the hunger for power, even when it is the power to do good, and exercised only in imagination: that the existence and rights of other individual human beings are overshadowed. The human cost of establishing utopia has long created unease in readers of Plato's

Republic, an unease perhaps culminating in Popper's magisterial study, *The Open Society and its Enemies*.[120] The attractions of a new beginning, making a clean sweep, are insidious, and Rasselas is right to resist the temptation even in fantasy. Nevertheless, this chapter doesn't put an end to what Imlac calls 'visionary schemes';[121] and it would also be true to say that the darker aspect doesn't predominate to the exclusion of humour. As it has been often remarked, the wonderful absurdities of *Don Quixote* also flavour Johnson's fiction,[122] whenever Rasselas engages with his companions in 'the dangerous prevalence of imagination'.

Yet, as the philosophical tale draws towards its close, solemnity rather than cheerfulness keeps breaking in. The discourses on old age and on the nature of the soul confront the group with awareness of mortality, and cause them to reassess their values in the light of eternity.[123] Certainly the encounter with the old man is much less devastating than Swift's satire when he brings Gulliver face to face with the Struldbruggs; but it is no less effective in its understated dry irony at the expense of those 'who expect that age will perform the promises of youth' – the words Johnson addressed to his putative readers at the very beginning of *Rasselas*.[124] Johnson is far from idealising the state of even virtuous longevity, as some utopian writers do. Given his state of mind, this venerable man might in fact be a suitable candidate for euthanasia in certain utopias, such as de Foigny's Australia (though not in More's commonwealth).[125] Here, as he says himself, he can only wait patiently 'and hope to possess in a better state that happiness which here I could not find, and that virtue which here I have not attained.'[126] This sentiment is deeply in the grain of Johnson's thinking. Happiness in the truest sense is not only not local; it is not earthly. Even if the sombre tone lightens with the wry remark registering the collapse of another utopian illusion – 'he rose and went away, leaving his audience not much elated with the hope of long life'[127] (a beautiful litotes) – the same tone sounds again in the meditation upon death arising from the visit to the catacombs. The utopian quest becomes, as the princess says of the choice of life, 'less important; I hope hereafter to think only on the choice of eternity.' The gravity of the phrasing has the whole weight of Johnsonian commitment behind it. Yet it isn't literally fulfilled within the work itself. There remains the famous final chapter, 'The conclusion, in which nothing is concluded',[128] which not only proves that closure is itself an illusion, on this side of the grave at least, but which also presents the last judgment within the text on the utopian imagination and the fictions that it creates.

Interestingly, this chapter briefly epitomises utopian types that are prominent in eighteenth-century fiction. It's worth quoting in its entirety the passage in which the three younger members of the group, having acquired education through observation and experience, re-formulate their 'various schemes of happiness':

> Pekuah was never so much charmed with any place as the convent of St Anthony, where the Arab restored her to the princess, and wished only to fill it with pious maidens, and to be made prioress of the order: she was weary of expectation and disgust, and would gladly be fixed in some unvariable state.
>
> The princess thought, that of all sublunary things, knowledge was the best: She desired first to learn all sciences, and then purposed to found a college of learned women, in which she would preside, that, by conversing with the old, and educating the young, she might divide her time between the acquisition and communication of wisdom, and raise up for the next age models of prudence, and patterns of piety.
>
> The prince desired a little kingdom, in which he might administer justice in his own person, and see all the parts of government with his own eyes; but he could never fix the limits of his dominion, and was always adding to the number of his subjects.[129]

Rasselas antedates the publication of *Millenium Hall* and *Munster Village*, but the versions of a utopian community chosen by Pekuah and the princess closely correspond to the fictional utopias described by women writers, with their emphasis on religion and learning and, most importantly, the idea of female leadership. If both institutions were to be amalgamated, they would parallel the prototype in Mary Astell's *Serious Proposal*. Moreover, the parallels aren't only in the work of women writers, for Pekuah's convent also resembles Sir Charles Grandison's notion of a Protestant nunnery in Richardson's novel, and Nekayah's college recalls Defoe's project of an academy for women. What is striking about the 'visionary schemes' in this context is how much they differ from the ones put forward by Pekuah and the princess in the earlier chapter, where they were playing at being queens or shepherdesses.[130] The intervening narrative, with its increasing sense of a longer perspective and life's latter end, might account for a new level of maturity (though not all critics would share this view).[131]

As for Rasselas, who has already shown signs of mature assessment of his previous utopian scheme, he does not radically change the nature of his aspirations. He adheres to the conventional masculine concept of a political utopia, a model kingdom in which power and the administration of justice should be entirely under his own control – in short, the kind of governorship that Crusoe had the opportunity of realising on his island. However, the flaw in this vision is ironically highlighted by the inability to set limits to this imaginary domain. Rasselas, unlike Crusoe, has no natural brake on his freewheeling imperialist fantasy.

In discussing this chapter, Paul Fussell has argued that 'each wish betrays the secret lust for power over others which, among decent, cultivated people like these, cloaks itself in proclaimed motives of beneficent intention.'[132] While not disputing an element of truth in this observation, I wouldn't go so far as to state that the 'beneficent intention' is only the *ostensible* motive, a cover-up for the *real* motive, the 'lust for power'. Both motives seem to me to be genuine and inseparable: together, they explain a great deal about the psychology of utopian imagination. In addition, as is generally accepted, the crucial key to interpretation is the clear-sighted acknowledgement that imagination must not be confused with reality, that utopia is no-place as well as (sometimes) good place: 'of these wishes that they had formed they well knew that none could be obtained.'[133] They have entered into the spirit of the sentence from Aristotle that Aldous Huxley uses as the epigraph of his utopian novel, *Island*: 'in framing an ideal we may assume what we wish, but should avoid impossibilities'.[134] What differentiates these schemes from earlier ones is the absence of illusion.

The most un-illusioned of all are Imlac and the astronomer, who conform to the conventions of the oriental tale rather than utopian fiction in their attitude of total acceptance: they are 'contented to be driven along the stream of life without directing their course to any particular port'.[135] Their acquiescence, and the metaphor that expresses it, might seem reminiscent of Johnson's rhetorical question in *The Vanity of Human Wishes*, published a decade earlier: 'Must helpless Man, in Ignorance sedate, / Roll darkling down the Torrent of his Fate?'[136] But Imlac and the astronomer are ignorant only in the Socratic sense – their wisdom consists in knowing that they know nothing – and their choice is rather to follow Johnson's own advice in his poem, 'Enquirer, cease . . . leave to Heav'n the Measure and the Choice'.[137]

In 'The conclusion, in which nothing is concluded', all the divergent lines meet in a single point. To put it another way, the narrative has completed a circle, which is perhaps the natural shape of utopia. Many utopian fictions end with a homecoming of some sort, and often irony and uncertainty deny closure so far as the reader is concerned; but this must be one of the simplest and most disputed endings of all: 'they deliberated a while what was to be done, and resolved, when the inundation should cease, to return to Abissinia.'[138] The journey to utopia, at least in its traditional form, is as much a journey to the past as to the future. *Rasselas*, neither novel nor satire, returns to the roots of a discourse that spreads through and colonises eighteenth-century fiction, in spite of all attempts to weed it out or to shrivel it with contempt. Writing close to the middle of his century, Johnson analyses the essence of everything that is most alluring and most unreliable in the utopian ideal: yet he doesn't patronise the human need for that ideal. He brings his own massive sanity and style to the subject, seeing in it a locus for his favourite study, human nature. And while occasionally streaking his narrative with individual colours, he restores utopian fiction to the grandeur of generality where it began. If the novelists and satirists, such as Defoe and Swift, signpost the literary way ahead for the nineteenth and twentieth centuries, it is Johnson's philosophical tale that keeps the genre true to its origins in classical and Renaissance civilisation.

Notes and references

1.   v C.-L. de S. Baron de Montesquieu 1721/1973 Letters 11–14 pp. 53–61: Voltaire 1759/1968 chs XVII–XVIII pp. 73–84: S. Johnson 1759/1990 vol. 1 chs i–ii.

2.   The French translation *Les Mille et Une Nuits* is by Antoine Galland: for discussion of its influence v P. L. Caracciolo 1988 (ed.) intro pp. 1–6. For the genre v Butt's intro in Voltaire 1747–1756/1964 pp. 7–8: R. L. Mack 1992 (ed.) intro pp. vii–xix: Kolb's intro in S. Johnson 1759/1990 pp. xxxiii–xliv.

3.   S. Johnson 1759/1990 vol. II ch. xxx p. 112.

4. cf E. W. Said 1978/1985 pp. 1–28: also the post-*Orientalism* debate (v R. L. Mack 1992 pp. liv–lv). For the Orient as both Old and New World 'in the mind's geography' v E. W. Said 1978/1985 p. 58.

5. v C.-L. de S Baron de Montesquieu 1721/1973: O. Goldsmith 1762/1934.

6. v M. de Montaigne 1580–1588/1991 pp. 240–1: J. Addison 1709–1712/1970 *The Spectator* no. 50 Friday 27 April 1711 pp. 176–9: of course both judgments are within the discourse of European culture.

7. v Voltaire 1747–1756/1964 pp. 96–8 (however Zadig voices humanity's protest against counsels of perfection in the all-important 'but'): cf Addison's use of the supernatural in the 'Vision of Mirzah' *The Spectator* no. 159 Saturday September 1 1711. In J. Addison 1709–1712/1970 pp. 319–24.

8. J. Boswell 1791, 1799/1934–50 vol. I pp. 447–8 1763 Aetat. 54.

9. J. Boswell 1791, 1799/1934–50 vol. II pp. 228 1773 Aetat. 64.

10. J. Boswell 1791, 1799/1934–50 vol. III pp. 291–3 1778 Aetat. 69.

11. J. Boswell 1791, 1799/1934–50 vol. II p. 118 1770 Aetat. 61.

12. v D. J. Greene 1960/1990 pp. 252–8: S. Johnson 1977 intro. For a modified view v H. Erskine-Hill 1984. In I. Grundy (ed.) pp. 107–36.

13. cf S. Johnson 1759/1990 p. 103 n. 4: also cf J. Boswell 1791, 1799/1934–50 vol. II p. 60 1768 Aetat. 59. Pope voices a similar pragmatism in *Essay on Man* Epistle iii ll 303–4 (A. Pope 1733–4/1950 pp. 123–4).

14. J. Boswell 1791, 1799/1934–50 vol. II p. 102 1769 Aetat. 60: Green's intro in S. Johnson 1977 p. xxix.

15. S. Johnson 1750–2/1969 vol. 3 *Rambler* no. 2 Saturday 24 March 1750 p. 10: cf J. Boswell 1791, 1799/1934–50 vol. III p. 53 1776 Aetat. 67 ('Life is a progress from want to want, not from enjoyment to enjoyment').

16. e.g. his comment on 'desire for knowledge': J. Boswell 1791, 1799/1934–50 vol. I pp. 457–8 1763 Aetat. 54: cf the review of Soame Jenyns's *Free Enquiry*. In S. Johnson 1757/1825 vol. VI pp. 53–7.

17. S. Johnson 1750–2/1969 vol. 3 *Rambler* no. 6 Saturday 7 April 1750 pp. 30–5.

18. S. Johnson 1735/1985 pp. 3–4.

19. S. Johnson 1735/1985 p. 44.

20. S. Johnson 1735/1985 p. 90.

21. S. Berington 1737 pp. 143, 160.

22. S. Johnson 1735/1985 p. 51.

23. J. Boswell 1791, 1799/1934–50 vol. I p. 89 1734 Aetat. 25.

24. v J. R. Moore 1954: E. Leyburn 1955: G. J. Kolb 1958: D. M. Lockhart 1963: Kolb's intro in S. Johnson 1759/1990 pp. xxvi–xxxi. Tillotson proposes another influence, the 'Persian Tales' (G. Tillotson 1942 pp. 111–16).

25. J. Boswell 1791, 1799/1934–50 vol. I p. 89 1734 Aetat. 25: for the mythic element in *Rasselas* with reference to Plato v T. M. Curley 1976 pp. 151–2.

26. For *Rasselas* as anti-utopia v S. Rose 1974 pp. 56–8.

27. S. Johnson 1759/1990 vol. I ch. i p. 7.

28. v S. Johnson 1735/1985 intro pp. xxvi–xxxii, xlii–xlv.

29. v S. Johnson 1735/1985 pp. 210–11.

30. In R. L. Mack 1992 (ed.) pp. 1–113: cf dedication p. 3: intro pp. xix–xxvii.

31. v S. Johnson 1759/1990 vol. I ch. ii pp. 11–12.

32. v S. Johnson 1750–2/1969 vol. 5 *Rambler* nos. 204–5 Saturday 29 February 1752, Saturday 7 March 1752 pp. 296–305: for links between the history of Seged and *Rasselas* v S. Johnson 1759/1990 intro pp. xxxv–xxxvii: also v J. R. Moore 1954 pp. 37–8.

33. S. Johnson 1759/1990 vol. I ch. ii pp. 11–12: contrast Plato 1955/1987 pp. 158–9.

34. v F. Rabelais 1564/1991 Book I chs 52–7 pp. 116–27.

35. S. Johnson 1759/1990 vol. I ch. i p. 11: the comparisons are to Jeremy Bentham's *Panopticon* (1791) and Orwell's *Nineteen Eighty-Four* (1949).

36. S. Johnson 1759/1990 vol. I ch. xii p. 55: cf P. New 1985 pp. 110–11.

37. S. Johnson 1759/1990 vol. I ch. xvi pp. 64–5: v p. 64 n. 6.

38. New notes however that 'in fact they quickly find that money is of very great use' (P. New 1985 p. 134).

39. S. Johnson 1759/1990 vol. I ch. ii p. 12.

40. v G. J. Kolb 1958 p. 13.

41. S. Johnson 1759/1990 vol. I ch. i p. 9: the secular idea of utopia and the religious image of Eden converge.

42. S. Johnson 1759/1990 vol. I ch. ii pp. 13–14: contrast the arguments of the theriophilists (v G. Boas 1933).

43. S. Johnson 1759/1990 vol. I ch. v p. 21.

44. S. Johnson 1759/1990 vol. I ch. iii p. 15.

45. S. Johnson 1759/1990 vol. I ch. iii p. 16.

46. Review of Soame Jenyns's *Free Enquiry*. In S. Johnson 1757/1825 vol. VI p. 57.

47. S. Johnson 1759/1990 vol. I ch. iv p. 18.

48. F. Bacon 1605–1627/1906 *Advancement of Learning* Book 2 p. 153.

49. S. Johnson 1759/1990 vol. I ch. vi p. 23.

50. v S. Johnson 1759/1990 vol. I ch. vi p. 22 n. 1.

51. v F. Bacon 1605–1627/1906 p. 295.

52. cf S. Johnson 1779–81/1905 vol. 1 Life of Milton pp. 99–100: for Johnson's attitude in relation to artificial human flight v L. A. Landa 1970 pp. 161–78.

53. v F. Bacon 1605–1627/1906 p. 297.

54. S. Johnson 1759/1990 vol. I ch. vi pp. 27–8.

55. v S. Johnson 1759/1990 vol. I ch. vi pp. 28–9 ns 2, 3.

56. S. Johnson 1753–60/1963 *Adventurer* no. 45 Tuesday 10 April 1753 p. 357 (cit. Kolb in S. Johnson 1759/1990 vol. I ch. vi p. 29 n. 3): cf T. Shadwell 1676/1966 pp. 44–5 II:ii:29–36: also intro p. xix.

57. For comparison between Johnson's use of dialogue and that of More and Swift v P. New 1985 pp. 96–100.

58. v H. Fielding 1742/1967 Book II ch. iii: 1749/1974 vol. 1 Book VIII chs. x–xv.

59. S. Johnson 1759/1990 vol. I ch. viii p. 34.

60. v P. New 1985 p. 143.

61. S. Johnson 1759/1990 vol. I ch. xi p. 50.

62. For Imlac's view of poetry and the poet v S. Johnson 1759/1990 vol. I ch. x pp. 38–45: for critical divergences v p. 38 n. 1: also v P. New 1985 pp. 100–1. Cf in the case of More R. S. Sylvester 1977 in R. S. Sylvester, G. P. Marc'hadour (eds) pp. 290–301: G. M. Logan 1983 pp. 53, 111–30: T. More 1516/1989 intro p. xx.

63. v S. Johnson 1759/1990 vol. I ch. xi p. 46.

64. S. Johnson 1759/1990 vol. I ch. viii p. 32: v n. 8.

65. S. Johnson 1759/1990 vol. I ch. xi p. 47.

66. S. Johnson 1759/1990 vol. I ch. xiii p. 57.

67. S. Johnson 1759/1990 vol. I ch. viii p. 31.

68. S. Johnson 1759/1990 vol. I ch. xii p. 53.

69. v J. H. Hexter 1952 Part I.

70. v S. Johnson 1759/1990 vol. I ch. xvi p. 64.

71. v S. Johnson 1759/1990 vol. I ch. xvi p. 68.

72. v S. Johnson 1759/1990 vol. I chs xvii, xviii: 'life led according to nature'
 v title of ch. xxii (vol. I p. 83: v n. 1).

73. v S. Johnson 1759/1990 vol. I chs xix, xx, xxi, xxiv: vol. II ch. xxvii.

74. v S. Johnson 1759/1990 vol. I ch. xxv: vol. II chs xxvi, xxviii, xxix.

75. S. Johnson 1759/1990 vol. I ch. xxiii (title) p. 89.

76. S. Johnson 1759/1990 vol. I ch. xxv p. 92.

77. S. Johnson 1759/1990 vol. II ch. xxvi p. 95: v n. I.

78. S. Johnson 1759/1990 vol. II ch. xxx p. 110.

79. v S. Johnson 1759/1990 vol. II ch. xxvi pp. 95–8: ch. xxix pp. 108–9.

80. S. Johnson 1759/1990 vol. II ch. xxvi p. 99.

81. S. Johnson 1759/1990 vol. II ch. xxviii pp. 103–4: v n. 8: cf ch. xxix
 p. 107 n. 1.

82. S. Johnson 1759/1990 vol. II ch. xxviii p. 106.

83. S. Johnson 1759/1990 vol. II ch. xxix p. 106 (also subsequent quotation).

84. S. Johnson 1759/1990 vol. II chs xxxviii–xxxix: for polygamy v ch. 6 n. 47
 above: for Johnson's treatment of the harem cf A. J. Weitzman 1969 pp.
 50–4.

85. C.-L. de S Baron de Montesquieu 1721/1973 Letters 2, 6, 20–2, 26–7,
 64–5, 147–61: cf A.J. Weitzman 1969 pp. 50–1.

86. e.g. C.-L. de S Baron de Montesquieu 1721/1973 Letter 26 pp. 75–7.

87. v C.-L. de S Baron de Montesquieu 1721/1973 Letter 56 p. 120.

88. v C.-L. de S Baron de Montesquieu 1721/1973 Letter 62 p. 129.

89. R. Burton 1621/1972 Pt 3 Sec. 3 Mem. 2 p. 284.

90. R. Burton 1621/1972 Pt 3 Sec. 3 Mem. 4 Subs. 2 p. 298.

91. J. Boswell 1791, 1799/1934–50 vol. II p. 121 1770 Aetat. 61: cf p. 440
 1776 Aetat. 67.

92. Weitzman emphasises the point: v A. J. Weitzman 1969 pp. 50–1.

93. S. Johnson 1759/1990 vol. II ch. xxxix p. 139.

94. S. Johnson 1759/1990 vol. II ch. xxxix p. 140.

95. For the repeated animal analogy v S. Johnson 1759/1990 vol. I ch. xxv p. 92: vol. II xxxix p. 138. The evidence for Johnson's attitude to women's intellectual achievements varies, including positive and negative elements: cf the account of his contact with the Blue-Stockings in J. Boswell 1791, 1799/1934–50 vol. IV pp. 108–9 1781 Aetat. 72.

96. v S. Johnson 1759/1990 vol. II ch. xlvi pp. 159–60.

97. v S. Johnson 1759/1990 vol. I ch. xxi pp. 80–3.

98. v S. Johnson 1759/1990 vol. II ch. xxxv pp. 125–8: cf. S. Richardson 1751/1972 Part 3 vol. VI Letter iv pp. 7–9.

99. v S. Johnson 1759/1990 vol. II ch. xxxvii p. 130: ch. xlvii p. 164.

100. v T. More 1516/1965 intro. pp. xlv–xlvi.

101. S. Johnson 1759/1990 vol. II ch. xlvii p. 164.

102. S. Johnson 1759/1990 vol. II ch. xlvii p. 165.

103. F. Bacon 1605–1627/1906 *Advancement of Learning* Book 2 p. 97 (here Bacon refers specifically to poetry).

104. S. Johnson 1759/1990 vol. II ch. xxxii p. 118.

105. v S. Johnson 1759/1990 vol. II chs xl, xliv.

106. J. Swift 1726/1965 Part III ch. ii p. 165.

107. J. Dryden 1681/1972 p. 10 ll 163–4.

108. v S. Johnson 1759/1990 vol. II chs xlvi, xlvii.

109. S. Johnson 1759/1990 vol. II ch. xli p. 144.

110. S. Johnson 1759/1990 vol. II ch. xli p. 145: cf ch. xliii p. 148. New also remarks that this is 'very precisely a utopian vision' and compares the astronomer's utopianism with that of Rasselas (P. New 1985 pp. 145–8).

111. S. Johnson 1759/1990 vol. II ch. xliii p. 148.

112. S. Johnson 1759/1990 vol. II ch. xlii p. 146.

113. S. Johnson 1759/1990 vol. II ch. xliv p. 150 (title).

114. S. Johnson 1759/1990 vol. II ch. xliv p. 152.

115. v S. Johnson 1759/1990 vol. II ch. xliv p. 153.

116. S. Johnson 1759/1990 vol. II ch. xliv p. 153.

117. S. Johnson 1759/1990 vol. II ch. xliv p. 153.

118. cf. Johnson's remark in *The Preceptor* cit. Kolb in S. Johnson 1759/1990 vol. II ch. xxviii p. 105 n. 6.

119. S. Johnson 1759/1990 vol. II ch. xliv p. 153.

120. v K. R. Popper 1945/1966 vol. 1.

121. S. Johnson 1759/1990 vol. II ch. xliv p. 153.

122. v T. M. Curley 1976 pp. 152–3: F. J. Keener 1983 p. 232: cf Kolb's connection between Imlac's phrase and Johnson's passage on Don Quixote in *Rambler* no. 2 (in S. Johnson 1759/1990 vol. II ch. xliv pp. 153–4 n. 7).

123. S. Johnson 1759/1990 vol. II chs xlv, xlviii.

124. S. Johnson 1759/1990 vol. I ch. i p. 7.

125. cf G. de Foigny 1676/1693 pp. 58–9, 104–6: T. More 1516/1989 Book II pp. 80–1.

126. S. Johnson 1759/1990 vol. II ch. xlv p. 156.

127. S. Johnson 1759/1990 vol. II ch. xlv pp. 156–7.

128. S. Johnson 1759/1990 vol. II ch. xlix p. 175 (title).

129. S. Johnson 1759/1990 vol. II ch. xlix pp. 175–6: cf New's commentary on this passage in relation to the structure of *Rasselas* and its utopianism (P. New 1985 pp. 149–51).

130. S. Johnson 1759/1990 vol. II ch. xliv p. 153.

131. e.g. P. New 1985 pp. 150–1: he does however concede that much has been learned (pp. 152–3).

132. P. Fussell 1971/1972 p. 241.

133. S. Johnson 1759/1990 vol. II ch. xlix p. 176.

134. A. Huxley 1962 p. 6.

135. S. Johnson 1759/1990 vol. II ch. xlix p. 176.

136. S. Johnson 1749/1971 pp. 91–2 ll 345–6.

137. S. Johnson 1749/1971 p. 92 ll 349, 352.

138. S. Johnson 1759/1990 vol. II ch. xlix p. 176: v n. 4.

Bibliography

Where more than one date is given, the date of publication of the original edition(s) is followed by the date of the text used for reference.

Adams, P.G. *Travelers and Travel Liars 1660–1800* (University of California Press, Berkeley 1962).

Adams, P.G. *Travel Literature and the Evolution of the Novel* (University Press of Kentucky, Lexington 1983).

Adams, R.P. The Social Responsibilities of Science in *Utopia, New Atlantis* and After. *Journal of the History of Ideas* (**10**(3): 374–98 1949).

Adams, R.P. *The Better Part of Valor: More, Erasmus, Colet, and Vives, on Humanism, War, and Peace, 1496–1535.* (University of Washington Press, Seattle 1962).

Addison, J. 1709–1712 (Allen R.J. ed.) *Addison and Steele: Selections from The Tatler and The Spectator* 2nd edn (Holt, Rinehart and Winston, New York 1970).

Albinski, N. *Women's Utopias in British and American Fiction* (Routledge 1988).

Aldridge, A.O. Polygamy in Early Fiction: Henry Neville and Denis Veiras. *Publications of the Modern Language Association* (**65**(4): 464–72 1950).

Alexander, P., Gill, R. (eds) *Utopias* (Duckworth 1984).

Andreae, J.V. 1619 (Held F. E. tr. and ed.) *Christianopolis* (Oxford University Press 1916).

Aristotle (Everson, S. ed.) *The Politics* (Cambridge University Press: Cambridge Texts in the History of Political Thought 1988).

Armytage, W.H.G. *Heavens Below: Utopian Experiments in England 1560–1960* (Routledge & Kegan Paul Studies in Social History 1961).

Astell, M. 1694–1706 (Hill, B. ed.) *The First English Feminist: Reflections Upon Marriage and Other Writings by Mary Astell* (Gower/Maurice Temple Smith 1986).

Atwood, M. *The Handmaid's Tale* (Virago Press 1987).

Bacon, F. 1597–1625 (Pitcher, J. ed.) *Francis Bacon: The Essays* (Penguin Books: Penguin Classics 1985–1987).

Bacon, F. 1605–1627 (Case, T. intro) *The Advancement of Learning and New Atlantis* (Oxford University Press: The World's Classics 1906).

Baker-Smith, D., Barfoot, C.C. (eds) *Between Dream and Nature: Essays on Utopia and Dystopia* (Rodopi, Amsterdam 1987).

Baker-Smith, D. *More's Utopia* (HarperCollins Academic: Unwin Critical Library 1991).

Barr, M., Smith N.D. (eds) *Women and Utopia: Critical Interpretations* (University Press of America, New York 1983).

Baruch, E. 'A Natural and Necessary Monster': Women in Utopia. *Alternative Futures* 2(1): 29–48 1979.

Bate, W.J. *Samuel Johnson* (The Hogarth Press 1978/1984).

Battestin, M.C. Tom Jones and 'His *Egyptian* Majesty': Fielding's Parable of Government. *Publications of the Modern Language Association* (**82**(1): 68–77 1967).

Battestin, M.C., Battestin, R.R. *Henry Fielding: A Life* (Routledge 1989).

Beauchamp, G. Gulliver's Return to the Cave: Plato's *Republic* and Book IV of *Gulliver's Travels*. *Michigan Academician* 7: 201–9 1974.

Behn, A. 1688 Oroonoko. In Todd, J. (ed.) *Oroonoko, The Rover and Other Works* (Penguin Books: Penguin Classics 1992).

Bell, I.A., *Defoe's Fiction* (Croom Helm 1985).

Bell, I.A., *Literature and Crime in Augustan England* (Routledge 1991).

Bergerac, C. de (see Cyrano)

Berington, S. *The Memoirs of Signor Gaudentio di Lucca* 1737.

Bierman, J. Science and Society in the *New Atlantis* and other Renaissance Utopias. *Publications of the Modern Language Association* **78**(5): 492–500 1963.

Boas, G. *The Happy Beast in French Thought of the Seventeenth Century* (The Johns Hopkins Press, Baltimore 1933).

Boswell, J. 1791, 1799 (Hill, G. B. ed., Powell, L. F. rev. ed.) *Boswell's Life of Johnson* (6 vols) (Clarendon Press 1934–50).

Boucé, P.G. (ed.) *Sexuality in Eighteenth-Century Britain* (Manchester University Press 1982).

Boucher, P.P. *Cannibal Encounters: Europeans and Island Caribs, 1492–1763* (The Johns Hopkins University Press, Baltimore 1992).

Brady, F. (ed.) *Twentieth Century Interpretations of Gulliver's Travels: A Collection of Critical Essays* (Prentice-Hall, Englewood Cliffs, New Jersey: Twentieth Century Interpretations 1968).

Brant, C., Purkiss, D. (eds) *Women, Texts and Histories 1575–1760* (Routledge 1992).

Brophy, E.B. *Women's Lives and the Eighteenth-Century English Novel* (University of South Florida Press, Tampa 1991).

Brown, H.O. The Displaced Self in the Novels of Daniel Defoe. *English Literary History* **38**(4): 562–90 1971.

Brown, J. *An Estimate of the Manners and Principles of the Times* 2nd edn (1757).

Brown, L. *Ends of Empire: Women and Ideology in Early Eighteenth Century Literature* (Cornell University Press, Ithaca 1993).

Brunt, S. 1727 (Nicolson, M. H. intro) A Voyage to Cacklogallinia (Columbia University Press, New York facsimile reprint 1940).

Brunt, S. 1727 A Voyage to Cacklogallinia. In Welcher, J.K., Bush, G.E. (eds) Gulliveriana vol. 4 (Delmar, New York Scholars' Facsimiles & Reprints 1973).

Burney, F. 1782 (Sabor, P., Doody, M. A. eds, Doody, M. A. intro) Cecilia (Oxford University Press: The World's Classics 1988).

Burton, R. 1621 (Jackson, H. ed.) The Anatomy of Melancholy (Dent: Everyman's University Library 1972).

Campanella, T. 1602, 1637 (Elliott A.M., Miller, R. tr., Morton, A.L., intro) The City of the Sun (La Città del Sole/Civitas Solis) (The Journeyman Press (Chapbook Series) 1981).

Caracciolo, P.L. (ed.) The Arabian Nights in English Literature (Macmillan 1988).

Carnochan, W.B. Lemuel Gulliver's Mirror for Man (University of California Press, Berkeley and Los Angeles 1968).

Case, A.E. Four Essays on Gulliver's Travels (Princeton University Press, Princeton, New Jersey 1945).

Castle, T. Why the Houyhnhnms Don't Write: Swift, Satire and the Fear of the Text. Essays in Literature (7(1): 31–44 1980).

Cavendish, M. Duchess of Newcastle, Natures Pictures Drawn By Fancies Pencill 1656.

Cavendish, M. Duchess of Newcastle, The Description of a New World, called The Blazing World 1666.

Cavendish, M., Duchess of Newcastle, (Lilley, K. ed.) The Description of a New World called the Blazing World and Other Writings (Pickering & Chatto: Pickering Women's Classics 1992).

Cervantes, M. de 1604–1614 (Cohen, J. M. tr.) The Adventures of Don Quixote (Penguin Books: Penguin Classics 1950).

Champion, L.S. (ed.) Quick Springs of Sense: Studies in the Eighteenth Century (University of Georgia Press, Athens, Georgia 1974).

Christie, J., Shuttleworth, S. (eds) Nature Transfigured: Science and Literature 1700–1900 (Manchester University Press 1990).

Coetzee, J.M. Foe. (Penguin Books 1986/1987).

Cohn, N. 1957 The Pursuit of the Millennium (rev edn. Maurice Temple Smith 1970).

Copley, S. (ed.) Literature and the Social Order in Eighteenth-Century England (Croom Helm: World and Word Series 1984)).

Cornelius, P., Languages in Seventeenth and Early Eighteenth Century Imaginary Voyages (Librairie Droz, Geneva 1965).

Cowley, A. (Waller, A.R. ed.) Abraham Cowley: Poems (Cambridge University Press (Cambridge English Classics) 1905).

Cowley, A. (Waller A.R. ed.) Abraham Cowley: Essays, Plays and Sundry Verses (Cambridge University Press: Cambridge English Classics 1906).

Cowper, W. (Spiller, B. ed.) *William Cowper: Poetry and Prose* (Rupert Hart-Davis: The Reynard Library 1968).

Crane, R.S. The Houyhnhnms, the Yahoos and the History of Ideas. In Mazzeo, J.A. (ed.) *Reason and the Imagination: Studies in the History of Ideas, 1600–1800* pp. 231–53 (Columbia University Press, New York 1959/1962).

Curley, T.M. *Samuel Johnson and the Age of Travel* (University of Georgia Press, Athens, Georgia 1976).

Cyrano de Bergerac 1657 (Strachan, G. tr. and intro) *Other Worlds (L'Autre Monde)* (Oxford University Press 1965).

Damrosch, L. *God's Plot and Man's Stories: Studies in the Fictional Imagination from Milton to Fielding* (University of Chicago Press, Chicago 1985).

Davis, J.C. *Utopia and the Ideal Society: A Study of English Utopian Writing 1516–1700* (Cambridge University Press 1981).

Defoe, D. *An Essay Upon Projects 1697* (Scolar Press Facsimile 1969).

Defoe, D. *The Consolidator: or, Memoirs of Sundry Transactions from the World in the Moon.* 1705.

Defoe, D. 1719 *The Life and Strange Surprizing Adventures of Robinson Crusoe: The Farther Adventures of Robinson Crusoe* (The Shakespeare Head Press 1927).

Defoe, D. 1719 (Shinagel, M. ed.) *Robinson Crusoe: An Authoritative Text, Contexts, Criticism* 2nd edn (W.W. Norton, New York (A Norton Critical Edition 1994).

Defoe, D. 1720 (Aitken, G.A. ed.) *Romances and Narratives of Daniel Defoe* (16 vols) vol. 3 *Serious Reflections during the Life and Surprising Adventures of Robinson Crusoe With his Vision of the Angelic World* (Dent 1895).

Defoe, D. *The Protestant Monastery 1726.*

Defoe, D. 1728 (Schonhorn, M. ed.) *A General History of the Pyrates* (University of South Carolina Press, Columbia, South Carolina, and Dent 1972).

Desfontaines, M. (l'Abbé) (tr.) *Voyages de Gulliver* (2 vols). Paris 1727.

Desfontaines, M. (l'Abbé) (Lockman, J. tr) *The Travels of Mr John Gulliver, Son to Capt Lemuel Gulliver* (2 vols). 1730/1731.

Diodorus Siculus (Oldfather, C.H. tr) *Diodorus of Sicily* (12 vols) (Heinemann and Harvard University Press, Cambridge, Mass (Loeb Classical Library) 1933–67).

Doody, M.A. *A Natural Passion: A Study of the Novels of Samuel Richardson* (Clarendon Press 1974).

Doody, M.A. *Frances Burney: The Life in the Works* (Rutgers University Press, New Brunswick, New Jersey 1988).

Doody, M.A., Sabor, P. (eds) *Samuel Richardson: Tercentenary Essays* (Cambridge University Press 1989).

Downie, J.A. Defoe, Imperialism, and the Travel Books Reconsidered. *Yearbook of English Studies* (**13** Part I Colonial and Imperial Themes 66–83 1983).

Downie, J.A. *Jonathan Swift: Political Writer* (Routledge & Kegan Paul 1984).

Dryden, J. 1681 (Swedenborg, H.T., Dearing V.A. eds) *Absalom and Achitophel.* In *The Works of John Dryden: Poems 1681–1684* (vol. II) (University of California Press, Berkeley and Los Angeles 1972).

Dryden, J. 1673 (Crane, D. ed.) *Marriage A-la-Mode* (A & C Black (New Mermaids) 1991).

Dudley, E., Novak, M.E. (eds) *The Wild Man Within: An Image in Western Thought from the Renaissance to Romanticism* (University of Pittsburgh Press, Pittsburgh. Pa 1972).

Dymond, A. *The Law on its Trial* (Alfred W. Bennett 1865).

Eaves, T.C.D., Kimpel, B.D. *Samuel Richardson: A Biography* (Oxford University Press 1971).

Eddy, W.A. 1923 *Gulliver's Travels: A Critical Study* (Peter Smith, Gloucester, Mass 1963).

Ehrenpreis, I. *Swift: the Man, his Works, and the Age* (3 vols) (Methuen 1962–83).

Eliade, M. Paradise and Utopia: Mythical Geography and Eschatology. In Manuel, F.E. (ed.) *Utopias and Utopian Thought* (Houghton Mifflin, Boston 1965).

Eliav-Feldon, M. *Realistic Utopias: The Ideal Imaginary Societies of the Renaissance 1516–1630* (Clarendon Press (Oxford Historical Monographs) 1982).

Elliott, R.C. *The Shape of Utopia: Studies in a Literary Genre* (University of Chicago Press, Chicago 1970).

Ellison, L.M. *Gaudentio di Lucca*: A Forgotten Utopia. (*Publications of the Modern Language Association* 50(2): 494–509 1935).

Euhemerus (see Diodorus)

Fabricant, C. *Swift's Landscape* (The Johns Hopkins University Press, Baltimore 1982).

Fausett, D. *Writing the New World: Imaginary Voyages and Utopias of the Great Southern Land* (Syracuse University Press 1994).

Ferguson, J. *Utopias of the Classical World* (Thames & Hudson (Aspects of Greek and Roman Life) 1975).

Fielding, H. 1742 (Battestin, M.C. ed.) *Joseph Andrews* (Clarendon Press (The Wesleyan Edition of the Works of Henry Fielding) 1967).

Fielding, H. 1743 (Goldgar, B.A., Amory, H. eds) *A Journey from This World, to the Next.* In *Miscellanies by Henry Fielding Esq* (vol. 2) (Clarendon Press (The Wesleyan Edition of the Works of Henry Fielding 1993).

Fielding, H. 1749 (Battestin, M.C., Bowers, F. eds) *The History of Tom Jones A Foundling* (2 vols) (Clarendon Press (The Wesleyan Edition of the Works of Henry Fielding) 1974).

Fielding, H. 1751 (Zirker, M.R. ed.) *An Enquiry into the Causes of the Late Increase of Robbers and Related Writings* (Clarendon Press (The Wesleyan Edition of the Works of Henry Fielding) 1988).

Fielding, H. 1751 (Battestin, M.C. ed.) *Amelia* (Clarendon Press (The Wesleyan Edition of the Works of Henry Fielding) 1983).

Fielding, H. 1752 (Goldgar, B.A. ed.) *The Covent-Garden Journal and A Plan of the Universal Register-Office* (Clarendon Press (The Wesleyan Edition of the Works of Henry Fielding) 1988).

Filmer, R. 1680 (Sommerville, J.P. ed.) *Patriarcha and Other Writings* (Cambridge University Press: Cambridge Texts in the History of Political Thought 1991).

Fink, Z.S. 1945 *The Classical Republicans* (Northwestern University Press, Evanston: Northwestern University Studies in the Humanities 1962).

Fischer, J.I., Real, H., Woolley, J. (eds) *Swift and His Contexts* (AMS Press, New York 1989).

Flynn, C.H., *The Body in Swift and Defoe* (Cambridge University Press: Cambridge Studies in Eighteenth-Century English Literature and Thought 1990).

Foigny, G. de 1676 *A New Discovery of Terra Incognita Australis, or the Southern World by James Sadeur a French-man* (*La Terre australe connue*) 1693.

Foucault, M. 1964 (Howard, R. tr.) *Madness and Civilization: A History of Insanity in the Age of Reason*. Tavistock Publications 1967).

Foucault, M. 1975 (Sheridan, A. tr.) *Discipline and Punish: The Birth of the Prison* (Penguin Books 1977).

Foucault, M. 1976 (Hurley, R. tr.) *The History of Sexuality: an Introduction* (Penguin Books 1981).

Foucault, M. 1984 (Hurley, R. tr.) *The Use of Pleasure: The History of Sexuality* (vol. 2) (Viking 1986a).

Foucault, M. 1984 (Rabinow, P. ed.) *The Foucault Reader* (Penguin Books: Peregrine Books 1986b).

Foucault, M. 1984 (Hurley, R. tr) *The Care of the Self: The History of Sexuality* (vol. 3) (Penguin Books 1990).

Frye, N. Varieties of Literary Utopias. In Manuel, F.E. (ed.) *Utopias and Utopian Thought* (Houghton Mifflin, Boston 1965).

Fussell, P. 1971 *Samuel Johnson and the Life of Writing* (Chatto and Windus 1972).

Garnier, C.G.T. (ed.) *Voyages imaginaires, songes, visions, et romans cabalistiques* (39 vols) (Amsterdam and Paris 1787–95).

Gay, J. 1728 (Loughrey, B., Treadwell, T.O. eds) *The Beggar's Opera* (Penguin Books: Penguin Classics 1986).

Gibson, R.W., Patrick, J.M. (eds) *St Thomas More: A Preliminary Bibliography of his Works and of Moreana to the Year 1750* (Yale University Press, New Haven 1961).

Gill, J.E. Beast over Man: Theriophilic Paradox in Gulliver's 'Voyage to the Country of the Houyhnhnms'. *Studies in Philology* (**67**(4): 532–49 1970).

Girdler, L. Defoe's Education at Newington Green Academy. *Studies in Philology* (**50**(4): 573–91 1953).

Godwin, F. *The Man in the Moone: or A Discourse of a Voyage thither by Domingo Gonsales* 1638.

Goldsmith, M.M. *Private Vices, Public Benefits: Bernard Mandeville's Social and Political Thought* (Cambridge University Press 1985).

Goldsmith, M.M. Liberty, luxury and the pursuit of happiness. In Pagden, A. (ed.) *The Languages of Political Theory in Early-Modern Europe* (Cambridge University Press 1987).

Goldsmith, O. 1762 (Church, R. intro) *The Citizen of the World: The Bee* (Dent (Everyman's Library) 1934).

Goldsmith, O. (Lonsdale, R. ed.) *The Poems of Thomas Gray, William Collins, Oliver Goldsmith* (Longman Annotated English Poets 1969).

Goodwin, B., Taylor, K. (eds) *The Politics of Utopia: A Study in Theory and Practice* (Hutchinson 1982).

Gott, S. 1648 (Begley, W. tr. and ed.) *Nova Solyma* (2 vols) (John Murray 1902).

Gove, P.B. 1941 *The Imaginary Voyage in Prose Fiction . . . with an Annotated Check List . . . from 1700–1800* (rev edn) (Peter Holland 1961).

Greenblatt, S. Invisible bullets: Renaissance authority and its subversion, *Henry IV* and *Henry V*. In Dollimore J., Sinfield, A. (eds) *Political Shakespeare: New Essays in Cultural Materialism* 1985.

Greenblatt, S. *Marvelous Possessions: The Wonder of the New World* (Clarendon Press 1991).

Greene, D.J. 1960 *The Politics of Samuel Johnson* (Yale University Press, New Haven 1990).

Grundy, I. (ed.) *Samuel Johnson: New Critical Essays.* (Vision and Barnes and Noble 1984).

Grundy, I., Wiseman, S. (eds) *Women, Writing, History: 1640–1740* (Batsford 1992).

Halewood, W.H. Plutarch in Houyhnhnmland: A Neglected Source for Gulliver's Fourth Voyage. *Philological Quarterly* (**44**(2): 185–94 1965).

Hall, J. 1605 (Healey, J. tr.) *The Discovery of a New World (Mundus Alter et Idem)*? 1608.

Hall, J. 1605 (Wands, J.M. tr. and ed.) *Another World and yet the Same: Bishop Joseph Hall's Mundus Alter et Idem* (Yale University Press, New Haven 1981).

Hamilton, M. 1778 (Baylis, S. intro) *Munster Village* (Pandora Press: Mothers of the Novel 1987).

Hammond, B. *Gulliver's Travels* (Open University Press: Open Guides to Literature 1988).

Harrington, J. 1656 *The Commonwealth of Oceana.* In Pocock J.G.A. (ed.) *The Political Works of James Harrington* (Cambridge University Press 1977).

Hay, D., Linebaugh P., et al 1976 (eds) *Albion's Fatal Tree: Crime and Society in Eighteenth-Century England* (Penguin Books: Peregrine Books 1988).

Haywood, E. *Memoirs of a Certain Island Adjacent to the Kingdom of Utopia* (2 vols 2nd edn) 1725/1726.

Haywood, E. *The Unfortunate Princess*. 1741.

Heidenreich, H. *The Libraries of Daniel Defoe and Phillips Farewell, Olive Payne's Sales Catalogue 1731* (im Selbstverlag, Berlin 1970).

Herodotus, 1954 (Selincourt, A. de tr., Burn, A.R. ed.) *The Histories* (rev edn) (Penguin Books: Penguin Classics 1972).

Hexter, J.H. *More's 'Utopia': the Biography of an Idea* (Princeton University Press, Princeton, New Jersey 1952).

Higgins, I. Swift and Sparta: the Nostalgia of *Gulliver's Travels*. *Modern Language Review* (**78**(3): 513–31 1983).

Hill, C. 1965 *Intellectual Origins of the English Revolution* (Clarendon Press 1980).

Hill, C. 1972 *The World Turned Upside Down: Radical Ideas during the English Revolution* (Penguin Books: Peregrine Books 1984).

Hobbes, T. 1651 (MacPherson, C.B. ed.) *Leviathan* (Penguin Books: Pelican Classics 1968).

Holstun, J. *A Rational Millennium: Puritan Utopias of Seventeenth-Century England and America* (Oxford University Press 1987).

Hulme, P. *Colonial Encounters: Europe and the native Carribean, 1492–1797* (Methuen 1986).

Hume, D. 1882 (Green, T.H., Grose, T.H. eds) *David Hume: The Philosophical Works* (4 vols) (Scientia Verlag Aalen 1964).

Hunter, J.P. *The Reluctant Pilgrim: Defoe's Emblematic Method and Quest for Form* (The Johns Hopkins University Press, Baltimore 1966).

Hunter, J.P. *Before Novels: the Cultural Contexts of Eighteenth-Century English Fiction* (Norton, New York 1990).

Huxley, A. 1932 *Brave New World* (Chatto & Windus 1950).

Huxley, A. *Island* (Chatto & Windus 1962).

Iambulus (see Diodorus)

Johnson, S. 1735 (Gold, J.J. ed.) *A Voyage to Abyssinia (Translated from the French)* (Yale University Press, New Haven (The Yale Edition of the Works of Samuel Johnson vol. 15) 1985).

Johnson, S. 1749 The Vanity of Human Wishes. In Fleeman, J.D. (ed.) *The Complete English Poems* (Penguin Books: Penguin English Poets 1971).

Johnson, S. 1750–2 (Bate, W.J., Strauss, A.B. eds) *The Rambler* (3 vols) (Yale University Press, New Haven (The Yale Edition of the Works of Samuel Johnson vols 3–5)1969).

Johnson, S. 1753–60 (Bate, W.J., Bullitt, J.M., Powell, L.F. eds) *The Idler and The Adventurer* (Yale University Press, New Haven, and Oxford University Press (The Yale Edition of the Works of Samuel Johnson vol. 2) 1963).

Johnson, S. 1757 Review of a Free Enquiry into the Nature and Origin of Evil. In *The Works of Samuel Johnson, Ll.D* (vol VI) (Talboys and Wheeler/W. Pickering (Oxford English Classics) 1825).

Johnson, S. 1759 (Kolb, G.J. ed.) *Rasselas and Other Tales*. (Yale University Press, New Haven (The Yale Edition of the Works of Samuel Johnson vol. 16) 1990).

Johnson, S. (Greene, D.J. ed.) *Political Writings* (Yale University Press, New Haven (The Yale Edition of the Works of Samuel Johnson vol. 10) 1977).

Johnson, S. 1779–81 (Hill, G.B. ed.) *Lives of the English Poets* (3 vols) (Clarendon Press 1905).

Jones, M. Swift, Harrington, and Corruption in England. *Philological Quarterly* **53**(1): 59–70) 1974.

Jones, R.F. 1936 *Ancients and Moderns* 2nd edn. (Washington University Press, St Louis 1961).

Kay, C. *Political Constructions: Defoe, Richardson, and Sterne in Relation to Hobbes, Hume, and Burke* (Cornell University Press, Ithaca 1988).

Keats, J. (Page, F. ed.) *Letters of John Keats* (Oxford University Press: The World's Classics 1954).

Keener, F.J. *The Chain of Becoming: The Philosophical Tale, the Novel, and a Neglected Realism of the Enlightenment: Swift, Montesquieu, Voltaire, Johnson and Austen* (Columbia University Press, New York 1983).

Kelly, A.C. After Eden: Gulliver's (Linguistic) Travels. (*English Literary History* **45**(1): 33–54 1978).

Kelsall, M.M. Iterum Houyhnhnm: Swift's Sextumvirate and the Horses *Essays in Criticism* (**19**(1): 35–45 1969).

Kinkead-Weekes, M. *Clarissa* Restored? *Review of English Studies* (n s **10**(2): 156– 71 1959).

Kinkead-Weekes, M. *Samuel Richardson: Dramatic Novelist* (Methuen 1973).

Knapp, J. *An Empire Nowhere: England, America, and Literature from 'Utopia' to 'The Tempest'* (University of California Press, Berkeley and Los Angeles 1992).

Kolb, G.J. Johnson's 'Dissertation on Flying' and John Wilkins' *Mathematical Magic. Modern Philology* (**47**(1): 24–31 1949).

Kolb, G.J. The Structure of *Rasselas. Publications of the Modern Language Association* **66**(5): 698–717 1951.

Kolb, G.J. The 'Paradise' in Abyssinia and the 'Happy Valley' in *Rasselas. Modern Philology* (**56**(1): 10–16 1958).

Korshin, P.J. The Intellectual Context of Swift's Flying Island. *Philological Quarterly* (**50**(4): 630–46 1971).

Korshin, P.J. (ed.) *Studies in Change and Revolution: Aspects of English Intellectual History 1640–1800*. (Scolar Press 1972).

Kramnick, I. *Bolingbroke and his Circle: The Politics of Nostalgia in the Age of Walpole* (Harvard University Press, Cambridge, Mass 1968).

Kumar, K. *Utopia and Anti-Utopia in Modern Times* (Blackwell 1987).

Kumar, K. *Utopianism* (University of Minnesota Press, Minneapolis: Concepts in Social Thought 1991).

Kupperman, K.O. *Settling with the Indians: the Meeting of English and Indian Cultures in America 1580–1640* (Rowman and Littlefield, Totowa, New Jersey 1980).

Landa, L.A. Johnson's Feathered Man: 'A Dissertation on the Art of Flying'

Considered. In Bond, W.H. (ed.) *Eighteenth-Century Studies in Honor of Donald F Hyde* (The Grolier Club, New York 1970).

Lasky, M.J. 1976 *Utopia and Revolution* (Macmillan 1977).

Laslett, P. *The World We Have Lost* (Scribner, New York 1965).

Laslett, P. 1971 *The World We Have Lost Further Explored* (Methuen, 1983) (rev edn of Laslett, P. 1965).

Leavis, F.R. 1952 The Irony of Swift. In *The Common Pursuit* (Penguin Books (Peregrine Books) 1962).

Lefkowitz, M. Only the best girls get to. *The Times Literary Supplement* (May 5–11: 484, 497 1989).

Leslie, E.E. 1988 *Desperate Journeys, Abandoned Souls: True Stories of Castaways and Other Survivors* (Macmillan 1989).

Lévi-Strauss, C. 1964 (Weightman, J., Weightman, D. tr.) *The Raw and the Cooked: Introduction to a Science of Mythology* (vol. 1) (Jonathan Cape 1970).

Levin, B. *A World Elsewhere* (Jonathan Cape 1994).

Levin, H. 1969 *The Myth of the Golden Age in the Renaissance* (Oxford University Press 1972).

Leyburn, E. 'No Romantick Absurdities or Incredible Fictions': the Relation of Johnson's *Rasselas* to Lobo's *Voyage to Abyssinia* (*Publications of the Modern Language Association* 70(5): 1059–67 1955).

Lock, F.P. *The Politics of 'Gulliver's Travels'* (Clarendon Press 1980).

Locke, J. 1690 (Laslett, P. ed.) *Two Treatises of Government* (Cambridge University Press: Cambridge Texts in the History of Political Thought 1988).

Locke, J. 1693 (Yolton, J.W., Yolton, J.S. eds) *Some Thoughts Concerning Education* (Clarendon Press 1989).

Lockhart, D.M. 'The Fourth Son of the Mighty Emperor': the Ethiopian Background of Johnson's *Rasselas*. (*Publications of the Modern Language Association* 78(5): 516–28 1963).

Logan, G.M. *The Meaning of More's 'Utopia'* (Princeton University Press, Princeton, New Jersey 1983).

Lovejoy, A.O., Boas, G. *Primitivism and Related Ideas in Antiquity* (The Johns Hopkins University Press, Baltimore 1935).

Lucian (Harmon, A.M. tr.) *A True Story* (8 vols, vol. 1) (Heinemann and Macmillan, New York: Loeb Classical Library 1913).

Lukács, G. 1920 (Bostock, A. tr.) *The Theory of the Novel* (Merlin Press 1971).

Macfarlane, A. *Marriage and Love in England 1300–1840* (Blackwell 1986).

Mack, R.L. (ed.) *Oriental Tales* (Oxford University Press (The World's Classics) 1992).

McKeon, M. *The Origins of the English Novel 1600–1740* (The Johns Hopkins University Press, Baltimore 1987).

Maddox, J.H. Interpreter Crusoe. *English Literary History* (51(1): 33–52 1984).

Mandeville, B. 1705–1725 (Kaye, F.B. ed.) *The Fable of the Bees: or, Private Vices, Publick Benefits* (2 vols) (Clarendon Press 1924).

Mandeville, B. 1705–1725 (Harth, P. ed.) *The Fable of the Bees* (Penguin Books: Penguin Classics 1989).

Manley, D. *Secret Memoirs and Manners of Several Persons of Quality, of Both Sexes. From the New Atalantis, an Island in the Mediterranean* 1709.

Manley, D. 1709 (Ballaster, R. ed.) *New Atalantis* (Penguin Books: Penguin Classics 1992).

Mannheim, K. (Wirth, L. and Shils, E. tr.) *Ideology and Utopia* (Harcourt, Brace, and World, New York 1936).

Manuel, F.E. (ed.) *Utopias and Utopian Thought* (Houghton Mifflin, Boston 1965).

Manuel, F.E., Manuel, F.P. *Utopian Thought in the Western World* (Harvard University Press, Cambridge, Mass., and Blackwell 1979).

Marin, L. (Vollrath, R.A. tr.) *Utopics: Spatial Play* (Humanities Press, Atlantic Highlands, New Jersey, and Macmillan (Contemporary Studies in Philosophy and the Human Sciences) 1984).

Mathias, P. (ed.) *Science and Society 1600–1900* (Cambridge University Press 1972).

Mezciems, J. The Unity of Swift's 'Voyage to Laputa': Structure as Meaning in Utopian Fiction. *Modern Language Review* **72**(1): 1–21 1977).

Mezciems, J. Utopia and 'the Thing which is not': More, Swift, and Other Lying Idealists (*University of Toronto Quarterly* **52**(1): 40–62 1982).

Mezciems, J. Swift and Orwell: Utopia as Nightmare. *Dutch Quarterly Review of Anglo-American Letters* (**15**(3): 189–210 1985).

Milton, J. (Wolfe, D.M. et al eds) *Complete Prose Works of John Milton* (8 vols) (Yale University Press, New Haven 1953–82).

Milton, J. 1674 (Fowler, A. ed.) *Paradise Lost* (Longman: Longman Annotated English Poets 1971).

Montaigne, M. de 1580–1588 (Screech, M.A. tr. and ed.) *The Essays of Michel de Montaigne* (Allen Lane 1991).

Montesquieu, C-L de S de 1721 (Betts, C.J. tr. and ed.) *Persian Letters* (Penguin Books: Penguin Classics 1973).

Moore, J.R. *Rasselas* and the Early Travellers to Abyssinia. *Modern Language Quarterly* (**15**(1): 36–41 1954).

Moore, J.R. *A Checklist of the Writings of Daniel Defoe* (Indiana University Press, Bloomington 1960).

More, T. 1516 (Surtz, E., Hexter, J.H. eds) *Utopia* (Yale University Press, New Haven (The Complete Works of St Thomas More vol. 4) 1965).

More, T. 1516 (Logan, G.M., Adams, R.M. eds) *Utopia* (Cambridge University Press: Cambridge Texts in the History of Political Thought 1989).

More, T. 1516/1551 (Robinson, R. tr., Warrington, J. intro) *Utopia* (Dent: Everyman's Library 1974).

Morgan, A.E. *Nowhere was Somewhere* (University of North Carolina Press, Chapel Hill 1946).

Morris, W. 1891 (Redmond, J. ed.) *News from Nowhere* (Routledge & Kegan Paul: Routledge English Texts 1970).

Morton, A.L. *The English Utopia* (Lawrence & Wishart 1952).

Murdoch, I. *The Fire & the Sun: Why Plato Banished the Artists* (Clarendon Press 1977).

Myers, S.H. *The Bluestocking Circle: Women, Friendship, and the Life of the Mind in Eighteenth-Century England* (Clarendon Press 1990).

Neale, R.S. *Bath 1680–1850: A Social History: or A Valley of Pleasure, yet a Sink of Iniquity* (Routledge & Kegan Paul 1981).

Negley, G., Patrick, J.M. (eds) *The Quest for Utopia: An Anthology of Imaginary Societies* (Henry Schuman, New York 1952).

Negley, G. *Utopian Literature: a Bibliography with a Supplementary Listing of Works Influential in Utopian Thought* (Regents Press of Kansas, Lawrence 1977).

Neville, H. 1668 *The Isle of Pines*. In Henderson, P. (ed.) *Shorter Novels: Jacobean and Restoration* (Dent (Everyman's Library) 1930).

Neville-Sington, P., Singion, D. *Paradise Dreamed: How Utopian Thinkers Have Changed the Modern World* (Bloomsbury 1993).

New, P. *Fiction and Purpose in Utopia, Rasselas, The Mill on the Floss and Women in Love* (Macmillan 1985).

Nicolson, M.H. *Voyages to the Moon* (The Macmillan Company, New York 1948).

Nicolson, M.H. 1956 *Science and Imagination* (Archon Books (The Shoe String Press) Hamden, Connecticut 1976).

Nokes, D. *Jonathan Swift, A Hypocrite Reversed: A Critical Biography* (Oxford University Press 1985).

Novak, M.E. *Economics and the Fiction of Daniel Defoe* (University of California Press, Berkeley and Los Angeles 1962).

Novak, M.E. *Defoe and the Nature of Man* (Oxford University Press 1963).

Novak, M.E. Imaginary Islands and Real Beasts: the Imaginative Genesis of *Robinson Crusoe. Tennessee Studies in Literature* (**19** Eighteenth-Century Literature Issue: 57–78 1974).

Novak, M.E. *Realism, Myth, and History in Defoe's Fiction* (University of Nebraska Press, Lincoln, Nebraska 1983).

Nussbaum, F. *The Brink of All We Hate: English Satires on Women 1660–1740* (University Press of Kentucky, Lexington 1984).

Orwell, G. *Nineteen Eighty-Four* (Martin Secker & Warburg 1949).

Ovid (Innes, M.M. tr.) *Metamorphoses* (Penguin Books: Penguin Classics 1955).

Pagden, A. (ed.) *The Languages of Political Theory in Early-Modern Europe* (Cambridge University Press 1987).

Paltock, R. 1750 (Bentley, C. ed., Turner, J.G. intro) *The Life and Adventures of Peter Wilkins* (Oxford University Press: The World's Classics 1990).

Patch, H.R. *The Other World, according to Descriptions in Medieval Literature*

(Harvard University Press, Cambridge, Mass (Smith College Studies in Modern Languages) 1950).

Patrick, J.M. Robert Burton's Utopianism. *Philological Quarterly* (**27**(4): 345–58 1948).

Patrick, J.M. *Nova Solyma*: Samuel Gott's Puritan Utopia. *Studies in the Literary Imagination* (**10**(2): 43–55 1977).

Pearlman, E.H. Robinson Crusoe and the Cannibals. *Mosaic* (**10**(1): 39–55 1976).

Perry, R. *The Celebrated Mary Astell: An Early English Feminist* (University of Chicago Press, Chicago 1986).

Petronius, 1965 (Sullivan, J.P. tr. and ed.) *The Satyricon* rev edn (Penguin Books: Penguin Classics 1986).

Philmus, R.M. The Language of Utopia. *Studies in the Literary Imagination* (**6**(2): 61–78 1973).

Plato (Cornford, F.M. tr. and ed.) *The Republic of Plato* (Clarendon Press 1941).

Plato (Lee, D. tr. and ed.) *The Republic* rev edn (Penguin Books: Penguin Classics 1955/1987).

Plato (Lee, D. tr. and ed. with an appendix on *Atlantis*) *Timaeus and Critias* rev edn (Penguin Books: Penguin Classics 1965/1977).

Plato (Saunders, T.J. tr. and ed.) *The Laws* rev edn (Penguin Books: Penguin Classics 1970/1988).

Plato (Gill, C. ed.) *Plato: The Atlantis Story: Timaeus 17–27; Critias* (Bristol Classical Press 1980).

Plutarch (Perrin, B. tr.) *Lycurgus*. In *Lives* (11 vols: vol. 1) (Heinemann and G.P. Putman's Sons, New York (Loeb Classical Library) 1914).

Pocock, J.G.A. Machiavelli, Harrington and English Political Ideologies in the Eighteenth Century. In *Politics, Language and Time: Essays on Political Thought and History* (Methuen 1971/1972).

Pope, A. 1733–4 (Mack, M. ed.) *An Essay on Man* (Methuen (The Twickenham Edition of the Poems of Alexander Pope) 1950).

Popkin, R.H. (ed.) *Millenarianism and Messianism in English Literature and Thought 1650–1800* (Brill, Leiden 1988).

Popper, K.R. 1945 *The Open Society and Its Enemies* (2 vols) rev edn (Routledge & Kegan Paul 1966).

Potter, H. *Hanging in Judgment: Religion and the Death Penalty in England from the Bloody Code to Abolition* (SCM Press 1993).

Prévost d'Exiles, A.F. *The Life and Entertaining Adventures of Mr Cleveland, Natural Son of Oliver Cromwell, Written by Himself* (5 vols). 1734.

Probyn, C.T. (ed.) *The Art of Jonathan Swift*. (Vision Press 1978).

Probyn, C.T. *Gulliver's Travels* (Penguin Books: Penguin Critical Studies 1987/1989).

Rabelais, F. 1564 (Frame, D.M. tr. and ed.) *The Complete Works* (University of California Press, Berkeley 1991).

Rawson, C.J. *Gulliver and the Gentle Reader* (Routledge & Kegan Paul 1973).

Rawson, E. *The Spartan Tradition in European Thought* (Clarendon Press 1969).

Reichert, J.F. Plato, Swift, and the Houyhnhnms. *Philological Quarterly* 47(2): 179–92 1968.

Ribeiro, A. Dress in Utopia. *Costume: The Journal of the Costume Society* (21: 26–33 1987).

Richardson, S. 1747–8 (Ross, A. ed.) *Clarissa or The History of a Young Lady* (Penguin Books: Penguin Classics 1985).

Richardson, S. 1751 (Butt, J. intro) *Clarissa or, The History of a Young Lady* (4 vols) 3rd edn (Dent (Everyman's Library) 1962).

Richardson, S. 1751 (Harris, J. ed.) *The History of Sir Charles Grandison* (3 Parts) (Oxford University Press (Oxford English Novels) 1972).

Richetti, J.J. *Defoe's Narratives: Situations and Structures* (Clarendon Press 1975).

Ricoeur, P. (Taylor, G.H. ed.) *Lectures on Ideology and Utopia.* (Columbia University Press, New York 1986).

Rizzo, B. *Companions Without Vows: Relationships among Eighteenth-Century British Women* (University of Georgia Press, Athens, Georgia 1994).

Rogers, P. (ed.) *Defoe: The Critical Heritage* (Routledge & Kegan Paul 1972).

Rogers, P. Crusoe's Home. *Essays in Criticism* (24(4): 375–90 1974).

Rogers, P. *Robinson Crusoe* (Allen & Unwin (Unwin Critical Library) 1979).

Rohrlich, R., Baruch, E. (eds) *Women in Search of Utopias: Mavericks and Mythmakers* (Schocken Books, New York 1984).

Rose, S. The Fear of Utopia. *Essays in Criticism* 24(1): 55–70 1974.

Ross, J.F. *Swift and Defoe: A Study in Relationship* (University of California Press, Berkeley and Los Angeles 1941).

Ruppert, P. *Reader in a Strange Land: the Activity of Reading Literary Utopias* (University of Georgia Press, Athens, Georgia 1986).

Said, E.W. 1978 *Orientalism* (Penguin Books: Peregrine Books 1985).

Samuel, I. Swift's Reading of Plato. *Studies in Philology* 73(4): 440–62 1976.

Sargent, L.T. Women in Utopia. *Comparative Literature Studies* 10(4): 302–16 1973.

Sargent, L.T. 1979 *British and American Utopian Literature 1516–1975: an Annotated Bibliography* 2nd edn (Garland, New York 1988).

Sargent, L.T. (ed.) *Utopian Studies* (vol. 1 -) (Society for Utopian Studies, Department of Political Science, Hampton University, Hampton, Virginia 1990).

Schoeck, R.J. More, Plutarch, and King Agis: Spartan History and the Meaning of *Utopia. Philological Quarterly* (35(4): 366–75 1956).

Schonhorn, M. *Defoe's Politics: Parliament, Power, Kingship, and Robinson Crusoe* (Cambridge University Press: Cambridge Studies in Eighteenth-Century English Literature and Thought 1991).

Scott, S. 1762 (Spencer, J. intro) *Millenium Hall* (Virago Press: Virago Classics 1986).

Seeber, E. Ideal Languages in the French and English Imaginary Voyage. (*Publications of the Modern Language Association* **60**(2): 586–97 1945).

Sekora, J. *Luxury: the Concept in Western Thought, Eden to Smollett* (The Johns Hopkins University Press, Baltimore 1977).

Shadwell, T. 1676 (Nicolson, M.H, Rodes, D.S. eds) *The Virtuoso* (Edward Arnold (Regents Restoration Drama Series) 1966).

Shakespeare, W. 1623 (Kermode, F. ed.) *The Tempest* 6th edn (Methuen: The Arden Shakespeare 1961).

Shakespeare, W. 1623 (Muir, K. ed.) *King Lear* (Methuen: The Arden Shakespeare 1985).

Skinner, Q. *The Foundations of Modern Political Thought* (2 vols) (Cambridge University Press 1978).

Skinner, Q. Sir Thomas More's *Utopia* and the Language of Renaissance Humanism. In Pagden, A. (ed.) *The Languages of Political Theory in Early-Modern Europe* (Cambridge University Press 1987).

Smallwood, A.J. *Fielding and the Woman Question: the Novels of Henry Fielding and Feminist Debate 1700–50* (Simon & Schuster) 1989.

Smith, F.N. The Danger of Reading Swift: the Double Binds of *Gulliver's Travels*. *Studies in the Literary Imagination* (**17**(1): 35–47 1984).

Smith, F.N. (ed.) *The Genres of Gulliver's Travels* (University of Delaware Press, Newark, and Associated University Presses 1990).

Spadafora, D. *The Idea of Progress in Eighteenth-Century Britain* (Yale University Press, New Haven 1990).

Spencer, J. *The Rise of the Woman Novelist: from Aphra Behn to Jane Austen* (Blackwell 1986).

Starnes, C. *The New Republic: a Commentary on Book 1 of More's Utopia showing its relation to Plato's Republic* (Wilfred Laurier University Press 1990).

Starr, G.A. *Defoe and Spiritual Autobiography* (Princeton University Press, Princeton, New Jersey 1965).

Sterne, L. 1759–1767 (Ricks, C. ed.) *The Life & Opinions of Tristram Shandy* (Penguin Books: Penguin English Library 1967).

Stone, L. *The Family, Sex and Marriage in England 1500–1800* (Weidenfeld and Nicolson 1977).

Stone, L. *Road to Divorce: England 1530–1987* (Oxford University Press 1990).

Stone, L. *Uncertain Unions: Marriage in England 1660–1753* (Oxford University Press 1992).

Stone, L. *Broken Lives: Separation and Divorce in England 1660–1857* (Oxford University Press 1993).

Suvin, D. Defining the Literary Genre of Utopia: Some Historical Semantics, Some Genology, a Proposal and a Plea. *Studies in the Literary Imagination* (**6**(2): 121–45 1973).

Swift, J. (Davis, H. et al eds) *The Prose Works of Jonathan Swift* (14 vols) (Blackwell 1939–68).

Swift, J. 1726 (Davis, H. ed., Williams, H. intro) *Gulliver's Travels* rev edn (Blackwell: *The Prose Works* vol. 11 1965).

Swift, J. 1726 (Landa, L.A. ed.) *Gulliver's Travels and Other Writings* (Houghton Mifflin, Boston: Riverside Editions 1960).

Swift, J. 1726 (Turner, P. ed.) *Gulliver's Travels* (Oxford University Press: The World's Classics 1986).

Swift, J. (Williams, H. ed.) *The Correspondence of Jonathan Swift* (5 vols) (Oxford University Press 1963–5).

Sylvester, R.S., Marc'hadour, G.P. (eds) *Essential Articles for the Study of Thomas More* (Archon Books, The Shoe String Press, Hamden, Connecticut 1977).

Tacitus (Mattingly, H. tr., Handford, S.A. rev) *The Agricola and the Germania* (Penguin Books (Penguin Classics) 1948/1970).

Tavor, E. *Scepticism, Society and the Eighteenth-Century Novel* (Macmillan 1987).

Temple, W. *A Vindication of Commerce and the Arts . . . being An Examination of Mr Bell's Dissertation upon Populousness* 1758.

Thomas, K. *Man and the Natural World: Changing Attitudes in England 1500–1800* (Allen Lane 1983).

Thomas, K. The Utopian Impulse in Seventeenth-Century England. *Dutch Quarterly Review of Anglo-American Letters* (15(3): 162–88 1985).

Tillotson, G. 'Rasselas' and the 'Persian Tales'. In *Essays in Criticism and Research* (Cambridge University Press 1942).

Todd, J. *Women's Friendship in Literature* (Columbia University Press, New York 1980).

Todd, J. *The Sign of Angellica: Women, Writing and Fiction, 1660–1800* (Virago Press 1989).

Traugott, J. A Voyage to Nowhere with Thomas More and Jonathan Swift. *Sewanee Review* (69(4): 534–65 1961).

Trotter, D. *Circulation: Defoe, Dickens, and the Economies of the Novel* (Macmillan 1988).

Tuveson, E.L. *Millennium and Utopia: A Study in the Background of the Idea of Progress* (University of California Press, Berkeley and Los Angeles 1949).

Unsworth, B. *Sacred Hunger* (Hamish Hamilton/Penguin Books 1992).

Upham, A.H. Mary Astell as a Parallel for Richardson's Clarissa. *Modern Language Notes* (28(4): 103–5 1913).

Uphaus, R.W., Foster, G.M. (eds) *The 'Other' Eighteenth Century: English Women of Letters 1660–1800* (Colleagues Press 1991).

Vairasse, D. d'A 1675–9 *The History of the Sevarambians: A People of the South-Continent. In Five Parts . . . Translated from the Memoirs of Captain Siden (L'Histoire des Sévarambes)* 1738.

[Vairasse, D. d'A] *Travels into Several Remote Nations of the World by Capt. Lemuel Gulliver* vol. 3 part 2 *A Voyage to Sevarambia.* 1727.

Van Marter, S. Richardson's Revisions of *Clarissa* in the Second Edition.

Studies in Bibliography 26: 107–32. Bibliographical Society of the University of Virginia 1973.

Van Marter, S. Richardson's Revisions of *Clarissa* in the Third and Fourth Editions. *Studies in Bibliography* 28: 119–52. Bibliographical Society of the University of Virginia 1975.

Veiras (see Vairasse)

Venturi, F. *Utopia and Reform in the Enlightenment* (Cambridge University Press 1971).

Vickers, B. (ed.) *The World of Jonathan Swift* (Blackwell 1968).

Vickers, B. (ed.) *Essential Articles for the Study of Francis Bacon* (Archon Books, The Shoe String Press, Hamden, Connecticut 1968b).

Virgil (Lee, G. tr.) *The Eclogues* rev edn (Penguin Books: Penguin Classics 1980/1984).

Vlastos, G. Was Plato a feminist? *The Times Literary Supplement* (March 17–23: 276, 288–9 1989).

Voltaire, 1747–1756 (Butt, J. tr. and intro) *Zadig/L'Ingenu* (Penguin Books: Penguin Classics 1964).

Voltaire, 1759 (Butt, J. tr. and intro) *Candide* (Penguin Books: Penguin Classics 1968).

Watt, I. 1951 *Robinson Crusoe* as a myth. *Essays in Criticism* 1951 1(2): 95–119. Reprinted in Clifford, J.L. 1951. (ed.) *Eighteenth Century English Literature: Modern Essays in Criticism* (Oxford University Press, New York: A Galaxy Book 1959).

Watt, I. 1957 *The Rise of the Novel: Studies in Defoe, Richardson and Fielding* (Penguin Books: Peregrine Books 1968).

Watts, C. *Literature and Money: Financial Myth and Literary Truth* (Harvester 1991).

Webster, C. (ed.) *Samuel Hartlib and the Advancement of Learning* (Cambridge University Press 1970).

Webster, C. The Authorship and Significance of *Macaria*. *Past and Present* (56: 34–48 1972).

Webster, C. *The Great Instauration: Science, Medicine and Reform 1626–1660* (Duckworth 1975).

Weitzman, A.J. More Light on *Rasselas*: the Background of the Egyptian Episodes. (*Philological Quarterly* 48(1): 42–58 1969).

Welcher, J.K., Bush, G.E. (eds) *Gulliveriana* (6 vols) (Delmar, New York: Scholars' Facsimiles & Reprints 1970–6).

Welcher, J.K. (ed.) *Gulliveriana VIII: An Annotated List of Gulliveriana 1721–1800* (Delmar, New York: Scholars' Facsimiles & Reprints 1988).

White, T.I. Aristotle and *Utopia*. *Renaissance Quarterly* 29(4): 635–75 1976.

Wilkins, J. 1638 *A Discovery of a New World . . . in Two Parts* (5th edn 1684).

Williams, H. *Dean Swift's Library* (Cambridge University Press 1932).

Williams, K. *Jonathan Swift and the Age of Compromise* (Constable 1958/1959).

Winstanley, G. 1651 (Hill, C. ed.) *The Law of Freedom and other Writings* (Cambridge University Press 1983).

Wollstonecraft, M. 1787 (Todd, J., Butler, M., Rees-Mogg, E. eds) *Thoughts on the Education of Daughters* (William Pickering (*The Works of Mary Wollstonecraft* vol. 4) 1989).

Wollstonecraft, M. 1792 (Todd, J., Butler, M., Rees-Mogg, E. eds) *A Vindication of the Rights of Men: A Vindication of the Rights of Woman: Hints* (William Pickering (*The Works of Mary Wollstonecraft* vol. 5) 1989).

Xenophon (Marchant, E.C. tr.) *Constitution of the Lacedaemonians*. In *Scripta Minora* (G.P. Putnam's Sons, New York, and Heinemann: Loeb Classical Library 1925).

Zirker, M.R. *Fielding's Social Pamphlets* (University of California Press, Berkeley 1966).

Index